The German Army at Passchendaele

In proud and loving memory of my grandfathers
William Bailey Sheldon
Corporal, Northumberland Fusiliers
and
Robert Kerr Aitken
Sergeant, Royal Army Medical Corps
Both of whom marched away to the Great War
and
Both of whom returned

The Author

Dr. Jack Sheldon retired from the British Army in 2003 after a thirty-five year career as a member of the Queen's Lancashire Regiment. He is a graduate of the German Command and Staff College in Hamburg and he held numerous international appointments, including that of Military Attaché Berlin.

For the past eight years he has been living in the Dauphiné Alps of southeast France, researching and writing his acclaimed German Army in The Great War series. These have already become the standard works on the subject for both the specialist and the general reader.

Jack Sheldon, a member of the British Commission for Military History, the Douglas Haig Fellowship and the Western Front Association, is in demand for his expertise on all aspects of the German military during the First World War.

By the same Author:

The German Army on the Somme 1914 -1916, *(also in paperback)*

The German Army at Passchendaele, *(also in hardback)*

The German Army on Vimy Ridge 1914 – 1917, *(also in paperback)*

The German Army at Cambrai

The German Army at Ypres 1914

The German Army on the Western Front 1915

The Germans at Beaumont Hamel *(Battleground Europe Series)*

The Germans at Thiepval *(Battleground Europe Series)*

All are available through www.pen-and-sword.co.uk

The German Army
at Passchendaele

Jack Sheldon

Pen & Sword
MILITARY

First published in Great Britain in 2007
and reprinted in this format in 2014 by
Pen & Sword Military
an imprint of
Pen & Sword Books Ltd
47 Church Street
Barnsley
South Yorkshire
S70 2AS

ISBN 978 1 78346 182 0

A CIP catalogue record for this book is
available from the British Library.

Typeset in Ellington by
Phoenix Typesetting, Auldgirth, Dumfriesshire

Printed and bound by CPI Group (UK) Ltd, Croydon, CRO 4YY

Pen & Sword Books Ltd incorporates the imprints of Pen & Sword Aviation, Pen & Sword
Maritime, Pen & Sword Military, Wharncliffe Local History,
Pen & Sword Select, Pen & Sword Military Classics and Leo Cooper.

For a complete list of Pen & Sword titles please contact
PEN & SWORD BOOKS LIMITED
47 Church Street, Barnsley, South Yorkshire, S70 2AS, England
E-mail: enquiries@pen-and-sword.co.uk
Website: www.pen-and-sword.co.uk

Contents

Foreword

For some ninety years now, Passchendaele – the name widely given to the Third Battle of Ypres after that engagement's murderous final phase – has been collectively regarded by the British and Commonwealth public as a synonym for all the hardships and suffering borne by the front-line soldier in the First World War. This was particularly the case in the years following the publication of Lloyd George's *War Memoirs* in the 1930s. In the unabridged version of his *Memoirs*, the former wartime Prime Minister predicted that the 'slaughter of Passchendaele', together with Verdun and the Somme, 'will always rank as the most gigantic, tenacious, grim, futile and bloody fights ever waged in the history of war'. Defining Passchendaele as one of the war's 'greatest disasters', Lloyd George pronounced that no soldier of any intelligence would now defend 'this senseless campaign'. As Ian M Brown has pointed out, Lloyd George, with the active assistance of Basil Liddell Hart, devoted over one hundred pages of his *War Memoirs* to Passchendaele as against twenty-seven to the battles of August to November 1918, when the Allies actually won the war. Lloyd George's largely negative, and often venomous, views on the conduct of the battle by the British High Command were reinforced in the late 1950s by the appearance of Leon Wolff's *In Flanders Fields*, a book which heralded another round of 'Haig bashing', though Professor Brian Bond has wisely reminded us that Lloyd George, as Prime Minister at the time of Haig's 1917 Flanders offensive, 'had the constitutional responsibility to stop it if he deemed it to be failing or too costly in casualties'. It is probably fair to say that, since the early 1970s, the Somme offensive of 1916 has supplanted Third Ypres as the battle which is popularly judged to have had the most significant impact, and to have inflicted the deepest physical and psychological scars, upon the British army and society as a whole. Nevertheless, Passchendaele has never lost its power to shock even the most hardened student of the Great War and, to many people, it remains the quintessential symbol of the horrors of the fighting on the Western Front.

In the last twenty years or so, there has been a steadily increasing flow of new books, essays, doctoral theses and battlefield guides covering virtually every aspect of the war from a British and Commonwealth standpoint, and especially the nature and conduct of the struggle on the Western Front. Historians such as Martin Middlebrook, Denis Winter, Bill Gammage, Desmond Morton, Tony Ashworth, Lyn Macdonald, Peter Liddle, Richard Holmes, Malcolm Brown, Nigel Steel and Peter Hart – to name but a few – have presented us with a highly detailed picture of the experiences and attitudes of British and Dominion junior officers and other ranks. Others – including Tim Bowman, Terence Denman, James W Taylor, K W Mitchinson, Jill Knight and Helen McCartney and Mark Connelly – have published important socio-military studies of various formations; Paddy Griffith, Bill Rawling, Martin Farndale and Jonathan Bailey are among those who have considerably enhanced our understanding of tactical developments and improvements in the British Expeditionary Force (BEF); numerous new unit histories have been produced; and – thanks to the recent scholarship of Gary Sheffield, Ian Beckett, Andy Simpson, John Bourne, Simon Robbins, Chris Pugsley, Chris McCarthy, John Lee, and Robin Prior and Trevor Wilson – we also have a much more precise idea of how operations were planned, and how command and control really functioned at different levels, in the BEF between 1914 and 1918. However, as Richard Holmes indicated in his Foreword to Jack Sheldon's previous book, *The German Army on the Somme 1914-1916*, we are distinctly less well catered for in terms of serious works, in English, on the German army in the First World War. As a result, our perception of the major operations on the Western Front, and of the lot of the ordinary soldier there, has inevitably become more than a trifle Anglocentric.

The same can be said of even the best recent works on Messines and Third Ypres. Apart from two short essays in the 1997 collection *Passchendaele in Perspective*, edited by Peter Liddle, most of the studies of these battles which have appeared since 1990 – notably by Robin Prior and Trevor Wilson, Nigel Steel and Peter Hart, Chris McCarthy, John Lee, Ian Passingham, Rob Thompson, Ian Beckett and Andrew Wiest – have looked at the fighting in Flanders in 1917 primarily, if not exclusively, from the British side of the wire. While *some* useful and important works on the German army have also been published – including studies by Timothy Lupfer, Bruce Gudmundsson, Dennis Showalter, Martin Samuels, John Lee, Martin Kitchen, Robert Asprey and Christopher Duffy – they have focused mainly upon the German High Command and upon strategy and tactics rather than upon the daily, and nightly, ordeals of the *Feldgrauen* in their trenches, pillboxes and muddy shell-holes. With the distinguished exception of Christopher Duffy – whose *Through German Eyes: The British and the Somme 1916* was published in 2006 – Jack Sheldon has, almost single-handed, begun to rectify this situation and to restore some sort of balance to the historiography of the First World War by furnishing us with a vivid and invaluable record of the men on the other side of No Man's Land, first in *The German Army on the Somme* and now in *The German Army at Passchendaele*. For this all serious students of the Great War are hugely in his debt.

So long as the German nation and the German army chose to maintain their occupation of large tracts of Belgium and northern France, the Allies, in their turn, had no *realistic* option other than to attack the Germans on the Western Front in an attempt to eject them, whatever the cost. To claim that, for the Allies, there was a viable alternative to the Western Front is to ignore or misunderstand the cardinal importance of logistics in the First World War. For the British it was just feasible to supply a massively-expanded BEF across the English Channel to France, where it could utilise the relatively sophisticated and extensive infrastructure of the French road, rail and waterways network. But, even on the Western Front, it was not until 1917-1918 that the BEF possessed an administrative and supply system which truly enabled it to begin to exploit the concurrent strides it was making in the spheres of operations and tactics. Bearing in mind the Royal Navy's commitment to the blockade of Germany and to the absolutely vital task of anti-submarine warfare, it would surely have been well-nigh impossible to sustain a major army in a decisive land campaign through the mountainous Balkans or beyond Alexandretta and across the inhospitable Anatolian plateau, where communications were notoriously poor. If, then, the Germans had to be defeated on the Western Front, Jack Sheldon's latest book - with its numerous accounts of resolute, heroic and skilful German defensive actions – makes it abundantly clear that this would *never* be quickly or easily accomplished by the Allies. As Jack Sheldon underlines, moreover, the BEF was not the only army undergoing a process of learning and tactical improvement in 1917. Changes in German platoon organisation for example, as described in the extract from the history of Infantry Regiment 418, appear to have been based on the same principles as those adopted by the BEF early in 1917.

What also immediately becomes clear from this book is that not all the pain was felt by one side at Passchendaele. We have perhaps become so accustomed to reading studies of the battle written from a British or Commonwealth viewpoint that we forget, all too frequently, the suffering of the men in field grey in what General Hermann von Kuhl, the chief of staff to Army Group Crown Prince Rupprecht, called 'the greatest martyrdom' of the war. In devoting so much time and effort to the debate on the performance of Douglas Haig and his Army commanders at Third Ypres, historians have correspondingly paid too little attention to the problems and mistakes of the German High Command in 1917. The awesome power of the British artillery at Passchendaele, as described in so many of the personal accounts selected by Jack Sheldon, is a very far cry indeed from the patchy and thinly-spread fire support available to the BEF on the Somme on 1 July 1916. These accounts likewise suggest that most historians have underestimated or underplayed the difficulties created for the German defenders by British aircraft, especially in a ground-attack role, at both Messines and Third Ypres. When analysing and criticising the handling of the battle by Haig and his subordinates, it is worth considering the point emphasised by Jack Sheldon in Chapters 4, 5 and 6, namely that, despite making successive modifications to their defensive tactics after 20 September 1917, the German High Command could find no effective answer to Plumer's limited-objective, 'bite and hold' attacks until the weather intervened in October. The reader is left in little doubt by the end of this book that, regardless of the long-disputed casualty figures on both sides, a critical strain was placed on *German*, as well as Allied, manpower resources by Passchendaele.

In addition to the relentless drain of trained soldiers from its ground-holding and *Eingreif* divisions alike, the German army's freedom of action was severely restricted. The British offensive in Flanders not only prevented the Germans from taking full advantage of the weakened state of the French army, following its wave of mutinies, but, as Ludendorff himself subsequently confessed, it also obliged the Germans to delay the transfer of divisions to Italy and to postpone its own planned offensive in the East at Riga. Nor was the balance sheet of divisions committed totally unfavourable to the Allies. According to Crown Prince Rupprecht, 88 German divisions were engaged in the battle, a quarter of them twice. By my calculations, 54 British and Dominion divisions, and up to six French divisions – a total of 60 – took part in operations at Third Ypres, although well over half of these were involved in more than one attack.

One of the principal problems for the BEF was that, however successful Plumer's methodical 'bite and hold' tactics had proved in overcoming the German system of elastic defence in depth, the British Second Army's step-by-step approach was subject, in the conditions of late 1917, to the law of diminishing returns, with each step costing more casualties for a smaller gain of ground than the preceding one. Although the dogged German defence obviously had a great deal to do with this, it is also arguable that Plumer's methods were, in several respects, ultimately self-defeating. While the British remained incapable of capturing substantial numbers of German guns, the BEF could not achieve the complete artillery dominance, or attain the high operational tempo, required to produce the decisive results which Haig sought. The colossal bombardments, drumfire and multi-layered British barrages graphically described here progressively damaged the already precarious drainage system of the Ypres Salient and destroyed the very roads and tracks needed to move guns, ammunition and troops forward for the next bound, thereby creating an almost impassable swamp and crater field once the rain returned on 4 October. The BEF may have solved the problem of breaking into the German defences but had not yet learned how to *break out*. It was only in the latter half of 1918 that the right combination of logistical, strategic and tactical conditions existed for the BEF to launch a rolling and successful series of limited-objective attacks on an almost daily basis and to achieve the necessary higher operational tempo by shifting the main point of assault apparently at will.

To the vast majority of the Tommies and *Feldgrauen* engaged in the bitter struggle for survival and supremacy in the morass of the Salient, the more mobile operations and semi-open warfare of 1918 would have seemed like an impossible dream. The British war correspondent Philip Gibbs famously wrote that after Passchendaele, for the first time in the war, 'the British Army lost its spirit of optimism, and there was a sense of deadly depression among the many officers and men with whom I came in touch'. Jack Sheldon shows in these pages that, by October 1917, the incessant fighting and the deteriorating weather was also beginning to affect the morale and motivation of some German troops. That said, anyone reading this excellent book cannot fail to be impressed by the courage, fortitude, and devotion to duty displayed by the junior officers, NCOs and men of the German army at Passchendaele. Indeed, in the final analysis, one remains full of admiration for the self-sacrifice and powers of endurance manifested by the front-line soldiers of *both* sides in this terrible battle.

Peter Simkins
January 2007

Introduction

Like every other book with the name 'Passchendaele' in the title, this one covers a much longer period than the six week fight for that unfortunate village. It concentrates on the period from 31 July 1917 onwards, but also includes its precursor, the Battle of Messines, and there is also mention of the intervening six weeks when, all doubt having been removed from the minds of commanders and staffs, the German army prepared for the forthcoming defensive battle with such thoroughness that, on its opening day, the army group commander, Crown Prince Rupprecht of Bavaria, could note in his diary, 'I find that I can face this offensive in a calm frame of mind, because never before have we had deployed along a front under attack such strong reserve forces, which have been so well trained in their role.' It was to be several weeks before his confidence was dented.

After the British success at the Battle of Messines, the Flanders front ran southwards from Diksmuide via Hooge, the northern edge of Hollebeke where the Yser Canal bent away from the Ypres – Comines railway, then as far south as Deûlémont and along the line of the River Lys. The countryside between Diksmuide and the Lys was criss-crossed by a network of streams and drainage ditches, most of which flowed more or less west, being crossed by the Ypres-Lys canal running north – south. It was flat countryside; swampy and only viable as agricultural land, thanks to a complex system of drainage. Before the area was hit by war, it had comprised a huge green expanse of fields, meadows and orchards. The enclosures were generally small and surrounded by hedges. Neat woods dotted the landscape, as did smaller stands of trees and tall rows of poplars. The spaces between the network of villages were filled with farms and farmhouses, large country houses and numerous chateaux belonging to the Belgian nobility.

In the south of the area, the farming tended to be especially prosperous, due to the fertility of the soil. Important cash crops included cereals, vegetables, animal feed and flowers. To the north, the dominant feature was Houthulst Wood, split in two by the main road from Diksmuide to Poelkapelle and criss-crossed with many tracks and rides. Underfoot it tended to be boggy, like so much of the remainder of the entire area. To the east of Ypres, there were numerous smaller woods: Nonne-Bossen, Polygon Wood and several others south of the Ypres-Menen road, which were to gain notoriety during the battle. In 1917 there were still a great many hedges, rows of trees and copses which cut down visibility dramatically and provided excellent concealment for the many strongpoints. Nevertheless there were vantage points at various places along the ridges which ran in an arc north to south through east and were generally about sixty metres high at their highest points. Possession of this high ground had always been strongly disputed during the three years the Ypres Salient had been in existence and this was to remain the case throughout the autumn of battles.

Obstacles to attack included the villages themselves, which were mostly already in ruins when battle was joined, liberal use of barbed wire and the natural defences formed when the damaged ditches and partially canalised streams burst their banks to produce impassable bogs and swamps. It had proved over the years impossible to dig worthwhile defences in this area, so the German army had created large numbers of concrete pillboxes and blockhouses, which were sited individually, or in groups and arranged for mutual support. Poor foundations and unparalleled quantities of super-heavy calibre artillery fire meant that the protection they offered was not always of a high order. Nevertheless, where they were well-placed and resolutely defended, they represented a considerable problem for the British army which, if it was to achieve its strategic objective of a general advance to the ports along the Belgian coast, it was going to have to overcome.

The defence designed by the German army was multi-layered and multi-faceted. In addition to the front line itself, by the beginning of the battle the main lines had been constructed in some depth. Roughly two kilometres to the rear, the *Albrecht Stellung* [Albrecht Position] was the furthest forward, then came in succession, at similar intervals, the *Wilhelm Stellung* [Wilhelm (William) Position] and the *Flandern Stellungen* I, II and III [Flanders Positions 1, 2 and 3]. The infantry units manning these lines were backed by artillery massed to the rear and behind the Geluveld Plateau. Plentifully supplied with ammunition, it exacted a high price from the British army during the long slog up the Passchendaele Ridge. Despite the progress made by the British army during the battle, when it was finally called off, the line of advance had only reached the *Flandern III* line east of Passchendaele on about a two kilometre front. It could be said that defence in depth had proved its utility.

Experience gained at Verdun and on the Somme in 1916, followed by the loss of Vimy Ridge in April 1917 and other setbacks during the Battle of Arras, were the cause of a great deal of heart searching to the German chain of command. The vulnerability of the Flanders area to attack was a constant preoccupation during the spring of 1917 and there was great concern that there might be another Allied attack in that area before they had had a chance to develop a counter to the use of massed artillery and sophisticated fire plans. The tactical solution, they eventually decided, was to adopt a system known as Flexible Defence. This idea, which was originally floated at the end of 1916, involved a chequerboard area defence in depth, conducted by ground-holding formations, which were backed by strong forces held back in reserve and located beyond the worst of the artillery barrage, but not so far back that they could not intervene effectively within a few hours. This operational procedure meant that attackers frequently made rapid progress against weakly held forward positions, but gradually their attacks were halted by a stiffening defence. Then, just as the artillery of the attackers ceased to be effective, the stalled attacks were hit by counter-strokes designed to throw them all the way back to their starting points.

The formations responsible for the counter-strokes were known as *Eingreif* divisions. *Eingreif is* generally translated as 'counter-attack', but this does not capture the sense of the word fully. To a German it includes a sense of 'intervening decisively', or 'becoming closely involved with' because, although these forces could be used in counter-attacks, it was not their only, or even main, role. At that time, the German army differentiated clearly between *Gegenangriff* [counter-attack] and *Gegenstoss* [counter-stroke]. During the Great War the difference was in the timings. A *Gegenangriff* implied a formal, deliberate attack with full preparatory artillery fire. A *Gegenstoss* was launched automatically, triggered by the moment when the enemy broke into the defensive position.

The principal task of an *Eingreif* division, therefore, was to conduct a meeting engagement in the form of a *Gegenstoss*. The operation would have been planned and rehearsed in advance and the formation would have launched it in a fully co-ordinated manner but, once it was underway in a particular sector, it would be integrated into the overall defensive effort under the command of the formation *in situ*. Sometimes, for example, these operations amounted to no more than simply plugging gaps or setting up blocking positions. In this book the word remains untranslated, leaving it for the reader to infer what type of operation the force was undertaking in each case.

'Bite and Hold' tactics, which had been used previously with success at Vimy Ridge and during the opening phase of the Battle of Messines, as well as elsewhere on a small scale, were brought into general use at the end of September 1917 and effectively put a stop to this method of use of the *Eingreif* divisions. No longer could they close up on a still-advancing, over-extended Allied attack. Instead, even if they could break though the protective barrages, they found that the attackers had gone over to a solid form of defence before they arrived. Lacking the means to conduct large scale counter-attacks, their *Eingreif* tactics stymied; towards the end of the battle the German army was reduced to hanging on grimly, assisted by the weather, until winter came to their rescue. It was just as well for the defence that there were so many lengthy pauses between the phases. The British, for example, may have used the gap between the Battle of Messines and the opening of the bombardment prior to 31 July 1917 to build railways lines and associated infrastructure, in order to move their artillery and dump ammunition forward, but that was nothing compared with the frenzied preparations on the German side, as additional forces were rushed to Flanders, trained and rehearsed in their particular roles. Delays later in the battle, for whatever reason, used up valuable campaigning weather and, in the end, the British army ran out of time.

When a regiment went into the ground-holding role alongside the other two regiments of its division, its three battalions undertook separate roles. Right forward was one battalion; its commander designated the *Kampftruppen-kommandeur (KTK)* [Commander of the Forward Troops]. The place where it was deployed was known as the *A-Stellung* [A Position]. 600 – 800 metres in rear was the support battalion, whose commander was nominated the *Bereitschaftstruppen-kommandeur (BTK)* [Commander of the Supporting Troops]. It manned the *B-Stellung* [B Position]. In the event of an attack, the supporting battalion generally pushed forward a further three hundred metres or so, ready to participate in the defence in whatever way events dictated they were needed. Finally, the third battalion occupied the *C-Stellung* [C Position] in the depth of the regimental position, located near to the regimental commander and ready to react to tasks in the forward area. Their commander was the *Reservetruppenkommandeur (RTK)* [Commander of the Reserve Troops], but the title *RTK* seems to have been used very little in comparison with *KTK* and *BTK*.

Without any doubt, the key man in each sector was the *KTK*. His command responsibilities went well beyond that of a normal battalion commander. Whenever possible he and his small staff (including an artillery liaison officer) were located in a concrete blockhouse, preferably of reasonable size, between the main defensive line and the gun lines. Rarely the *KTK* might operate from a trench or shell crater, but this was an emergency measure. Some sort of covered accommodation and communications were essential for the proper exercise of command. The *KTK* had complete devolved power of command in his sector, which was sometimes up to 500 metres wide and 700 metres deep, but was usually kept to a width of 400 metres in order to ease command and control difficulties. Throughout the battle this was the zone where all the critical events occurred. Due to the immense difficulty of communicating on this battlefield, the regimental, brigade and divisional commanders were not in a position to react swiftly enough in the face of enemy attacks. The supporting troops were always near at hand, at the disposal of the *KTK*, and the companies of the reserve battalion were usually within easy reach as well. It was up to the *KTK* to decide when and where to deploy the supporting troops and, from the moment they were committed, they came under his direct command. The same applied to the reserve battalion if it was called for, but the deployment of this unit was a decision for the regimental commander in the first instance.

The forward troops looked to the *KTK* for all aspects of their support. He directed where the artillery main effort was to be from minute to minute and was responsible for all aspects of resupply, casualty evacuation and reporting. This last responsibility was of critical importance. Crucial decisions were made further up the command chain on the basis of what the *KTKs* reported. It was far from easy in the midst of a raging battle, with shells raining down all around, for cool appreciations of the situation to be made. Yet it was essential if a successful defence was to be conducted. It was quite wrong for the *KTK* to call for additional reserves when he himself had the means to defeat an attack; equally, decisive and, above all, timely requests for support when the situation demanded it were essential.

The rank of the *KTK* was of secondary importance. For the German army a man's appointment was what gave him his authority. Thus it was entirely proper for the *KTK* to issue written orders to the commanders of reserves behind him and he did so, knowing that they would be obeyed, even if the commander to his rear was senior to him in rank. This responsible role called for highly experienced, calm and cool commanders. They needed what the Germans referred to as *Fingerspitzengefühl*; that is to say, they had to blend experience with instinct, in order to conduct operations professionally and successfully. Of course *KTKs* made mistakes. There were setbacks and disasters. However, bearing in mind that the rank of these men was generally Hauptmann, it is remarkable how well they coped with the unprece-dented demands of the Flanders battlefield. As a group they probably did more to thwart Allied ambitions than any other.

Whereas in the Middle Ages it was the norm for the heralds of the opposing armies to get together after battles and agree on the nomenclature to be handed down to history, there was no such meeting of the minds following the Great War. The German names for the campaign in Flanders in 1917 and its various major battles are entirely different from those the Allies used. This can be quite confusing. The Battle of Messines, for example, was known as the *Kampf um den Wijtschatebogen* [The Battle of the Wijtschate Salient]. As far as operations from the end of July to November are concerned, the Germans referred to what the Allies called the Third Battle of Ypres, as the *Flandernschlacht* [Battle of Flanders]. Post-war, they identified twelve major attacks, which they regarded as being particularly significant and hard-fought. They considered that there were also five main phases to the battle, which, for them, did not finally end until 5 December 1917, when Crown Prince Rupprecht issued a special Order of the Day – although, well before then, their attention had turned primarily to the Battle of Cambrai. There is not complete unanimity in the literature about the dates but, as an indication, here is an approximate chronology, with the equivalent Allied designation for the battle which opened the phase:

31 July	First Battle of Flanders	Battle of Pilckem Ridge
16 August	Second Battle of Flanders	Battle of Langemarck
20 September	Third Battle of Flanders	Battle of the Menin Road
9 October	Fourth Battle of Flanders	Battle of Poelcappelle
22 October	Fifth Battle of Flanders	Second Battle of Passchendaele (preliminary operations)

Useful though these artificial divisions are as we look back on the events of 1917, the terms would have meant nothing to the men who lived through the unspeakable conditions and horrors of the Passchendaele battlefield. On the defensive, the German army spent almost the entire length of the battle reacting to events. In consequence the *Feldgrauen* in their pillboxes and water-filled shell holes did not even have the satisfaction of preparing for the next big push behind the lines, well-fed and in reasonable comfort. Instead, soaking wet, chilled to the bone and exhausted, they just had to soldier on – despite everything that a determined enemy and the malevolent weather could throw at them. Uncertain if they would live to see the next day or the next hour; uncertain if they would be able to beat off the next attack when it came; uncertain, even, where their next meal or drink was coming from, they simply endured and went on enduring, until death, wounds or relief provided them with an escape from their purgatorial surroundings.

This is their story.

Jack Sheldon
Vercors, France October 2006

jandl50@hotmail.com

Author's Note

Certain eye witness accounts and other descriptions in the text are linked to a particular locality on the battlefield. Each chapter includes at least one map of the area. The figures on the 'Eyewitness Maps' relate to the numbers in bold associated with that section of the relevant chapter. In some cases different witnesses were located in the same area, so they share a number. The only exception comes in Chapter 7, which contains three detailed maps of the Passchendaele area, but no numbers appear.

Place names are something of a problem when describing events in Flanders. The familiar names of Ypres, Messines and Passchendaele have been retained, but other places have been rendered in their modern Flemish forms.

The Germans never differentiated between English, Scottish, Irish or Welsh soldiers and units, referring to them all as Engländer. This usage was frequently extended to contingents from the Dominions as well. Engländer has been translated throughout as 'British' for troops from the United Kingdom and usually adjusted where other nationalities were involved.

German time, which was one hour ahead of British time, is used throughout the book. Thus, the mine blasts which marked the opening of the Battle of Messines went off at 4.10 am.

Acknowledgements

Because of the loss of the Prussian archives in a bombing raid in 1945, it is completely impossible to reconstruct the Great War battles from the German perspective without recourse to the many hundreds of regimental histories which appeared during the interwar period. I fully acknowledge the debt that I owe to the authors of these books. My work would be impossible without theirs to draw on. I should also like to thank Professor Peter Simkins for writing the Foreword. Professor Simkins has devoted a lifetime of scholarship to the Great War and we are all indebted to him for his immense contribution to the historiography of the period. Once again my wife Laurie has drawn the maps for this book and sustained me through my research through her loving support. My editor, Nigel Cave, has proved once more to be a fount of knowledge concerning all manner of obscure detail and has made sure that what I have written has the ring of truth to it. Nevertheless, I remain responsible for any errors which may remain. After almost a century has passed, this account can, at best, only be an honest approximation of the German side of this landmark battle. Alex Fasse in Germany has helped me again with material and advice, Lieutenant Colonel Phillip Robinson and Ian Jones of the Durand Group kindly provided me with the technical background concerning mining in the area and the explosives used in the Hill 60 craters and I am most grateful to the Director and staff of the *Kriegsarchiv* in Munich for their assistance in obtaining primary source material. My thanks are also due to all at Pen & Sword books. I have tried to avoid infringing copyright in the writing of this book. Should I have done so inadvertently, I ask that my apologies be accepted.

CHAPTER ONE

June and July 1917

T he night of 6/7 June 1917 was comparatively quiet after several days of an intense bombardment, which had involved the use of over three million shells. All along the German front line in Flanders, sentries came and went, officers moved silently around their positions, checking that all duty personnel were alert and the occasional flare shot up in the sky, casting harsh and grotesque shadows on the desolate strip of territory between the lines that was No Man's Land. The night wore on, dawn approached and tired company officers, their rounds and their paperwork complete for the night, were thinking of snatching a nap before the dawn stand-to when suddenly, at 4.10 am [3.10 am British time], the largest man-made explosion in history up until that moment was unleashed. From Hill 60 forward of Klein-Zillebeke in the north, to St Yves, east of Ploegsteert Wood in the south, nineteen massive mines, prepared in total secrecy over many months, blew up simultaneously.

The noise was heard up to two hundred kilometres away. Many thought that there had been an earthquake. Hundreds of German soldiers had no time to think anything. Killed instantly by the concussion, sent spinning into the air by the force of the blasts or vaporised by the intense heat in the centre of the explosions, they died in droves, swept away and forgotten, as the curtain rose on a battle which was to last five months, claim the lives of tens of thousands of soldiers on both sides, test men to the uttermost limit of human endurance and cast a long shadow over the lives of millions in the years to come.

The Messines ridge, known to the German Army at the *Wijtschatebogen* [Wijtschate Salient] had been a thorn in the side of the British army for three years. From its heights much of the Ypres salient could be overlooked and guns placed on it could bring down aimed enfilade fire on any point within it at will. For their part, the Germans were continually worried about the intrinsic vulnerability of the *Wijtschatebogen*. Concerns about the potential for attacks against it were a staple pre-occupation in the weekly situation reports issued by Staff Branch Ic of the Headquarters of Army Group Crown Prince Rupprecht during the early months of 1917.[1] As a result, news that a preparatory bombardment had opened against it on 20 May came as no surprise to the defence.

From north to south of Group Wijtschate, commanded at the time by General der Kavallerie von Laffert, the 204th (Württemberg), 35th, 2nd and 40th (Saxon) Divisions, huddled in their dugouts, pillboxes and blockhouses, could only hold their positions and endure whatever the British artillery, directed by a large number

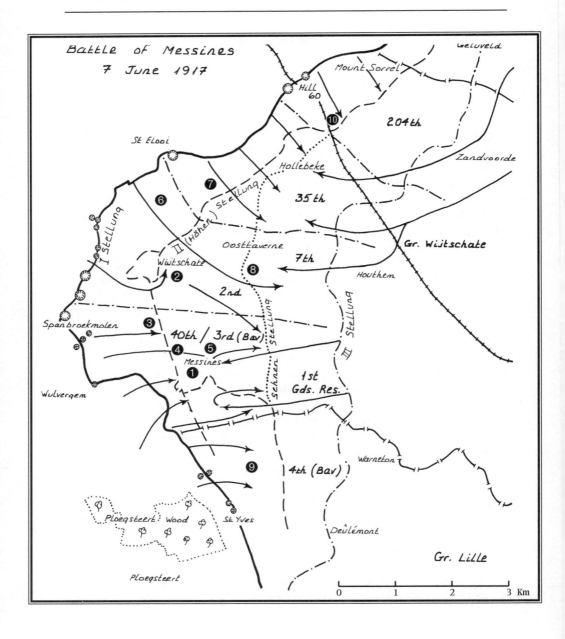

of aerial observers, could throw at them. There are numerous accounts of the trauma of this bombardment. One of the observers of Field Artillery Regiment 32 of 40th Infantry Division, for example, has left us a graphic account of the manning of an observation post as the shells rained down around him: **1**

"Until the end of May manning our observation post in Messines was still a fairly pleasant job. The British had started to engage Messines with heavy calibre shells, but they left the monastery, where we were located, alone. Day by day, this situation altered to our disadvantage. Suddenly, one day a shell landed right in front of us. It was only light calibre, so it had very little effect on our concrete pillbox. The following day a direct hit landed right on top of us. Once again it was only light calibre, thank heavens. Tiles and pieces of concrete landed on the wooden planks, but we still felt that it was a chance hit. Because of the increasing number of shells each day, it was quite possible that one had found its way accidentally in our direction. We were about to learn better.

"Gradually the light calibre rounds gave way to 280 mm shells, which crashed down with massive detonations, sending up huge pillars of earth and dust. Initially they landed beyond us, but gradually they crept closer. It dawned on us that our observation post was being deliberately targeted with super-heavy calibre rounds. As a result, for an hour at a time, two or three times a day, we were engaged with identically heavy shells. Our concrete pillbox heaved and swayed with each close impact by the shells. Thick powder smoke filled the room whenever a shell exploded really close, windows shattered, tiles and chunks of concrete rained down; the interior of our post often looked very rough indeed.

"It was noticeable that, whenever we directed a shoot against the mortars that were hammering our trenches, we in turn came under fire. It was perfectly obvious that the British had realised that there was an observation post here and were able, therefore, to bring effective fire down on it. There was not much left of Messines. What had once been an attractive village was reduced to a heap of ruins. The British, nevertheless, did not have all the luck when they engaged the village. Had they been more fortunate, they would have managed to land a direct hit on our post and snuff out all life. Try as they might, they never managed it. Not until the very last day before the attack did they manage to crush half of it with a direct hit." [2]

Reserve Oberleutnant Scheele Adjutant 2nd Battalion Grenadier Regiment 4 [3] **2**

"Our *KTK* (Leuthen) [(Command Post of the) Kampftruppen-kommandeur = Commander of the Forward Troops][4] was nothing more than a heap of ruins. We lost all four corners in the early days of the bombardment. An extremely heavy dud landed right on the roof of the blockhouse and wedged there with its tip hanging directly above the entrance; not that that reduced the number of visitors. The *Pappelhof* was also badly hit but, despite that, it remained in remarkably good condition. The daily air battles were most interesting. It was far from rare to see the enemy flying in battle formations of sixty to seventy aircraft. We were not in a position to put up so many sorties but, when we did, the British tended to stay away.

"Leutnant Wellhausen was seriously wounded in the *KTK*. A shell landed right outside, sending showers of splinters through the small window and hitting Wellhausen. We were clustered close together round a table, because the pillbox only measured 1.5 x 2.5 metres and were almost blinded by debris, dust and flying earth. I ignored the firing and headed off out carrying my discipline files, which the regiment had sent forward to me. The British landed shells just behind me, but I escaped their effect behind the next traverse, having first thrown my case containing the files there. I rounded up some stretcherbearers for Wellhausen here.

"The British did not fire on the stretcher bearers carrying the stretcher. [After that] we stayed where we were and did not attempt to return to *KTK* Leuthen before it went dark. It was, of course, still engaged at night, but not with aimed fire. The air battles continued to entertain us. The aircraft made a special effort to destroy balloons. If one of the latter was shot down, the observers used to jump and descend to earth by parachute. When the aircraft fired phosphorous [incendiary] bullets, they left long trails of flame and made a most interesting sight. Those of us on the ground were frequently the targets of enemy aircraft; the boldest of these came down to twenty metres to fire at us.

"It went on like this day after day. By then we were worn down so much that, finally, careful watchfulness in the face of danger gave way to complete indifference. None of us believed any longer that we should escape this witch's cauldron in one piece, so it was all the same to us if we met our fate a few days earlier than we otherwise might have done. Our situation was desperate, but it did draw us together. We went into our letter cases and drew out letters and photographs of our relatives to show to one another, [but] our conversation tended to be confined to speculation about when we should be hit."

Reserve Leutnant Wolk, 3rd Battalion Field Artillery Regiment 1 [5]

"Swarms of enemy aircraft enhanced the efficiency of the artillery. They interdicted the rear areas by day and night, attacking all manner of live targets with bombs and machine gun fire. It was clear to us all what lay before us and everyone held his breath, waiting for the infantry assault which just had to come. In order to counter what was going on, our artillery counter-battery fire also increased in intensity. Despite high losses of men and materiel in the batteries, we plastered enemy batteries and mortar positions industriously. Our Green Cross gas shells [filled with phosgene, or chloropicrin, or a combination of the two] certainly silenced many a 'Tommy' battery."

The 40th Division had returned to its sector of the Wijtschate front on 21 April after a brief rest and, between that date and 3rd June, had lost 1,300 men to various causes. Those who remained were tired out and overdue for replacement. In consequence, the 3rd Bavarian Infantry Division was moved forward to relieve it.

The relief was due to be completed by the morning of 7 June, but the final stages of the process were overtaken by events.

Leutnant Dickes Bavarian Infantry Regiment 23 [6] **3**

"During the night 5/6 June 1917 the 3rd Bavarian Infantry Division relieved the 40th infantry Division in the Wijtschate area. Once more Bavarian Infantry Regiment 23 was heading for the trenches ... The 1st Battalion was stationed forward, the 2nd Battalion was in reserve and the 3rd Battalion was on stand-by and was not involved in the relief until the night 6/7 June ... At midnight on 5/6 June [the regimental staff] set off for the regimental command post southeast of Wijtschate. Already, on the far side of Tenbrielen (eight kilometres east of Wijtschate), heavy shells droned overhead and red, yellow and greens flares could be seen up ahead. In single file we pressed on past innumerable shell holes – the going seemed to be far worse than anything experienced on the Somme or at Arras – through gas-filled hollows as far as the command post, which was housed in two concrete blockhouses. The party finally arrived for the relief, dog-tired and soaked with sweat. Everyone could see that this was a real hot spot, but nobody realised just how bad things would turn out ...

"At 4.15 am [*sic*] on 7 June,[7] the earth suddenly shook violently, which made everything tremble ... thinking that it had been caused by heavy shells landing nearby, Hauptmann Klahr, having shouted in vain to his batman, leapt outside. The sky was full of smoke and dust and thousands of British gun barrels were pouring out death and destruction. It suddenly dawned on everyone that the British, having mined forward over a long period, had blown up the entire front and launched the anticipated attack. What could our men outside possibly do? They had hardly arrived. They did not yet know the ins and outs of the position. Utterly overwhelmed by such explosions, what could be expected of them? Simultaneously, down came the British artillery fire, which further damaged the shattered remnants of the trench garrison lucky enough to have survived the explosions. Split into small nests of resistance, they held out forward. No support could get forward through it. The defensive artillery batteries had been neutralised and the battalions at readiness could not get to the front.

"About 5.00 am, the first report arrived from the front line. It stated that the British had blown up the positions held by 1st, 2nd and 3rd Companies Bavarian Infantry Regiment 23, had overrun them and that the *Kaiserschanze* (1,500 metres southwest of Wijtschate and located between the First and Second Positions), which was being defended by 4th Company Bavarian Infantry Regiment 23, had also been taken. In other words, the forward battalion had ceased to exist. At that point Reserve Leutnant Kliegel, commander of 9th Company, who, despite the fire, had managed to get forward, reported in. He was ordered to occupy the crest line to our front and the remaining reserve companies under Major Koch (Infantry Regiment 104) received the same order. To have delayed longer would have been dangerous.

"The two concrete blockhouses which housed regimental headquarters were visibly shaking from the impact of exploding shells. It appeared that the British rolling barrage had reached this line and was about to move on. The sound of small arms fire could be heard clearly in the blockhouses. Reserve Leutnant Heerget went forward to the crest and spotted that the British were only fifty metres away. There was no sign of support; some of our men had already pulled back. Reserve Leutnant Diehl was still up on the crest line, firing a machine gun for all he was worth and could not be persuaded to withdraw. 'I have never seen targets like it,' he said. But what could he and his machine gun achieve alone? He stayed where he was and was captured.

"The decision was now made to evacuate the command post. To have stayed any longer would have been tantamount to committing suicide. As we left the command post the British poured small arms fire at our small group at virtually point-blank range but, amazingly, nobody was hit. After racing away in bounds of hundred metres and fifty metres, the withdrawal continued at a walk; the wall of dirt and dust cutting out all visibility ... The British rolling barrage was quite distinct, but our artillery was completely silent. We passed battery positions where the guns were still there and ammunition lay ready. Only the crews were missing. As we made our way to the rear, we did not hear our artillery fire a single round. Our airmen were also completely absent, whilst those of the British circled above and fired at us from close range. Finally, at 7.17 am, we arrived at

Villa Kugelheim (a farm two kilometres to the east of Wambeke), which was the headquarters of 88 Infantry Brigade. Here we reported what had happened …

"Next morning, the 8th June, the regiment assembled near to Korentje (six kilometres east of Messines). There were about 600 altogether. Apart from one officer (Reserve Leutnant Seeburger), three men and the mortar platoon, the 1st Battalion was destroyed. Only a few remnants remained of the 3rd Battalion, which had been surprised on the march forward. The 2nd Battalion suffered the least … Within perhaps half an hour the regiment had lost twenty nine officers and more than 1,000 men. The great majority fell victim to British weaponry; a few were captured."

Oberleutnant Eugen Reitinger,
Adjutant 3rd Battalion Bavarian Infantry Regiment 17 [8] (**4**)

"Beginning on 4 June, 3rd Bavarian Infantry Division began to relieve 40th Infantry Division. Bavarian Infantry Regiment 23 was located on the right, with Bavarian Infantry Regiment 17 in the centre and Bavarian Infantry Regiment 18 on the left. Each regiment was deployed with one battalion forward, one close behind in support and one resting. These regiments from the Pfalz knew the ground well, having spent time there in 1914/15. Following the bloody battles around Ypres in November 1914, trench warfare had begun. Very quickly a vigorous policy of sapping and mining was put in place by both sides. Over time this reduced in intensity and later came to a complete standstill. In the past few weeks, the 40th Infantry Division had not detected the slightest sign which might have caused them to think that the enemy was engaged in mining. They had been subject to a fatal deception … During the night 5/6 June, Bavarian Infantry Regiment 17 under its proven commander, Major Ritter von Kohlmüller, had taken over as reserve battalion. The following night it moved forward to relieve the forward battalion in the front line. Enemy artillery fire had wrecked or flattened the trenches and, all around, the ground looked like a freshly ploughed field. The garrison settled down to establish itself here as well as possible and prepared to face the forthcoming enemy assault.

"The command post for both forward and reserve battalions was a large concrete blockhouse, named *Thümmelschloß* [Castle Thümmel] after its builder. The staffs of the relieved and relieving battalions were here during the early hours of 7 June – it was Corpus Christi – fully occupied with the hand over details. In the front line the relief was in full swing; when suddenly, at 4.00 am, there was an almighty roar and the earth began to quake and everything flew off the chairs: explosion! Attack! Both officers and men poured out of the entrance into the open air. An awe-inspiring and appalling sight met their eyes. The hills from Wijtschate to Messines were enveloped in a great sea of flames. Fourteen [*sic*] fiery volcanoes and masses of earth erupted vertically into the sky colouring it a blood red. Then the great masses of earth crashed back down to the ground and, simultane-ously, drum fire of unprecedented violence crashed down. Time passed worryingly then, at about 5.00am, a runner arrived from the front, with dreadful news: '3rd Battalion Bavarian Infantry Regiment 17 has been blown sky high'

Major von Kohlmüller blanched as he absorbed the news that his beloved battalion had been destroyed. But, a moment later, he opened his mouth and said firmly, 'All personnel in *Thümmelschloß*, listen to my orders!' He then proceeded to give out a full set of orders for the defence of the command post. In the meantime [we discovered that] the reserve battalion, which had been occupying positions in shell holes forward of the bunker, had been almost completely annihilated by the drum fire and the remnants had been overrun by the assaulting British troops. The first of the British troops were starting to appear on the hill behind which the *Thümmelschloß* stood, but they were quickly halted by the determined fire of the courageous defenders. Unfortunately the enemy were able to deviate left and right and encircle the *Thümmelschloß*. Cut off on all sides, further defence appeared to be hopeless. There were faint-hearted calls for the attempt to be made to break out towards the rear, but Major von Kohlmüller had only one reply to that: 'I have been brought up to hold the position with which I have been entrusted. We are either going to die here or be relieved from the rear. I am not pulling out!' At this both officers and men were filled with renewed courage.

"Meanwhile the British had redoubled their efforts to clear this toughly defended pocket of resistance. After drum fire lasting half an hour, several British companies launched a further attack about 7.00 am. This developed into hand to hand fighting, during which Major von Kohlmüller set a shining example to all. The attack was beaten back several times, but this had cost us much blood. Only five lightly wounded officers, two machine guns and a few men remained to give battle. Despite that, having moved the wounded into the shelter of the blockhouse, this brave little band prepared to fight on, but the odds were too great. Once more artillery fire was concentrated on the bunker. Casualties continued to mount then, at about 7.30 am, a shell blew Major von Kohlmüller to pieces. Towards 8.00 am the British renewed the attack. Once all the officers and most of the men were no longer able to continue to fight, they finally succeeded in taking the *Thümmelschloß* Thümmel. Only a few wounded men were taken prisoner."

The loss of Major Hans Ritter von Kohlmüller was a further serious blow to the regiment on this day of almost unrelieved disaster. He had been awarded the Knight's Cross of the Military Max Joseph Order for his heroism during the defence of the Hohenzollern Redoubt during the Battle of Loos at the end of September 1915 and was a strong and charismatic leader. Only one officer, Leutnant Brander, escaped capture after this incident, bringing news of the disaster. Hauptmann Senn, commander 1st Battalion Bavarian Infantry Regiment 17, was severely wounded in this action and died of his wounds in British captivity.[9] Leutnant Reitinger was seriously wounded, captured, but survived to provide virtually the only first-hand witness account of the fight for the *Thümmelschloß*.

Reserve Leutnant Hermann Kohl, Liaison Officer Bavarian Infantry Regiment 17 [10] 5

"Oberst Auer (Commander, Bavarian Infantry Regiment 17) was going forward to complete the relief when his move was overtaken by events and he was ordered by Brigade Headquarters to remain where he was. About midday [I found him] in front of his command post, looking like a broken man. He had no contact whatsoever with his troops and knew only that few of them were left. Tears glistened in his eyes. It was my task as liaison officer to brief him about the tactical situation and the complicated chain of command along the front. I had a bicycle, but most of the time I carried it and walked cross country. The approach roads were crammed and under attack from enemy aircraft. Guards Reserve Regiment 1 was making its way forward under the blazing midday sun. It was high time that the British flood tide was dammed up by fresh troops.

"My route took me in to the area of the *Barbarahof*. The farmhouse was totally wrecked, standing in the midst of a sea of ploughed-up destruction, with the farm buildings reduced to smouldering ruins. The fields around looked like an endless chessboard covered with overlapping craters. It was the work of one hard day; one single day. Everywhere I bumped into stragglers from the division: leaderless and wandering like lost sheep from a scattered herd. Totally apathetic, they lay in shell holes or by the side of the road. They were waiting for orders. The boldest were forward in the *Sehnen Stellung* and had joined the counter-attack. There were Saxons, too, [presumably from 40th Infantry Division] scattered around the terrain. At the *Barbarahof*, I came across a Saxon Leutnant, who had obviously suffered a nervous breakdown. He kept bawling at me that I ought to be in the front line and taking part in an attack. His spoke incoherently and in a pitifully agitated fashion. I was just waiting for him to draw his pistol … But I had no time to engage him in a drawn-out debate about the importance of my mission and no breath to spare either.

"Heavy artillery fire was coming down behind the *Barbarahof*. The explosion of a couple of heavy shells crashed into the ground to my front, showering me with earth and sending me flying into a huge crater hole, complete with bicycle and causing me to sprain both my arms. My arrival was greeted with curses and complaints from below, where a Prussian brigade staff was trying to get set up. The adjutant was as red as a lobster with anger; he had made sharp contact with the handlebars of the bicycle. The general calmed him down. In the end falling into the crater was a stroke of luck. The staff was able to assist me in the fulfilment of my task and to set me off in the correct direction. Half-right, over there in the *Burghof*, was where the commander of the new Guards front line regiment was located. This would make it easy to obtain the information I needed. I presented the Guards with the wrecked bicycle, exchanged a few words and set off …

"The *Burghof* was not exactly an inviting sight. A heavy shell had just landed nearby smashing the remaining rafters to matchwood and giving it a rather drunken silhouette. An enemy aircraft suddenly crashed to the ground right next to it in the crater field. I took prisoner the British officer who was flying it and went with him down into a musty cellar, where I introduced myself and handed him over to the Guards. A Prussian Oberst, who was wearing the *Pour le Mérite*, was sitting bent over spread out maps and was dictating an attack order. The orderly jumped up and offered me the obligatory coffee. The candle flames guttered from the overpressure of shells busting in the ruins of the *Burghof*. Nobody took any notice; there were more important issues to be dealt with.

"Openly and with concise seriousness, the Oberst gave me a briefing about the fighting to the front, the objectives of the attack, the organisation of the forces involved and the chain of command. The remnants of the Bavarian troops were fighting with the Guards! With a few strokes of the pen a sketch was produced and half an hour later it was in front of my Oberst. He was extremely grateful and shook my hand several times. At last the nightmare of uncertainty was lifted from him."

That day Bavarian Infantry Regiment 17 suffered total casualties of thirty four officers, 1,151 junior ranks and three horses – and the picture was much the same for Bavarian Infantry Regiment 18.

Leutnant Wilhelm Handrich 5th Company Bavarian Infantry Regiment 18 [11]

"The 3rd Bavarian Division, having been successful in the role near Arras, had been intended for use as an *Eingreif* division. It demonstrated its counter-attacking skills on exercise areas near Oudenaarde and Wervik; in the latter place in front of General der Infanterie Sixt von Armin and dozens of other generals. So the division was skilled and practised in that role. Suddenly, on 4 June, came the order to relieve a ground-holding division. Bavarian Infantry Regiment 18 was responsible for the sector running southwards from Messines to the valley of the Douve and 2nd Battalion moved forward during the night 4/5 June. 5th Company was stationed in Messines itself ... The German positions, back as far as the Third, were being heavily gassed and British artillery fire of all calibres was hammering down on the German positions and the ground in between ... During the early morning [of 6 June] the weight of artillery fire increased considerably.

"Throughout the day British aircraft flew at extremely low level over the German positions and rear areas; directing the British artillery fire and dropping bombs on all identified targets ... including Messines, which also received an especially generous allocation of super-heavy calibre shells. The medical aid post received a direct hit, which penetrated straight through the concrete overhead cover. At the time the post contained Oberarzt Finkenauer (3rd Battalion), Unterarzt Kellermann (2nd Battalion)[12] and fifteen stretcher bearers. Unfortunately only five of the stretcherbearers were saved – by Infanterists Jakob Schwarz, Michael Lieb and Karl Nolting (all of 5th Company), who set about rescuing them immediately, despite the extremely heavy fire. The two doctors and the other stretcherbearers were beyond help. The dugout became their grave.

"In the meantime, the drum fire continued heavier than ever, which meant that the attack was imminent. In actual fact it began at 4.15 am [*sic*], 7 June. Within an hour, out of all the elements of the powerful 3rd Bavarian Division which had been deployed, only shattered remnants remained. Setting off sixteen to eighteen [*sic*] massive explosions from the canal northwest of Hollebeke to the valley of the Douve, the enemy launched their attack. The ground trembled and complete sectors of the front were blown up. Entire companies were destroyed and wide gaps were ripped in the defences. The British initially poured through these gaps, then widened them.

"Places where there were no mines, such as the village of Messines itself, were kept under fire longer. When the barrage moved on and the defenders from the 18th emerged from the concreted defences, they found that overwhelming masses of British [*sic*] troops had effectively already surrounded them.[13] This made defence in most areas completely impossible ... The four companies of the 3rd Battalion, which had been manning the front line, were as good as wiped out at a stroke by the explosions. 5th Company did manage to maintain a spirited defence in Messines itself for some considerable time to come; earning itself honourable notices in the British press. The final remnants of the company did not surrender until the company commander was seriously wounded. The other three companies of 2nd Battalion, which had been deployed in the Second Position, did their utmost to hold off the British who had penetrated the position but, finally, they were attacked by overwhelming force from the rear, bringing resistance to an end. Only the odd individual was able to break through the smoke and dust and escape to the rear.

"Thanks to the extraordinary artillery preparation and the blowing of the mines, the British took the first two positions in their initial assault, but the attack came to a halt in front of the *Sehnen Stellung*, the line which connected the two ends of the Wijtschate salient ... They had insufficient strength to rush the position and had to dig in in front of it. Thanks to the number of airborne artillery observers, the British artillery continued to engage the German batteries so successfully that the fire of the latter was further reduced. Command and control of the British artillery was quite excellent. Newly-arrived German batteries had hardly begun to open up before they were engaged by counter-battery fire by the British. The companies manning the *Sehnen Stellung* were also subject to increasing fire. A thrust attempted by the British at about midday was driven off, but increasing casualties meant that the defenders of the *Sehnen Stellung* found themselves ever more threatened.

"The 1st Guards Reserve Division, amongst others, was launched in a counter attack. Two battalions of Guards Reserve Regiment 1 and a battalion of Bavarian Reserve Infantry Regiment 5 advanced through the area of Bavarian Infantry Regiment 18, but could not get beyond the *Sehnen Stellung*, so they stayed to reinforce the seriously weakened companies of 1st Battalion Bavarian Infantry Regiment 18 there, so that at least this position could be held. As it went dark enemy activity died away. Apart from a few concentrations of artillery fire, the night passed off peacefully. The next morning Bavarian Infantry Regiment 18 was withdrawn completely from the position ... Its losses had amounted to 1,100 men and those of the division 98 officers and 3,600 men."

As has been noted, the relief of the 40th Division by the Bavarians was not complete when the mines were detonated. This meant that numerous members of the Saxon Infantry Regiments 104, 134 and 181 were still in the forward area when the battle began. The 24th Saxon Infantry Division, which had been relieved on 5th June, was further away, having already begun its move to a rest area, but the minute the offensive was launched, all its units still within range were rushed back to the endangered sector.

Major Oschatz, 3rd Battalion Infantry Regiment 133 [14]

"On 7 June 1917 occurred the long-expected blowing of the entire Wijtschate salient. The British, operating at depths of up to sixty metres,[15] had mined right beneath our lines as far as the Second Position, the so-called *Sehnen Stellung*.[16] In a series of massive explosions, the entire defensive position was blown into the air and, with it, thousands of the soldiers of its garrison. Our regiment was fortunate because it was part of 24th Infantry Division, which had been holding the position since the previous December and had suffered heavy casualties during the systematic bombardment by the British and, therefore, had had to be relieved a couple of days earlier. The troops were making their way on foot to a rest area to the south east of Lille, when during the early hours of the morning we heard a dull rolling roar, which sounded like an earthquake. This was followed immediately by the noise of enormously heavy drumfire.

"My 3rd Machine Gun Company was halted on the march by motorcycle despatch rider from divisional headquarters. Loaded onto one of the numerous narrow gauge railways, they were rushed back to the area we had just left. The machine guns were prepared and, because the huge explosions meant that losses were so severe that insufficient reserves were on hand, the arriving troops were thrown straight into the battle. The objective was to reinforce the Third Position which was still being defended by a few remnants, to prevent the British who had pushed forward over the heights of Wijtschate from advancing further and to throw them back by means of a counter-attack. Heavy British artillery fire and lack of cover in this open area meant that we suffered severe casualties. Thanks to the arrival during the next few days of *Eingreif* divisions, it was possible to hold the British in the course of heavy fighting, despite the fact that incessant British artillery fire destroyed the routes to the rear and cut all the telephone lines, so that it was impossible to bring up hot rations for the troops."

To the right of 3rd Bavarian Infantry Division and guarding the northern shoulder of the Wijtschate Salient, the regiments of 2nd Infantry Division were subjected to no fewer than seven of the great mine explosions. Once more, their forward elements suffered extremely severely. The final six days of the bombardment had cost Infantry Regiment 44 the lives of Leutnants Wülpert and Eggert, together with fifty five junior Ranks. There were, in addition, three officers and 195 men wounded.[17] Grenadier Regiment 4 and Füsilier Regiment 33 recorded similar figures. In this area, although many commented on the fact that the hours before the explosions were calm for the forward companies, extensive use of gas and large quantities of high explosive shells had already cut them off from the positions containing their supports and reserves.

Reserve Oberleutnant Scheele Adjutant, 2nd Battalion Grenadier Regiment 4 [18] **2**

"It was the night 6-7 June. Once more we spent the night in the *Pappelhof.* The ration party was unable to get through again, so we made do with a little tinned meat – all our bread was finished – and we lay down to rest. The night was strangely quiet. About 4.00 am, a violent shaking threw me from my desk and on top of my friend Reschke. Simultaneously, intense drumfire began. We looked with horror at one another, believing initially that there had been an earthquake but then, finally, we realised, because of the drumfire, that we had experienced the explosion of mines marking the start of a great offensive. Going to the entrance of our dugout, we looked out at a massive cloud of dust which was rolling towards us. This was lit up by a great firework display of light signals and we noted that the battlefield around us was eerily empty apart from dead horses, dead men and wrecked wagons which littered its surface, the top two to three metres of which was completely ploughed up.

"Here and there the odd wounded man or courageous survivor was trying to pick his way towards the rear. It seemed impossible and, indeed, most were killed in the attempt. The Major, Sergeant Schmeer and I crept out of the dugout and, despite the fire, made our way along the line of what had been *Puitsgraben.* Deviating first to the left, then to the right, we headed towards the front. The rolling barrage drew closer and closer. We forced a way to within 100 to 200 metres from the advancing line of British infantry. Our route to the rear was cut off by the barrage and our nerves were on edge. With the aid of a two metre long periscope which, together with the most important maps and orders we had brought with us from the *Pappelhof,* I spotted the fact that the enemy was signalling at short intervals to their artillery with coloured rockets and that the fire was coming down in the areas indicated by the rockets. We adjusted our position so that we were always within the arc of the rockets, but just far enough distant from the enemy. To do this we leapt from one deep shell hole to the next, which was not difficult because the craters were mostly overlapping.

"Suddenly I saw a runner from our 8th Company and called to him to come over. The commander, Leutnant Gartenmeister, reported that he had launched a counter-attack, but that he was being pressed hard by the British. What could he do against such overwhelming odds? Whenever there was a brief gap in the endless clouds of dust and smoke we could make out massive numbers of attackers, followed by dismounted cavalry leading their horses. I could not tell if our artillery was firing in support of us; it was impossible to distinguish particular sounds, due to the appalling racket. I certainly saw no artillery observers. We rallied the few men who made it back and formed a rough defensive line, determined to sell our lives dearly. I kept my pistol permanently in my hand and took the odd pot shot at enemy pilots who engaged us from a height of ten to twenty metres. Then, in the distance, I could see British commanders standing upright in the midst of the lines of attackers. It was quite clear that the entire battalion must have been lost. Firing rapidly, we attempted to keep these attackers and others from the left flank at bay. A runner from the forward headquarters of the Saxon regiment on our right told us, as he was passing, that their commander was about to burn all the maps, because he was sure that they were about to be captured. Although the enemy did not seem to be making much effort to push on, we came to the conclusion that we could not save the situation. Our 8th Company, too, was surrounded and had to surrender after a fierce and desperate battle. We were on our own without our rifle companies. What were we to do? The choice was capture or an attempt to break through the appallingly heavy box barrage.

"We chose the latter course of action. At the first attempt I was blown off my feet by the concentration of enemy shells and loose earth that was being thrown in all directions. Behind me, Sergeant Schmeer grabbed me by the collar with his great gloved hand and hauled me to my feet once more. Major Simpson was hit on the helmet by a shell splinter and knocked out for several minutes. But we pressed on through the showers of earth and shell splinters from shell hole to shell hole, making for the rear. Shells with delayed action fuzes were hurling fountains of earth up as high as houses. We were resigned to our fate. A Leutnant from the regimental staff was killed just next to us. He had been trying and failing to get forward. There was not a trace of the remainder of the staff.

"Eventually, towards 5.00 pm, after being continuously on the move for thirteen hours after the explosions, the Major, Sergeant Schmeer, a telephonist and I arrived in the *Sehnen Stellung*, which was occupied by clerks, chefs, wagon drivers and batmen. We carried on through the line and reported to the regiment, who ordered us to take over one of the sectors of the *Sehnen Stellung*. The enemy arrived at this position during the late afternoon and launched an attack preceded by a rolling barrage and supported by tanks but, prior to that, reserves had been rushed forward and relieved us. The enemy did not get far beyond the *Sehnen Stellung*. We were given orders to withdraw to Werwik where the remnants of the Division were assembling. At roll call the following morning it transpired that my commander and I were the only officers of the battalion left. The remnants of the companies, comprising the ten to twenty men of the ration parties who had been unable to get forward during the night, were led to the rear by NCOs of the Quartermaster's department. Our hearts were filled with sorrow. After the war some prisoners explained that the enemy had blown five or six craters, 100 to 150 metres in diameter, in the regimental sector."

When, on 8 June, Grenadier Regiment 4 was withdrawn, a mere forty four returned from the forward companies. The casualties in the twenty four hours of fighting had been forty six officers and 1,370 men killed, wounded or captured,[19] whilst Füsilier Regiment 33 reported seventeen officers and 1,106 men missing.[20] Infantry Regiment 44, for its part, had missing no fewer than thirty two officers and 992 junior ranks, of whom more than one third were killed.[21] Very often survival was a matter of mere chance. The men of 12th Company Füsilier Regiment 33 just happened to be making their way to the rear in the early hours of 7 June, having just been relieved.

Füsilier Paul Schumacher, 12th Company Fusilier Regiment 33 [22] **6**

"Just before we reached the *Kortestollen*, I looked to the rear and suddenly noticed from the British side star flares being fired along the entire line from Messines to St Elooi. This struck me immediately as odd and I drew the attention of my friend Thormann to it, saying, 'Look out, those dogs are up to something;' but Thormann just laughed. We hurried on, puffing and sweating towards the *Kortestollen*. I asked the time; it was exactly 4.00 am. Then suddenly there was an enormous flash, just where we had come from, to the right by St Eloi and to the left at Messines. Blood-red flames shot up into the sky and a dull crack and boom penetrated the roar of the guns. The earth heaved and rocked as though it was trying to tear itself apart. Like lightning the thought rushed through my head: the British have blown mines and are about to attack! Simultaneously, a hail of hundreds of shells rained down on the Wijtschate salient. The entire position, from front to rear, was brought under the most intense drum fire.

"There was complete confusion as shells landed around us. Fusiliers crawled out of the dugout and took cover against the appalling fire. All the orders that the officers tried to give to restore order from chaos were drowned out by the terrible din. Suddenly I felt as though a weight was pressing on my lungs. I could get no air and I fell forward. Just a minute, I thought, 'those dogs are firing gas shells!' and so they were. I yanked my mask out, put it on and immediately felt better. My equipment, in which I kept the camera which had accompanied me for so long, went flying. At that precise moment I could not have cared less. If I emerged alive from this, I could collect it later, but I gave it no more thought.

"What company are you from?' demanded a young Leutnant, bawling through his mask. 'The 12th', I replied. 'Go left and extend the 4th Company line!' was the next order I received. I could not find my Leutnant (Hoffmann), or my company. There was no sign of Thormann; perhaps he was already dead. Anyway I pressed on and attached myself to the left flank of 4th Company, whilst shells landed all around us with ear-splitting crashes. Split into small groups, we moved forward to occupy the crest in front of the *Kortestollen*. The entire time we were stumbling into shell holes, were sprayed with earth and filth, screaming shell splinters flew through the air and shrapnel balls whistled around us. All hell seemed to have broken loose. Sweating and shivering from the excitement, we ducked down into shell holes and let this hellish fire pass over us. I lay behind a small mound and pressed myself down on the ground. My thoughts raced, as did my pulse and my head ached. I must have laid there for hours. Because of the dirt, my watch had not been working for days, so I had no idea of the time. To my left, about thirty metres away, was a machine gun. From time to time I could hear it being fired to test that it was still working. Above me, enemy aircraft were climbing and diving, circling and spiralling, as they ignored the hail of fire of their batteries and swooped low to see where any living beings might still be concealed.

"I cursed them, I cursed the sun which had now risen in all its radiant glory and was shining down mercilessly on this murderous scene. I squirmed lower into the sand to try to escape the gaze of these enemy birds of prey. A shell burst just in front of me and clods of earth hit me painfully on my back and helmet. For a moment I was conscious of the thought that my last hour had come; but this soon passed. I rolled over on to my other side, removed my gas mask and rolled further a few metres into a shell hole, where I saw some steel helmets moving about. Two of my comrades from 4th Company were lying there and waiting for the British assault. I asked the time. It must have been about 8.00 am. Still the fire continued. The pillars of earth from the shell bursts flew up in the air, as high as houses. Above the general tumult and din, steel shells could clearly be heard exploding with a shrieking clatter. A splinter tore my left sleeve and a small fragment cut my right cheek, making it bleed, but nothing else happened to me. Cursing and swearing, the three of us crouched in the crater, wracked by thirst and with our senses reeling, as we let everything pass over us. Gradually we could not care less what happened. I became quite indifferent to my fate and just waited for something to happen.

"The machine gun to our left suddenly opened up, as did another to our right and there they were, hard up against the curtain of fire. Grey monsters drew slowly towards us, spitting fire. They were British tanks and flashes were coming from them. Between them we could see infantrymen with steel helmets, the flat type, who were wearing khaki. The three of us fired like mad men. To our right and left, out of all the shell holes the enemy was being fired at. Closing in on the tanks, which continued to grind forward, they advanced on us. Now we could see them clearly. They were blacks, probably British colonial troops, swinging short curved knives in their hands. We looked on with horror as they cut down every living thing in front of us and now we knew what awaited us. However they did not try to take us on. From their wild cries and the animal savagery with which they hacked at everything, they seemed to be completely drunk.[23] Amongst them were white infantrymen, rifles in their hands, who advanced steadily, only hitting the ground when the machine guns to our left and right sent their 'blue beans'[24] cracking across the ground. We fired on, but began taking careful aim and economising on bullets, which became fewer and fewer. A heavy shrapnel round burst overhead, pouring its blessing down on our hole. My two comrades suddenly shrieked; one collapsed and seemed to have been mortally hit, whilst the other was apparently severely wounded. Blood spurted from his back and he soon lay still next to me.

"What was I to do? The last of the rounds would soon be fired and then …? Was I to let myself by murdered by the blacks? – never. 'Just a moment', I thought, 'why not try to link up with the left hand machine gun that was still firing about forty metres away?' No sooner thought than done. I crawled up the side of the shell hole on stiff, painful limbs and was just about to dash to the left when I was confronted by a tall figure dressed in khaki and wearing a flat steel helmet and puttees. He was without doubt an officer. He yelled something at me which I did not understand. Instinctively I raised my gun, but received a heavy blow to the left upper arm at the same instant. The British soldier had shot and wounded me. I had to hit him before he could get a second shot off. He was only fifteen to twenty paces away; I could not miss. The shot rang out; the tall figure collapsed, spun round and disappeared into a shell hole, but it was over for me. My arm was terribly painful, blood was pouring down my sleeve and my rifle fell to the ground. Closer, ever closer came the yelling blacks. It was high time to be off. Once more into the hellish fire! Boiling hot, stumbling and running I made it back to the *Kortestollen.*

"What a sight it was! There were bodies lying everywhere and a sickening smell hung over everything. I stopped for a bit of a breather, applied a field dressing to my arm, then pushed on further into the raging fire. The artillery fire was coming down kilometres to the rear; it was no easy thing to come through it. I leapt from shell hole to shell hole, pursued by enemy aircraft which kept firing at me. Diving down like hawks from one hundred metres, they picked off the wounded with machine gun fire. A shrapnel ball cut through my trousers and grazed my leg, but I just kept on going. Just onwards, ever onwards, through the hellish fire – and I succeeded, despite the British machine gun fire which was already sweeping the area from positions in Messines."

Only one offensive mine blew up within the sector boundaries of 35th Infantry Division, which was responsible for the Hollebeke area. It hit the extreme left flank of the divisional frontage, which meant that several eyewitnesses in other parts of the forward battle area were able to get a clear view of the momentous events

Leutnant Meinke Infantry Regiment 176 [25] **7**

"Suddenly, what was it? The earth roared, trembled, rocked – this was followed by an utterly amazing crash and there, before us in a huge arc, kilometres long, was raised a curtain of fire about one hundred metres high. The scene was quite extraordinary; almost beyond description. It was like a thunderstorm magnified one thousand times! This was followed by thousands of thunderclaps, as the guns opened up simultaneously, adding their contribution to the power just unleashed. The wall of fire hung in the air for several seconds, then subsided to be replaced by the flashes of the artillery muzzles, which were clearly visible in the half light. For an instant we just stood, mesmerised by the spectacle. There was no question of returning to the rear to have wounds dressed, because hardly had the wall of fire died away to nothing than the entire earth seemed to come to life. Scrabbling their way forward from hundreds of starting points, came steel-helmeted men. Line upon line of infantrymen emerged and the enemy launched forward."

Unteroffizier Köhler 9th Battery Field Artillery Regiment 1 [26] **8**

"At 4.00 am on 7 June the earth seemed to groan then, an instant later, there was an appalling crash. The Tommies had blown everything up! Hardly had we recovered our senses than the battery came under a murderously destructive fire from shells of all calibres. Some one bawled 'Man the guns! Defensive Fire!', but his voice could barely be heard, such was the racket. From that moment the howitzers had to fire as quickly as possible. We opened around 4.00 am at 4,600 metres and shortened by 7.00 am to 3,100 metres.

"In broad daylight and amidst extraordinarily heavy enemy fire, our teams galloped up at about 9.00 am. The ammunition column arrived in the position to replenish us. What daring! We ran over to the wagons and tore the ammunition boxes off them, then they raced away. What a miracle; not a man was wounded. Only the battery simpleton came unstuck. He missed the wagons as they raced away and had to make his way back to the horse lines in Comines on foot. The artillery fire decreased in intensity slightly after 10.00 am.

"About 3.30 pm a fresh bombardment began; the British storming forward behind its shelter. We replied with defensive fire once more. Suddenly, a 280 mm shell crashed down next to us and, a split second later, another to our front ... then there was a third 280 mm round which exploded, heaved the gun off its mountings and flung it, barrel facing to the rear, against the concrete blockhouse in which we were sheltering. After that only the right hand section of 9th Battery could continue to fire. At about 5.00 pm came the order, 'Evacuate the position!'...We fired no more ... The infantry brigade commander who had observed the gallant arrival of the ammunition drivers and the unloading of the shells that morning by the gun crews is supposed to have asked later, 'What has happened to the brave gunners of 9th Battery?'"

Kanonier Schütze 9th Battery Field Artillery Regiment 1 [27] **8**

"Although our 9th Battery had often been under heavy fire, it was nothing to compare with the horror of that morning when we had to man the guns under such a dreadful weight of fire. Inevitably each man was extremely conscious of the proximity of death, but each reacted differently, depending on his inclination. One might turn to prayer; another might throw himself aggressively to his duties on the gun and yet a third, optimistic to the last, might simply hope for the best. But every man stood to his post and did his duty! Our gun fired round after round. After an hour of constant firing and the crash of enemy shells exploding in the vicinity, the three men who were serving our gun were all completely deaf! This was an advantage, because it blocked out the devilish racket of the enemy drum fire; we hardly heard anything of it ...

"Around 5.00 pm our gun jammed during loading and I had to race 400 metres through the wall of fire to the armourer. However this stoppage was never cleared, because a Leutnant entered the gun pit and ordered us to evacuate it. Everyone grabbed what was valuable or important to him; first and foremost his weapon of course. We pulled back and formed a rough infantry firing line in rear of our position, but the officer who had ordered us to adopt it, sent us further back, because we could not have achieved much with our 88 pattern weapons. We had a terrible job getting back through the enemy curtain of fire to our horse lines. I dragged or carried a wounded infantryman, who had lost both eyes due to a shell splinter, all the way to Houthem. All the way there he kept begging me to shoot him. It was simply dreadful."

Amidst scenes of confused, heavy fighting and severe losses, there were also lucky escapes and astonishing coincidences on the battlefield that day, as this short account of a meeting between father and son near the *Sehnen Stellung* demonstrates.

Pionier Jakob Schneider Bavarian Landsturm Pionier Company 11 [28] **9**

"At evening roll call on 6 June, we were ordered to go out that night and repair the many shell holes in the roads around Wijtschate, so that ammunition and rations could be brought forward. The battle was going at full blast. About 4.00 am there was a thunderous noise, like an earthquake. Because of all the smoke and dust, you could not see the sun rise. There we were in heavy shell fire and we were given a load of work to do during the night. When dawn began to break, the wounded started to come back from the battles, moving past us in small groups. My son was with Bavarian Infantry Regiment 9. There were lots of the 9th there. I asked them, 'What's happening to the 2nd [Company]?' The answer was that they were coming too. My son was in that company. Then more wounded came past, I asked them again and someone told me that the 2nd Company was in the fighting. Our Unteroffizier ordered us to go to the other road that ran to the front.

"Wounded men were coming down this road too: 9th, 5th and the other Bavarian regiments. I kept asking about the 2nd Company when the 9th came by. Then I was by a big shell hole. I could see a single wounded man coming from a long way off. I thought: 'That it is one of the 9th.' We were wearing steel helmets and, because of the hard work, I never thought any more about this soldier. With my pick in my hand, I was working on the shell hole and suddenly heard a voice. 'Good morning, father!' I looked up in shock and there was my son, covered in blood. He had been hit last evening at 8.00 pm by a shell splinter, which had gone through his helmet and wounded him in the head. He had laid there at the aid post from evening to morning, covered in blood and in great pain. He asked me, 'Father have you got something to drink?' I said, 'My dear son, I shall go with you to the next village. There is a canteen there.'

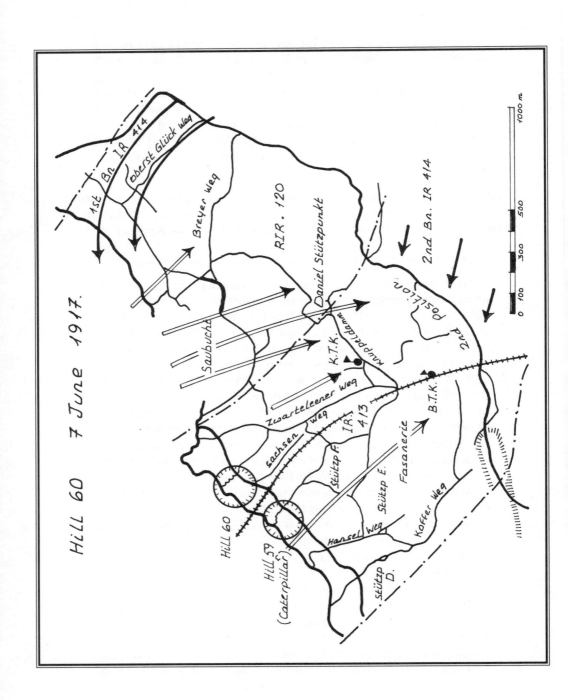

Hill 60   7 June 1917.

"At that moment there was a big air attack and we were ordered, 'Take cover!' We sat together under a willow tree and talked about this amazing meeting, which happened through a miracle. Then my son said, 'Father I've got to get to the nearest hospital. I can't stand this pain anymore.' Then we parted with a heavy heart. Three weeks later I visited him in Lomme, near Lille. That same evening he had to go back in the trenches. On 30 September 1918, he died a hero's death for the Fatherland."

Somewhat further to the north, Infantry Regiment 413 was occupying the left forward sector of 204th Infantry Division, with its 2nd Battalion in forward trenches on Hill 59 [The Caterpillar] and Hill 60, the location of the two most northerly offensive mines. Hill 60 had been the site of mining by both sides since early 1915, so the fact that the mines here achieved surprise is, in itself, remarkable. According to the history of Infantry Regiment 413, during the early days of June, the amount of destructive artillery fire directed at this small sector had removed any doubt about a forthcoming major offensive so, by order of higher head-quarters, all the German sappers and miners were withdrawn from the area. It was felt that no more useful work could be achieved before the attack was launched and they did not want to hazard the lives of their valuable underground experts. However, even after the engineers had withdrawn, the infantry in this location detected the sound of mining activity here between 1 to 4 June, but it was felt that it must be coming from shallow galleries five to eight metres deep.[29]

Quite apart from any other consideration, the German miners had experienced great difficulty in dealing with the water-bearing strata, which on their side of the line was fifteen to twenty metres thick and had all the characteristics of quicksand. It was not until September 1916, after many fruitless endeavours, that this 'Kemmel' quicksand was driven through by means of ferro-concrete shafts – a cumbrous, time-consuming process. The Germans assumed that the British and Dominion miners were likewise baulked, but in this assessment they were quite wrong. With a combination of engineering ingenuity, the use of 'tubbed shafts' and hard work, the BEF miners had penetrated through to the hard, blue, Ypresian clay at a much earlier stage and had already placed most of the mines, at depths of thirty metres or more, before the Germans were in a position to develop defensive galleries at that depth. With few sounds of working to be heard, it would have been mostly a matter of luck if they had found any of the waiting charges. Suspicions were voiced, notably by Oberstleutnant Füsslein, the engineer officer responsible for mining in the area, but the prospect of a substantial mining attack was largely discounted by the experts, creating that most dangerous of situations – an immense threat from a totally unexpected source.

Of course, even if the German defenders had known of the presence of the deep mines, they were caught on the horns of a dilemma.[30] If they had pulled back from the heights to avoid the danger of being blown up, they would instantly have ceded the advantage of the observation in all directions which was possible from the crest line. In the event, the choice was to sit tight and await further developments – a decision which cost hundreds of lives and did not prevent the loss of the summit of Hill 60. Also deployed forward and to the right of Infantry Regiment 413, was Reserve Infantry Regiment 120, which was also badly affected by the Hill 60 mine. When it exploded, two of its companies were wiped out and a third scattered. It is interesting to note that Reserve Infantry Regiment 120 reported later that, although this particular mine produced a wide blast of flame and made the ground churn and quake, in contrast to the others, it did not send up a great column of smoke, fire and rubble.[31] Whatever the facts, the effect was still devastating and, when the great mines were detonated, the adjutant of 2nd Battalion Infantry Regiment 413 and one of the platoon commanders of 2nd Company found themselves well placed to witness everything that happened.

Reserve Leutnant Wendler Adjutant 2nd Battalion Infantry Regiment 413 [32] **10**

"During the night 6/7 June the 2nd Battalion was deployed in the front line. About 2.00 am a sudden stillness descended but, as we later learned, it was just the calm before the storm. I remained awake throughout the night in a dugout, intending to get some sleep about 4.00 am, provided that nothing out of the ordinary occurred. About 3.45 am I went up once more into our observation post, from where it was possible to survey the entire front. Everywhere was deadly quiet. Suddenly, at about five minutes to four, red flares were fired from the sector to our left, but there was no response from our artillery. I immediately despatched a runner to the neighbouring *KTK* to find out what was happening. In the meantime I prepared my signal pistol, in case we needed to relay the message and alert the guns.

"Suddenly, at exactly 4.00 am, explosions, accompanied by drumfire occurred. The effect of the explosions was massive. Everything swayed and huge clods of earth were blown as far as our dugout. Of course, there was no need for me to alert the men in the dugout; all the shaking woke everyone up. All our attempts at telephoning [units on] either side were fruitless, because all the lines had been broken immediately. We had no luck either with our message dogs. One of them returned wounded immediately and the other was so scared it would not go out at all. Our wireless operator also tried to establish contact, but they explained that they had had no success. All we had left were our carrier pigeons, which did sterling service that day in keeping divisional headquarters informed.

"To begin with we had no idea what was actually happening in the front line trenches. We could only assume that the four forward companies and the machine gun company had been totally destroyed by the explosions. As a result, just after the explosions, I was given the task by Major von Legl personally to go to the reserve companies of the 1st Battalion, which were located by the corduroy road [to the rear] and order them to launch some of their numbers against the enemy and to occupy the strong points between the First and Second Positions with the remainder. Equipped only with gas mask and pistol, I ran through the drum fire to the companies of the 1st Battalion. I could never understand later how I found my way there and back. All I knew was that every few metres I fell, or was blown, over obstacles and into trenches, before arriving bleeding, my uniform ripped but otherwise intact, to report to my commander that my task had been completed.

"In fact nothing happened, because it was completely out of the question for the companies of the 1st Battalion to leave their pillboxes and dugouts in that torrent of fire. They would have been cut to shreds. However, when at about 6.30 am the British advanced from the *Saubucht* [about 500 metres east of the Hill 60 mine crater] towards the *Daniel Stützpunkt* [Strongpoint Daniel, about 600 metres behind the front line], we established that elements of the 1st Battalion were manning the line of the corduroy road to prevent the British from progressing further. Oberleutnant von Wachter and his batman entered the *KTK* blockhouse and I explained to him that I still had one serviceable machine gun with plenty of ammunition and that, therefore, I did not intend to abandon the position for the time being. If the British did, in fact, surge forward once more, there would still be ample opportunity to pull back to the corduroy road. Not only that, but there was an aid post containing about thirty seriously wounded men just next to my dugout and I did not want to abandon them to capture by the enemy.

"From then on, for the remainder of the day, four of us defended the dugout, reinforced from time to time by runners. Our tactics were for two of us at a time to man the observation post and the machine gun in rotation. Because it was only possible to move around the position by crawling, we put a length of rope on the machine gun and dragged it some way back behind the command post. As soon as the British showed themselves near the *Daniel Stützpunkt*, we fired a few rounds, then swiftly changed position, so that the British would think that heavier forces were occupying the position. In this way we moved to and fro all day long and our efforts at deception were successful, because no British soldier dared to push forward.

"During the afternoon, fourteen men from Infantry Regiment 414 under Leutnant Arnold appeared along the railway track. They had been ordered to advance to the *Daniel Stützpunkt*. Fortunately I spotted them at the last minute, or they would have blundered into the hands of the enemy. As soon as I explained the situation to Leutnant Arnold, he decided to stay with us, which meant that our fighting strength had gone up to twenty. About 5.00 pm a runner arrived from Major von Legl, who was occupying a dugout in the rear, ordering me to assemble the remnants of the 2nd Battalion, once it had been properly relieved later that evening, and to report to him. With a heavy heart I had to inform him that the remnants of the 2nd Battalion comprised just myself and a few others.

"The hope we nursed that a number of stragglers from the battalion would turn up the following day turned out to be a false one. Our forward sector, which had a width of 240 metres, had been hit by two mines, each of which had left a crater between eighty and one hundred metres wide. Those who were not killed or wounded had been captured and the following day it was established that we could muster only twenty seven men, almost all of them from 7th Company. They had not been caught by the explosion and had been able to avoid capture by pulling back through the neighbouring sector."

Reserve Leutnant Freiherr Kreß von Kressenstein
2nd Company Infantry Regiment 413 [33] **10**

"Around midnight I was standing outside, listening intently to the guns of both sides firing, noticing how high in the sky the trajectory of the super-heavy shells was ... They arrived in pairs from the direction of Ypres, soaring overhead to land in Menen or Kortrijk. Fired at intervals of three minutes, one salvo after another hit the German rear area. Suddenly there was an almighty flash, as an enormous quantity of German ammunition blew up. It later transpired that several trainloads of ammunition in the station at Menen had exploded. Then there was an eerie stillness; the British seemed to be satisfied with the result of their shooting. Only the occasional flare sputtered up into the sky, exposing the outlines of Hills 60 and 59. With slight concern, I lay down for a short rest, next to my men, who were already snoring.

"A massive earthquake, coupled with a thunderous noise from under-ground, brought me back to my feet. On Hill 60/59 a huge pillar of fire, a good hundred metres high, had shot into the sky. It was obvious that the British had set off an explosion and, immediately, the entire hill was cloaked in smoke and flames as drum fire smashed down on it. Our batteries came under an enormous weight of fire. The entire earth and the air trembled with all the explosions. Machine guns opened up all along the line, sending ricochets whining around us. I rushed to my platoon: *Take cover and stand-by!* We strained our eyes to watch the appalling spectacle and the adjacent heights. All we could see was smoke and pillars of fire.

"To begin with the platoon was outside the main zone of fire but, as the rattle of the machine grew louder, it was clear that the enemy was having success. Sometimes we could even make out their silhouettes through the smoke ... Suddenly gas shells began landing in our midst and I ordered my platoon to move to the Second Position to escape the clouds of gas. No sooner had we done this, however, than our new location was engaged by howitzer fire. My men crawled off into concrete pillboxes, but I stayed where I was in the open trench; I did not think the pillboxes would be proof against shells of that calibre. In fact it was not long until a direct hit on a crammed bunker by a delayed action shell collapsed the whole thing and buried everyone inside it.

"Shortly afterwards I was jammed in a narrow section of trench by the explosion of a shell, but I was freed by some of my men ... the drum fire continued to fall with undiminished ferocity, creeping ever closer to us. Here and there we could see the British advancing, individually or in small groups. We entered the trenches on 4 June with eighty five men, but the company was now reduced to about half of that ... The company commander, together with seven men, was occupying a large, deep, shell hole in the centre of the company sector ... I took cover there too and was amazed at the confidence that Leutnant Merz was radiating. A large smile on his face showed that he was the master of the situation. We were bombarded with clods of earth and steel splinters were whizzing everywhere. Machine guns hammered away and the earth trembled and swayed with the constant huge explosions. Shells went on bursting, showering us with fragments, nose caps and shrapnel, so our original group of nine kept getting smaller.

"Once, following a dreadful crash, came the shrieks of many voices in pain and fear. Chunks of concrete, steel splinters, fire and filth cascaded over us. Men scattered as though a herd of wild animals had been disturbed and went in search of fresh cover and one man, with his left arm dangling, was racing around the cratered area like a lunatic. There was a twelve centimetre gash in my steel helmet, but my head was untouched. One man lay still in the powder-blackened crater, his body lacerated by innumerable wounds, another let out his final bellow of agony and voices called out for medical orderlies – but none were in sight. I raced off after the company clerk, Unteroffizier B___, grabbed him and forced him back into the trench. In a state of collapse he leaned back against the wall of the trench as I amputated his arm, where it was wounded just below the shoulder, with my pocket knife and applied a tourniquet made from the strap of my map case to the stump, to prevent him from bleeding to death ...

"Throwing him across my back I set off through the trench, sweating profusely, over the wire and through the craters and soon arrived in one piece at the *KTK*, where there was a doctor. B___ had lost consciousness by now and I handed him over to the professionals. Unfortunately he could not be saved; he had lost too much blood. Scheer, the adjutant, took me into his pillbox and poured me a huge measure of schnaps, which I certainly needed, because I was close to collapse myself. During the short five minute breather I spent there I experienced heavy shells knocking large holes out of the roof, so I needed no persuasion to go back into the Hell outside. Death in the open air seemed to me to be preferable to one under a collapsed pillbox.

"I dashed back the same way I had come to my platoon, which had suffered even more casualties. At 10.00 am I was ordered to occupy the *Daniel Stützpunkt*. On the way there the company lost Leutnant Schmidt to a direct hit.[34] ... When we reached [it], we saw that the British were standing shoulder to shoulder in it. Machine gun fire forced them to take cover. I left a machine gun there and returned with my men to the Second Position, where we linked up with a few others. Some Prussian troops arrived at midday to reinforce us ... So the day continued. The battle ebbed and flowed. Death swung its scythe and danced on the crater field, in the trenches, the pillboxes, on the troops at readiness and the artillery batteries. Finally I was hit in the groin by a large piece of concrete and could hardly stand, let alone walk. Finally night cast a protective cloak over us."

What became known as the Battle of Messines continued until 12 June, during which time the German ability to recover rapidly from setbacks meant that resistance increased and Allied losses mounted before the battle was finally called off. It had been a significant victory for the men under General Plumer, a fact which stands out clearly between the lines of German communiqués and Orders of the Day, which were published whilst the fighting was still continuing.

Army Daily Communiqué issued by GHQ 8 June 1917 [35]

"Western Theatre of Operations:
Army Group Crown Prince Rupprecht:

"Attacks launched by the British between Ypres and Ploegsteert Wood, north of Armentières, were beaten off yesterday southwest of Ypres by troops from Lower Saxony and Württemberg. At the same time the enemy succeeded after a series of enormous mine explosions along the line St Elooi, Wijtschate and Messines, in breaking into our positions and driving forward, after a hard battle of changing fortunes, via Wijtschate and Messines. A powerful counter-attack by Bavarian troops threw the enemy back to Messines. Further to the north an attack was brought to a standstill by a counter-attack … "

Crown Prince Rupprecht of Bavaria – Diary Entry 9th June [36]

"The British Army communiqué is celebrating the victory of General Plumer at Wijtschate. It is said that the detonation of the gigantic mines could be heard in London. Some of the mine galleries were completed a year earlier. In the first rush, the British troops succeeded in overrunning the German lines and by midday both Wijtschate and Messines were in their hands. All around Messines the ground was said to have been covered by the bodies of Bavarian soldiers (our poor, brave 3rd Division!)."

Fourth Army Order of the Day 10 June 1917 [37]

"The hard fought battles of 7 June have cost us our forward positions in the Wijtchate salient. That is regrettable, but we now know that the enemy were only able to achieve their success by means of the use of over-whelming strength and the massive exploitation of a wide range of technical military means.

"That which was achieved by the German forces of all arms and services, of each unit and formation, through the most obstinate defence and ener-getic counter-attack and at the cost of severe casualties makes this a Day of Honour for us.

"My warmest thanks and fullest recognition go to all those who partici-pated in the battles of 7 June. At the head of such troops I can face the future with solid confidence.

The Commander
Signed: Sixt von Armin, General der Infanterie"

As the fighting died away and the defence consolidated along the line St Yves – Wambeke – Hollebeke, there began a period which was referred to by General der Infanterie Hermann von Kuhl, Chief of Staff at Army Group Crown Prince Rupprecht, as 'a lengthy period of anxious waiting.' [38] The German chain of command recognised that the initiative had been yielded to the Allies and that, for the time being, they could only study the situation, attempt to prepare for the most obvious contingencies and stand by to react to events. In the wake of the disaster of Messines, Group Ypres issued an order relating to the holding of forward positions.

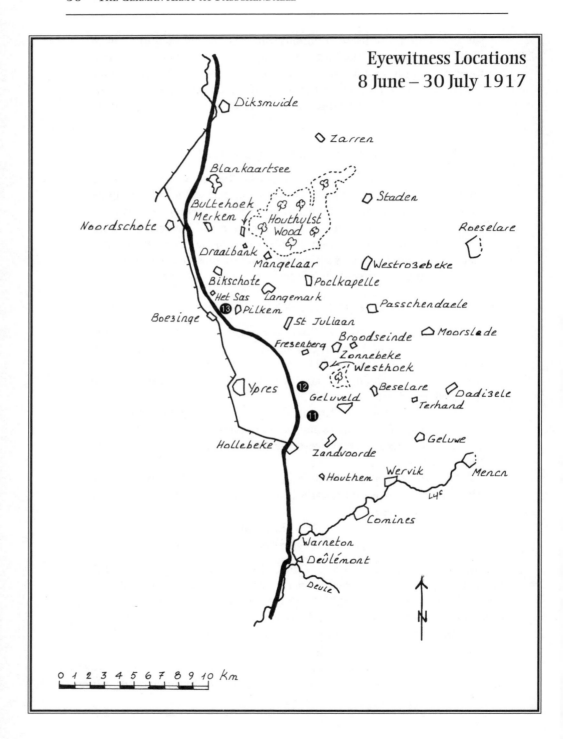

Eyewitness Locations
8 June – 30 July 1917

Diksmuide

Zarren

Blankaartsee

Bultehoek
Merkem   Staden
Noordschote
                Houthulst
                Wood   Roeselare

Draaibank
        Mangelaar
Bikschote   Westrozebeke
Het Sas   Poelkapelle
        Langemark
Boezinge ⑬ Pilkem   Passchendaele

        St Juliaan
                Broodseinde   Moorslede
        Fresenberg
                Zonnebeke
                Westhoek
        Ypres   ⑫
                Geluveld   Beselare   Dadizele
                ⑪   Terhand

Hollebeke   Geluwe
        Zandvoorde
        Houthem   Wervik   Menen
                            Lys

                    Comines
        Warneton
        Deûlémont

        Deule   N

0 1 2 3 4 5 6 7 8 9 10 km

Group Ypres [III Bavarian Army Corps] Order Ia Nr. 3/Juni dated 12 June 1917 [39]

"In order not to sacrifice the front line garrison unnecessarily, strong forces must not be kept in the threatened area. The real battle line is to be withdrawn about 300 metres behind the front line. Token security forces only are to be maintained in the former front line and given the task, together with patrols along the length of the front line and operating forward in the direction of the enemy, of deceiving the enemy about these measures. There is little risk that the enemy will attempt to establish a presence at some point in the position; he will wish to avoid occupying positions beneath which he has placed mines. In any case, we shall have to accept that slight risk."

A week later, the commander issued an explanatory note concerning the above.

"In order that there may be no doubt about which line is to be fought for in the course of a defensive battle, I direct that this is to be the front line trench, which we are currently only occupying with sentry posts … this type of garrison meets the needs of the defensive battle and is derived from the experience of battles around Arras …"

General der Infanterie Hermann von Kuhl
Chief of Staff Army Group Crown Prince Rupprecht [40]

"During the second half of June 1917, there was complete clarity on the German side that a major British offensive in Flanders was to be expected. The axis of the attack against the sector Bikschote-Deûlémont (either side of Ypres) was also known with reasonable certainty. What was completely uncertain, however, was when the offensive was due to begin. It was obvious that the British had imposed an operational pause, in order to complete all their preparations with the utmost thoroughness."

Towards the end of June, there was a large increase in aerial activity. At one point the men of Bavarian Reserve Infantry Regiment 6 counted 139 aircraft in the sky above them. It was a tremendous boost to morale for the German soldiers to see the predominantly red aircraft of Richthofen's squadron operating above them. Inevitably some German aircraft were shot down during the dogfights that occurred on a daily basis. One particularly noteworthy victim was Leutnant Karl Allmenröder, who had thirty victories to his name. With considerable difficulty, 4th Company later recovered his body from the crash site in No Man's Land.[41]

Dr. Schnitzler Bavarian Reserve Infantry Regiment 6 [42] **11**

"Early on the morning of 27 June, Infanterist Max Feuerstein of 4th Company was on guard in a shell hole. Immediately next to him was a concrete blockhouse covered with earth, in which his comrades were sleeping or cleaning weapons. The Flanders sky was hidden by low cloud which covered both sea and land. Then the first of the British aircraft arrived on the scene and circled around low for the next thirty minutes. Suddenly, like bolts of lightning, the blood red one-seaters, so well known to the Flanders soldiers, came diving down out of the clouds, pouring fire into the British hornets. They scattered in all directions, accompanied by the rattle of machine gun fire. A tangled dogfight quickly developed and it was not long before the first of the red white and blue fighting cocks was going down in flames over his own lines, wreathed in black smoke. The battle picture then altered as the enemy planes sought the safety of their own lines, pursued by one of the red aircraft.

"The red aircraft was soon on its way back, under heavy fire from anti-aircraft guns and small arms fire. It was hit and splinters were seen to be flying off ... the red machine rocked and banked steeply. One wing broke off, black smoke started coming from it then, suddenly, it was enveloped in a tongue of flame. The aircraft plunged out of control. The broken wing fell with a crash into the mud right by the blockhouse and the remainder of the fuselage crashed to the ground in flames, not one hundred metres from the British lines. Nobody could do anything to help. The aircraft was in full view of the British, who were putting down curtains of machine gun fire all round the area.

"That same day Oberleutnant Sorge, the company commander, received the news that the shot down pilot was none other than Fliegerleutnant Karl Allmenröder, a member of Richthofen's Fighter Squadron 11 and holder of the *Pour le Mérite* [Blue Max]. The squadron commander, Baron von Richthofen himself, had urgently requested that the body of their fallen comrade be recovered. Unteroffizier Reinhold Voxberger, a calm and very practical frontline soldier, set about forming a team of volunteers and attempting to carry out the mission. Once it went dark, he and three others crawled forward into No Man's Land, but were unable to approach the wreckage, which was still burning. The lit-up circle was kept under constant British machine gun fire from Hill 60. The patrol spent the entire night near the wreck, but never reached it."

Unteroffizier Reinhold Voxberger
4th Company Bavarian Reserve Infantry Regiment 6 [43] **11**

"As it went dark on the second night, we set off once more and this time we reached the crash site relatively quickly. I knew where it was from the previous night and the three men with me, Infanterists Georg Hutzler, Georg Müller I and Max Feuerstein were first class. When we reached the target I put out two men as sentries left and right, well forward of the site, so that we should not be surprised by enemy patrols. What we found was that the engine and cockpit had driven down deep into the ground. The wingtips, and tail assembly, together with the control surfaces, lay around broken and scattered. After a preliminary examination, we set about digging the earth away left and right of the cockpit. The worst feature of this was the appalling smell of rotting corpses, which interfered with our ability to work. The aircraft had crashed into a battlefield cemetery, containing the bodies of comrades who were killed in 1915 and 1916. Decaying limbs and other body parts lay strewn about everywhere. After a long hard struggle, lasting about two hours, we had finally recovered the dead airman. We placed his body in a groundsheet that we had brought for this purpose.

"The two sentries were withdrawn and they carried him back. Müller I crawled in front, followed by the others who crawled back carrying the load. I brought up the rear, ready to fend off the enemy. After about 150 – 200 metres we were able to risk abandoning crawling and moved upright. We were soon back at our own lines, with the recovery complete. Having reported to the company commander, we were ordered to transport the body back to battalion headquarters. We did this and were ordered to take the body to regimental headquarters. From there we were told to carry it to divisional headquarters, but for us, after two sleepless nights and the indescribable strain and fatigue of it all, that was too much. I went to see the regimental adjutant and explained the circumstances. An ambulance was made available, we loaded in the mortal remains of Leutnant von Allmenröder into it and a medical orderly assumed responsibility for this important duty. We returned to the front."

A few days later a special army order was published:

IIa Nr. 1360 dated 7 July 1917: Fourth Army Routine Order 1127 [44]

"I wish to express my especial recognition of Unteroffizier Voxberger and Infanterists Hutzler, Müller I and Feuerstein of 4th Company Bavarian Reserve Infantry Regiment 6 for their courage and for the care with which they carried out the recovery of the body of Leutnant Allmenröder of Fighter Squadron 11, who was mortally wounded in aerial combat and who crash-landed in front of our lines near Klein-Zillebeke.

"The entire *Fliegertruppe* [Flying Corps] passes on its warmest thanks that they made possible the burial of our well-known pilot and comrade in the Homeland.

"For their heroism and on behalf of His Majesty the Kaiser, I have awarded the Iron Cross First Class to Unteroffizier Voxberger and Infanterist Müller I and the Iron Cross Second Class to Infanterists Hutzler and Feuerstein.

> Signed: Sixt von Armin, General der Infanterie
> Commander in Chief

Unteroffizier Voxberger, somewhat taken aback by his award, later said, 'We just went forward again and did our duty.' One of the others who was involved, added, 'We certainly did not expect any reward. We thought it only natural that we should help to fulfil the wishes of the squadron commander and the parents that the body of their loved one should be returned home for burial.'

General der Infanterie Hermann von Kuhl
Chief of Staff Army Group Crown Prince Rupprecht [45]

"From the beginning of July the signs began to multiply that the offensive was approaching. The enemy preparations were being driven ahead quite openly. Railways were built, the number of battery positions increased and the number of troops along the British front increased. But still there was no attack. The situation of Army Group Crown Prince Rupprecht was difficult and required the Commander in Chief to make serious choices. Concerned, he had to turn his attention to the other fronts; to the Lens area, to Arras and St Quentin where, at any time, there could be an enemy thrust – even if it was designed simply as a diversion or secondary attack.

"The previous year on the Somme it had proved possible to hold the Anglo-French offensive only because the other fronts had been seriously weakened to enable force to be placed at the decisive point. Even a relatively modest enemy attack elsewhere could have had the most serious consequences. We had to reckon with the possibility of such attacks in the summer of 1917, after the army group had ordered all the men and materiel which could be spared to be moved to Flanders and put at the disposal of Fourth Army for the forthcoming defensive battle.

"Out of the blue, Sixth Army reported the arrival of railway guns, an

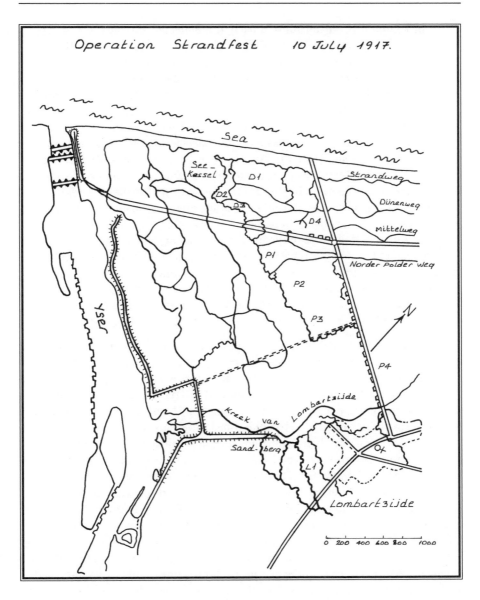

increase in heavy batteries, the placement of thirty five tanks south west of Arras and other signs, which caused them to assess 'with certainty that a seriously large attack was to be resumed.' In its present state, the army was not in a position to counter such an attack; it could not release any more troops for Flanders and it needed artillery reinforcements. Crown

Prince Rupprecht did not allow himself to be deflected. Having checked the reported indicators, he decided that, whilst it was entirely possible that a strong secondary attack could occur, the British had regrouped their forces for a major offensive in Flanders. Nevertheless the Sixth Army could not be weakened any more; reserves must be maintained behind it, but not used if at all possible and kept for deployment in Flanders.

"This process brought to the fore the question, which to our cost we had failed to answer prior to Wijtschate, and to decide whether or not to learn from experience and avoid the first blows of the forthcoming offensive in Flanders by conducting a planned withdrawal. This was examined during a conference at the end of June and led to the decision that, given the particular local circumstances, it would not be advantageous to do this. In order to have forced the enemy to re-locate their artillery it would have been necessary to withdraw to the great *Flandern Stellung* [Flanders Position] in the rear and, in so doing give up the entire depth of the current defensive system. In addition, the *Flandern Stellung* was still not ready. The local commanders were also unanimous that the current system of positions was eminently suitable for defence from both an infantry and an artillery point of view and that the deployment of reserves had been well prepared." [46]

When, on 19 June, a patrol action by the 3rd Marine Infantry Division produced eleven prisoners from the British 32nd Division, the fears of Admiral von Schröder, commander of Group North and the Marine Corps, who was responsible for the defence of the coast, were confirmed. It appeared as if the British had taken over this sector as a preliminary to some form of amphibious landing later in the summer. Increasing artillery and air activity underlined these perceived intentions as well, so approval of the Army High Command was sought and granted to conduct a pre-emptive operation to seize the bridgehead east of the River Yser from the Lombardzijde Creek to the sea. The entire operation, codenamed *Strandfest* [Beach Party],[47] which was to be conducted by regiments of the heavily reinforced 3rd Marine Infantry Division, with the 199th Infantry Division in reserve, was placed under command of General der Infanterie von Quast, Commander of the Guard Corps, who assumed responsibility for the land element of Group North on 30 June.

Several units of the 3rd Marine Infantry Division were withdrawn from the line during the last two weeks of June to rehearse for the forthcoming operation, which was to feature both a frontal assault and the use of fire support by eleven large torpedo boats from the sea. In order to ensure that the attack would have every chance of success, seventy three additional batteries, comprising field artillery, light and heavy howitzers, supplemented by a small number of super-heavy calibre weapons and three railway guns, were deployed and allocated 300,000 rounds of ammunition.[48]

Originally the operation was planned to begin at 8.00 pm on 9 July but, at 6.10

am that day, the preliminary bombardment having begun ten minutes earlier, orders arrived that, due to the wet and stormy weather, a delay of twenty four hours had been imposed. This was hardly a contribution to operational security and surprise. The men of the British 32nd Division, which had now been joined by elements of the 1st Division, were alerted to the fact that something was in the air and at 12.30 am on 10 July a violent raid was launched against 7th Company Marine Infantry Regiment 1, which was manning Sector P3, approximately 600 metres west northwest of the centre of Lombartzijde. In the course of a sharp action and mostly due to shell fire, 7th Company lost thirteen killed, including Gefreiter Müller and Seesoldat Poweleit, who through their bravery at a key machine gun post, had played a large part in beating back the raid.[49] Fifty one members of the company were also wounded so, although the raiders suffered fairly severe losses, it was not a good start to the day.

10 July dawned stormy, but dry. With strong, gusting winds from the north northeast, air operations were hindered and, from the sea, the planned support by the torpedo boats had to be cancelled. Nevertheless, the decision was taken to go ahead, the bombardment began to crash down at 11.00 am and the remainder of the day was spent on final preparations. It was the heaviest use of artillery ever in the area of the dunes and there was only a feeble reply from the British guns, largely due to counter-battery fire and extensive use of gas on the gun positions.[50] When the assault was launched, only one gap in the wire was under significant shrapnel fire. The final hour of the bombardment was a frenzy of gun fire, which completely wrecked the British positions and sent sand flying in all directions. Whipped by the wind, this reduced visibility dramatically and made effective resistance by the defence a near impossibility.

Launched forward in two long waves, close behind their bombardment and supported by aircraft machine-gunning the defences from low-level, the marines stormed forward. In an almost completely one-sided action, the 3rd Marine Division had captured all its objectives in a matter of minutes. Following up, waves three and four, whose role was to man overlooking positions to suppress any enemy interference from the west bank of the Yser and to carry forward and install engineer supplies, were able to carry out their tasks completely unimpeded. By 8.45 pm all the positions had been consolidated and work had even begun to free some of the defenders from their dugouts, whose entrances had been blown in. Only in isolated places had there been any real resistance; one such being a command post, which was tackled by 10th Company Marine Infantry Regiment 1.

Hauptmann Engholm 10th Company Marine Infantry Regiment 1 [51]

"Here Vizefeldwebel Ley performed in an outstanding manner. Armed only with a flare pistol, he forced his way into the dugouts and winkled one

British soldier after another from his hideout. It was a really comic sight, which I shall never forget, to see how this first-rate man, speaking in his Baden dialect and with raised pistol, which he fired from time to time, not so much to alert our artillery, but out of glee, directed the trembling British to the rear. It was essential to take the greatest care with the clearance of one particular dugout which had more than one entrance. There was no reply to a shout, so two hand grenades were thrown into the entrances. Ley stood there in expectation, like a cat in front of a mouse hole. A tall, senior officer, wounded in the hand, emerged, gave himself up and made as if to head for the rear – but he was barking up the wrong tree.

"Dissatisfied with one prisoner, suspicious too that the roomy dugout probably held other occupants, Ley sent him back inside to bring out the rest. This was not unsuccessful and four other officers followed him. These turned out later to be a complete regimental staff, with the commander at its head. Here the company captured the complete contents of the regimental command post: very valuable files, orders, secret pamphlets, carrier pigeons, aerial photographs, several telephones and telegraphic equipment, as well as arms and ammunition. Later, when the company had been through the whole position, prepared it for defence and had gone over to normal routine, great was the joy when entering an undamaged dugout we found it equipped as an officers' mess. On the table was the finest food, fruit and drinks."

With the exception of four officers and approximately thirty five men, who dumped their weapons and equipment and swam back across the Yser, only to be caught in the German bombardment falling on the west bank, the entire garrison of the bridgehead was either killed or captured.[52] Marine Infantry Regiment 2, alone, captured nineteen officers and 662 junior ranks of the 1st British Division and the division as a whole took a total of thirty one officers and 1,253 junior ranks prisoner. Given the weight of the bombardment, this figure was a tribute to the strength of the British dugouts and the ability of the sand dunes to absorb high explosive shell fire. German casualties were extremely low and most of them were caused by their own artillery fire dropping short.

Daily Report Army Group Crown Prince Rupprecht 11 July 1917 [53]

"In the area of the Marine Corps, following a thorough and effective artillery bombardment, units of the battle-tested Marine Infantry assaulted the strongly constructed defence line between Lombartzijde and the sea. These positions, which had been constructed by the French, were taken over recently by the British. The enemy was thrown back over the Yser. More than 1,250 prisoners, thirty seven [sic] of them officers, were captured. British casualties in the area between the coast and the river were very high, but the number is not yet known. Once more our airmen contributed greatly to the complete success of the operation, despite the severe weather."

Delighted by the outcome of this efficiently conducted operation, the Kaiser himself despatched a telegram to Crown Prince Rupprecht.[54]

"Field Marshal Hindenburg has briefed me about the significantly successful offensive operation by the Marine Corps against the British on the 10th of this month. I wish to express my special recognition to the Commander of the Fourth Army and the Headquarters of the Guards and Marine Corps, for the well-planned and careful preparation of this operation. I congratulate the courageous 3rd Marine Division for the exemplary and daring way this attack was conducted and for the success it achieved. You have my personal thanks and that of the Fatherland. Wilhelm"

It was not only the Kaiser who was pleased at the outcome. Morale in the 3rd Marine Division was sky high after this success. An officer of Marine Infantry Regiment 3, identified only as 'Leutnant F.', wrote home after the operation:

"What an operation that was! The British were occupying the dunes about a kilometre north of the Yser. Around Lombartzijde the distance back to the Yser was about one and a half kilometres. The distance from our trenches to those of the enemy, with the exception of a boggy area west of Lombartzijde, was everywhere no more than fifty to one hundred and fifty metres. The trenches on both sides were well constructed. The aim and objective of our operation, code named *Strandfest*, which took place on 10 July, was to deny the British an area of ground on this side of the Yser which would have been an outstanding start point for an offensive and to recapture a section of the first and second trench lines near to Lombartzijde. The operation went according to plan and succeeded completely.

"At 5.00 am, supported by observers in aircraft and balloons, our artillery began to bombard the bridges over the Yser. At 8.00 am the rest of the artillery joined in. Destructive fire from the super-heavy guns (240 – 420 mm) was brought down against the rearward communications of the enemy from 10.00 am, directed mostly against Nieuport-Bains. After that, at 11.00 am, every gun and mortar brought down fire for effect and, with the exception of three planned pauses, continued to fire throughout the day ... From 8.00 pm the artillery fire crept forward at timed intervals and after 9.00 pm it gradually reduced to harassing fire, which continued through the night. British artillery fire was never more than moderate at any time.

"The infantry attack in several waves was launched at 8.00 pm. The artillery preparation was so thorough, both in terms of the number of heavy guns and the quantity of ammunition available, that the only resistance was put up by small pockets of the enemy in the dunes. Everywhere else the enemy was so demoralised that they simply surrendered without a fight. The disarmed enemy were then despatched to the rear in great groups. Because of the ease with which we advanced, we felt that the artillery lifts were too slow. Already by 8.25 pm an infantry cooperation aircraft was able to radio to the divisional headquarters that all the objectives had been reached.

"Amongst the prisoners taken were some individuals, who had only left Dunkirk at 6.00 am that day by truck and had been rushed forward as reinforcements. Our aircraft did not only conduct reconnaissance flights during the pauses in the bombardment, they also supported the infantry attack with fire. The officially reported total of approximately 1,250 prisoners has subsequently been increased to about 1,600.[55] As far as the enemy who were occupying the dunes themselves were concerned, it appears that not one single man returned. Bearing in mind the very favourable outcome of this operation, our own casualties must be regarded as extremely low. Would that that were always the case!" [56]

The previous year, during the Battle of the Somme, it had become clear to the German army that the corps level of command was critical to the conduct of the contact battle and that the pressures of modern major battles required a flexible approach. Each of the corps was renamed a 'Group' and was so organised as to be able to take under command varying numbers of divisions as they rotated through the battle area. From time to time they themselves would be relieved, but they were expected to carry out longer tours of duty, to build up expertise over a particular area and thus provide essential continuity. The same system was adopted on the Flanders front.

During July, from Diksmuide to Warneton, the Fourth Army sector was divided into three. In the north, Group Diksmuide was based on XIV Army Corps, commanded by General Châles de Beaulieu. The south was the responsibility of IX Reserve Corps, was known as Group Wijtschate and was commanded by General Dieffenbach. In the centre and the most important of the three, was Group Ypres, formed from III Bavarian Army Corps under General Freiherr von Stein. The responsibility for Group Ypres was taken over in September 1917 by the Guard Corps and it also proved necessary, as the battle went on, to insert a fourth group between

Groups Ypres and Diksmuide. This was Group Staden, commanded by General Freiherr von Marschall and based around the Guards Reserve Corps. Despite all the pressures and crises that were to come, this organisation proved itself to be equal to the immense demands placed on it.

As July wore on, both the forward and the rear areas, too, suffered increasingly. Movement was rendered extremely difficult in the face of bold air attacks and re-connaissance flights deep behind the lines, whilst liberal use of gas-filled mortar bombs and artillery shells poisoned the air often for as much as six kilometres into the depth of the German positions. All movement forward was badly restricted and the supply of rations, ammunition and trench stores was completely halted at times. Taken together with the appallingly squalid condition of the few dugouts and the pillboxes available, it was small wonder that the nerves of the trench garrison, which shrank day by day as the battle casualties and the sick lists grew, were badly stretched.

Reserve Leutnant Rau 6th Company Grenadier Regiment 89 [57] **12**

"The position we were allocated was saturated and the walls of the trenches were only secured with wooden hurdles. The shelters were made of huge concrete blocks and they had very little space inside. The British soon increased the tempo of their shelling. It was easy to see that large masses of guns, of every calibre from small to super-heavy, were being pressed into service to bombard our position. That fact, linked to the constantly increasing amount of aerial activity, meant that we soon recognised that the enemy was preparing an offensive of huge proportions. After three to four weeks of this, our position was just a crater field, such as we had never before experienced.

"Not a single communication trench was passable, the concrete pill-boxes all stood out clearly, making marvellous targets for the enemy. This meant that we had to move out of them and take cover in the craters, which themselves were under constant fire. Unfortunately the water table was so high that they soon filled with water, ruling out all thoughts of a rest, no matter how short. Ceaseless rain, gas attacks, constant raiding and patrol activity, the need to lug forward stores and build wire obstacles by night wore our men out physically and lowered their morale badly.

"The transmission of orders was extraordinarily difficult, because the telephone lines were being cut all the time and could only be substituted by runners ... Of these courageous comrades, I should like to praise especially Gefreiters Soltau and Brandt. Their exemplary bearing made them very models of front line soldiers. Gradually the company losses started to make themselves felt. The average strength dropped to between twenty and forty men. As a result of lack of sleep, insufficient food and over-exertion they became so completely apathetic, that the officers were extremely concerned about their ability to counter attacks launched by fresh British assault troops."

Hauptmann von Wulffen 3rd Battalion Grenadier Regiment 89 [58] **12**

"Individual pillboxes in the front line were now half-full of water and an appalling stench filled the rooms. Nevertheless the outpost troops did not abandon them. They lay on planks just above the water and just below the ceiling, which meant that, for the time being, they had some protection from fire and the elements. The entire artillery zone, together with all tracks, roads, buildings, woods and copses as far back as the Passchendaele-Beselare road were under constant fire by the enemy. The village of Zonnebeke itself was frequently the target of heavy and super-heavy batteries. The enemy used mortars firing gas-filled bombs against the forward regiments, causing painful casualties amongst the outposts. The enemy airmen had air superiority and directed fire against all the important targets. In addition enemy squadrons often penetrated to the rear areas and dropped bombs on the stations and other important installations."

It would be wrong to assume that activity during the closing days of July was restricted to Allied artillery fire, directed against defenders huddled helplessly in trenches, craters and pillboxes. Locally there were numerous raids, many of them launched to check if the German defenders had withdrawn from particular sectors. The German army, too, carried out a number of similar operations, often to improve their positions. Some were successful, other less so. One such minor battle occurred at the end of July to the west of Pilkem in the Boezinge area, where units of 49th Reserve Division, Reserve Infantry Regiment 226 in particular, having been seriously weakened by the bombardment, were forced to pull back from the west bank of the Yser canal.[59] Once this had been observed by British aerial reconnaissance, this withdrawal permitted the British Guards Division to cross over on 27 July and subsequently to launch its attack on 31 July from a start line on the east bank.

Within hours of the British movement forward across the canal, the German army launched a counter-attack, intended to push the enemy troops back whence they had come. It was not well planned or conducted. It was launched hastily and particular difficulty was experienced in passing orders and coordinating the various units involved, some of whom – the exhausted remnants of 49th Reserve Division – were in no fit state to attack anything. It was effectively broken up by artillery fire and came nowhere near to its objective of regaining the west bank of the canal.

Vizefeldwebel Wellhausen 3rd Company Fusilier Regiment 73 [60] **13**

"During the morning of 28 July 3rd Company Fusilier Regiment 73 was deployed in a series of shell holes on the western edge of *Artilleriewald* [Artillery Wood]. My platoon formed the battalion right flank, but there was no contact with the unit to my right. Our company commander, Leutnant Sanvoß, was located in a concrete blockhouse known as the *Armleuchter* [Chandelier]. It was a beautiful day. The larks were singing and rejoicing up in the sky as shells fell on the *Artilleriewald*. The earth heaved and rocked. It was like hell on earth. We could see nothing of what was happening at the front. From time to time stretcher bearers came past us carrying their heavy burdens. British airmen circled endlessly above us, machine gunning continuously. About 3.00 pm my platoon commander, Leutnant Ehlert, Vizefeldwebel Schnell and I were ordered to report to the company commander. We were directed to set off for the front line at 9.30 pm where, assisted by the remnants of Reserve Infantry Regiment 226, we were to throw the British back across to the western side of the canal. Hand grenades were fetched. Every man received two each …

"About 9.30 pm we headed off in single file. Leutnant Sandvoß was in the lead with his runners. Despite hellish artillery fire, we had no trouble getting forward but, unfortunately, we were spotted by a British captive balloon crew. No sooner had we reached the *Tauentzien-Stellung* than a hail of shellfire, far worse than anything we had experienced on the Somme, came down on us … At 10.35 pm, there was still another fifteen minutes to go. Shells, shrapnel balls and their pots rained down around our heads. With watches in hand, we waited in feverish tension as the last moments ticked away. Finally: ready! Go! Let us get out of this hellish fire! After about 150 metres we were clear of the *Dobschützwald* and thus out of the fire. I still had ten men with me. Press on! Suddenly: 'Halt who goes there?' – Ehlert's platoon! Leutnant Ehlert still had eighteen men with him. There was no trace of the 3rd Platoon. We spread out widely and continued for another 400 metres. Suddenly flares went up, followed by the rattle of small arms fire. It seemed as though, instead of a few isolated soldiers, we had come up against something more like a battalion. Nevertheless there we were in front of the British trench. With shouts of *Hurra*, we launched ourselves forward, but we were too weak. We could not get close and we had to huddle in cover before the trench. Unteroffizier Nolte patrolled forward, but hardly made twenty metres … In the end we occupied an abandoned German position in and around a blockhouse, one hundred metres east of the road along the canal.

"Leutnant Ehlert ordered us to occupy a semi-circular position in the shell holes. In total there were twenty five to thirty of us. To our left we could distinctly hear small arms fire and see the British constantly firing flares. It was just the same for us. We thought that it might be 1st Company Fusilier Regiment 73. Leutnant Ehlert immediately sent a full situation report back to battalion. It was past midnight and the British artillery began to fire gas throughout the entire rear area. The easterly wind blew the gas back over us towards the British. Our eyes were streaming, we could hardly speak for coughing, but we could not mask up; otherwise we should not have been able to see anything in the darkness. Finally dawn broke.

"Leutnant Ehlert decided to hold the position during the day. We soon spotted the British trench, which was fully developed and located ten to twenty metres before the canal road and was not being fired at by our guns. Hardly had we noted that fact than a British aircraft arrived. Our men nick-named it the 'trench inspector'. It was there to direct the artillery fire by means of signals and, having dived to roof top height, soon spotted us. I could clearly see the crewman photographing us and taking notes, before flying over to the British trench to throw out a report. It then continued to circle for a long while, about 400 metres to our left. It then fired a smoke signal towards the British trench and, within a short time, we saw rein-forcements arriving. The Tommies emerged out of cover. I saw more about 200 metres away trying to get round to our rear and went over to the concrete blockhouse, where I quickly fired a green flare to call for harassing fire; but none came. Then I found myself stuck behind the blockhouse and unable to get back to my men. I managed to irritate the British by holding an old helmet out on a rifle first left, then right of the blockhouse. Each time it was fired at.

"I made a dash for it and rejoined my men. Within only twenty minutes there was no enemy to our left. I could not see any men of the 76th to our right and all was quiet there. We sent two volunteers back to battalion head-quarters. The first was hit and fell, but Fusilier Heise got through to the *Dobschützwald*. The British had now worked their way round to our rear. In order to avoid certain capture, Leutnant Ehlert decided to withdraw. He gave the order: 'Split up, make your own way back and rendezvous where we began the attack!' Leutnant Ehlert leapt into a shell hole to give orders to Unteroffizier Nolte, then I heard him shout, 'Everyone pull back half left!' Hardly had he attempted to get back to the next shell hole, than he fell; killed by a shot to the head. The British were standing up and shooting at anything that moved. Most of the men were hit by rifle and machine gun fire. I called my men around me and we fired madly then, using fire and manoeuvre, we withdrew from shell hole to shell hole. In a nearby crater I found the body of Leutnant Ehlert, lying dead on the rim of the crater.

"Suddenly, I saw a large black cloud approaching and it began to rain very heavily. We continued to withdraw, sometimes dashing, sometimes crawling; pursued by the British with fire, but eventually I got through to the *Dobschützwald* with six or eight unwounded men, where we met up with Leutnant Sandvoß and about twenty men. Five or six others trickled in later wounded and some men stated that they had seen four or five others being led away by the British, but all the rest were missing. Later that afternoon Leutnant Jünger arrived with the remainder of 8th Company Fusilier Regiment 73 as reinforcements, but the British continued to fire on us with all calibres up to super-heavy."

On 29 July Field Marshal Hindenburg received a telegram from the Kaiser, who was visiting the Eastern Front at the time. Its contents were distributed immediately down to all regiments, including those enduring the closing days of the preparatory bombardment.[61]

"From the battlefields of Galicia, where our forces have added to their laurels through continuous advances and success upon success, my thoughts turn, with a grateful heart, to the unforgettable deeds of the armies of the west; which, through their sacrificially tough endurance, are holding back the enemy. Having read the accounts of their marvellous offensive spirit in yesterday's communiqué, I am thinking especially of the courageous troops in Flanders, who have already been under heavy artillery fire for weeks, unflinchingly awaiting the coming storm.

"You have my complete trust, together with that of the entire Fatherland, whose borders you are defending against enemies from all over the world. *Gott mit uns!*"

As the day set for the opening of the offensive approached, the massive bombardment ground on, far heavier and more concentrated than that used before the opening of the Battle of the Somme, or even before Messines in May and June 1917. 1,000 medium or heavy guns and howitzers and more than 2,000 field guns fired four and a quarter million shells over a two week period into a waterlogged countryside and its precarious drainage system. As a result the British artillery, backed by the enormous output of the munitions factories and an efficient logistic chain, ensured that however much damage might have been done to the German defenders in the process, the forthcoming battle would certainly be fought in a swamp of their own making.

Notes
1. Kriegsarchiv München: HGr Rupprecht Bd 125 & Gen Kdo III AK Bd 135
2. Partzsch: History Field Artillery Regiment 32 pp 128-129
3. Dieterich: History Grenadier Regiment 4 p 750

4. The abbreviation *KTK* is used interchangeably to mean either the commander of the forward troops or the command post within which he was located.
5. Laeger: History Field Artillery Regiment 1 pp 269-270
6. Dellmensingen: *Das Bayernbuch vom Weltkrieg Bd II* pp 429-431
7. Dickes is in error. The explosions occurred at 3.10 am British time [4.10 am German time]. Almost all the eyewitnesses provide similarly inaccurate timings for the explosion of the offensive mines. With no reliable means of synchronising watches, disparities of this type are common in Great War personal accounts.
8. Riegel: History Bavarian Infantry Regiment 17 pp 118 – 120
9. Hauptmann Otto Senn died on 11 June 1917 and is buried in the German cemetery at Proyart Block 2 Grave 467
10. Kohl: *Mit Hurra in den Tod!* pp168 – 170
11. Dellmensingen: *op. cit.* p 431 – 433
12. Feldunterarzt Karl Kellermann is buried in the German cemetery at Langemark in the *Kamaradengrab.*
13. Messines was, of course an ANZAC battlefield, but the German historians rarely distinguished between the differing contingents.
14. Niemann: History Infantry Regiment 133 pp 68-69
15. This is an exaggeration. The truth of the matter, impressive enough, is that the deepest of the mine chambers was at St Elooi, where the charge was located at a depth of 38.5 metres.
16. Oschatz is mistaken about this. The *Sehnen Stellung* was well to the rear of the locations of the explosions.
17. Hoffmann: History Infantry Regiment 44 p 242
18. Dieterich: *op. cit.* pp 755-756
19. *ibid.* p 757
20. Liedtke: History Füsilier Regiment 33 p 300
21. Hoffmann: *op. cit.* p 245
22. Liedtke: *op.cit.* pp 296-298
23. German sources continually refer to drunkenness amongst attacking troops. Although there was usually a rum ration before attacks were launched, there are few authenticated cases of excessive consumption amongst forward Allied troops at any time during the Great War. It is also most unlikely that these were black troops.
24. 'Blue Beans' was a generic German slang expression for bullets and shells of all calibres.
25. Preusser: History Infantry Regiment 176 p 211
26. Laeger: History Field Artillery Regiment 1 pp 291-292
27. *ibid.* p 292
28. Dellmensingen: *op.cit.* p 431
29. Scheer: History Infantry Regiment 413 p 31
30. Most of the mines had been in place since 1916. During the battle of the Somme, Haig had considered firing them, in association with the major attack of 15th September 1916, in order to fix German troops in the Ypres Salient. With nothing but maintenance taking place at most sites, it is small wonder that nothing was detected.
31. Fromm: History Reserve Infantry Regiment 120 p 84. It is possible that the reason for the way this mine appeared to explode was that its charge contained 15% guncotton (over 3.5 tonnes out of a total of 24.3 tonnes). Gun cotton was often used as a primer to set off

ammonal, but this was a particularly large quantity. Ammonal detonates comparatively slowly at around 4,000 metres per second. It generates a large amount of gas, further augmented by the heating effect of the aluminium powder it contains. All this gas produces a considerable heaving effect, which makes it particularly suitable for mining. Gun cotton, on the other hand, detonates nearly twice as fast at 7,300 metres per second, which produces a much greater shattering effect. Instead of heaving, the violently released very hot gases from the gun cotton would tend to seek the weakest route to the surface, where the gases would vent. Mixed with atmospheric oxygen, this would cause a secondary flash, similar in principle to the muzzle flash of a gun, but on a much greater scale.

32. Scheer: *op.cit.* pp 46-47
33. *ibid.* pp 39-40. It is an interesting confirmation of the anomalous explosion of the Hill 60 mine that Kressenstein, who observed the event, later described seeing only *a pillar of fire.*
34. Leutnant Gustav Schmidt is buried in the German cemetery at Menen Block F Grave 949.
35. Kriegsarchiv München: Gen Kdo III AK Bd 83
36. Kronprinz Rupprecht *'Mein Kriegstagebuch' Vol2* p 191
37. Hoffmann: *op. cit.* p 246
38. Von Kuhl: *Der Weltkrieg 1914-1918 Band II* p 115
39. Kriegsarchiv München: Gen Kdo III AK Bd 100
40. Von Kuhl: *op. cit.* p 117
41. Karl Allmenröder had a meteoric career as a pilot with Jasta 11. Born in Solingen in 1896, he began the war as an eighteen year old gunner in the artillery. He was commissioned the following year, transferred to the German air service where he flew two-seater aircraft before joining Jasta 11 in November 1916. Allmenröder had scored nine victories by April 1917, but followed this in May with thirteen more. By the time he was shot down at the end of June, his score of confirmed victories had reached thirty and he had been awarded the *Pour le Mérite* on 7 June 1917, when he destroyed his twenty fourth aircraft. Allmenröder is buried in a modest grave in the Waldfriedhof in Solingen. Between the wars he was commemorated in various ways, including having streets named after him. Unfortunately, due to the use the Nazis made of the memory of such as he, these places were re- named after the Second World War and Allmenröder, who was an exceptional pilot, faded into obscurity.
42. Bezzel: History Bavarian Reserve Infantry Regiment 6 pp 156-157
43. *ibid.* pp 157-158
44. *ibid.* p 158
45. Von Kuhl: *op. cit.* p 118
46. Oberst (later Generalmajor) Friedrich von Loßberg, the noted German defensive expert, who was chief of staff to General Sixt von Armin at Fourth Army, apparently gave a brilliant and convincing presentation to the conference, which helped to carry the day.
47. This code name would have won no prizes for operational security. The use of names which could possibly betray the nature or location of a forthcoming operation is generally avoided by military planners.
48. Tannen: History Marine Infantry Regiment 3 p 207
49. Gefreiter Johannes Müller and Seesoldat Friedrich Poweleit are buried together in the German cemetery at Vladslo Block 3 Graves 2308 and 2307 respectively.

50. Goertze: History Marine Infantry Regiment 2 p 140
51. Kinder: History Marine Infantry Regiment 1 p 358
52. Tannen: *op.cit.* p 210
53. *ibid.* p 209
54. *ibid.* p 210
55. It is not possible to verify the accuracy of this statement. Nevertheless, for an operation conducted in a very confined area, the overall number of prisoners was clearly very large.
56. Foerster: *Wir Kämpfer im Weltkrieg* pp 392-393
57. Zipfel: History Grenadier Regiment 89 p 323
58. *ibid.* p 322
59. Rohkohl: History Reserve Infantry Regiment 226 pp 58-61
60. Voigt: History Füsilier Regiment 73 p 533
61. Kümmel: History Reserve Infantry Regiment 91 p 292

CHAPTER TWO

31st July 1917

T hroughout the night intense artillery and mortar fire continued to batter the German positions and rear areas, flaying the battlefield from north to south and in considerable depth. Air attacks on dumps, depots and installations in the rear areas went on non-stop, as did attacks on headquarters and billeting areas. British long-range artillery fire reached as far back as twelve kilometres behind the lines, interfering with defensive preparations and disturbing resting troops. The German artillery did its best to respond, but one major problem was the fact that whole concentrations of heavy and super-heavy batteries, making use of their range to remain some distance behind the front, were simply out of range of the German guns. Immune from counter-battery fire, they pounded the German infantry, making their life intolerable and preventing them from sleeping. Casualties continued to mount and the few remaining dugouts were smashed or buried. The remnants of trenches and barbed wire obstacles were simply swept away and the infantry was left clinging on precariously in isolated pill boxes, mud- and water-filled shell holes; there to face grimly whatever dawn would bring.

The trench garrisons did their best to find cover from the torrent of shells, but others were forced to spend the night on the move. A couple of days earlier, 52nd Reserve Division had been given the task of reinforcing the line held by the Bavarian 6th Reserve Division at Hooge astride the Ypres-Menen road. This ground-holding division had been hit extremely hard during the preparatory barrage, so the relief of its troops sub-unit by sub-unit had actually begun during the night of 29/30 July. This process continued during the night 30/31 July. It was an extraordinarily difficult operation. Elements of Reserve Infantry Regiment 239, for example, having been moved forward by motor transport met up with their guides from Bavarian Reserve Infantry Regiment 17 in Terhand and the march forward began. Harassing fire was coming down everywhere and large sections of the rear area were being drenched with chemicals from gas shells, forcing the marching troops to mask up and complicating the move even more. Within minutes the eyepieces of the masks misted up and that, coupled with the darkness, meant that it was generally almost impossible to see the man in front. Command and control difficulties were further exacerbated by the fact that the guides soon lost the way.

Despite this the 5th, 7th and 8th Companies arrived on the position at around 5.00 am and duly relieved the corresponding companies of Bavarian Reserve Infantry Regiment 17. The unfortunate men of 6th Company Reserve Infantry Regiment 239 had a far harder time of it. For hours on end that night they stumbled

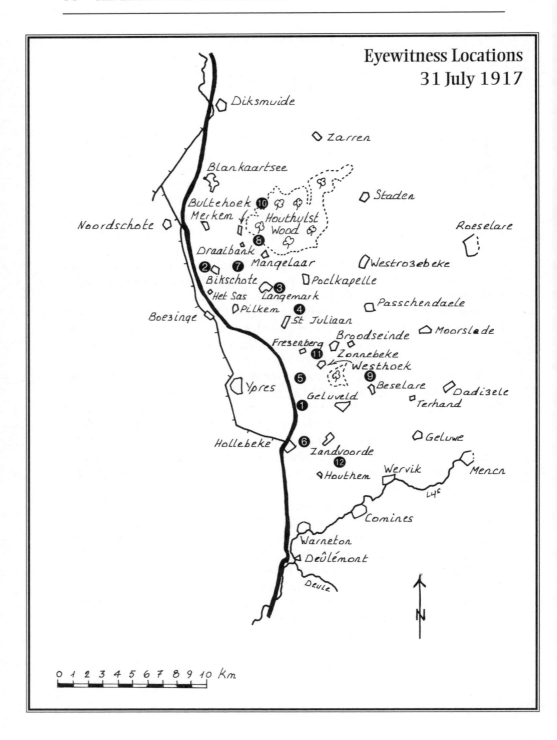

Eyewitness Locations
31 July 1917

around behind their guides through the cratered chaos of the battlefield. They suffered heavy casualties from artillery fire and were badly affected at one point by a gas attack. Lost, scattered and utterly exhausted the company was temporarily finished as a fighting body of troops. The handful of men still with Leutnant Marget, the company commander, took cover where they were and decided to wait for dawn. Unable to complete the hand over, the commanding officer of Bavarian Reserve Infantry Regiment 17 stayed in command and was in the process of sending desperate signals to the rear: *Own forces too weak; reinforcements urgently required* – just as red flares began to go up signifying that battle was about to be joined. It was hardly the most auspicious way to begin a life and death struggle.[1]

It was much the same story for the other regiments of 52nd Reserve Division. The very fact that a Prussian division was relieving a Bavarian one added to the problems, as it always did. There was often a quite irrational tension between units and sub-units whenever this happened. This manifested it in small ways, such as on this occasion when the company commander of 5th Company Reserve Infantry Regiment 240 was unhappy with the proposed route forward and method of movement to be adopted by his guides from Bavarian Reserve Infantry Regiment 20.

Leutnant Wiemes
Company Commander 5th Company Reserve Infantry Regiment 240[2] **1**

> "Never throughout the entire war was I involved in a relief in the line under such unfavourable circumstances. The guides (Bavarians) had only the haziest idea about the route forward and so with a heavy heart I had to abandon my tried and tested method, intended to avoid pointless casualties, of advancing by individual platoons. As a result I was full of concern … "

In the event the move forward went reasonably well, despite the fact the area was being swept with fire, which cause numerous casualties – especially when a large shell crashed down on the rear platoon, killing and wounding an unknown number of men. Leutnant Wiemes continues:

> "The information I obtained from the company commander, a young Leutnant, painted a far from rosy picture. The position no longer had a barbed wire obstacle. There was almost nothing recognisable as a trench. Orientation was impossible in the darkness of the night. The relief was complete by about 2.00 am. The company which, when we set off from Terhand, had a fighting strength of eighty eight rifles, had to occupy a sector approximately 300 metres wide – and not just the front line. The reserve line about seventy five metres in rear had to be manned as well. All of the destruction caused by the week-long bombardment meant that

there was no continuity within the company. As a result the sections were more or less isolated. There were no heavy machine guns in the company sector. The light machine gun which the company had taken over was destroyed by a shell shortly after the handover and its crew under Unteroffizier Herbertz was all killed or wounded. Equally serious was the almost total lack of hand grenades. The two reliable runners whom I despatched to battalion headquarters with the information never returned. This was the highly unfavourable situation in which the company found itself when the major British offensive broke over it during the morning of 31 July."[3]

Writing after the war in his magisterial account, *Der Weltkrieg 1914/18*, General der Infanterie Hermann von Kuhl succinctly summed up the violent chaos visited on the troops of Groups Wijtschate and Ypres that summer morning:

'In the early hours of 31st July a hurricane of fire, completely beyond anyone's experience, broke out. The entire earth of Flanders rocked and seemed to be on fire. This was not just drum fire; it was as though Hell itself had slipped its bonds. What were the terrors of Verdun and the Somme compared to this grotesquely huge outpouring of raw power? The violent thunder of battle could be heard in the furthest corner of Belgium. It was as though the enemy was announcing to the world: *Here we come and we are going to prevail!*' [4]

Few would have taken issue with von Kuhl but, interestingly, Hauptmann Prinz zu Solms, commanding officer 1st Battalion Infantry Regiment 94, defending the line near Zonnebeke – clearly a man in full control of his emotions and a master of understatement – contented himself with the simple remark: *Never before, during the entire campaign, had I had an opportunity to witness such a bombardment.*[5] The commander of Infantry Regiment 164, one of the forward formations of 111th Infantry Division which was occupying positions around Bikschote, would have been in full agreement.

Oberstleutnant Freiherr von Forstner, Commander Infantry Regiment 164 [6] **2**

"The night [30/31 July] was the worst I ever experienced. The fire increased to an intensity that was simply beyond our power to compre-hend. Our blockhouse and a nearby mortar battery received more than 1,000 large calibre shells. The earth trembled, the air shimmered. My pillbox heaved and rocked as though it was going to collapse. Almost by a miracle it received no direct hits. Everyone who dared to go out was wounded. Stabsarzt Katte resorted to issuing opium.

"At 6.00 am there was a gas alarm. I went outside and watched as a cloud of gas ten metres thick drifted slowly by. The entire pill box stank of it. I had every tiny gap wedged up with wet cloths. At 7.00 am the firing reached a peak of intensity. It was simply ghastly. The men in the outer room were wounded or died of gas poisoning. The small reserve of gas masks was exhausted because many men needed replacements for masks which had been shot through. The enemy followed up behind the gas cloud. I received a report about 10.00 am that the regiment had evacuated the *Prinz Heinrich Stellung.* The news arrived that the enemy had pushed on and had reached the *Querriegel* [Cross Trench]. My regiment pulled back to the *Draaibank Stellung.*

"Throughout the entire time extraordinarily destructive fire by heavy and super-heavy calibre guns came down on all the defence lines. All the formations were shattered by it. I no longer had a regiment, just wreckage. By 10.00 am I probably was reduced to:

> 100 men and two machine guns in the *Draaibank Stellung.*
> About 200 men with eight machine guns in the Crater Position
> One platoon of 4th Company with two machine guns.

"I transferred command over the *Draaibank Stellung* to Battalion Goesch and the Crater Position to Hauptmann Schultze-Schmidt of Infantry Regiment 76. Leutnant Bode commanded the remainder of 4th Company. There was still contact to the right with Infantry Regiment 181, but it was in the midst of relief by Infantry Regiment 134.[7] To the left we were meant to have contact with Infantry Regiment 76, but the regiment only had ninety men left. Around midday information arrived that 2nd Guards Reserve Division was on the march ..."

Infantry Regiment 181 was in an equally bad way. Not only was it soon out of contact with Infantry Regiment 164 on its left, but its companies, severely weakened by the number of gas casualties, had also lost contact with one another. All links to the rear failed, runners could not get through and the wireless could not be made to work. Then just before the main assault began and at a time when it seemed that matters could get no worse, no fewer than twenty seven men of 11th Company Infantry Regiment 181 were killed or wounded by a single 320mm shell.[8]

Although the troops holding the forward positions were on the receiving end of the worst of the shelling, the rear areas where the *Eingreif* divisions were located were far from safe. Reserve Infantry Regiment 213, which was part of 207th Infantry Division, one of the formations in reserve behind Group Wijtschate, left its billets at 5.00 am to take part in a brigade exercise, but soon found itself caught up in events.

Leutnant Höllwig 10th Company Reserve Infantry Regiment 213 [9]

"We rode off to the training area. Suddenly drum fire began to come down all along the front and there was suddenly an enormous number of red and green flares in the sky, calling down German defensive fire. The entire horizon was lit up and a dreadful rumble filled the air. Leutnant Boldt was riding next to me. He raised his hand and pointed to the west: 'That is the start of the Battle of Flanders, Höllwig. I shall be amazed if we spend tonight back at our quarters!' I laughed, not wanting to believe him. We rode on and the fire continued with undiminished violence … When we reached the assembly area it was already light … We sat and waited. Above Menen we could see an infantry cooperation aircraft flying very low. We chatted away about nothing in particular. I took another look at the aircraft then shouted, 'Everyone take cover!' What we had assumed was an infantry cooperation aircraft was – a Tommy, who immediately engaged us from 200 metres with a machine gun. God be praised! Nobody was hit. A couple of moments later I saw Leutnant Peters come racing across the field towards us. He signalled us to gather in and I realised that this meant not only the cancellation of the exercise, but also the opening of the great Battle of Flanders."

The divisional codeword for the opening of the battle, *Scharnhorst*, [10] was flashed in all directions as the formations and units of the German Fourth Army began to manoeuvre to put the new doctrine of flexible defence to its first real test. Meanwhile those who had the misfortune to be deployed right forward to delay and channel the surging offensive were engaged in a desperate fight for survival against the odds. For fear of mines, the forward sub-units of Bavarian Reserve Infantry Regiments 16, 17 and 20 of 6th Bavarian Reserve Division defending the sector astride the Ypres-Menen road at Hooge, had been thinned out considerably in accordance with the new operational doctrine of flexible defence, leaving them no alternative but to give ground gradually when the attacks came in. Nevertheless, in the course of hard fighting, the presence of the reinforcing regiments of 52nd Reserve Division stabilised the situation and the Bavarians had their moments of success too. In close quarter fighting by the edge of the Herenthage Park, about two kilometres southeast of Hooge, a gun team of 2nd Machine Gun Company Bavarian Reserve Infantry Regiment 17 was awarded a prize of 500 marks by the Bavarian Ministry of War for knocking out a tank that day. [11]

The war diaries and other documentation of the regiments of 52nd Reserve Division went missing after the war, but fortunately when the time came for them to write up their histories, numerous eyewitnesses were able to contribute graphic accounts of the events of the opening day of the battle.

Leutnant L, Peper, Commander 6th Company Reserve Infantry Regiment 240 [12] **1**

"My predecessor left me [at 2.00 am] with the warning that the British appeared to have moved forward into our old front line and seemed to be about to do something. A fighting patrol under an experienced leader went forward, but returned not having discovered anything suspicious ... About 5.00 am a terrible drum fire crashed down on the entire line. In expectation of an immediate attack, I called for artillery defensive fire and saw flares going up also to my left and right. Here there was only a weak response by the artillery and even this fire slackened off after about ten minutes. But now I could hear heavy small arms fire from the front and simultaneously I could see shadowy figures moving across country to our left. Their numbers swiftly increased and, as it became lighter, I could clearly recognise them as British, who must have broken through in the neighbouring sector.

"In the meantime the men of my blockhouse had been stood to and I gave them the order to open fire. This must have been effective because the attack faltered; some men took cover, others fired back and more still even pulled back. To our front things seemed to be going well and a prisoner was brought in. The attack seemed to have been beaten off and I expected to be able to round up those who had broken in. Suddenly a fresh attack was launched directly at us in much greater strength from the left flank. If we had only had a machine gun! It would have had dreadful effect. On the other hand, what could we do with a few rifles, even though we fired until the barrels glowed red hot?

"Once more some of the enemy engaged us in a fire fight, as soon as they realised that they were under fire from a flank. Already we had dead and wounded and our numbers kept reducing. Others attempted to encircle us and cut us off from the rear. Possibly earlier we might have been able to avoid this danger, because the ground to our right appeared to be free of enemy, but in the heat of battle we had never given it a thought. At that time we were not really familiar with the concept of mobile defence. In the meantime the front line positions were lost. After putting up an obstinate defence and taking serious casualties, the remainder had surrendered. The only man to get through to us was Vizefeldwebel Huxdorf and the noose gradually tightened around us.

"All of sudden came a shout, 'They are on the roof' (of the blockhouse). Initially there were only two or three of them. I brought one down with a shot and two hand grenades drove the others away ... How long we held out I cannot say. In such a situation it is easy to lose track of time. In any case our watches were stolen as soon as we were captured. Finally we were completely cut off. The British approached to within fifty metres, despite our counter-fire. I gave the order to cease fire and waved a towel as a sign of surrender. There were only about eight of us still able to fight."

Peper was probably right to judge the moment to surrender when he did. Defence, especially by machine gunners, continued to the very last minute generally meant that the surviving defenders were shot out of hand. The few remaining members of 5th Company Reserve Infantry Regiment 240 had a very narrow escape a short distance away.

Leutnant Wiemes Commander 5th Company Reserve Infantry Regiment 240 [13] **1**

"Terrible destructive fire had raged throughout the night, increasing to drum fire of unimaginable intensity during the early hours. Protected by this utterly unprecedented weight of fire, the British advanced out of cover in dense attacking waves, with the aim of breaking through our lines. Unfortunately by this time the constant artillery fire had caused the company considerable numbers of casualties. Several of my best Unteroffiziers were killed or wounded. Despite this my men all grabbed instinctively for their rifles as soon as the khaki-clad British waves hove into view. The first of them were halted by the defenders' rifle fire, but ever larger attacks were repeatedly launched against our positions. Two courageous men, Gefreiter Rücken and Landsturmmann Best were seriously wounded close to me during a battle with hand grenades and about seventy five metres away a heavy British tank rumbled across the trenches of the neighbouring regiment (Infantry Regiment 94).

"Towards 5.45 am the tiny garrison which had heroically fended off the attacking enemy was partially outflanked and overwhelmed. Eyewitnesses told me later that my courageous platoon commander, Vizefeldwebel Jaffke and the remainder of his men were bayoneted to death. I myself, along with three or four of my men, was surrounded by a pack of undisciplined British soldiers. Some of them were very drunk and they came at us with fixed bayonets.[14] At this highly dramatic moment a British corporal leapt between us and his men, whom – and this must be said in his praise – he energetically kept in check. I believe that it was entirely due to [his intervention] that we were not cut down."

Infantry-tank cooperation was starting to come into its own in 1917 and in many instances the tanks did good work in assisting the attacking infantry by eliminating strong points, block houses and nests of resistance within the defence. By this stage of the war the artillery firing in the direct role over open sights was regarded as the primary anti-armour defence, but here and there it was still possible for the infantry to inflict damage on these early tanks, providing that it had easy access to quantities of S.m.K. ammunition [*Spitz-Munition mit Kern* = armour piercing bullets with hardened steel cores]. Sufficient weapons, preferably machine guns, to fire it were also essential.

Leutnant Göldner, Commander 7th Company Reserve Infantry Regiment 240 [15] 1

"[Having beaten off early attacks] the company morale was excellent. Our rifle and machine gun fire was outstandingly effective. Our light machine gun kept jamming, unfortunately, but the heavy machine gun proved its worth constantly. Its crew behaved in an exemplary manner. It directed its fire wherever the British assault troops were mostly densely massed but, because of the fire, it had to change position regularly. The company defended its sector heroically and here the attempt at a breakthrough fell apart.

"Suddenly, at about 7.30 am, the first British tanks appeared: first four then six. They crept towards us like great monsters, but they could not put the wind up us. We had come across them on the Aisne and had seen them littered about knocked out.[16] *Let them come!* We opened a lively fire at them with armour-piercing rounds. We soon got through the ammunition in our pouches and had to break into the reserves. A complete case of armour-piercing ammunition was our salvation as the bullets clattered against the armour of the tanks. We succeeded in bringing two tanks to a halt, one of them immediately bursting into fire. Like lightning the crew baled out, but we shot them down with rapid fire. The other tanks were dealt with later by artillery and machine guns.

"We found the fire of the tanks very unpleasant indeed. At about 2.00 pm the enemy renewed the assault against our forward strong point, attacking *Königin Olga-Weg* [Queen Olga Way] simultaneously from a flank. Two new tanks headed in the direction of Herenthage Wood, making use of the low ground to its front. Fresh assault troops, for whom they were intended to provide cover, advanced behind the tanks, but these attacks too were halted by a combination of small arms and artillery fire. The last of the tanks turned to escape and unfortunately they got away."

Further to the north, from the Pilkem area south, regiments of 3rd Guards Division were in the process of conducting a relief in the line, so that the battered troops of 23rd Reserve Division, who had suffered particularly heavily during the bombardment, could be withdrawn. The Fusilier Guards occupied the right hand half of the divisional front, the Lehr Infantry Regiment the left half, with Grenadier Regiment 9 initially back in reserve. The following extract of the Group Ypres Situation report of the following day summarises the desperate fighting in this area very clearly. [17]

"3rd Guards Infantry Division: The tough and obstinate defence of the forward troops under *K.T.K* Struyve made an outstanding contribution to the overall defence. 1st Battalion Lehr Infantry Regiment was in the middle of relieving 3rd Battalion Reserve Infantry Regiment 392. At 7.00 am the Stuyve sector was attacked hard from the south by enemy who had already thrust beyond the *Albrecht Stellung*. Once the first position had been overwhelmed by the numerically superior enemy, the remainder of the two battalions closed in around the command post, which was under attack by the enemy from all directions. Thanks to the extreme bravery displayed by the two commanders and their staffs it was possible repeatedly to keep the enemy at bay by means of continuous close-quarter fighting.

"Major Scheffer, commanding officer 3rd Battalion Reserve Infantry Regiment 392, his adjutant and, in addition Hauptman Hinstedt from the Lehr Infantry Regiment, who personally led a successful counter-attack as far as the *Albrecht Stellung*, were all killed, as were numerous courageous NCOs and men, who were involved in the battle with hand grenades. Major Franz, commanding officer of 3rd Battalion Lehr Infantry Regiment, was one of those seriously wounded. Not until the ammunition and hand grenades had run out at about 10.00 am and the command post was deeply outflanked on both sides did the few survivors find themselves with no alternative but to attempt to breakthrough back to the Steenbeek whence, in the meantime, our infantry had fallen back. The two battalion medical officers stayed with the wounded. The remainder, led by the one remaining officer, Leutnant Braun of 3rd Battalion Infantry Regiment 392, pulled back to our lines."

Fate and chance always play a role in battle. The forward troops of the outstanding Lehr Infantry Regiment were wiped out almost to a man during the day, but some had lucky escapes. In the case of Fusilier Häbel, he was elsewhere when the blow fell; Vizefeldwebel Berndt of the Mortar Platoon was simply lucky.

Fusilier Guard Häbel, Mortar Company Lehr Infantry Regiment [18] **3**

"During the evening of 29 July we advanced via Poelkapelle and Langemark to the First Position. Our luck was in and we got through without casualties. Our platoon took cover in various poor quality dugouts. During the night the British artillery fire slackened somewhat, only to return with increased intensity the following morning. At times like this it is a matter of keeping calm – very calm, for each moment may be the last. All of a sudden a shell exploded in front on the dugout, then another next to it; then two or three to the rear, to the right and to the left: shell upon shell and all of super-heavy calibre! Sometimes there was a lull in the firing for a quarter of an hour. When this happened we climbed out of the dugouts to stretch our limbs. Once the pause was over we just heard explosion after explosion. It was as though the earth itself was bursting. Wherever an individual was seen, British airmen were on hand to direct the fire of their guns on to him. A sentry stood stock still, hidden by a groundsheet so that he could not be seen from the air in front of each dugout. Every few moments someone called to him to see if he was still alive. From time to time one of these men was hit and collapsed: either silently, or groaning, to the ground.

"Whenever the fire was lifted, everyone rushed out. Now the attack, the relief from this hell must be upon us! But this hope was frequently replaced by disappointment. Dozens of British aircraft circled over our positions, watching for any movement and so we ended up again in an even bigger mess than before. The British were trying to extinguish all signs of life. Towards morning the British fire tended to reduce in intensity and both friend and foe used the time to recover and evacuate the wounded. We called this the, 'First Aid Hour'. This was [the reality of] the Battle for Flanders.

"As dawn broke on 1 August, [*sic*. Häbel means 31 July] the order came: 'Collect rations.' Nobody wanted to go so Fusilier Guard Zufall and I volunteered for the duty. We left bearing some water bottles, mess tins and sandbags. Was it fate or providence that the two of us went? Certainly as a result, we were the only two of our platoon to come through the battle unscathed. Moving from shell crater to shell crater, which were full to the brim with filthy water, we made our way to the rear; passing the *Wilhelm Stellung* [Wilhelm Position] and heading for the shot up village of Langemark. Near to the church we found what we were looking for: sacks of bread and buckets filled with butter, cheese, sausages, jam, tea and coffee. We loaded ourselves up with as much as we could carry and then got clear of the village, which was under constant fire, as swiftly as possible.

"We had hardly turned our backs on the village when the British fire came down extremely heavily. The pen strives in vain to describe its effect. It was coming down in all its fury on the *Wilhelm Stellung*, the gun positions and the approach roads. Zig-zagging we raced to the *Wilhelm Stellung*. As we were just leaving its trenches, we met our Leutnant, who had been wounded in the thigh and was making his way to the rear. We shouted to him and he shouted back, 'Move back and to the left!' I replied, 'No, Herr Leutnant, the British are already heading that way!' He paid no attention to me, moved to the left and was taken prisoner. As we arrived in the Second Position we shouted, 'The Tommies are coming!' Major Franz leapt up into a firing bay and looked to see what direction the enemy might be coming. Crack! He fell slowly back, hit by a shell [splinter]. The battle began in earnest for 1st Battalion, Lehr Infantry Regiment. We could only throw hand grenades, whilst our own artillery fire became weaker and weaker.

"It was an unequal battle. We soon pulled back through Langemark with the remnants of 1st Battalion, Lehr Infantry Regiment. What a sight it was. A complete company of ours and one of the *Maikäfer* [Cockchafers – nickname of the Fusilier Guards] lay scattered on the ground: destroyed – dead! It was no better on the gun positions. Wrecked guns were sunk in the mud; hardly any were still firing. A group of gunners and sappers was trying to pull a heavy gun out of the morass, but it was hopeless. An empty ammunition column transported us back to Westrozebeke. We were saved!"

Vizefeldwebel Berndt 2nd Mortar Platoon Lehr Infantry Regiment [19] 3

"It must have been about 5.00 am when the sentry shouted, 'Defensive fire!' Everyone rushed out to the mortar. With sights set on 700 metres, we trusted to luck and opened fire. Whether or not we were successful was impossible to say. We just kept firing to help our comrades up front. One mortar was knocked out by a shell and there were dead and wounded. Then they started trickling back one by one. This included Vizefeldwebel Müller of 8th Company, whom I knew well. He was wounded and was trying to make his way to the rear. What he had to say was a terrible blow. Just at the moment of relief, the Tommies charged forward and overran the front line. Three heavy machine guns arrived at our bunker. We hastily constructed a nest of resistance, with one gun on the roof and the two other left and right covering out to the flanks.

"We suddenly found that we were in the front line. I had this reported to the rear by signalling lamp, in the hopes that someone would pick up the information. The seemed to be another machine gun nest about 300 metres to our left. One of our guns was knocked out by an enemy shell. A British airman circled above us. Having spotted us he dived to ten metres and flew over us, spraying us with a hail of lead. The strength of our little group continued to shrink then, towards 8.00 am, a deeply echeloned line of enemy infantrymen crossed the small fold in the ground to our front. At long last we had a clear target and we fired, either lying or with our rifles resting against the uprights which had once supported our barbed wire obstacle. But the enemy did not even seem to take note of his losses; the gaps were quickly filled. By some wretched luck tanks were also making

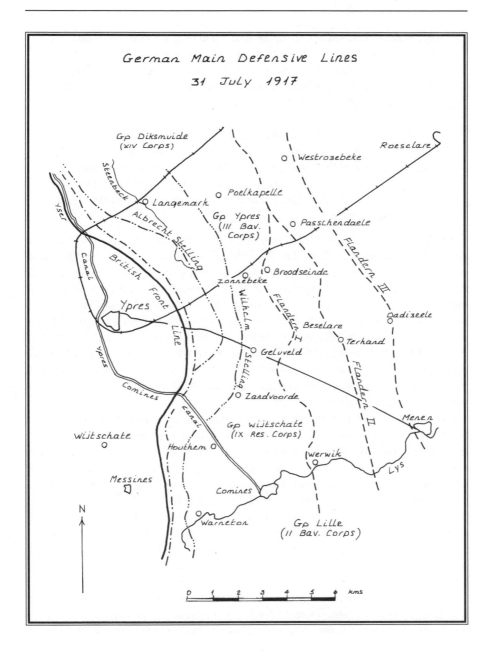

German Main Defensive Lines
31 July 1917

their way forwards. They were the first I had ever set eyes on. Using our last intact mortar we tried to hit one of these great tracked objects. All the enemy fire was now being concentrated on us. As I was taking aim my splintered rifle was suddenly torn out of my hand. A shell had suddenly torn off two of my fingers and simultaneously bored through my upper arm.

"We were down to five or six defenders, but we held on. One of my comrades bound my wounds then I headed off to the rear. I had hardly taken a step beyond the bunker when a shrapnel ball smashed through my left elbow joint. I noticed no pain and just kept going as fast as my feet would carry me. At long last I reached the lines of the counter-attack division. I was saved."

The Fusilier Guards, the other regiment of the division deployed right forward, also had an extremely difficult day. In their area the artillery fire intensified from 4.15 am to drum fire along their entire front, whilst the rear areas were gassed. From 5.00 am smoke and flame weapons were also used against their positions. All means of communications failed, patrols were despatched, but failed to return, runners did not reach their destinations and a short while later a massive British attack developed, especially against their left flank and their left hand neighbours. A breakthrough there was quickly followed by attacks which developed from all directions, including the rear. Desperate all round defence was attempted, but even having fired off all their ammunition, nothing could be done against the overwhelming weight of the enemy attack.

Eventually there was nothing else for it, but for the remnants of the two forward battalions to try to break back through the British barrage and reform in the rear. Few made it and a number remained on the position badly wounded or simply too exhausted to move. Those who survived were all captured. There was, however, one amazing escape. Leutnant Eisenträger, commander of 1st Company, was wounded by shrapnel and unable to move. He would undoubtedly have been taken prisoner, but for the extraordinary courage and physical strength of his batman, Fusilier Guard Musolf, who hoisted him onto his back and somehow, dodging the fire and avoiding the British barrage, carried him to safety through the muddy, cratered landscape. This daring feat was quite rightly rewarded by an immediate Iron Cross First Class; a rare award for a junior rank.[20]

Whilst the infantry battle continued to be sharply contested, the German artillery was doing its best to respond to calls for defensive fire and to contribute to breaking up the attacks. Such was the weight of counter battery and suppressive fire that in many cases the fire, when it came at all, was somewhat desultory and lacking in effect, but in others, useful work was done, despite all the difficulties.

Reserve Leutnant Pohl
Forward Observer Sector 'Hummel' [Bumble Bee] [21] *Field Artillery Regiment 6* [22] **4**

"The enemy had been firing gas since 2.00 am. Again and again waves of gas rolled up to where we were observing with the tripod binoculars, forcing us to mask up. Luckily none of the gas shells found their way onto the plank roof of our observation post. Then – it was probably around 5.00 am – drumfire came down with a crash on our front line trenches. Simultaneously swarms of flares rose in the morning sky. I did not need to give an order. My observer was ready with the flare pistol and soon our signals were also going up. Within seconds came the howls of greeting of our shells as they bored forward over our observation post. We all breathed a sigh of relief, as the appalling tension of the destructive British bombardment began to ease. Day dawned. The area was cloaked with thick mist, which rendered observation impossible. Hours of terrible uncertainty followed then the village of St Juliaan to our front could be seen through the binoculars followed, a little later, by parts of the *Albrecht Stellung*, above which a British aircraft could be seen circling at low altitude.

"Further to the front could be seen dark figures, who threw themselves to the ground, then advanced again, heading for our *Albrecht Stellung*. Patchy fog interfered with observation from time to time and our eyes attempted to bore through it. Then we saw more figures. There was no doubt that they were British. At the very same instant there came a knock on the door. 'Leutnant, the British are 200 metres away!' At that one of my telephonists risked his life to carry this important message through intense fire to the 6th Company – the line had long since been cut. Once again we manned the binoculars. It was all very tense. Our eyes were still stinging from the gas, but we paid no attention. The same question kept running through my mind. Would the report get through or not? But then we could make out, from the different colour of the smoke, where our rounds were landing. It was well-directed and was coming down in the midst of the swarms of British soldiers. In the meantime the tireless signallers had laid a new line between the battery and the observation post.

"Good grief! What's that? exclaimed an Unteroffizier, who was using a hand-held telescope to keep a general eye open. A huge oval box seemed to be moving along behind a row of trees. There was another – and a third! The telephone receiver had never been pulled from its mounting more quickly than at this moment. 'Battery! three tanks! Direction 150; Range 1,600. Fire a salvo!' I shouted down the telephone. 'Where is the fall of shot? Why have they not fired?' I could hardly maintain my patience.

Finally they arrived, but they were plus of the target. 'Drop 200!' Now a round landed right behind a tank, which had slewed broadside on and was engaging our infantry with its machine gun. My next order was swallowed up by a deafening crash. Powder smoke and dust enveloped our view, which was simultaneously cut out by flying lumps of clay and splintered timbers. Immediately afterwards a shell impacted on the side of our observation post; the overpressure sending telephone, maps and flares flying all over the place in a mad dance.

"Luckily nobody was injured, though a beam made the acquaintance of an unteroffizier's head. Right, everybody out! It was preferable to observe in the open than to run the terrifying risk of being buried alive! We carried on observing over the parapet of an infantry trench. In the meantime, the damned tanks had made off. One battalion of Infantry Regiment 454 moved up to reinforce – but what hope had one battalion against the advancing British masses? They drew ever closer, until they could be recognised by their flat steel helmets with the naked eye. Runner after runner raced to the battery in order to provide fire corrections and repeatedly they returned through the hail of fire. It had now become pointless to try to continue to observe. The enemy troops were within 100 metres of the *Wilhelm Stellung*. We headed back to the 6th Battery with a final report, leaping from crater to crater, through the roar of battle and amidst a crazy maelstrom of shells, shrapnel and small arms fire. Nevertheless we all got through to the battery unscathed, there to find that only one gun was still capable of firing. With its barrel red hot, it fired off the last few rounds."

To the south of the recently formed 235th Infantry Division,[23] the formations and units of 38th Division performed extremely well and so were also mentioned in the 1 August Group Ypres situation report:[24]

"38th Infantry Division: (5) During the heavy British attack Infantry Regiments 94 and 95, which obstinately defended their positions and Infantry Regiment 96, which launched a series of counter-attacks, all distinguished themselves, as did Field Artillery Regiment 19 which intervened in the battle on its own initiative. Hauptmann Prinz zu Solms, 1st Battalion Infantry Regiment 94, launched a powerful counter-attack with his battalion against the enemy, which had broken into our positions in several places and ejected them. 3rd Battalion Infantry Regiment 96 and 1st Battalion Infantry Regiment 95 under Majors Behrens and Bohm respectively counter-attacked vigorously the enemy which had broken into the *Albrecht Stellung* then held on obstinately despite being outflanked on both sides by the enemy, until they were replaced by other newly arrived elements of the division.

"7th Company Infantry Regiment 94 under Leutnant von Tümpling, together with elements of 3rd Battalion Infantry Regiment 94 operating near *Kaffee-* and *Quergut* held their positions in the face of repeated enemy attacks. Finally encircled later by superior numbers of enemy, they managed under his leadership to break out. Hauptmann Klassen, 3rd Battalion Infantry Regiment 95, beat off the enemy, which repeatedly launched attacks against the *Schwabenhof* from positions which deeply outflanked him to his right. Supported by the radio station commanded by Gefreiter Chrznowski of Divisional Radio Detachment 19, which carried out its duties in the forward trench to the last in an exemplary manner, he succeeded in passing a constant stream of messages concerning the enemy which was pressing forward, north of the railway and also in passing to the artillery information, which led to the destruction of the advancing tanks.

"Thanks to the heroic efforts of the observers and the men manning the radio and light signalling equipment, higher command was kept almost continuously informed about the situation. Hauptmann Oberdeck, 1st Battalion Field Artillery Regiment 19, engaged the enemy who were advancing in dense columns with excellently directed fire. One of his batteries was temporarily captured by the enemy, who suffered extremely heavy casualties from one of its guns which went on firing to the very last minute, but the counter-attack by our infantry, which was organised very swiftly, found it a simple matter, because of the enemy casualties, to re-capture the lost guns.

"Leutnant Schmeichel, who assumed command of 2nd Battery Field Artillery Regiment 19, after his battery commander was killed, knocked out three tanks and, despite being surrounded by the enemy, continued to keep his battalion commander fully informed through a series of excellent observations. Similarly Leutnant Heimann, commander of 1st Battery Field Artillery Regiment 19, distinguished himself when our infantry was overrun by dense enemy columns, by conducting an obstinate close-quarter defence with his guns at ranges under 600 metres and forcing them to dig in to his front and on either flank."

It is quite clear from the record that all the regiments and units of 38th Division performed aggressively and well throughout the day. They had counter-attacked in a timely and effective manner, which was precisely in line with the latest tactical and operational thinking. They were rightly proud of what they had achieved in quite unfavourable circumstances, as this account from a member of Infantry Regiment 96 makes clear.

Leutnant Faßhauer 4th Company Infantry Regiment 96 [25] 5

"Drum fire continued to come down in undiminished strength; the company area being subjected mainly to heavy calibre shelling. Because heavy machine gun fire could be heard, the company despatched a reconnaissance patrol, comprising Gefreiter Matthaei and Musketiers Oertel and Berg forward. [This] established the fact that the British had overrun the *Heckenstellung* [Hedge Position] and had penetrated the *Albrecht Stellung*. On order of the battalion, the 4th Company moved to the 3rd Battalion sector and relieved 9th Company. A short time later a further order arrived from the battalion: 'The enemy has reached the *Albrecht Stellung*. 3rd Battalion Infantry Regiment 96 is to hold the *Wilhelm Stellung*, left flank on the *Gutscherweg* [the road running along the northern edge of Polygon Wood]. 1st Battalion Infantry Regiment 96 is to extend the line to the south; 1st Company Infantry Regiment 96 is to occupy the front line, with 4th Company Infantry Regiment 96 to its left. 4th Company is to establish contact with 2nd Battalion Reserve Infantry Regiment 238 (Hauptmann Richter). The battalion is to join in the attack during the advance on the *Albrecht Stellung*.'

"Before the company even reached the *Wilhelm Stellung* it suffered its first fatal casualty. Gefreiter Fischer, one of the very best stretcherbearers, who had been with the company ever since the outbreak of the war, was killed when he was hit in the chest by a shell splinter.[26] The advance was conducted in columns and passed through extraordinarily heavy artillery fire and without further casualties we reached the northwest edge of Polygon Wood. There, in order to avoid later additional movement, the company was forced to wait until 3rd Battalion Infantry Regiment 96 and 1st Company arrived. [Once they had arrived] 4th Company, (deployed in the order 1, 2 and 3 Platoons), occupied positions to the left of 1st Company in the *Wilhelm Stellung*, which was under extremely heavy shell fire. Vizefeldwebel Humburg with 3 Platoon on the left of the company was ordered to link up with Reserve Infantry Regiment 238, but in the process of moving to his left, Vizefeldwebel Humburg was wounded in the arm.

"Simultaneously Vizefeldwebel Sachs, commander of 1 Platoon, was wounded by shrapnel in his upper thigh and unable to continue. Thereafter 1 Platoon was combined with 2 Platoon under Vizefeldwebel Förster and Leutnant Lukas took over 3 Platoon. As soon as the sector was occupied, the company was ordered to push men forward and so arrange itself in depth. 1st Company did the same: it was not a moment too soon, because a few minutes later the entire *Wilhelm Stellung* as far as the eastern edge of

Nonne-Bossen came under extremely heavy artillery fire of all calibres. Despite this [dispersion], within a very short time the company had already suffered considerable casualties. Taking cover in a shell hole with the company commander were Unteroffizier Bermpohl and Tambour Petermann. Shortly after the drum fire began, Bermpohl was hit by a shell splinter which pierced his steel helmet and his forehead. Despite being in great pain and losing a lot of blood, Bermpohl constantly urged Tambour Petermann to keep a sharp look out to the front ...

"The order to attack arrived from battalion, but such was the weight of artillery fire that to attempt to advance was out of the question for the time being. This fact was reported to battalion. Gefreiter Hintsch, one of the bravest runners in the company throughout the hardest of days, was seriously wounded in the back as he carried the message. Whilst this was occurring, Vizefeldwebel Förster, Unteroffiziers Diercks and Paalhorn and about ten men pushed out to the left to complete the link up to Reserve Infantry Regiment 238, which had not been achieved up until then. Diercks then volunteered to work his way forward half-left, in order to see what was happening at Nonne Bossen. He returned a little later with the report that all that was left there were the remnants of Reserve Infantry Regiment 238, who were rallying. Despite the pain in his leg, caused by a dud, Gefreiter Conrad volunteered to pass this information to the company commander.

"Throughout the period of drum fire, the *Wilhelm Stellung* was also under heavy machine gun fire. The stretcher bearers under the tried and tested Sanitätsunteroffizier Oberdick earned high praise by ignoring the fire and going forward from crater to crater to find and tend to the wounded. A short time after 12.00 pm the British lifted their fire to the rear. This was the yearned-for moment when we could get forward ... As we approached the Hanebeek, we came under machine gun fire from the right and left, tank fire from the left and some individual riflemen fired from directly to our front. Tambour Petermann, the last of the company headquarters on his feet, was knocked out of the battle here with a machine gun bullet wound to the upper arm. The advance continued as individuals sprang from crater to crater towards the Hanebeek. This swampy ground, pitted with shell holes, could only be traversed in a few places and then only with extreme difficulty.

"Nevertheless the company pushed on until it arrived at the southern corner of the wooded area, northeast of Point 585 [German reference point] and deployed to the north. Having gone firm on this line, the company came under fire from the right from the *Eksternest* strongpoint and from the left from a tank which was located to the west of Hill 64. All of a sudden rifle fire opened up at very close range. Unteroffizier Mitschke, together with Gefreiters Raithel and Oettler, Wehrmann Wallesh and Musketiers Weber and Drescher, dashed forward cautiously in bounds, as far as the *Steingraben*, at the point where the barbed wire obstacle of the *Albrecht Stellung* cuts the *Steingraben*. The British had barricaded themselves in the *Steingraben*. Opening well-aimed fire from twenty metres, [the German group] was successful in neutralising this outpost. The effect of the fire was clear from the dead British soldiers, whom Gefreiter Raithel brought in later as it went dark. Removing letters, epaulettes and gasmasks from them, he took these valuable items via the company back to battalion.

"Every Tommy who raised his head above the trench was dealt with, but they fought back. It was during this time that Gefreiter Oertler was severely wounded in the chest. Vizefeldwebel Förster worked his way forward through the fire and linked up with Unteroffizier Mitschke and his men. Because Mitschke had taken casualties and was likely to suffer more, but because the ground had to be held at all costs, he sent Gefreiter Raithel back to fetch the platoon forward to occupy the *Albrecht Stellung*, which lay about thirty metres in rear of Unteroffizier Mitschke ... Because the platoon had nobody to its left or right, Vizefeldwebel Förster sent Unteroffizier Becher along the *Albrecht Stellung* in a northerly direction and Unteroffizier Kühne off to the left to try to remedy this. Within a short time Kühne was back to report that Infantry Regiment 46 was about seventy metres to the left of the company and he was despatched once more to maintain contact.

"Becher, however, reported that the right flank was in the air. This report was sent on to the company commander. There was then a personal discussion with Leutnant Ehmer and Leutnant Posseldt, 2nd and 3rd Companies Infantry Regiment 96 respectively, at which the following was decided: 2nd Company would fill the gap between 4th and 6th Companies. 3rd Company would maintain contact with Infantry Regiment 46 and echelon the remainder of the company to the left as flank protection. Although some doubt was cast on the matter, until it was confirmed by an infantry cooperation aircraft later in the day, 4th Company was the first sub-unit to reach the *Albrecht Stellung*.

"The infantry cooperation aircraft earned the highest praise that day. Already in the early dawn when the positions were shrouded with thick fog, they repeatedly overflew the *Wilhelm Stellung* at very low altitude. The liaison which they achieved, despite coming under heavy machine gun fire, was brilliant. Lacking air recognition panels, as soon as one appeared, 4th Company Infantry Regiment 96 laid out maps, report forms, pieces of newspaper, hand towels and handkerchiefs. Waving, the crew of the aircraft made it clear that they had established where our line ran. The photographs they took confirm that 4th Company Infantry Regiment 96 really had reached the line of the *Albrecht Stellung* right at the beginning [of the counter-attack]"

Located north and south of Hollebeke and astride the Ypres-Comines canal the 10th Bavarian Division, like so many others, had suffered acutely during the bombardment. Its ability to conduct a cohesive and effective elastic defence was compromised from the start by damage to its positions and the near-destruction of all means of command and control, as this short passage from the history of Bavarian Reserve Infantry Regiment 8 makes clear:

> "To the rear there was almost no means of communication. The message dogs were wounded; the telephones and radio equipment were destroyed. It was impossible to use light signals, because the receiving station, which was co-located with the commander of the reserve troops, had been wrecked, along with the command post itself. Two of the four carrier pigeons were despatched with situation reports and requesting air support. Green flares and signal rockets were fired, but were not observed by the artillery. Very few runners could get through because of the enormous weight of fire. Finally, at 9.45 am, an infantry cooperation aircraft appeared overhead. The commander of the forward troops laid out air panels, which read: *There is a battalion command post here. The enemy has broken in to the right and in the centre. Support is needed.*" [27]

The message was photographed, delivered to the division and acted upon, but it was evening before support arrived and the general exhaustion of the troops made a counter-attack out of the question. To their immediate north, the men of Bavarian Reserve Infantry Regiment 6 were embroiled in a bitter struggle, which at times descended to hand-to-hand fighting. Despite the lack of support, this regiment was only forced to give up a relatively small amount of ground, but the cost in casualties was extremely high.

Oberstleutnant von Baligand Commander Bavarian Reserve Infantry Regiment 6 [28] **6**

> "The front line established in the crater field was gradually yielded after an obstinate defence. In fact it had to be, because the British were enfilading it from the right flank, where they had pushed on deep into the sector of the neighbouring Prussian regiment [Reserve Infantry Regiment 82, 22nd Reserve Division]. The line there was in any case too weakly held. The many dead British soldiers lying scattered around the blockhouse on our extreme right flank near the Prussian front line bore silent witness

to how determined our defence of it had been. A further thirty dead British soldiers lay in one small space near the railway embankment in Sector K. Point *Lichterfelde* had to be abandoned temporarily."[29]

It was much the same story on the front of the 16th and 18th Divisions deployed slightly further to the south. Hauptmann Sieveking of Reserve Infantry Regiment 86 (18th Res Div) reported to his regimental commander at 10.50 am: 'My centre has been driven in by the enemy. Our light machine guns are all out of action. I request a resupply of light machine guns and two platoons as reinforcements. All my means of communications are destroyed. Ask the artillery to keep a sharper look out for flares requesting defensive fire.' This was followed at 12.14 with, 'Parts of our front line have been lost. Casualties are heavy, I urgently request reinforcement.'[30]

In the very nick of time assistance arrived and, by dint of desperate fighting throughout the remainder of the day, with artillery supporting fire brought down at regular intervals, the regiment succeeded in holding on to its positions through counter-attacks. Nevertheless, it was touch and go and the cost was high. One platoon despatched to close the gap to the neighbouring Reserve Infantry Regiment 31 was as good as annihilated before night fell. Away to the north between Bikschote and Langemark, Fusilier Regiment 73 and Infantry Regiments 76 and 164 of 111th Infantry Division were also being forced back, but continued to put up a vigorous defence until they were threatened with total encirclement and capture. Already by 8.00 am the situation was beginning to unravel. Leutnant König, commander of 9th Company Infantry Regiment 76, arrived at the command post of the *KTK* to report, 'The enemy has broken in to the sector of Fusilier Regiment 73 on my left and the attack continues to make progress. To my right the picture is the same. My entire company is either destroyed or scattered.' [31] During a day of heavy casualties, many men of the division were captured. A high proportion of them were wounded but some, outmanoeuvred, had no choice but to surrender. Nevertheless there were numerous examples of hairbreadth escapes.

Vizefeldwebel Kober 6th Company Fusilier Regiment 73 [32] **7**

"In the crater next two me, I saw two filthy figures pick themselves up, knocking the earth off a machine gun. They fiddled around with the muzzle, checked the working parts and finally pissed into the cooling jacket, which had no water left in it. Then they brought the machine gun into action and tack! tack! – off whistled the bullets amongst the British. However, because the 6th Company was threatened with being encircled and destroyed, the company commander, Leutnant von Solemacher, gave the order to scatter and for each man to make his way to the rear individually. The two machine gunners did the same. One swung the gun over his shoulder and the other carried two boxes of ammunition. Then they calmly made their way back. What a pair of outstanding men! They were from the 3rd Battalion."

Hauptmann Goesch 2nd Battalion Infantry Regiment 164 [33] **7**

"I decided to evacuate the command post. Having destroyed all maps and documents I set off in a northeasterly direction with about thirty riflemen. I placed Vizefeldwebel Jacob 5th Company Infantry Regiment 164 in charge of the rearguard. I took up a blocking position behind a hedge along the Bikschote-Hilgendorff road. At that moment the 3rd Machine Gun Company under Leutnant Dürking arrived complete with all its weapons."

Schütze Fletge 2nd Machine Gun Company Infantry Regiment 164 [34] **7**

"Because I had received a slight head wound three days earlier and had not gone to the rear due to the heavy fire, Feldwebel Hobrecht sent me in the morning with a report of the commander of the fighting troops. Hardly had I left our blockhouse than I came under fire of the British out of the trees. I had to cover a lot of distance crawling or dashing, because the British always fired especially heavily at individuals moving alone. I took a short cut from the track through the corner of a wood. There I came across a battery to my front, but there were only dead men around the guns. I quickly left this evil place. I could hear heavy small arms fire behind me. On the way to battalion headquarters, I came across a good comrade, the Battalion runner Heins, who was seriously wounded. I placed him over my shoulders and carried him to the battalion where his wounds were dressed. This place looked awful. Around the blockhouse lay many dead. They had been carried, seriously wounded, to the command post and had died there. The remainder of our two machine gun platoons and Feldwebels Waldhelm and Hobrecht were all captured."

Whilst the forward troops gave ground gradually, or fought hard to defend particular strong points so as to delay the Allied advance, the other main component of the new flexible defensive tactics was ordered into action. The six *Eingreif* divisions (2nd Guards Reserve in the north, 221st and 50th Reserve behind Group Ypres and 207th, 12th and 119th in support of Group Wijtschate), were about to face a stern test. Their role was to advance to the line occupied by the ground holding divisions then counter-attack enemy incursions forward of the German lines and throw them back, thus restoring the original line held before the attack began. The immediate difficulty they faced was the fact that the Allied artillery now had the capacity more or less to seal off the battlefield, by bringing down continuous intense barrage fire designed to cut off all movement in or out of the forward battle area. The regiments involved achieved varying success that day, but they all experienced great problems caused by suppressive fire and air attacks. Receiving from Group Diksmuide at 5.10 am the order *Friedrich*, the regiments of 2nd Guards Reserve Division went to immediate readiness. This was followed at 6.20 am with the code word *Wilhelm* and the companies and battalions set off marching towards their assembly areas via the southern part of Houthulst Wood. It was the start of a day of order, counter-order and considerable confusion and, for the men of 8th Company Reserve Infantry Regiment 77, even this initial move forward was to prove memorable for all the wrong reasons.

Unteroffizier Euling 8th Company Reserve Infantry Regiment 77 [35] **8**

"The company commander (Reserve Leutnant Weiterer) and I ran from 3 Platoon where we had been originally, forward to 1 Platoon. We had hardly gone twenty five metres when four heavy shells – the worst high-explosive shells I had come across – passed over our heads with a fearful roar. One of them landed right in the middle of 3 Platoon, exploding with a violent detonation, sending out an appalling pressure wave, killing eleven dear comrades and seriously wounding ten more. Here are the names of those faithful comrades who lost their lives at this place: Offizierstellvertreter Wilke, Unteroffizier Hahn, Unteroffizier Schwabe, Siemering, Kellner, Weyer, Rohde III, Wodk, Gefreiter Hanekamp, Gehring and Schlüter – Deeply shocked we stood and looked at this scene of dreadful destruction.[36] But there was no time to complain or mourn! It was a soldier's fate! We hurried forward at assault pace to counter the attacking enemy!"

The regiments of the 119th Infantry Division, in support of Group Wijtschate, were also launched forward early but, as the experience of Reserve Infantry Regiment 46 demonstrates, moving forward without clear orders or objectives simply exposed men to needless risks for little gain.[37]

Vizefeldwebel Pötschke Reserve Infantry Regiment 46 [38]

"At 5.00 am on 31 July the alarm was raised near Dadizeele. In the distance we could hear the sound of the guns, which had been pounding away ceaselessly for weeks. At 5.30 am the state of alarm was lifted, but then, around 9.00 am, everything really broke loose. It was a grey day; the sky was full of low rain clouds. We remained in wait behind some bushes, whilst to our front an artillery battle raged as the British attacked. The plan was to deploy us to the north of the Ypres railway. After we had eaten we headed for the front ... and it began to rain. We halted for some hours by a house alongside the road. An aeroplane stuck its neck out, flying very low and close to us beneath the low cloud ceiling and attempting to press on to our rear. There were two German aircraft around and in seconds they had shot down the enemy. It sank down, trailing a bright stream of flame from the rear of its fuselage. A British tri-plane appeared a few minutes later at high speed. It was very well handled. The anti-aircraft guns could not hit it and, within a quarter of an hour heavy artillery fire was coming down on the road. Motor vehicles were bringing casualties from Infantry Regiments 41 and 1 from the front. It was pouring with rain. We were soaked to the skin and we looked for shelter for the night in some wooden huts. It rained the whole night. The artillery battle raged on; apparently there were 420 mm guns [*sic*] in the vicinity.

"The next morning we were still dodging artillery fire. About twenty Scottish prisoners were escorted to the rear. Fresh troops were heading for the front. The battalion moved through the pouring rain further to the right. We spent that night in the open lying in thick mud. At about 2.00 am we moved further to the left and pulled back slightly. The stink of dead horses fouled the air. It was pitch black and nobody knew the correct route. We wandered lost amongst a sea of shell holes, stumbling and falling up to our knees in mud all the time. We kept edging forward. We cannot have been far off falling into the hands of the British! Enemy fire was coming down everywhere It began to get light.

"Finally we reached our goal! Behind some hedges, we stretched out our groundsheets to try to make tents and we looked for shelter from the rain there and behind the remains of a ruined wall. It went on raining all day. Our filthy, saturated clothing stuck to our skin. I took a good look round. I knew this place from before, but what a state it was in now! Crater upon crater – all full of water. Houses and woods had all been swept away by the hail of iron. It was a dreadful sight. So, without shelter, we were stuck here until 4 August. It hardly ever stopped raining. A direct hit robbed me of one of my very best comrades; a man I had marched away with.

"Finally on the morning of 5 August we headed for the rear. Never had we so longed for it! The rain had protected us from even worse casualties, but many had to report sick. In Koekelare, north of Diksmuide and near Leke, we finally had a well-earned rest. The great Battle of Flanders had been another day of glory for our 119th Infantry Division. Two of its regiments had launched a counter-attack. Its commander received the *Pour le Mérite* [Blue Max]; our Hauptmann the Iron Cross First Class. Our artillery played the biggest part in the success. The amount they fired was almost unbelievable. The British must have taken enormous casualties. They seemed especially to fear our gas shells! Enraged they fired upon villages and towns well behind the front and frequently launched air attacks on stations during the night."

It is, of course, wrong to draw general conclusions from individual accounts, so the strange meanderings of Vizefeldwebel Pötschke are probably not typical – not even within 119th Infantry Division. As Pötschke mentions, the Division was directed to counter-attack in behind 38th Infantry Division where there had been deep enemy incursions and Infantry Regiment 46 which, somewhat confusingly, was part of the same division as Reserve Infantry Regiment 46, played a leading role in it. The code word to launch the operations was *Näher ran* [Get closer]. The regimental commander had tested the transmission of the codeword during the night 30/31 July and by 5.45 am on 31 July it was clear that passage of information had been patchy. Nevertheless, whilst the commander was moving between his 1st and 2nd Battalions to discuss the matter, the regimental adjutant rode up from brigade with the real version: *Näher ran! The enemy has apparently broken through to Geluveld.*

The battalions rushed to complete their preparations, then, at about 10.00 am, the following order arrived from brigade: 'The regiment is to advance immediately to the area of the *Wilhelm Stellung*, using covered routes as far as possible to avoid being spotted from the air. 1st Battalion: southern edge of Polygon Wood; 3rd Battalion: roughly between the Baden House and Geluveld chateau; 2nd Battalion: area of Westhoek. Regimental command post is to be in the ruined house on the hill to the west of Beselare. Establish communications there immediately; report arrival as soon as possible. 4th Battery Field Artillery Regiment 237 and MG Lehrkursus [Training Course] are to adopt covered positions about 400 metres south of the church in Beselare.'[39]

This attack was reasonably successful, but throughout the day there was considerable confusion on the battlefield, due to an almost complete failure of communications. From his hill top position, the commander was able to observe the movement of his battalions personally, which enabled him to make adjustments as necessary, but with only runners and the occasional rider able to pass messages, situation reports and orders, the headquarters of the ground-holding 6th Bavarian Reserve Division were completely unaware of how the attack was progressing, which in turn meant a serious lack of coordination between the movements of the German units in the area. Furthermore it was quite impossible to report back to 119th Division at all until the following day. Despite all these vicissitudes, the important point from the perspective of the defence was that the critically important Hooge sector was firmly in the hands of the *Eingreif* troops of 119th Infantry Division as night fell.

The overcast wet conditions that day meant that air activity was severely curtailed, as it had been for artillery spotting aircraft during the bombardment, nevertheless the German air force made a huge effort to get airborne and to support the ground –holding and counter-attack divisions to the maximum extent possible.

"During the entire day of battle only individual enemy aircraft were observed. Despite thick ground mist and low cloud our own airmen made repeated attempts to get to the front. They then flew over the battle zone throughout the entire day, succeeding repeatedly in locating our front line of own troops, despite the fact that it changed constantly. Where no air panels had been displayed they descended lower and lower until they could recognise men waving at them from shell holes. An abundance of reports about the battle situation was the result of all these flights. The infantry cooperation aircraft were able to do their work thanks to protection delivered by aircraft of the fighter squadrons, which in turn meant that our infantry were helped by the fact that the attacking enemy was subject to a great deal of machine gunning and bombing.

"Reconnaissance flights, which were rendered difficult, but not impossible, because of the weather revealed that the enemy was not moving reserves forward. Poor light conditions made it impossible to conduct photo reconnaissance. Despite the low altitude and the extent of enemy defensive counter-measures, aircraft losses were extremely low. Vizefeldwebel Paul of Air Detachment 213 was wounded in the back, but still succeeding in landing back safely at base with a report. The enemy lost one aircraft, shot down by Leutnant Götsch of *Jasta* [*Jagdstaffel* = Fighter Squadron] 8

"Although visibility was reduced to less than three kilometres, due to thick mist and low clouds, all the Group balloons were airborne until the rain set in during the afternoon, in order not to miss any opportunity to observe if the visibility improved."[40]

Not everything which occurred in the southern area appeared to be suffering so badly from the confusion of the battlefield. The commander of 1st Battery Field Artillery Regiment 20, for example, was most impressed by what he saw unfolding before his eyes that day from his firing position near to Beselare.

Hauptmann Petzel, 1st Battery Field Artillery Regiment 20[41] **9**

"The firing position of 1st Battery was about two kilometres to the north of the other two of the 1st Battalion and located around a farm. The gun sections were located left and right of the farm buildings, tucked away into dense hedgerows. The men occupied the stable, the officers and the telephones were established in the kitchen and a further small room, none of which was even splinter proof. Concrete blockhouses near to the battery were full of infantry reserves. Initially the entire setting was idyllic. The Tommies pounded targets all around us; sometimes with large calibre shells, sometimes with gas, but they left us alone. We were silently triumphant, believing either that we had not been discovered, or that we were assumed to be located elsewhere. We were not even suspicious about the high-burst shrapnel above us, even though these were doubtless ranging rounds.

"The first rays of dawn on 31 July brought us a rude awakening. At 5.00 am British drum fire suddenly came down all along the front. Within seconds we had manned the guns and began to fire the first defensive fire mission but, before it was even complete, the Tommies brought us under fire. One of the first shells was a direct hit on Number 1 gun, then rounds began to land all over the position. A pile of ammunition blew up; there was a direct hit on the officers' quarters then another on Number 4 gun. Gefreiter Dartsch of Number 1 gun suffered serious wounds, from which he later died.[42] Unteroffizier Nagel and Kanonier Maaß were also badly wounded and the gun was knocked out.

"The shell which landed on Number 4 gun, burst under the trails; upending it and sending Gefreiter Pilhop flying over the adjacent hedgerow, which was three metres high. After a long search we found him lying unconscious twenty metres from the gun. It later transpired that, apart from a few bruises, he had escaped miraculously unhurt. Kanonier Kronkowski was also slightly hurt. The shell which burst in the officers' quarters caused nothing more than minor damage, because everyone had already raced to the guns. We lost no time in moving house. Because the infantry reserves had moved on, we occupied the three blockhouses 150 metres in front of the battery position and arranged the guns around them. The battery occupied this site until 24 September, without suffering serious losses, despite frequently coming under heavy fire. The accommodation was not a matter of unalloyed joy, however; the blockhouses shook badly every time we came under fire ...

"It was a great sight to see the advance of the *Eingreif* divisions during the morning of 31 July. All such major battles are marked by a degree of uncertainty at first, because hard news arrives only slowly from the front. Only gradually is it possible to build up a picture about what is actually happening. Up until that point there is always anxiety that there may have been a breakthrough somewhere, so it lifted our spirits to note, as midday approached, that the entire terrain from the rear areas forward was filled with columns of marching infantry and fresh batteries going into position. We were full of admiration for this amazing display of organisation and we knew straight away that the British Flanders offensive was doomed to fail."

It was not only the troops of the *Eingreif* divisions which were moving that day. With the artillery firing at intense rates, for example, the question of resupply became of pressing importance very early on, with additional columns having to be improvised at short notice to battle their way forward.

Leutnant Leiding Ammunition Column
1st Battery Bavarian Foot Artillery Regiment 5 [43] **12**

"Although columns and resupply teams were already on their way, I received orders at 12.30 am on 31 July to bring forward another five wagons loaded with 200 shells to our furthest forward position, about two kilometres west of Timbriele. By 1.15 am I was ready to move off with my vehicles. At a lively trot we headed to the ammunition dump at Geluveld via Menen. After some time, it may well have been 4.00 am, we had loaded the ammunition up and had set off for the firing position. The night was relatively quiet and the weather pleasant. Towards 5.00 am I had reached the farmhouse, which was later to become the command post of Group *Dichtelei*, about one kilometre east of Amerika [a hamlet midway between Kruiseke and Wervik]. At that point the ground began to rise, which was exceptional. I called a halt there in order to allow my horses to rest a while, prior to the final difficult part of the journey.

"At that moment the British began to bring down an unprecedented weight of fire of all calibres on our sector. Believing that it could not possibly last very long, I extended the pause. A short while later Offizierstellvertreter of the 1st Column came up to me and said, 'It is impossible to go further.' He had already delivered his ammunition to the gun positions and was delighted to have escaped the witch's cauldron. In the meantime day had dawned and there was no sign of a let up in the heavy fire. I then despatched an Unteroffizier to Group to request new orders in view of the changed situation. After a while an order came from the artillery commander, who by then had been briefed about our situation: 'The ammunition is to be got forward.' With a word of encouragement to everyone, I gave the order to advance. My men followed me in good order, my grey setting off at a good trot. Within a few moments we were in the middle of the witch's cauldron.

"Anybody who has experienced fire like this on the way to a position would agree that the final 100 metres before the actual centre of the fire is the worst part. I call this area the cold zone. It almost comes as a relief to be amongst it. My NCOs and men followed me courageously and we headed for Timbriele. The closer we came to the position, the worse the fire became. Timbriele was now to our rear. We now found ourselves on a narrow road. Right and left of us were water-filled trenches. Shell holes and abandoned vehicles blocked our way. The movement stalled; the situation was critical. Luckily a wayside farm offered us some cover. After considering the matter for a short while, I decided in order to avoid losses to men, horses and material to empty the wagons and to move them to the farm. We succeeded in doing this. At that moment Fahrer Hirth was killed.[44] His horse was severely wounded as were other horses slightly. At that I pulled my teams back two kilometres to where the fire was less intense. This cost me my best draught horse, one belonging to Fahrer Göpfert. A shell splinter sliced off his left foreleg.

"We took shelter in an empty stable. We watered the horses and fed them some turnips, which was the best we could do. For my two unteroffiziers and nine drivers I begged half a loaf off another unit. That was all we ate until 4.00 pm. At about 1.00 pm, I called together my men in order to complete the task. I left the NCOs' mounts and the wounded horse behind and we trotted forward. We cleared the road with pick and shovel and then loaded one wagon after the other and despatched them forward to the position. That left me with only my driver, so I got stuck in myself as well. It was great to work alongside men who were giving it their best. I still remember how Gefreiter Schneider came up to me and asked, 'May I drive the last wagon forward?' Of course I agreed to allow this. By 2.30 pm all the ammunition was on the gun position and we had added to it because plenty of ammunition of the same calibre was lying around where it had fallen from overturned vehicles.

"The driver is the gunner's right hand man. Furthermore, whilst the driver has no possibility of doing so, the gunner can at least return enemy fire. This means that when the driver behaves courageously, his conduct must be regarded as doubly laudable. At 3.00 pm I informed the artillery commander that all the ammunition was on the position. He duly praised us for our efforts. During our return journey we came across the field kitchen, so we enjoyed a tasty meal by the roadside and discussed the events of the day. I firmly believed that not a single one of my drivers had faltered as we resupplied ammunition on 31 July. It was a very hard job on an unforgettable day."

As has already been noted, communications between *Eingreif* and ground holding troops were fraught with difficulty, but the same problem applied to coordination of activities between the regiments of the *Eingreif* divisions, who needed to act as one in order to produce the synergy which could only come from timely exchange of information. One of the staff of Reserve Infantry Regiment 77 has left us a harrowing account of his attempts to conduct a mounted reconnaissance to locate and discuss the forthcoming counter-attack by 2nd Guards Reserve Division in the area of 111th Infantry Division late on the afternoon of 31 July.

Reserve Leutnant Alfred Wohlenberg,
Orderly Officer, Reserve Infantry Regiment 77 [45] **10**

"I climbed up on a miserable-looking nag belonging to the cavalry troop subordinated to us. Two Uhlans were detailed to accompany me. Riding using a cavalry saddle was an unaccustomed experience, but a bad ride is always better than a good walk. In a few moments at a sharp trot we reached *Friedrichstrasse*. The driving rain lashed our faces. My dripping wet coat slapped my legs. Water soaked slowly but surely through my clothes until I was soaked to the skin. However I took no notice of these minor inconveniences. The artillery fire and the [need to negotiate] uprooted trees demanded the highest state of alertness. Each time a shell landed nearby or a shrapnel round exploded, the old nag reared up sharply. A short dig with the heels and a calming word made it see sense again. It all got very unpleasant as we moved along one of the rides in the wood which led northwards parallel to the *Friedrichstrasse*. Artillery rounds of heavy and super-heavy calibre were crashing down. Tree trunks, as thick as a man, were ripped out of the ground as though by a ghostly hand and thrown down on their sides. There must have been batteries nearby, for which the fire was intended. The rotting corpses of dozens of dead horses lay all over the place and inside them, oblivious to the din of battle, the rats were at their disgusting work.

"One shell made a direct hit on a magnificent beech tree. With a crash the top of the tree fell to the earth immediately in front of us. One of the troopers lost control over his horse, which leapt to one side and fell into a very large shell-hole. In no time both horse and rider were sinking in the mud. Jumping swiftly off my horse, I was joined by the second Uhlan. Together and only with the utmost effort, we were just able to pull our comrade out of the morass. The horse was beyond help. We were not even able to put it out of its misery by shooting it. Only a spray of mud showed us that the horse was fighting and losing the battle against suffocation. Soldiers: Carry on! The two of us galloped on. The animals trembled and foamed with fear. No wonder in that dreadful racket! We raced along one ride after another. The map which might, perhaps, have enabled us to orientate ourselves, had long since dissolved in the mud and rain. Suddenly, shortly after 6.00 pm, the artillery fire eased and we came across a corduroy road which led us to the regimental headquarters of our fellow countrymen of Infantry Regiment 164. Here we discovered that it was not the 15th [Reserve Infantry Regiment 15], but the 164th which was responsible for the junction point at the *Sachsenbrücke* [Saxon Bridge]. I briefed them on our situation and the men from Hameln guaranteed that they would be pushing their forward posts out to the *Sachsenbrücke*. The mission was completed, despite the difficulties and we rode back at a gentler pace."

The very fact that Wohlenberg was expecting to link with Reserve Infantry Regiment 15, and found instead that Infantry Regiment 164 had been given the task is yet another example of how confusion could reign, even between formations of the same division. It was one outcome of the decision to subordinate the remnants of 111th Infantry Division to 2nd Guards Reserve Division, but on the ground it caused immense confusion. It is small wonder that this planned counter-attack by 2nd Guards Reserve Division, which was intended to restore the line of the *Albrecht Stellung*, stalled short of its objective.

As has already been noted, the move forward of Reserve Infantry Regiment 77 was affected from the start by severe casualties caused by long-range artillery. These losses continued throughout the march forward and were equally problematic for the other regiments; Reserve Infantry Regiment 15, for example, lost Leutnant Kuhlmann of 2nd Company killed[46] and eight of his platoon seriously wounded to a single 380 mm shell landing in the forward assembly areas in the Houthulst Wood.[47] These were serious losses amongst troops not yet committed to counter-attack; they cannot fail to have taken the edge off the attacking zeal of the remainder of the unit.

Leutnant Lützen 2nd Company Reserve Infantry Regiment 15 [48]

"The first platoon had just traversed Jonkershove unscathed as an [unfortunate] situation developed to our rear. I sensed that something was wrong and raced back to the second platoon. I met Leutnant Kuhlmann coming towards me. 'I have been wounded!' he said. I said calmly, 'It should not be too bad. There is no blood to be seen.' It was probably just a stone. However, when I reached the crossroads I was met by a dreadful sight. I was able to shake hands, for the last time I felt, with the first class Unteroffizier Rosengarten, who had been with the company since it marched away to war. Fortunately he was in fact saved.

"Whilst I waited there in the middle of the crossing to warn the third platoon, two direct hits crashed down, but no splinters hit either me or the numerous wounded men who were lying there. Just as I was crossing the danger point with the third platoon I heard that Leutnant Kuhlmann, located on the edge of the wood, had been killed by a shell splinter."

Meanwhile 3rd Battalion Reserve Infantry Regiment 15 was struggling to get forward through Houthulst Wood as well, but by a different route. Under constant fire, but urged on by their commanders, the move was delayed and the troops were split into small groups, who eventually, despite the difficulties, arrived at Bultehoek, four kilometres west of the Wood, by 12.30 pm.

Hauptmann Biermann,
Commander 11th Company Reserve Infantry Regiment 15 [49] **10**

"I gave a short speech mounted on my horse. *The Fatherland demands the faithful fulfilment of his duty by each and every one of you!* All I could see before me were faithful determined faces! In the meantime battalion orders had been issued:

Companies are to move from the assembly area to Bultehoek, collecting supplies of hand grenades along the road Staden-Stadenreke.

Order of march: 1, 2 and 3 Platoons at 100 metre spacing.

We set off and took a one hour break for final individual preparations. The road was not under fire, but the wood most certainly was … One man played his harmonica, others danced and sang. Did they not believe that this was serious? Finally everything was prepared and we advanced cross country towards the wood. Through previous reconnaissance, I knew the place as well as my favourite hunting area back home. We advanced along game trails in single file.

"There were endless halts to keep everyone together and for orientation purposes. Within the wood a great many trees had fallen victim to shells. Before we even arrived at the main wood there were incidents to our left and right. I rode forward, ordering the men to stay calm, maintain their positions and keep their distance. My horse was wounded by a shell splinter, but it had done its duty and its care could be entrusted to our rear echelon. The company arrived, considerably delayed, but without casualties, at the rendezvous, which was already occupied by battalion headquarters, 9th and 12th Companies. The 10th Company was still not present. It had been intended to provide the left flank guard, with 11th Company in reserve after the first contact with the enemy.

"Further delay was, however, out of the question, so 11th Company assumed the task of the 10th. 'Company! Deploy!', but there was another short pause. A battalion of Reserve Field Artillery Regiment 20 went into action and opened fire immediately, just as though they were on exercise. It certainly put heart into the troops! They had total confidence in their gunners – Forward! 1 and 2 Platoon under Vizefelwebels Kesselmeier and Brückmann respectively shook out in the lead and I followed up with 3

Platoon deployed in reserve under Offizierstellvertreter Weber"

"Fortunately for us Bultehoek was an island of calm amidst all the artillery fire, but hereafter the platoons were hit by an absolute torrent of it ... As we pushed to the west we began taking casualties immediately. Our target was the *Draaibank Stellung* [Draaibank Position]. Everything had been reconnoitred in advance and carefully thought through, but in this hail of shells, things did not turn out as expected. We seemed to attract fire from the west like magnets. The line of forward troops lost direction as a result of this. I spotted it immediately and rushed forward shouting and waving. Thank heavens I was understood and the 11th swung round more to the south.

"Suddenly a *Stollenknicker* [dugout smasher – presumably a large calibre shell] crashed into the damp clay one or two metres from me and I fell unconscious to the ground. Vizefeldwebel Weber and Brand rushed over and brought me round. In the meantime the word raced round the battalion, 'the commander of the 11th has been killed!' They wanted me to be taken to the rear because I must have been wounded. I checked myself over. There was no blood to be seen, just a terrible whirring in my head. I must have been struck by a large clod of earth, which knocked me down without injuring me. My face was absolutely filthy.

"I decided to carry on. Where was the company? We soon found it. The hail of iron had brought it to a halt and everyone had sought cover in holes and folds in the ground. 'Lads this will not do!' Let us get to the *Draaibank Stellung* and then we shall take stock of the situation.' At that the company followed its commander further to the south. The other companies saw what was happening and conformed to our movement in a southerly direction. This meant that the 11th found itself on the right flank and the 12th on the left. We worked our way forward through a great swampy expanse of ground that had been drenched with gas. There was not a sign of the enemy, just this endless torrent of fire of all calibres hammering down from the right.

"Suddenly overhead came the sound of cracks and whistles. The newcomers checked, wondering what it was. 'Lads, it's small arms fire! We shall soon be amongst them!' bawled Offizierstellvertreter Weber. Extremely heavy machine gun fire cracked overhead, having been fired from Bikschote in the direction of Bultehoek, where we had just come from! Fortunately it was all too high."

The experience of 11th Company was mirrored throughout the regiment. The cratered ground and intense fire was producing precisely the effect that the Allies intended; namely to break up and disrupt the forward movement of large reserves.

It was a near impossibility, in the clinging sodden clay soil of the crater field, for the battalions to maintain cohesion and direction and, in the meantime, casualties continued to rise. Nevertheless men of Infantry Regiment 134, pulling back, stressed that the enemy was possibly already forward of Bikschote. There was nothing for it but to press on. In the effort to fulfil their mission, units and sub-units did their best, but the advance was inevitably un-coordinated and consequently weak. By the time the various elements had straggled into the *Draaibank Stellung* the companies were seriously weakened and already down to an average of sixty riflemen. This was an inauspicious start to a difficult operation. The commander of 11th Company takes up the story:

Hauptmann Biermann,
Commander 11th Company Reserve Infantry Regiment 15 [50] **8**

> "We reached the *Draaibank Stellung* and the men took cover in deep holes. I sought out an intact concrete pillbox which contained a machine gun sharpshooter troop and was overflowing with wounded men and tried to clarify the situation. 'Is it possible to cross the Steenbeek? Are there any German troops forward of it? Where is the enemy?' Nobody could provide any information. All they could say was that they had lived through the Battle of Messines and that that was child's play in comparison with what they had experienced here.
>
> "I looked around outside the bunker and spotted Loof. We shook hands. As I looked at him I was sure that death had marked him out, but he did not in fact die a hero's death here; that occurred some weeks later at Passchendaele as he was moving into position. There did not seem to be any chance of crossing the swollen stream here, despite all the careful preparations we had made earlier. Without exception all the [pre-positioned] bridging materiel had been destroyed by shell fire."

The company commanders fanned out along the line of this obstacle trying to locate a way of forcing a crossing, but it was hopeless. Hauptmann Biermann continues,

> "The infantry was not in a position to repair the crossings. Fire was concentrated on all the crossing points to which the sections were drawn. Diversions, bunching and jams were the result. In the crowded confusion the shells and shrapnel took a heavy toll ... Suddenly Kater, the battalion drummer, arrived: 'The companies are ordered to advance on Bikschote immediately and without fail!' Kater was briefed about the situation and sent back with a report. I decided to look for a crossing. 'Lads, who will come with me?' Brand did not say a word, but got to his feet. We pushed

on to the left, following the line of the stream. Nowhere could we locate a possibility and slowly, rushing forward in bounds from cover to cover, we arrived at another bunker *Lünette* [Skylight] *I* or *II*.

"A man was cowering in the entrance. 'Who is inside?' 'Two officers.' I went in and found two captains. I asked them what was happening and if any of their men were located on the far side of the stream. Both of them were at the end of their physical and mental tether. Their only reply to my questions was a gasped, 'Everyone is dead!'[51]

Orders and exhortations arrived throughout the afternoon and junior commanders struggled to carry them out, but the obstacles to progress were simply too great and the losses from continuous artillery fire too large for there to be any chance of retaking Bikschote from the French that day. Finally using two tree trunks to bridge gaps in a burnt out footbridge, some men of Reserve Infantry Regiment 15 succeeded in crossing the Steenbeek in the later afternoon. Shells exploding nearby continued to take a toll. Men were blown off the makeshift bridge and numbers of them drowned in the swamp below.

Hauptmann Biermann,
Commander 11th Company Reserve Infantry Regiment 15 [52] **7**

"The enemy themselves came to our aid. Their heavy shells had felled some strong trees over the stream. This offered us a possibility. I went back and fetched the companies. Man after man teetered over the tree trunks. This was far from easy and much harder than it is to write. Heavy shell fire continued to come down, sending up huge fountains. A number of men were thrown into the water – including me, but I was fortunate enough to be able to reach the far bank. Not that that prevented the rumour from reaching battalion headquarters 'The commander of the 11th has been killed!' A machine gunner fell into the stream, complete with his load, and it was not possible to save him."

The sections who had succeeded in gaining the far bank pressed on as best they could in the direction of Bikschote. Biermann found himself virtually alone with just a few men of his company. 'Where were 1 and 2 platoons?' he asked himself. 'Where were the other companies? What was to our right? Where, above all, was the 1st Battalion that was meant to be advancing to our right?' The companies advanced painfully forward 300 or 400 metres in places; as much as 800 in others, but there was no momentum to the attack. 2 Platoon under Feldwebel Brinkmann advanced the furthest, but before long Hauptmann Biermann and Leutnants Lützen, Lindau and Bonin went firm near Bullenstall and along a slight rise 300 metres to the southwest.

Hauptmann Biermann,
Commander 11th Company Reserve Infantry Regiment 15 [53] **7**

"Yet again the battalion commander sent us an urgent order to capture Bikschote. Division was demanding it and pressing. I was unwilling to give the order for an assault unless the 1st Battalion was properly in position with all its companies near to us, so I duly reported this to the rear. As soon as it began to go dark, I sneaked over to the right with Brand to check out previously observed movement. There I met Leutnant Lindau, together with his company. He had no idea where the other companies were. There was no link up to the right and he could not move without an order from Hauptmann Nitzsches.

"I could have overridden his objections and ordered him to move, but it would have been impossible to capture a large village with one and a half weak companies. Not only that, but the village was being bombarded intensely by our guns, whose shells howled overhead. Had we attempted it we should simply have been advancing blindly into our own artillery fire and the machine gun fire of the enemy. We weighed the options up carefully and decided against advancing on our own. We reported this to battalion headquarters and they stopped pressurising us. They had obviously recognised how matters stood ... Towards midnight Weber was overcome by gas. I tried everything to save him but it was no use. Vizefeldwebel Kessmeier was wounded, which meant that all three platoon commanders were out of action. We were utterly exhausted. The leg which I had injured in the Vosges and which had never really recovered hung like a huge deadweight from my body. I could hardly move. So I dragged myself off to battalion headquarters to report. Dr von Hinüber then sent me back to the rear."

The situation was no better for the other battalions of Reserve Infantry Regiment 15. The very fact that they gained the west bank of the Steenbeek at all was worthy of the highest praise in the circumstances, but as this report sent that day by Leutnant Wirth of 2nd Battalion shows, a combination of the condition of the battlefield and the efficiency of the Allied barrage simply defeated their best efforts.

"Because the bridges that were being used were destroyed during the crossing, I got separated from the company and had to make use of a bridge 400 metres further southeast. I still had my assault group comprising engineers and one machine gun team with me, but some were wounded and some could not keep up carrying their heavy loads. I went in search of my company, therefore; following the track of a light railway to the right. I bumped into a party from Infantry Regiment 164, who informed me that the French were a mere 300 metres away, that they were reduced to two sections and that they were withdrawing.

"I was able to confirm this, because I was under constant machine gun fire from the left and the front. I then pulled back to the bridge where I discovered that the wounded of 2nd Battalion were pulling back from the *Bullenstall*. Armed with this information I set off in that direction and met up with Leutnant Loof and 10th Company. He told me that he was digging in 400 metres forward of the Steenbeek. To his front were the remnants of 9th, 12th and 1st Companies which had suffered such heavy casualties that they were withdrawing.

"Back at the bridge I had met up with Vizefeldwebel Bommermann, who was leading five sections of 7th Company. I told him to push his men out to the right as far as the railway line. I have now returned to him and assumed command of the whole sector. All I have at my disposal are the five sections and three machine guns ... Because our right flank is in the air and because the only possible withdrawal route is back over a badly damaged bridge, I have decided that the position would be untenable in the face of a serious attack; there would certainly be no possibility of launching a counter-attack over a single bridge! I have just learned that two platoons of 5th Company are located behind the Steenbeek together with machine guns and mortars. I have ordered them to move forward and extend the line further to the right.

"A further advance with these disorganised and weakened forces is out of the question. [signed] Wirth, Leutnant." [54]

In sharp contrast, the 221st and 50th Reserve, the *Eingreif* divisions of Group Ypres, played a significant role during the day. Their interventions were most effective and were deemed worthy of public praise by Group Ypres:

"221st Infantry Division: **11** During the night 30/31 July this division was located five to eight kilometres behind our front line. It was hidden from aerial observation, dispersed around the area and ready to counter-attack. All staffs up to and including the divisional one were occupying their command posts. Already by the early hours of 31 July an advance party was put at the disposal of 38th Division, which was tangled up in hard fighting. These fresh and fully battle-ready battalions from East Prussia, supported by 1st Battalion Field Artillery Regiment 273, so strengthened the fighting power of 38th Division that the British thrust on the divisional left flank was soon halted. Around midday the division received its main mission of the day, which was to launch a counter-attack to repulse the British in the Verlorenhoek sector, who had already overrun the *Albrecht-* and *Wilhelm Stellung*, forced their way into the village of Zonnebeke and were closing in on the *Flandernstellung* [Flanders Position].

"The counter-attack was launched from southeast to northwest, with the aim of retaking Zonnebeke, then advancing on both sides of the Zonnebeke-Langemark road. It hit the British in the right flank and was a complete success. There was especially good fire support from 2nd and 3rd Battalions Field Artillery Regiment 273, which as far as the tactical situation allowed, pushed sub-units forward to the Gravenstafel area, in order to engage the British at the closest range possible. Several tanks were knocked out. The whole of the *Wilhelm Stellung* was back in our hands by the end of the afternoon. Reserve Infantry Regiment 60 was located to the north, Reserve Ersatz Regiment 1 to the south and here was contact with all flanking units.

"The order to retake the *Albrecht Stellung* then arrived. After a short, but heavy, barrage the attack was launched in one single mass, succeeding in retaking the right flank of the *Albrecht Stellung* and consolidating about 100 metres short of the position in shell holes. The counter-attack was conducted by Reserve Ersatz Infantry Regiment 1, Reserve Infantry Regiment 60, two battalions Field Artillery Regiment 273 and 1st Company Reserve Pionier Company 25. The British suffered very significant casualties as a result of our counter-attack. The British had pushed forward a great many small detachments, which were all dealt with. They held back our advance to some extent, but their main effect was to increase the number of British dead and captured." [55]

Although not individually mentioned by Group Ypres, around 9.00 am, Infantry Regiment 41, as part of the 221st Infantry Division, also received orders to move forward to occupy part of the *Wilhelm Stellung*, between Iron Cross and the Ypres – Roeslaere railway [i.e. a line north-south about 700 metres west of Dochy Farm]. The 1st Battalion came under the orders of Infantry Regiment 95 for this reinforcement mission, but as it advanced the orders changed. It was now to attempt to advance beyond this position and retake part of the *Albrecht Stellung*, where it crossed the Hanebeek more or less due north of Frezenberg.[56] Advancing through constant heavy artillery fire, then against a hail of small arms fire, the objective was reached at the cost of extremely heavy casualties, but the counter-attack was only a partial success. The remnants of two companies held on, though isolated, throughout the night 31 July/1 August. An attempted relief operation by Infantry Regiment 58 on 1 August failed, despite efforts continuing throughout the day and, having survived a further twenty four hours of continual losses the few men left were forced to withdraw to the *Wilhelm Stellung* during the night 2/3 August.

Writing later, an eyewitness from 1st Company Infantry Regiment 41 described the extraordinary bravery of his company commander during this attack.

"Reserve Leutnant Mann set a rare example of cold blooded courage. The battalion had deployed in rear of the *Wilhelm Stellung* ready to carry out a counter-attack. The 1st Company was set to take the lead, when suddenly the enemy brought down an extremely heavy barrage forward of the *Wilhelm Stellung*. Passing it was out of the question, but an hour later it was possible to begin moving. At that Mann, with total aplomb and disregarding the heavy hail of fire, moved along the front giving out his orders for the advance. Together with his two runners, he then hurried to his position at the head of the company. His example gave everyone courage. Just as if they were on exercise, the individual waves stormed forward one behind the other, crossing the *Wilhelm Stellung*, and heading across the low ground towards the *Albrecht Stellung*.

"Without pausing the company moved across the crater field and up the slope towards the *Albrecht Stellung*, oblivious to the enemy rifle and machine gun fire. Suddenly the company came under very heavy fire from the right from a machine gun located just west of Schwaben House. It would have been madness to attempt to cross the road which was being swept by fire. Mann ordered the company to take cover then, despite the torrent of fire, rushed over to the threatened flank to judge the situation for himself. Standing bolt upright, ignoring the fire, he searched the ground with a telescope. It was almost a miracle that he was not hit, but seconds later, where the machine gun had failed, an enemy sniper succeeded. A well aimed shot hit him in the forehead just above his right eye and threw him to the ground. There was a short groan and 1st Company had lost its commander.[57] Just as his two predecessors had done on the Somme and at Arras, Leutnant Mann met a hero's death at the head of his company." [58]

Reserve Infantry Regiment 229, as part of 50th Reserve Division, was called early on 31 July to counter-attack along the line Poelkapelle – Langemark – Pilkem. Despite heavy casualties, the enemy was ejected from Langemark around 1.30 pm and the regiment went firm along the line of the Langemark – Zonnebeke road. Fighting continued long into the night and, such were the penetrations achieved during this day of close-quarter fighting, that many units and sub-units found themselves fighting battle completely isolated or cut off. On a day when much courage was on display, one of the platoon commanders of 5th Company – Vizefeldwebel Ratay, was singled out for mention in the Group Ypres despatches for the day. His citation reads: 'This platoon (Ratay) held on to its new position under its commander, even though all contact to the right and left was lost. The position, which had been taken by counter-attack, was successfully defended against numerous assaults by an enemy vastly superior in strength. Ratay [who had been wounded] did not seek treatment for his wounds until all the attacks had been beaten off and then he resumed command of his platoon.'[59] This incident was only one of many on that day for the Reserve Infantry Regiments 229, 230 and 231 of 50th Reserve Division, whose exploits were also covered in some detail in the official reports that evening.

"50th Reserve Division: (3) 10th, 11th and 12th Companies, Reserve Infantry Regiment 229 succeeded in reducing a British pocket of resistance during the course of an attack on the Steenbeek. This strongpoint was based on a concrete blockhouse and was strongly equipped with machine guns. Once the assault battery of the regiment (6th Battery Reserve Field Artillery Regiment 50) had gone into action from a position immediately southwest of Langemark and had brought the strongpoint under sharp fire, the above mentioned companies captured it by means of a daring attack with bayonet and hand grenades. Cavalry advancing from the direction of Pilkem was completely wiped out by 4th and 9th Companies Reserve Infantry Regiment 229.

"About sixty British soldiers armed with Lewis guns had established themselves in the concrete blockhouses of the position of 1st Field Howitzer Battery of Field Artillery Regiment 81. Despite strong resistance 7th Company Reserve Infantry Regiment 230 surrounded the battery and captured the British. During the same operation, a company under Leutnant Lüders advanced from the *Albrecht Stellung* to the earthwork 800 metres northeast of Hill 33, capturing two battleworthy tanks in the process. Later, however, the company had to be ordered to return to the current position.

"Reserve Infantry Regiment 231: A vigorous counter-attack repulsed the enemy which had already penetrated in the *Wilhelm Stellung* to the east of Kerselaar. The regiment then kept the pressure on the enemy, throwing back across the Steenbeek those who had been checked by the arrival of fresh forces near St Juliaan and pursuing them to the *Albrecht Stellung*. The remainder of the enemy either fled or were mown down. Seventy prisoners and ten machine guns remained in our hands here. Thanks to the availability of a telephone team, which followed up right behind the attacking forces, it was possible to report the success of the attack immediately afterwards. This brilliant success owed as much to the close cooperation of Reserve Field Artillery Regiment 50 as to the aggressive nature of the thrust itself. Following up closely behind the assaulting infantry, the assault batteries, for example, 4th Battery Reserve Field Artillery

Regiment 50, opened fire at 600 metre at the enemy infantry and also succeeded in knocking out an enemy tank with a few rounds." [60]

With the coming of darkness the artillery fire slackened and the fighting died away as both sides reflected on the course of the events of the day. It is instructive to compare the summaries of the battle prepared at the corps and army level and to read both in combination with the diary assessment of Crown Prince Rupprecht.

Group Ypres (HQ III Bavarian Army Corps) Situation Report dated 1 August 1917 [61]

"At 6.00 am on 31 July 1917 after a massive artillery bombardment which lasted for days and preceded by one hour of drum fire of extreme intensity, the long-anticipated enemy infantry attack was launched. Thrusting forward swiftly and in overwhelming strength, supported by numerous tanks, the enemy succeeded in overrunning our weakly held outpost line. Even in the *Albrecht Stellung* the combined efforts of the numerically inferior front line and reserve battalions could not halt the powerful thrust. As a result, by midday the enemy had reached the line Langemark – St Juliaan – *Artillerie Gehöft* – *Almenhof* – Zonnebeke – Villa Hanebeek.

"At that moment the powerfully directed counter-strokes of the assault regiments and the two *Eingreif* divisions (50 Reserve Division and 221 Infantry Division), which had been moved up close behind the front line, began. During the course of bitter fighting in the early afternoon further enemy advances were prevented and, with outstanding support from the tough resistance put up by some of our individual advanced posts, it was possible to throw the enemy back across the Steenbeek and out of St Juliaan, the *Artillerie Gehöft*, the *Almenhof* and Zonnebeke.

"Our front line trace currently runs from the right hand Group boundary along the Steenbeek as far as the *Albrecht Stellung*, bends either side of the Ypres-Roeselare railway to the east of the *Albrecht Stellung*, follows the line of the *Pionierweg* [Sapper Way] to meet it once more in the southern Bellewaarde sector and then runs to the left hand Group boundary.

"The first great enemy attack has failed. In addition to extraordinarily heavy losses, it has delivered to us large numbers of prisoners and machine guns. Several knocked out tanks are stranded in front of our lines … "

Daily Report Headquarters Fourth Army 31 July 1917 [62]

"The enemy attempt at a breakthrough … can, according to reports from the land and air formations, be regarded as having failed. It seems that the assault was launched in depth with two and, in some places, three divisions following one another in waves. As a result of use of numerous tanks and large quantities of infantry accompanied by cavalry, we were temporarily pushed back from a line between Bikschote and Merkem, lost control of Langemark, were pushed back over the Langemark-Zonnebeke road and had to fight for Zonnebeke.

"Further to the south as far as the Lys, the break in was from one to two kilometres in depth, but our infantry, fighting heroically and supported superbly by our artillery and airmen, succeeded in the course of very bloody close quarter fighting in breaking the violence of the enemy attack. Counter-attacks succeeded in recapturing a considerable part of the lost territory.

"Army Headquarters expects there to be a resumption of the offensive, but faces the forthcoming violent battles with determined confidence ... "

Crown Prince Rupprecht of Bavaria: Diary Entry 31 July 1917 [63]

"This morning the attack, supported by a great many tanks, opened on a front of eighteen kilometres between Steenstraat and the Lys on the Flanders front. I find that I can face this offensive in a calm frame of mind, because never before have we had deployed along a front under attack such strong reserve forces, which have been so well trained in their role.

"By the evening it became clear that the enemy break in to the front of the line we hold: *viz*. Westhoek – east of Bikschote – Steenbeek valley – St Juliaan – west of Zonnebeke – Polygon Wood – West edge of Herenthaage Wood – Ypres – Comines canal, has been halted. In view of the massive enemy forces, in conjunction with the fact that experience shows that the initial blow is always the most dangerous, we can take particular comfort from the fact that the battle reserves of Group Wijtschate were barely utilised."

It is clear that in claiming outright that the Allied operations had been a failure, both headquarters were guilty of hyperbole. The defence had indeed acquitted itself well, but in places, as has been seen, Allied advances of up to three kilometres had been achieved. Not only that, but the way in which heavy artillery fire had severely cut up the well-practised regiments of 111th Infantry Division before they could close with their objectives, was an unpleasant foretaste of what was to come elsewhere later in the battle when artillery planning had gained in sophistication and complexity. In addition, two German defensive lines had been overrun and a third threatened before counter-attacks had partially restored the situation.

However it is correct to say that in the much more important Geluveld Plateau sector, the outcome of the fighting was nowhere near as promising for the Allies. Flexible defence had meant that the initial German positions had been pushed back and it is certainly true that they had lost some important observation posts along the Bellewaarde Ridge, but this was a poor return overall for Allied casualties which approached thirty thousand men that day. The power of the German counter-attacks, carefully planned and prepared and driven home with immense determination, had been underestimated by British planners and commanders. Furthermore, the fact that progress had been so limited in this sector rendered the Allied advance further north vulnerable to direct fire in enfilade and also to observed artillery fire in the coming days.

Overall, the forward placement of the *Eingreif* division, their decisive use and bold, courageous, leadership had meant that, thanks to earlier planning and rehearsal, they had been able, albeit at a high cost in casualties, to have a consider-able influence on the fighting. It ought, therefore, to have been clear to the Allied commanders that despite the immense preliminary expenditure of ammunition there were going to be no easy breakthroughs and that further progress across the Geluveld Plateau, if it was to come about, would only be achieved by means of labo-rious movement forward of the artillery, with the offensive renewed as and when further preparatory bombardments had been fired.

As the day drew to a close, the high command on both sides, nevertheless, took a sanguine view of events. The Allies felt that they had delivered the first of a series of crushing blows which would lead inevitably to German collapse; the Germans that they had held successfully the worst that the Allies were likely to be able throw at them and that they had spare capacity to deal with whatever the future might hold. The battles to come would reveal which of the viewpoints was closest to the truth.

Notes

1. Schatz: History Reserve Infantry Regiment 239 p 123.
2. Lennartz: History Reserve Infantry Regiment 240 p 292
3. *ibid.* p 293
4. von Kuhl: *Der Weltkrieg 1914-1918 Band II* pp 121-122
5. Hartmann: History Infantry Regiment 94 p 224
6. Forstner: History Reserve Infantry Regiment 15 p 101
7. This is not quite correct. According to Pflugbeil in the history of Infantry Regiment 181 (p 81), the relief did not even begin until the following night and took until 4/5 August 1917 to complete.
8. Pflugbeil: History Infantry Regiment 181 p 79
9. Tiessen: History Reserve Infantry Regiment 213 pp 522-523
10. Reymann: History: Infantry Regiment 62 p 156
11. Großmann: History Bavarian Reserve Infantry Regiment 17 p 82
12. Lennartz: *op.cit.* pp 293-294
13. *ibid.* pp 291-292
14. References to drunkenness amongst Allied troops are as frequent in the German litera-ture as they are improbable.

15. Lennartz: *op. cit.* pp 295-296
16. This is, of course, a reference to *French* tanks.
17. Kriegsarchiv München GenKdo III AK Bd. 83
18. Mülmann: History Lehr-Infantry Regiment pp 406-407
19. *ibid.* pp 410-411
20. Schulenburg-Wolfsburg: History Fusilier Guard Regiment p 181
21. Hummel was one of the two sub-sectors forward of Passchendaele at that time: *Hummel and Wieltje*. Hummel was the more northerly sub-sector.
22. History: Field Artillery Regiment 6 pp 202 – 204.
23. The 235th Infantry Division, which was formed on 16 January 1917, comprised Infantry Regiments 454, 455 and 456. Unfortunately, in common with many of the wartime regiments with high numbers, none of these formations produced a history post-war, so it is impossible to follow events in this sector from a German perspective in any great detail; their original records having been destroyed in 1945.
24. Kriegsarchiv München GenKdo III AK Bd. 83
25. Bölsche: History Infantry Regiment 96 pp 410-413
26. Gefreiter Oskar Fischer is buried in the German cemetery at Langemark Block G Grave 12502.
27. Wurmb: History Bavarian Reserve Infantry Regiment 8 p 113
28. Bezzel: History Reserve Infantry Regiment 6 pp 161-162
29. A vigorous counter-attack that same evening, led by Reserve Leutnant Böck of 9th Company Reserve Infantry Regiment 6, recaptured this point, but a further withdrawal by Reserve Infantry Regiment 82 to the north meant that the regained ground had to be abandoned once more.
30. Jürgensen: History Füsilier Regiment 86 p 238
31. Sydow: History Infantry Regiment 76 p 142
32. Voigt: History Füsilier Regiment 73 p 558
33. Mitkämpfer: History Infantry Regiment 164 pp 397
34. *ibid.* pp 396-397
35. Wohlenberg: History Reserve Infantry Regiment 77 p 291
36. All but three of these men are buried together in Graves 3061-3073 at the German cemetery in Hooglede. They are: Offizierstellvertreter Wilhelm Wilke, Unteroffizier Franz Hahn, Unteroffizier Willi Schwabe, Gefreiter Hermann Hanekamp, Paul Gehring, Johannes Kellner, Ludwig Schlüter and Peter Weyer. Rohde, Siemering and Wodk have no known grave.
37. Throughout the battle the Germans never managed fully to reconcile the requirement to move their *Eingreif* units and formations forward swiftly, with the need for troops to be properly briefed before they were launched into action. In their concentration areas, they generally had adequate means of communications, but once they began to move forward this was lost. Lightweight combat net radio would of course have been the answer, but the few wireless sets available at the time were simply too heavy, bulky and delicate to be moved and used in that manner. Weeks later, directives from the Army High Command were still attempting to address this issue.
38. Puttkamer: History Reserve Infantry Regiment 46 p 146
39. Zunehmer: History Infantry Regiment 46 p 288
40. Kriegsarchiv München GenKdo III AK Bd. 83

41. Benary: History Field Artillery Regiment 20 pp 300-302
42. Fritz Dartsch, whose rank is given officially as Kanonier, is buried at the German cemetery at Bousbecque Block 3 Grave 858
43. Dellmensingen: *Das Bayernbuch vom Weltkrieg Bd II* p 435-436
44. Fahrer Ulrich Hirth is buried in the German cemetery at Menen Block L Grave 2750.
45. Wohlenberg: History Reserve Infantry Regiment 77 p 302-303
46. Reserve Leutnant Edmund Kuhlmann is buried in the German cemetery at Hooglede Grave 3103.
47. Forstner: *op. cit.* p 105
48. *ibid.* p 105
49. *ibid.* pp 107-110
50. *ibid.* p 112
51. *ibid.* p 113
52. *ibid.* p 116
53. *ibid.* pp 117-118
54. *ibid.* p 122
55. Kriegsarchiv München GenKdo III AK Bd. 83
56. The objective was a large concrete blockhouse very near to the present day Bridge House CWGC cemetery.
57. Leutnant Hebert Mann is buried in the German cemetery at Menen Block K Grave 808.
58. Bülowius: History Infantry Regiment 41 pp 200-201
59. Wiedersich: History Reserve Infantry Regiment 229 p 92
60. Kriegsarchiv München GenKdo III AK Bd. 83
61. Kriegsarchiv München GenKdo III AK Bd. 83
62. Forstner: *op.cit.* pp 123-124
63. Kronprinz Rupprecht: *'Mein Kriegstagebuch' Band II* p 232

CHAPTER THREE

August 1917

In the immediate aftermath of the battles on 31 July 1917, Group Ypres lost no time in providing Fourth Army with a short appreciation of the situation and an overview of the fighting strength of its divisions.

Group Ypres Appreciation dated 2 August 1917 [1]

"Situation The long anticipated major offensive began on 31 July 1917. According to captured orders, the assault, or as the British refer to it, 'The Ypres Operation' was to have begun earlier. It has not proved possible to establish the reasons for the postponement. According to reports of prisoner interrogations and the content of captured orders, the attack in the sector of Group Ypres was carried out by six divisions (38th, 51st, 39th, 55th, 15th and 8th). The objective for the assault of 31 July 1917 appears to have been the *Wilhelm Stellung.*[2] In behind the wave which attacked on 31 July there are assessed to be a further six divisions (29th, 11th, 36th, 16th, 25th and one more, which is, as yet, unidentified).

"On 1 August the enemy renewed their attacks, but without success. Because only troops which had previously been deployed on 31 July were used, it appears to have been an attack designed simply to complete the missions allocated for the previous day and not a new major push. This is not expected until the second wave [of assaulting divisions] has been deployed. Up until that point further localised actions, such as those which occurred on 1 August, are to be expected. The enemy appears to be placing particular stress on [advances] towards Langemark and along the line of the Ypres-Roeselare railway.

"Fighting Strengths

3rd Guards Division. Casualties, approximately 3,000. The division needs to be relieved and given two to three weeks rest.

50th Reserve Division. Casualties, approximately 1,500. The division needs to be relieved in a few days time and then requires two to three weeks rest.

221st Infantry Division. Casualties, approximately 2,150. The division needs to be relieved in a few days time and then requires two to three weeks rest.

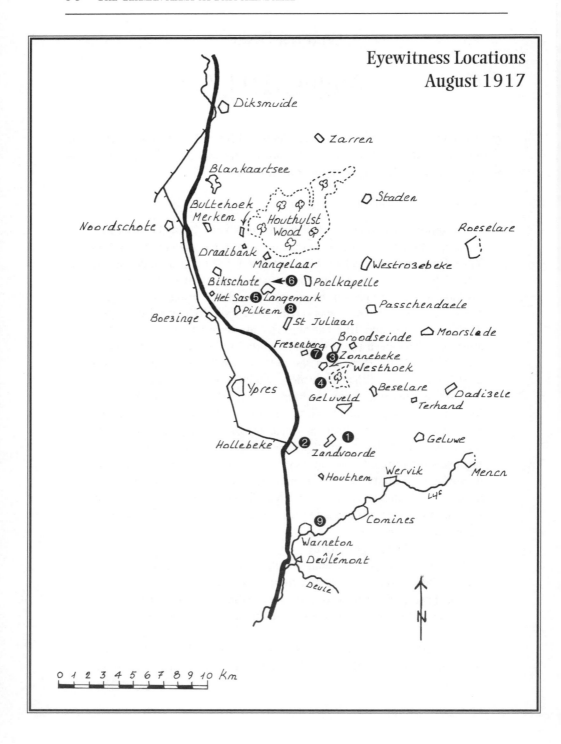

Eyewitness Locations
August 1917

Diksmuide

Zarren

Blankaartsee

Staden

Bultehoek
Merkem

Houthulst
Wood

Noordschote

Roeselare

Draaibank
Mangelaar

Westrozebeke

Bikschote ◄─ ⑥ Poelkapelle

Het Sas ⑤ Langemark

Pilkem ⑧

Passchendaele

Boezinge

St Juliaan

Broodseinde ⏢ Moorslede

Fresenberg ⑦ ③ Zonnebeke

Westhoek

Ypres

④

Geluveld

Beselare ⏢ Dadizele

Terhand

⑥ Geluwe

Hollebeke ⑫ ②

Zandvoorde

Houthem   Wervik   Menen

Lys

⑨ Comines

Warneton

Deûlémont

Deule

N

0 1 2 3 4 5 6 7 8 9 10 Km

38th Infantry Division. Casualties, approximately 4,000. The division needs to be relieved and given two to three weeks rest.

It is not possible at present to state if the casualty figures are completely correct.

79th Reserve Division and 3rd Reserve Division are both fully battle-worthy.

"State of Health: The poor weather has had an effect on the strength of the troops, especially those who have been stationed in the front line or have also had problems with rationing. However, because the counter-attack divisions have had to stand-to repeatedly in the open without shelter, they too have complained of nausea and diarrhoea."

Relieved and out of the line at Koelenberg, two kilometres west of Geluwe, one of the company commanders of Infantry Regiment 62, whose company had suffered terribly from the lacerating effect of concentrated British artillery fire, also attempted on 5 August to draw together the raw impressions of the past few days in a letter to his parents.

Reserve Leutnant Josef Boehm Commander 10th Company Infantry Regiment 62 [3] **1**

"Dear Parents, Once more with God's help I have safely negotiated a series of very hard days. All the dreadful experiences which I witnessed during the battles of the invasion, at Notre Dame de Lorette, the Somme and the Ancre have recurred in even more appalling form during the past few days of the Battle of Flanders. I shall now attempt to paint the picture for you and provide you with an impression of the recent past. It will have to remain an attempt, because nobody who has not personally experienced the terrifying reality of this hell can ever have any true conception about the meaning of the word 'war' ... At 2.00 am on 31 July I was ordered to advance to the artillery positions near Zandvoorde. That was all. There were no guides available, so in streaming rain and a pitch black night we set off across the trackless terrain under enemy artillery fire, heading for a place which I knew only by name ...

"We arrived towards 3.30 am and took cover in large shell holes, which were seventy five per cent full of water and the rest was clinging wet clay. There we remained, in pouring rain and under constant fire from super-heavy artillery, until 5.00 pm that day. At 5.00 pm I was ordered to advance the company in broad daylight 1,000 metres forward to where the positions of Infantry Regiment 71 had been wiped off the face of the earth by the enemy. Nobody could give me any hint what route to follow, or exactly where the British were located. I spread the company out wide and, luckily, we moved forward 1,500 metres without suffering casualties. I left the company in cover on the western edge of the so-called *Westfalenwald* [Westphalian Wood] and patrolled forward with a few men to locate the actual front line.

"About one hundred metres further on I came to the remains of an old farmhouse, the *Westfalenhaus* [Westphalian House] where I was waved at by an agitated group of men. This was obviously where our line was to be found. Suddenly a dreadful artillery concentration hammered down on the front edge of the wood where both mine and 12th Company were waiting. The British had obviously seen us move into the wood and were now engaging us. It was awful! My company was being shot to pieces in front of my eyes and there was not a thing which I could do to help. The firing went on for one and a half hours. There was then a short pause and a further thirty minute bombardment from 9.15 pm. The fire died away then and we could rally the survivors. The company had suffered nine killed, thirty five wounded and fifteen missing.

"I led the remainder forward; there were about thirty of them ... and moved up eighty metres beyond the house to the so-called front line, which was simply a line of craters full of water and it was still raining heavily. At daybreak, I pulled most of the men back to *Westfalenhaus* so that they could eat and drink and spend a few hours under a roof. There were only a few sentries forward. That night we re-occupied the craters. I simply cannot find words to describe our appearance or the conditions. Suffice it to say that two men of 11th Company drowned that night in the craters, because they could not free themselves from the clinging mud.

"*Westfalenhaus* had been under fire almost constantly, so the company had further soldiers killed and wounded. I gave up all hope of ever escaping this hell. In the end I was down to twenty two men. At 5.00 am on 3 August, as it became light and I was surveying the ground to the front in the direction of Klein-Zillebeke, I noticed dense columns of British soldiers advancing about 600 metres away over a hill. A gefreiter and I immediately brought a machine gun into action and opened fire. We were the only ones left who knew how to do this. Our firing was spot on target. The columns dispersed and pulled back over the hill. The attack was beaten off![4] I had fired off two belts of ammunition. In the meantime artillery fire which I had demanded by flare signal came down and dealt with the remainder.

"The order for our relief arrived that evening and as night faded into dawn on 4 August, I made my way back, harried by British artillery fire, but without any more casualties. We were supposed to be having three days' rest and are occupying positions near to our batteries, but we were stood-to again this morning, so there has not been much rest and tomorrow we are to move forward again. The men have stuck to it remarkably well. Just think: four days under the heaviest artillery fire in constant pouring rain, soaked to the skin, with insufficient food and drink, in shell craters in the mud! All I can think about are the countless unburied corpses along the approach routes and in the forward area. Oh the pity of it! Today I had the great pleasure of presenting three of my bravest Musketiers with Iron Crosses and then I wrote to the next of kin of all my fallen. I shall have to close now. There is drum fire along the front and we have been stood-to once more. It must mean an attack. Heartiest greetings to you both from your faithful son, Josef."

It is no surprise that there was early concern at high level about the demands the fighting in Flanders was going to place on the troops but equally, as this extract from the history of Infantry Regiment 418 shows, lessons had been learned and applied from the Battles of the Somme the previous year and Arras in April and May. As a result, troops arriving in Flanders were well briefed and trained in their new roles and confident that they had the measure of the Allied attackers:

"Our division [183rd Infantry Division], together with 3rd Reserve Division, formed the *Stoßdivisionen* [assault divisions, i.e. the *Eingreif* divisions] of *Gruppe Ypern* [Group Ypres]. It was located behind the right flank and 3rd Reserve behind the left flank of the Group. In accordance with the army order, our division was deployed in assembly areas in and to the south of Westrozebeke, which enabled it to conduct a frontal counter-stroke in a westerly direction, or a flanking one towards the southwest. So behind the actual defensive front there stood another: that of the *Stoßdivisionen*. What was their purpose?

"In the early days of positional warfare there had been an insistence on all-too-rigid holding of the very front line. The bulk of the defensive forces were deployed forward in places which were covered by the enemy artillery and were crammed into far too shallow an area. This caused a great many casualties and meant that the troops in rear were linked to deployment sectors which were much too limited. Now the ground holding divisions were deployed in greater depth and the main fighting strength of the infantry was held sufficiently far back to thwart the enemy's plans. The front line was reduced to a line of weakly held outposts, but the regiments of these divisions were still largely responsible for the prevention of break-throughs and expected to use their depth units to carry out counter-strokes against an enemy which had broken in.

"Major battles demanded an all-embracing form of protection of the front: the *Stoßdivisionen*. These were located further to the rear, generally outside the range of enemy artillery fire. As the state of readiness increased, they were moved forward into previously selected assembly areas. If it was necessary for them to intervene in the battle then, thanks to their ability to manoeuvre in any direction, they could be thrown into battle in the direction where they could have the greatest influence, or where their chances of a successful advance were greatest. Out of rigid defence a type of mobile warfare within the forward battle zone had developed.

"This reorganisation of the defence was by no means restricted to the infantry of the *Stoßdivisionen*. In future only their medium and heavy artillery would participate in the hellish drum fire concerts; the light field artillery was grouped with the infantry regiments into artillery assault groups. The assault batteries had to accompany the infantry assault in harness, ready to close up on the enemy and bring them under observed or even direct fire over open sights. Each of the three regiments of our division received a battalion of Field Artillery Regiment 183, each of two assault batteries. The 3rd Battalion was allocated to us, as was a platoon of the 16th Reserve Engineers.

"The lessons derived from the defensive battle, the introduction of new weapons and equipment and training in new operational techniques caused us to reorganise the rifle companies and designate and to train up specialist teams. Each of the three platoons was organised as follows: 1. An infantry rifle section; 2. An assault troop; 3. A grenade launcher troop; 4. A light machine gun section; 5. An infantry rifle section. Hand grenades grew in importance even more, as did coloured signal flares, which were by far the quickest means of passing messages, demanding artillery fire etc." [5]

Two days later Group Wijtschate followed the Group Ypres appreciation with an assessment which included, 'The enemy can only press their intended thrust to the northeast if they create sufficient room on the flank by forcing back the 52nd Reserve Division. This leads to the expectation that the push, which is likely to be launched with massive violence, will be directed against 52nd Reserve Division and 12th Infantry Division.'[6] All the regiments of 52nd Reserve Division reorganised to meet the expected attack, adopting a deeply echeloned formation with one regiment forward and the other two stepped back in support and reserve. These tactics were repeated elsewhere up and down the line and the artillery battle continued unabated, taking a steady toll of casualties amongst the forward ground-holding divisions and the German artillery units, as did a series of only moderately successful counter-strokes launched by the German army – mainly against Hollebeke.

The timing of the counter-attack launched on 5 August provides an interesting example of how battlefield intelligence could be exploited quickly if an opportunity appeared to present itself. The regiments of 12th and 207th Infantry Divisions, which had replaced the mauled units of 22nd Reserve Division after the heavy fighting on 31 July between Zandvoorde and Hollebeke, had been establishing a routine of relief in the line and carrying out minor operations, when they suddenly received the intelligence that a message recovered from an intercepted British carrier pigeon[7] and prisoner interrogation[8] had revealed that the British 41st Division had suffered such severe casualties that it had to be relieved without delay. The German army assumed that that meant that the relief would be carried out during the night of 4/5 August and they planned a counter-attack to improve their poorly placed positions. In fact the intelligence was only partially correct,[9] but it definitely provided a spur to action and an incentive to the assaulting troops.

The operation, planned under the code name *Sommernacht* [Summer Night], was scheduled for 5.20 am 5 August. Reserve Infantry Regiment 213 ran into difficulties even during the march forward, when a shell exploded amidst the advancing troops:

Leutnant Kath 6th Company Reserve Infantry Regiment 213 [10] **2**

> "We all landed in a heap in the saturated soft clay. I could hear groaning. Everybody who was able got to his feet and felt around. Someone was lying off to one side: It was Leutnant [Kurt] Boldt, who had been seriously wounded, as had been Keßenich of 6th Company. Everybody else seemed to be more or less in one piece. With immense difficulty, we carried Boldt through the narrow trench to a pillbox. My God, what a sight he was, with his face deathly pale and multiple wounds to his limbs. He was utterly still, almost as though he was going to fall asleep. A medical orderly chopped a bench in two with a hatchet to make splints for his limbs. I trickled the last drops of my cognac through the poor chap's bloodless lips. He fell asleep shortly afterwards. The incident hit us all like a nightmare." [11]

Following a short preliminary bombardment, Infantry Regiment 62 attacked with three companies of its 1st Battalion and captured its objectives on the ridge 1,000 metres north east of Hollebeke in less than fifteen minutes. The British troops, completely surprised, fell back a further eighty metres and eleven prisoners, two machine guns and a large quantity of materiel were secured. Even better for the attackers, the new positions were a considerable improvement over the previous ones. The shell holes were drier, the British troops could no longer overlook the area behind the front line and, as a result, casualties due to artillery fire were reduced during the coming days. Sergeant Gach of 1st Company Infantry Regiment 62 was promoted immediately in the field to Vizefeldwebel after this operation in recognition of his outstanding gallantry. Operating just to the south were elements of Reserve Infantry Regiment 209 and Reserve Infantry Regiment 213 of 207th Infantry Division. Here the tactics were for Reserve Infantry Regiment 213 to launch its own assault troops forward, followed up by further infantry reinforcements, but the village of Hollebeke itself, which was on the front of Reserve Infantry Regiment 209, was to be attacked by the Divisional Assault Company.

Leutnant Kath reported later: 'Our brave lads were a picture of calm. As though they were on exercise they moved forward into No Man's Land ... The Flanders fog was so thick that it provided us with the advantage that nobody could see a thing between 5.00 am and 6.00 am; the disadvantage was the fact that we could not make out where the worst of the swamps were as we tried to advance.'[12] Nevertheless the men of Reserve Infantry Regiment 213 did achieve their objectives, albeit at the cost of heavy casualties. Although the assault on Hollebeke was a divisional responsibility, the commander of the Assault Company happened to be an officer of Reserve Infantry Regiment 213, who wrote a detailed report subsequently.

Reserve Leutnant Sommerfeld,
Commander Assault Company 207th Infantry Division [13] **2**

"The assault company was split into three elements: left flank (Assault Platoon, Reserve Infantry Regiment 98), centre (Assault Platoon, Reserve Infantry Regiment 209) and right flank (Assault Platoon, Reserve Infantry Regiment 213). The flanks had the task of outflanking the village to the left and right, whilst the centre was to assault the village five minutes later. The right and left hand platoons were further subdivided into two detachments, one of which in each case was to thrust forward 150 metres west of the village, then swing in to the left and right towards the centre to clear the ground of any enemy. The other halves of the platoons were to launch converging attacks half left and half right, aimed at clearing the enemy out of concrete bunkers and ruined houses. The centre platoon (Reserve Infantry Regiment 209) was to clear straight through the village and on to the high ground to the west to link up with the other two platoons.

"Each of the three platoons of the assault company was allocated three sections of infantry from Reserve Infantry Regiment 209 [i.e. about twenty to twenty five men per platoon] as ammunition carriers. It was their job to follow up the assault company and to assist in the defence of the newly-captured positions until the following night. At about 4.50 am the individual platoons arrived on their separate start lines. The start line for the Reserve Infantry Regiment 98 platoon was on the left flank of Reserve Infantry Regiment 209. That of the Reserve Infantry Regiment 209 platoon was about 150 metres east of the fork in the road Hollebeke – Lock 5/ Hollebeke – Wilhelmshof and that of Reserve Infantry Regiment 213 was at Lock 6.

"Between 5.00 am and 5.20 am all the platoons worked their way forward under cover of the fog to their assault positions and launched their attacks at the time ordered. Just short of the enemy positions the platoons came under intense machine gun fire, but aggressive hand grenades tactics silenced all the guns in a very short time. Almost simultaneously the enemy position was in our hands. However most of the enemy troops were located in groups of up to thirty in the concrete blockhouses and they put up fierce, obstinate resistance. Once all these points had been knocked out and prisoners and captured materiel had been moved into a secure location, the company advanced forward of the village onto the heights as ordered. By 5.45 am, with all three platoons present, three flares were fired in succession to indicate that the objective had been seized as directed.

"Because mopping up the nests of resistance had used up so much ammunition, there were hardly any hand grenades left. This was exacerbated by the fact that the ammunition carriers of Reserve Infantry Regiment 209, who were already worn down before the attack even began, had not been able to follow up as swiftly as intended and, on the right flank, had not been able to get forward at all. By 8.00 am numerous enemy patrols were sighted and brought under fire. In the meantime the enemy artillery brought down heavy fire on our old A Line [the positions of the battalion deployed right forward]. Because of the failure of the three sections of 9th Company Reserve Infantry Regiment 209, it was impossible to establish link ups with the centre and the canal, especially because forward of the Reserve Infantry Regiment 213 sector enemy machine guns were in action. It was necessary to pull back about 150 metres behind the line ordered.

"Because it was impossible to hold a 1,200 metre frontage just with the assault company and the few members of Reserve Infantry Regiment 209 who made it forward, especially in view of the lack of ammunition, the commander had no alternative in the face of massed enemy thrusts, which were launched at about 8.45 am, but to order a withdrawal to the old A Line. Later the company was ordered to withdraw completely by an order from higher headquarters. Through its dash in the attack the company had been able to capture one German heavy machine gun, two British heavy machine guns, four Lewis guns, four officers and approximately fifty men. Enemy casualties were believed to amount to about 300. Company casualties were one officer (Reserve Leutnant Schanz) wounded, one vizefeldwebel, two unteroffiziers and six junior ranks killed. Four unteroffiziers and twelve junior ranks were wounded and three were missing. A good many of the friendly casualties were sustained during attempts to rescue wounded comrades. The fog was initially favourable to the operation, but later became so thick that it made orientation in the area, which was extremely difficult anyway, even worse."

The net result of the fighting on 5 August was that the front line presented a somewhat ragged picture. A gap had developed 400 metres wide between Reserve Infantry Regiment 209 and Reserve Infantry Regiment 213,[14] which the British sought to exploit. There then followed several days of inconclusive attack and counter-attack in this area, until this area too was caught up in the major day of battle on 10 August. Although locally significant, the fighting around Hollebeke was not of major importance. The army group commander had other concerns that day, which he confided to his diary.

Crown Prince Rupprecht of Bavaria – Diary Entry 5th August [15]

"The rainfall of the past few days was so heavy that not only is the crater field occupied by Fourth Army full of water, so are the trenches in places. Most of the soldiers are taking cover behind their flooded trenches or in shell holes. In the latter case, they are attempting to protect themselves from the wet conditions by huddling under planks or sheets of corrugated iron, daubed with mud. These conditions go a long way to explaining the speed with which the troops are being exhausted and having to be replaced. On average, each has suffered casualties of 1,500 to 2,000. During the Battle of the Somme, on the other hand, tours of duty usually lasted fourteen days, with, in general, about 4,000 casualties. Whilst the troops, as a result of those long deployments, suffered a great loss of sleep and required a very long period of rest and recuperation, the troops are generally recovering more quickly now. It is proving very difficult to transport food, rations and trench stores forward because of the amount of gas which the enemy is using. The carrying parties are generally not in a position to mask up sufficiently quickly. This explains the high number of gas casualties; 1,200 in the 6th Bavarian Reserve Division alone.

A great deal of low-level intelligence continued to be obtained by careless use of the telephone by the British army. The Germans, because of their knowledge of the capabilities of their intercept equipment, made use very early in the war of low-level code, but in August there was a further effort to provide communication security by means of veiled speech. The regimental history of Infantry Regiment 140 describes how it worked in practice.

"In order to reduce the risk of intelligence being gained from telephone interception a low grade field code system was introduced. It was designed to make tactical conversations sound like double Dutch. These lists of words included: snake = casualty, monkey = prisoner, walrus = Russian, carp – Frenchman, herring = black soldier, dried cod = British soldier, grey = wounded and black = died or dead. This system produced sentences such as: 'We had some snakes, but brought in several monkeys, including a walrus, a carp, a herring and a dried cod. One of the monkeys was grey, but turned black on the way." [16]

The method was probably proof against casual eavesdropping, but would not have had any value in the face of attack by properly constituted intercept teams.

By this stage of the month, the conditions were taking their toll on the efficiency not only of the infantry, but of the artillery also, as this description by a gunner from the 10th Bavarian Infantry Division shows.

Oberleutnant Brügelmann
Commander 2nd Battery Bavarian Field Artillery Regiment 20 [17] **2**

"No sooner had the British launched their first great attacks on 31 July, than a continuous downpour began. This certainly hindered their advance, but it largely flooded the field where our guns were located. The guns themselves were standing in water. It was impossible to dig protective pits, so the guns were completely exposed. There were no concrete blockhouses either, so the only bit of cover was provided by some wooden sheds. These kept out the worst of the weather, but were no use against enemy fire. The previous days of heavy fighting had almost wrecked the sheds, but it was still better to have a basic roof over one's head than to have to lie down on the saturated ground and [inside them] our worn out soldiers soon fell asleep.

"Suddenly there was another concentration of fire, but nobody was bothered by it. All were far too weary to react to a flurry like that. Then, with a crash, the whole shed shook from a great blow. A direct hit! What has happened? Is anybody wounded? – No reply. The shed was searched in case anyone was caught beneath the ruins. Yes, there is someone over there! He is beyond help; he is dead. He cannot be recognised either, because his head has been shot off. Who can it be? It could only be Weininger – poor chap! He was such a courageous, lively lad; one who took a full part in everything and stuck it out manfully. Now he had been caught whilst asleep and helpless – hit and killed! Nothing else could be done in the darkness. It was an unlucky accident and, hardened by plenty of similar events, everyone lay down in the same places as before and went back to sleep. Nothing else happened that night.

"As dawn broke, I went through the shed once again carefully and this time found, stuck to floor near the door like a plaque, half of poor old Weininger's head. He face was in repose, as if asleep. His skin was unmarked, just colourless. It was a shocking sight! The rest of his body was recovered. All the soldiers agreed that he had to be laid to rest immediately; that his mutilated corpse must not, contrary to orders, be transported back to a military cemetery. A grave was dug in a quiet corner of the field and his comrades paid him the last honours. It was a small, but moving ceremony. Then everyone went back to work."

The conditions during the first week of August, coming on top of the heavy fighting of 31 July, meant that the whole of the 10th Bavarian Infantry Division was relieved on 6 August. Lessons had been learned from the Battle of the Somme the previous year, so this time the supporting artillery was withdrawn for rest and reconstitution at the same time as the infantry regiments.

Oberleutnant Brügelmann
Commander 2nd Battery Bavarian Field Artillery Regiment 20 [18] **2**

"The very worst hours of the six week tour, which we had endured under constant fire by day and night, were those which led up to the relief that evening. Every heart was aching to be out of this hell, but duty demanded that we held on. Everyone wanted to get away, but could not. I sent off every man who could be spared, in order to avoid unnecessary casualties. Despite this the battery was still to lose Unteroffizier Bauer, that courageous gun commander, struck down by his gun and seriously wounded after firing ceaselessly for so long. At long last the new battery commander arrived during the afternoon and the officers repaired to one of the wooden sheds to hand over the files and other documentation: nowhere else was dry enough for the task. Suddenly there was a great crash and the shed collapsed like a house of cards. Surely there must have been an absolute bloodbath? But a miracle had occurred. All the officers and gunners climbed out of the ruins and stretched their limbs. They were somewhat shocked, but everyone was in one piece and nobody was missing!

"This miracle only came about because the good old British had to use such poor ammunition. The shell landed almost vertically, pierced the shed roof and floor, missing everyone, before exploding in the soft ground. A spray of filth and splinters of wood were blown out sideways, but no further damage was done. Time passed. It went dark, but the relieving guns had still not arrived. Instead the British fired concentration after concentration: mostly low trajectory shells which smashed violently into the hill behind the battery. What luck that we were not deployed there! Finally there was a pause in the firing and the guns got through. In seconds the whole place was swarming with men and horses. The guns were placed right up hard against the sheds, because the position of 2nd Section was so shot up that, although the guns could be extracted with difficulty, there was no way of locating the new ones there. Once again the British opened up. Shells burst closer and closer, until they were whistling over our heads and landing less than twenty metres away!

"The calmness and bearing of our men was remarkable. Despite the fact that they could have been hit at any moment, they sat on their horses as calmly as if they were on exercise. They wanted nothing more than to get away, but they could not; we had to drag our guns away and they were still two hundred metres distant. Grabbing hold of the leading horse of the first team, I shouted 'Forward, follow me!' and we set off in the darkness. The British began to mix gas with their high explosive. It was completely impossible to mask up at this time. It would have been impossible to see anything. Fortunately, as we learned during the past few days, the British gas was not all that bad. Suddenly a shell landed in our midst! Immediately the horses and gun teams were enveloped in a thick cloud. I grabbed hold of the leading horse and held it back. If they were to rear then head off, the journey would certainly finish in a shell hole and that would have been the end of the relief for that night. It was impossible to see anything in the cloud of gas. I called out and received a reply from the courageous Vizewachtmeister Reinhardt, who had not left us to struggle. Moving cautiously forward in the direction of the shouts I emerged from the cloud of gas and, with my head above it, was able to orientate myself with the aid of some trees ...

"Moving the second team was much harder. It was literally wedged in a shell hole. Enemy shells had landed all around it. Only the shell hole which contained the gun and its crew had been spared. It continued firing until the last minute, but in so doing the limber eyelet sheared. To repair this required the use of perfectly tied knots and none of the young gunners knew how to tie them; there had been no training time during the war for such niceties. Fortunately Gunlayer Dreyer, who had six years service behind him, did know what to do. He tied the knots correctly and they held whilst the six horse team strained with all their might to move the gun. Finally everything was ready to move ... The [relieving] Wachtmeister appeared and we could go. What a relief it was to leave this place where we had spent the hardest six weeks of the campaign! We passed a series of wrecked vehicles and freshly killed horses, but we were in luck. Nothing else happened and we emerged, God be praised, from the Hell of Flanders."

One of the first reinforcement divisions to be ordered north to Flanders after 31 July was 54th Infantry Division. Leading elements were already in the area by 2 August and the division was complete and ready to be deployed forward to the Zonnebeke-Polygon Wood area by 5 August. The divisional sector was 2,500 metres wide and manned initially with Infantry Regiment 84 right forward, Reserve Infantry Regiment 90 left forward and Reserve Infantry Regiment 27 in the *Eingreif* role within the division. The arrival in Flanders made an immediate impression on the entire division.

Offizierstellvertreter Alt, 4th Company Reserve Infantry Regiment 27 [19] **3**

"The performance of the artillery on both sides during this battle was just extraordinary. At night we often stood outside our billets and marvelled at the coloured light show that was being played out forward at the front. At all times we were ready to be called forward to take our place in the hell of the front …

"Finally we were stood to during the morning of 8 or 9 August and moved forward. Bombs were being dropped from aircraft all over the area, making the whole enterprise risky. We took cover in a roadside ditch just to the east of Zonnebeke and waited for whatever we might be called upon to do. All kinds of materiel and the bodies of dead horses were strewn here and there along the shot-up road. They were giving off an appalling stench. Stray shells fell in amongst the troops with terrible results; numerous men were killed or wounded. A direct hit amongst a pile of ammunition belonging to a battery stationed right by the road blew the whole lot up. Eventually we were moved back to the rear."

Despite the appalling weather, which saw twenty five millimetres of rain fall between 1 and 4 August, followed by a further ten millimetres on 8 August, the British were ready to renew the offensive against the Geluveld Plateau on 10 August. The battlefield was by now one great bog, fed by the sluggish flow of streams which had burst their banks and so cut up by shelling that movement was severely restricted. The attack by the British 18th Division went in as planned, but the bombardment had failed to deal with all the German strongpoints in the woods and copses to the west and southwest of Polygon Wood. As a result, although 74 Brigade, 25th Division took and held the hamlet of Westhoek, 1,500 metres west of the northwest tip of Polygon Wood, the defenders generally not only stood their ground, but launched counter-stokes, which sent the bulk of the British attackers back to their start lines. As an offensive thrust it was a complete failure; the German artillery massed on the reverse slopes of the Geluveld plateau had once more proved to be very effective, directed, as it was, by skilled and well-placed observers.

Reserve Leutnant Michalk 8th Battery Reserve Field Artillery Regiment 9 [20] **3**

"I quickly took my leave of the Hauptmann, packed a few necessary items in my rucksack and sent for my horse. As I was riding past the church in Dadizeele I met Leutnant Zenner, who asked me what my mission was. 'Well, you have landed on the pig's back again!' he said and shook me warmly by the hand ... Together with my batman I rode via Beselare in the direction of Zonnebeke. Protected by the dying rays of the sun I arrived at the observation post and relieved my predecessor. The observation post was situated about three kilometres behind the front line, one kilometre southeast of Zonnebeke and right next to the track leading south from Broodseinde. It was the most dominating point in the Group sector. As a result there were several other observation posts on this hill. I was to have been relieved after four days, but no word about this arrived, nor did any successor for the whole time I was there.

"The observation post was ideal. To our front was Ypres laid out like a landscape model and it provided views over all operational activity almost from Langemark to Wijtschate. That is probably the reason why the Division (8th Infantry Division; the 21st Infantry Division was deployed behind it) maintained observation there. There was a reasonable selection of telephones available to enable direct communications to be maintained, but inevitably the links were cut whenever the need for them was greatest. In addition radio equipment was available (transmitter only). This worked superbly and, as a result, all important reports were successfully sent to the rear. I was allocated two cavalrymen as assistant observers. Because the field of observations was so good, I was able to send numerous comprehensive reports back to the division. In addition, because the British were always up to something, the duty was extremely interesting; I felt like a little general. Even pleasant company was catered for. Hauptmann Braxator, commander of 4th Battery Field Artillery Regiment 273, was co-located with me. His battery was deployed not far to the rear and supplied us with rations; sometimes even with hot meals.

"Each day saw the same film repeated. At dawn an enemy attack would be launched somewhere or other. Then there would be a scurrying to and fro: counter-attack, renewed attack; advance of the *Eingreif* divisions and so on. If it had been a major attack, sometimes the two sides were locked in hand-to-hand fighting throughout the day. Frequently the units were so interlocked that only the artillery fire provided an exact picture of the front line trace. Evening was often a time for renewed drum fire and large-scale offensive manoeuvring – then night would fall at last ... From 4 to 6 August, it rained constantly; but rain was our friend here. It prevented the British from pressing their major offensive vigorously. None of the subsequent small-scale attacks brought them any success worth the name.

"The weather improved on 7 August and the British increased their activities immediately. Enemy artillery fire took on the characteristics of planned preparatory bombardment. The ground began to dry out and become easier to traverse. The fragmentation effect of exploding shells was greater. Columns of Tommies could be seen advancing along all the approach routes, even in broad daylight. Visibility was poor once more up until the afternoon of 9 August, then the skies cleared and there was extremely heavy shelling towards evening. As the sun went down, my batman Kautz appeared on a horse, (he had just learned to ride) having brought me, as he did every few days, some rations. Because we wanted to celebrate my birthday the following day, he had also brought up some bottles of red wine and a bottle of cognac. As soon as he had appeared, he disappeared once again: he faced a very unpleasant journey.

"During the night 9/10 August, extremely heavy enemy fire came down along the entire length of the Flanders front. We did not get much sleep, because it was clear to us that this would be followed by a major attack. We were also somewhat nervous, because a direct hit on a neighbouring obser-vation post the previous day had killed three of our comrades. In our area (left flank of Group Ypres) and on the right flank of Group Wijtschate the concentration of fire went on increasing. 54th Infantry Division was deployed to our front. Soon the grim dance would be beginning. Earlier than usual I rose from my straw palliasse, donned my coat, hung my gas mask round my neck and – I must have had a premonition – put on my steel helmet. Then we began observing the front with the naked eye. Just before 6.00 am red flares of our infantry started flying up and a hellish din began as all the guns on both sides poured out death and destruction. It was impossible to make out individual gun flashes; there was just one streak of red all along the front. Mortar bombs rose in the air like great glowing grapes; it all combined to produced a magical scene. We had to shout to make ourselves understood, even when we were right next to one another.

"It was about 6.15 am when I suddenly felt a violent blow on my upper thigh and fell to the ground from my elevated position. A high explosive shell made of the finest steel (which we called a *Razzer*) had landed just to our right and I had been hit by a splinter. My comrades carried me down to the dugout. My right leg felt warm and as I felt for the cause, I saw that it was covered with blood. I pulled the splinter, which had bored through my leg, out of the inside of my thigh and my comrades bandaged me up. Hauptmann Braxator congratulated me warmly on my birthday and poured me a beaker full of brandy.

"I sat there as everybody resumed their posts and waited to be moved back to the dressing station. After two or three hours, Hauptmann Braxator succeeded in obtaining a stretcher and four bearers from his battery. I was pleased to be being moved towards medical attention, but I cannot say that the journey there was pleasant. One stretcherbearer was much taller than the others, so I felt constantly as though I was going to roll off the stretcher. Every time we came under fire, they put the stretcher on the ground swiftly and crawled off into cover, whilst I had to lie there until it was time to move on. At the dressing station I was placed in an ambulance on my stretcher then, after a further period of waiting I was taken, together with others, further to the rear."

In preparation for further operations to the west of Zonnebeke, the night 9/10 August had seen a general increase in the amount of artillery fire. 'The guns of both sides ran through their whole repertoire; pulling out all the stops of their organs of violence. Sometimes they played *forte*, sometimes *piano*, adding in *crescendo* and *diminuendo* in one great hellish concert.'[21] Probing patrols were sent forward by the British army and some prisoners fell into the hands of the defenders. Their interrogation confirmed that an attack was imminent. At 5.30 am, drum fire came down all along the front of 54th Infantry Division, as well as the division to its left. It was quite clear that an attack was about to take place, so defensive fire was called for about 5.45 am. The attack by 74 Brigade of the British 25th Division began at 6.00 am, but the defensive fire was so well placed that the attack came to a standstill between the railway embankment and Villa Hanebeek and the machine guns of 1st Battalion Infantry Regiment 84 were able to engage an enormous array of targets as the British infantry flooded back to the rear.

The British attack enjoyed rather more success to the south, where the right flank of Reserve Infantry Regiment 90, held by the exhausted and seriously weakened 5th and 6th Companies, was penetrated and the companies of 2nd Battalion Reserve Infantry Regiment 90 were rolled up. There were numerous heroic acts as isolated groups of defenders sought to hold the attack, despite being surrounded. Vizefeldwebel Ottenheimer, for example, despite being wounded, was able to continue in command of his platoon, having had his wounds dressed, and then to return later to regimental headquarters and to pass on a coherent account of the events of the morning to the commander.[22] Vizefeldwebel Dauber continued to fire at the advancing attackers until the very last minute then, together with Musketiers Rabe and Müller and Krankenträger Brüll, attempted to break back through the British troops who were already swarming all over the area. Only Brüll got through and the story was similar in the 6th and 8th Companies, where casualties were so high after the encirclement that only Reserve Leutnant Düber, who was severely wounded, Reserve Leutnant Arnecke and approximately fifty men fought their way to the rear.

There were several reasons for the British success in this area. There was extremely thick mist that morning, which the British added to by liberal use of smoke towards the end of the preparatory fire. This meant that the defenders had no idea about the approach of the enemy until they were within a few paces of the forward positions. The machine guns in the forward positions were all destroyed, either during the bombardment, or later when the positions were surrounded and close-range fighting with hand grenades ensued.[23] In the meantime neither the machine guns nor any of the observers to the rear could see anything through the smoke and dust. The telephone links had all been destroyed during the drum fire and the light signalling stations were rendered ineffective by the general obscuration. The entire *Albrecht Stellung* was captured as far as the Hanebeek. The minute that runners arrived bearing news of the penetrations the 12th Company, which was back in the *Wilhelm Stellung*, was launched in a counter-stroke and the regimental headquarters of Reserve Infantry Regiment 90 sent a message by light signal to 108 Brigade, requesting reinforcement by Reserve Infantry Regiment 27.[24]

In the meantime several of the survivors related their experiences to the regimental staff:

Musketier Krummreich 6th Company Reserve Infantry Regiment 90 [25] **3**

"When the enemy was attacking in dense masses, I went out of the blockhouse together with Musketier Schuldt of 2nd Machine Gun Company, carrying the machine gun to a firing position. We then opened fire on the attackers, causing them heavy casualties – at least 200 – 300 men. This halted the attack, but suddenly we saw that we had been deeply outflanked to the left and were almost threatened from the rear. We tried to swivel our weapon round, but it fell off the blockhouse. There was no time to recover it and bring it into action again, so we pulled back from crater to crater and slowly shot our way back." [26]

Unteroffizier Kuhn 7th Company Reserve Infantry Regiment 90 [27] **3**

"When the attack began I was in a pillbox, near the door. The sentry, who had been posted outside in accordance with normal procedure, bawled, 'The British are coming!' I dashed out of the pillbox and fired a white flare, because it was still dark and foggy. My section deployed left and right along the position. The enemy was already within forty paces, hurrying forward in tight groups. I fired about twenty five rounds from my rifle and my section also fired rapidly. Musketier Ernst, who also broke out with me, threw about three hand grenades. One of them exploded short. I was going to tick him off, but there was no time. To our right the British were already in and around the position. A machine gun from Ottenheimer's platoon [2nd Machine Gun Company] which was located close to me was damaged and made unserviceable by a shell splinter. To my left a German machine gun went on firing until the British had closed right up to our craters. Despite the fact that a great number of them had fallen, there were so many that they forced their way into our lines. At that point Ernst and I made off for the rear. Despite the extreme danger from the British who were already in rear of us, we broke through."

Gefreiter Domsky 5th Company Reserve Infantry Regiment 90 [28] **3**

"The enemy came up on the left flank of Infantry Regiment 84 under the cover of some hedgerows and appeared at our right rear. My light machine gun had been buried by a direct hit, so I could only fire with my rifle. The enemy took heavy casualties from one of our regimental machine guns firing from 150 metres back. When I could clearly see the enemy behind me, I dashed over to a machine gun of 1st Machine Gun Company Infantry Regiment 84 and fired my rifle in support. We caused the British heavy, bloody casualties."

Musketier Fürst 8th Company Reserve Infantry Regiment 90 [29] **3**

"The British drum fire began suddenly at 5.30 am, landing fifty metres to our rear. The attack in dense columns followed immediately. We fired our rifles at the rapid rate and threw grenades, once the British had got close enough, causing them bloody casualties. But masses more kept appearing to fill up the gaps and we had to pull back. We headed back to the pillboxes, moving from crater to crater, firing and throwing grenades so that we were not followed too closely. We halted by the pillboxes and put down heavy fire. Suddenly we realised that we were outflanked from the right, so we had to pull back again. About 250 metres from the pillboxes I lay down in a shell hole with my comrade Cirsovius of 8th Company and we prepared to defend it. The British forced their way into the pill box and took everyone prisoner, then they continued to advance. To begin with we went on firing but, when they got close we lay down in the hole and let them go past us. British aircraft were flying down below fifty metres, shooting at our men with machine guns. During the day our artillery fired very successfully at the British who were digging in behind us. We were freed by the counter-stroke and were very pleased to be back in German lines."

Despite spirited leadership of the 12th Company counter-stroke by Reserve Leutnant Weitemeyer, heavy artillery fire meant that the company sustained serious casualties. As a result, it was able to force a way across the Hanebeek, but had to take shelter almost immediately in the wreckage of a group of semi-destroyed concrete pillboxes. In the meantime a more systematic counter-attack was being prepared, to be commanded by Hauptmann Kellner, from 3rd Battalion Reserve Infantry Regiment 90 and to include reinforcements from 10th and 11th Companies and four machine guns of the neighbouring Reserve Infantry Regiment 27, commanded by Reserve Oberleutnant Schwahn. It was a bright day of sunshine, but the war diary later recorded the continuation of the operation by stating:

> "The problems and difficulties which had to be overcome during the ensuing attack became absolutely indescribable. In the swampy ground men found themselves stuck up to their knees in mud, completely unable to move. Often it required outside assistance before they could finally work their way forward. During the attempt to cross the Hanebeek with its boggy banks, the companies received from the left flank (the 52nd Reserve Division sector) and the British positions, which were somewhat higher, extremely heavy and effective machine gun fire. As a result the attack stalled right from the start. Repeated attempts later to cross the Hanebeek enjoyed no more success, especially after the British brought the whole valley under heavy artillery fire." [30] (3)

As soon as the fighting began, the divisional reserves all began to move forward to stiffen the defence and add weight to the counter-attacks.

Musketier Bär, 7th Company Reserve Infantry Regiment 27 [31] **3**

> "Forwards we trudged through a hail of iron, pursued by bullets from the numerous British aircraft. The way forward that we had taken was marked by a trail of dead and wounded. We had just reached the *Wilhelm Stellung*. I was standing just in front of a concrete pillbox when suddenly a column of black smoke shot up. A direct hit had landed not five metres from me, blowing five men of 6th Company to bits. Sanitätsgefreiter Schöbe of 7th Company was seriously wounded in the arm. The same shell tore my rifle out of my hand, smashing it and at the same instant I received a heavy blow above the right eye and fell backwards to the ground as though I had been pole-axed. I got to my feet just as quickly, checked I could still see and put my hand up to my face. Blood ran through my fingers, but it was just a minor wound to the skin caused by a concrete splinter. Seized by fury I grabbed another rifle – there were plenty lying around – and stormed forward with 6th Company, alongside its commander, Reserve Leutnant Uderstadt, from crater to crater. Here, in front of the *Wilhelm Stellung*, we were in a murderous storm of shells and machine gun fire. Our losses were

very heavy, but we pressed on despite it to the Hanebeek, which had been transformed into a swampy sea. For the time being we could get no further and were pinned down in shell holes for hours, enduring a hail of heavy and super-heavy shells, rifle and machine gun fire. The British tried everything to force us back, because we formed the German front line at this point. This included a concentration of shrapnel fire, which exploded directly over the craters. This was a difficult period of time. It cost us much blood, but we did not yield."

Musketier Fritz Müller 6th Coy Reserve Infantry Regiment 27 [32] **3**

"Having pushed on further we arrived in the place where our heavy machine guns were located. Here an officer held us back because his guns were out of action. The remainder of our company continued on its way. Around 2.00 pm we were also permitted to carry on. Because we had absolutely no idea where our company was and because artillery fire was coming down with such intensity in our position, (it was very fortunate that so very many were duds) we went to the next machine gun position and sat down under some corrugated iron until it began to go dark. The monstrous artillery fire and the way the ground shook under us from the impact of the duds[33] had us making all kinds of plans under our corrugated iron. But the words of our gun commander held us back. 'You can go where you like and do what you want, but I am staying here and so is the gun ...'

"About 4.00 pm our battalion commander, Major Stubenrauch, appeared through the heavy fire and came up to us. Bearing in mind the heavy fire and the fact that Major Stubenrauch walked with a limp, we had to give him full credit for having achieved something that might not have been attempted by many a fit battalion commander. He told his orderly officer to take our names for shirking our duty. It was a pity that our company commander, who was well aware of the worth of our gun commander, was not there to put him right."

Defensive fire poured down incessantly on the old German positions in the *Albrecht Stellung* and British reinforcements continued to arrive. Unfortunately for the defence, the weight of the British fire was such that the German counter-attack ground to a halt in the boggy ground, without even having crossed the Hanebeek. It was decided, therefore, that no further attempt could be made until there had been a substantial period of artillery preparation. At 6.30 pm, after a long preparatory bombardment and a short period of drum fire on the *Albrecht Stellung* and the ground to the west of the Hanebeek, the attack was re-launched, this time with additional support from Reserve Infantry Regiment 238, but once again it soon stalled. It was simply impossible, given the state of the ground, the lack of cover and the excellent view from the *Albrecht Stellung*, to make any significant progress. Isolated parties did force their way forward of the Hanebeek, but their success was only temporary. On the extreme left (southern) flank an assault group led by Vizefeldwebel Runkel and Unteroffizier Lehmitz of 4th Company Reserve Infantry Regiment 90 stormed a British pocket of resistance in Nonne-Bossen, killing or capturing all the occupants. But, overall, it was a bad day for the regiment, which lost every officer of 1st Company, which was split up and scattered completely by a series of direct hits by shell fire.

Two accounts by eyewitnesses provide a vivid impression of the events that evening. The first was by a man who took part in the attack, the second by a member of the 1st Machine Gun Company, who brought down supporting fire from a high point of the *Wilhelm Stellung*, near to the northwest tip of Polygon Wood.

Musketier Bär, 7th Company Reserve Infantry Regiment 27 [34] 4

"Punctually at the appointed time we began the assault. Despite sinking at times up to our chests in water as we waded through the boggy Hanebeek, we headed in the direction of the Wupzaal up above us. There was nothing to be seen but a few destroyed houses and concrete pillboxes. We were greeted by a hail of bullets from British machine guns and took casualties as a result. However we were soon through the swamp and close up against the buildings. Although we were reduced to a small group, the British escaped to the rear. Had we received reinforcements at that moment, we should have been able to force our way back into the *Albrecht Stellung*. That was certainly the view of our officers, but unfortunately we were too weak; all we could do was to take up hasty defence and keep a sharp lookout, in order to ensure that we were not overrun by the enemy.

"They had taken up positions about 150 – 200 metres to our front. Suddenly I saw a British soldier, probably a runner, making his way to the rear carrying a large file. With one shot I brought him down. We spent a long time bringing fire down on the enemy. The British tried repeatedly to advance, but were unsuccessful."

Landsturmmann Troch
 1st Machine Gun Company Reserve Infantry Regiment 27 [35] 4

"Completely exhausted, about ten men of our company reached the valley at the correct time. There was a half-wrecked blockhouse, which perhaps would have offered us some protection against fragments and bad weather. The surroundings were thoroughly dismal. Everywhere dead men lay around ... Shells landing on them threw up into the air fragments of these half-decayed corpses, which fouled the air. Shell craters were full of stinking ordure and blood. All of us were seized by a deep seated anger to take revenge for our fallen comrades.

"But we had to be careful because the enemy position was not far off. We took it in turns to observe the enemy, but the Tommies were not asleep either: every time some of our comrades attempted to approach our block-house, they came under extremely heavy machine gun fire. Later, both our position and the ground to our rear were subjected to terrible artillery fire. Because of the explosions, our blockhouse swayed like a rowing boat on a rough sea. But our artillery was also sending over iron rations to the enemy. Whenever there was a direct hit, we could see all manner of items being thrown up in the air. We certainly have our artillery to thank that the attack was suppressed.

As late as 9.40 pm, just as it was beginning to go dark, yet another attempt was made to recapture the original positions, but it was impossible to make any impression on the British troops. The *Albrecht Stellung* was lost and the companies of Reserve Infantry Regiment 90 were reduced to maintaining a series of patrols forward throughout the night, in order to avoid being surprised by a resumption of the attacks. Musketier Bär once more:

"Finally peace descended with the arrival of darkness. Some of us satisfied our hunger and quenched our great thirst by removing food and drink from the British haversacks which lay all around, whilst others maintained a sharp lookout to the front. Despite the fact that we were dog tired and our nerves were jangling from the strain of the day, sleep was out of the question. The night passed slowly, but the artillery duel continued." [36]

The events of the day were summarised the following night, (evasively and inaccurately, as was often the case), in the official Army Communiqué for 11 August. The capture of Westhoek may not have been an enormously important gain for the British army. Nevertheless it had been achieved and, as night fell, the new position was being consolidated – despite the German artillery fire which was directed at the men of the British 25th Division well into the night. [37]

"The British attacks of yesterday morning were conducted by several divisions.[38] On a frontage of more than eight kilometres between Frezenberg and Hollebeke the enemy advanced but, despite the deployment of strong forces, they enjoyed no success. Initially the deeply echeloned assaulting enemy succeeded in breaking into our lines in several places, but they were thrown back once more by means of swiftly-mounted counter-attacks by our supports. In the case of Westhoek (where 54th Infantry Division was deployed) this was not until after long hard fighting."

After the almost total failure of operations on 10 August, there was an operational pause as preparations went ahead for the launching of the Battle of Langemark on 16 August. Naturally, amidst the continuing heavy artillery fire, attempts were made to improve positions locally and this saw the regiments of 79th Reserve Division involved in a series of minor skirmishes between Langemark and St Juliaan. One such occurred on 11 August in the sector of Reserve Infantry Regiment 261.

Leutnant Schwenk 11th Company Reserve Infantry Regiment 261 [39] **5**

"Along with the pitiful remnants of 11th Company, I was occupying a position near a concrete artillery emplacement down by the Steenbeek during the morning of 11 August. During the early hours of the morning, about 2.00 am, the British had attempted to probe forward in the area of 10th Company to our right, but were beaten back. We of the 11th Company could see no enemy to our front, but in the swampy area to our left, where it was impossible to maintain contact with the 12th Company, the British had infiltrated thirty to forty men and simply took us by surprise from the rear. This would have been about 5.00 am. My scattered sentries took the British for ration carriers; only at the last minute, when they attacked with hand grenades and Lewis guns, did they realise what was happening.

"So when I read in the extract of officers' appointments that I was wounded by a shell splinter on 16 August, this is actually a double error. In fact I was wounded by a ricocheting bullet fired from only twenty to thirty metres away as I attempted to get to the position of our one remaining machine gun on the concrete blockhouse. Our other weapon had been buried by a direct hit from an artillery shell the previous day. I lay with a serious wound to the thigh in a shell hole that was half full of water only twenty metres away from the British, who were making themselves comfortable in the concrete blockhouse. The British fired a green flare to the rear as a signal for a further advance, but nothing much seemed to happen. At that our comrade Blickensdorfer gathered a few men around him and together they threw themselves with fixed bayonets and loud *Hurras* at the Tommies. This counter-attack was completely successful; part of the patrol lay dead where they were and the remainder were captured.

"One of our 11th Company men, whose name I have unfortunately forgotten, was so fired up by the battle that he took aim at close range at me, as I attempted to sit upright in my crater. He lowered his rifle in response to my hand signals, but seconds later shot dead a Tommy who raced round the blockhouse and ran along a tree trunk which had been placed across the Steenbeek, in an attempt to escape. After that the brave chap came over to me then fetched a medical orderly. My own two first field dressings were insufficient to cover the size of my wound, so a large temporary one was applied and I was carried over to the road on my right, where I successfully used my English to obtain a drink of water from a Tommy.

"The cellar of a ruined house by the road was occupied by our comrade Kneher and there my dressing was renewed and improved. After that I was loaded into a groundsheet and taken back to Poelkapelle. On the way there, Hauptmann von Goerne (Commanding Officer 2nd Battalion Reserve Infantry Regiment 261) gave me a refreshing drink of mineral water. At the dressing station there Dr Rohlfs dressed my wound once more and, during the early evening of 11 August, he accompanied the stretcherbearers who carried me out to the wagon which brought me to Sprieht, where I was transferred to a motor vehicle which transported me to Isighem. Rohlfs was the last of my comrades in the field with whom I shook hands."

By the middle of the month the German army had mixed views concerning the progress of operations. On the one hand, the defensive successes which had been achieved were a source of satisfaction, but the price being paid in casualties, bearing in mind the pressure on manpower on all fronts, was becoming a cause of concern.

Crown Prince Rupprecht of Bavaria – Diary Entry 15th August [40]

"Yesterday General Ludendorff, who was visiting Fourth and Sixth Armies, stated that if we were to vacate Belgium we could have peace. He is for the time being, however, not amenable to the view that unless we do leave Belgium we shall never succeed in achieving peace. He is currently preoccupied with the plan for the capture of Riga. He said that in view of the French attacks on an eighteen kilometre front at Verdun, an offensive with six divisions around Mitau will only be possible if we can manage operations in Flanders from within our own resources ... We shall certainly attempt [to achieve this], but it remains a hazardous undertaking, because of our anticipated heavy losses and lack of replacements. The losses within my army group from 1 June to 10 August amount to no fewer than 2,020 officers and 85,508 other ranks ... There can be no question of Fourth Army recapturing Langemark; all that can be undertaken by them are a few minor operations to improve their positions.

"Today I spoke to His Majesty the Kaiser who, having toured the fortifications at Heligoland, had travelled to Zedelghem, near Bruges ... [He was] in the best of spirits. I did not miss the opportunity to inform him that our losses in Flanders were very significant. At the same time I had the occasion to meet the Chief of the Admiralty Staff, Admiral von Holtzendorff, who assured me that he was of the opinion that our U Boat campaign would defeat England by October. The gentlemen of the navy are dangerous optimists!"

It was not just the physical losses which were sapping the strength of the German army. The dreadful weather, the incessant artillery bombardments and harassment from the air were also taking their toll on the nerves and ability to resist of the defenders.

Reserve Oberleutnant Süßenberger,
Company Commander 3rd Company Reserve Infantry Regiment 263 [41] **6**

"When on the evening of 1 August we relieved the fought-out division, the 1st Battalion spent three days occupying a reserve position to the west of Poelkappelle. This, the so-called *Winterstellung* [Winter Position], reminded us strongly of the primitive positions at the start of trench warfare and probably dated back to that time. Now it was to see another moment of glory. A few metres in rear were our battery positions, which unfortunately meant that when they were 'blessed' by the British artillery we were too. These few days of rest in Westrozebeke were supposed to steel us for the forthcoming days spent in the crater field and, during the evening of 8 August, we made our way forward through the muddy fields which had been ploughed up by all the shells to the Steenbeek, which divided the British and German battle lines. Only those who were there can possibly understand what it meant to pick a way through the crater field of Flanders in the pitch black night under enemy artillery fire and they will look back on it with a shudder.

"The 1st and 4th Companies relieved the front line. 3rd Company was located 200 metres to the rear, whilst the 2nd Company was placed in the well-constructed *Wilhelm Stellung* about 800 metres further back. This last named was the main defensive line. The front line companies were distributed amongst shell holes; two small concrete pillboxes serving as command posts for the company commanders. The commanders of 1st and 4th Companies shared one and I occupied the other together with a light machine gun section. If I live to be one hundred, the memories of the days on the Steenbeek will never be extinguished. Here the true greatness of the defensive battle revealed itself in full. It requires enormous reserves of morale and courage to hold out in muddy shell holes for seven long days on end despite bad weather and ceaseless concentrated artillery fire. What each man in his lonely shell hole achieved deserves to be set down in letters of gold in the history of this war.

"There was not a speck of green left. As far as the eye could see it looked as though some appalling earthquake had torn the ground apart, leaving a ploughed up desert. In the midst of this men just had to hang on whilst his comrade next to him was killed and simply wait for the same fate to befall him. Death reaped a grim harvest. My original intention to move all our fallen comrades to the rear, in order to guarantee them a dignified burial, had to be abandoned. This caused me great pain, but what the stretcher bearers were achieving as they recovered the wounded was already super-human. To this day it is a mystery to me why my concrete pillbox, the only thing still left standing in this area, was not smashed to pieces. We were certainly bracketed by shells often enough and, with each successive explosion in the vicinity, the whole object shook, almost as though its foundations were sitting on a treacherous bog.

"A few hundred metres to our right we could see the remains of Langemark. I shall never forget seeing a constant stream of hellishly evil, flaming mortar bombs landing in the ruins and sending up jets of burning liquid into the sky. The British had a special way of ruining our nerves. Every morning towards 5.00 am the shelling was increased to a crescendo of drum fire. We were sure that the enemy were coming; we even wished they would come. We wanted to do something at long last; to fight, to defend ourselves, weapons in hand, anything rather than have to endure any longer this [rain of shells], which was slowly driving us all mad. We prepared for battle. We checked our ammunition, hand grenades and flares and laid them out where we could reach them easily. After about an hour the fire would stop – and the Tommies did not come. And so it went on, day after day. In the end they did come and in a way that had disastrous conse-quences for us – more of that later …

"During the afternoon of 15 August we received the news that we were to be relieved that night by Infantry Regiment 184. We breathed a sigh of relief; we had given our all both physically and spiritually. The military expression for this degree of exhaustion was 'fought out'. It summed up our situation exactly. The relief arrived after midnight. The company commander of 3rd Company Infantry Regiment 184 arrived at my dugout, bathed in sweat and at the end of his strength. He explained to me that he still did not have his whole company; a large number were still floundering in the mud. In view of the extreme difficulty of the task before him, he did not feel that this chaotic relief was a good omen.

"I had directed that, when the relief was complete, the move to the rear was to be by platoons. In the meantime I brought my successor up to date with all important information: general situation, terrain, organisation of the troops and so forth. Despite having completed the entire laid-down relief procedure, I remained longer. For one thing I had it on my conscience to make sure that the commander of the relieving company was absolutely *au fait* with his new situation and, for another, the fire was particularly heavy during this night and I thought that if I delayed my departure I should have an easier time of it as I moved to the rear. Instead of slackening, however, the fire continued with increased intensity. It was well past 4.00 am when I set off with company headquarters. This was not before time. If we had left it another half an hour, our fate would have been sealed.

"For the second time we made our way through the cratered landscape, which was much worse than the first time. Again and again one of us would sink in up to his knees and only be able to extract himself with help from other comrades. We were continually bumping into the relieving troops, in particular the machine gun teams, who simply could not get their weapons forward in this sea of mud. It was an appalling spectacle. Skirting around Poelkapelle, which was under heavy fire, we eventually reached the road to Westrozebeke. At that precise moment, with a great crash, a hurricane of fire which surpassed anything in our experience broke out. There could be no doubt. They had come at last! The British had had the good fortune to attack troops who were new to the position, did not know the layout and, due to the dreadful relief, were practically exhausted and almost incapable of putting up a defence. All of a sudden, as far as the eye could see, red flares went up all along the front – artillery defensive fire! ...

"We tucked ourselves away in the houses of Spriet. Then suddenly with a noise that made the streets resound, came battalion after battalion. It was the troops of the fresh *Eingreif* divisions, advancing to launch a counter-stroke. The sight of these men coming towards gave us heart. The British certainly would not break through. In Westrozebeke the remainder of the company who had survived the battle, assembled and went into bivouacs. I had set out with one hundred men and returned with barely fifty and, which was worse, Vizefeldwebel Becker, a really dependable prop within the company, had gone missing along with some other men during the relief operation. They had probably decided to wait for the fire to slacken before they set off and had been swept up in the attack. Their fate must have been death or capture.

"Whilst we slept the sleep of the dead for a few hours, the battle raged further forward. About midday a rumour went round that the British were in Poelkapelle and a little later an order arrived, directing every man who could carry a rifle to man the *Flandern Stellung* [Flanders Position]. Fortunately it transpired that the rumour was an exaggeration; nevertheless the enemy had broken through to the *Wilhelm Stellung* and beyond

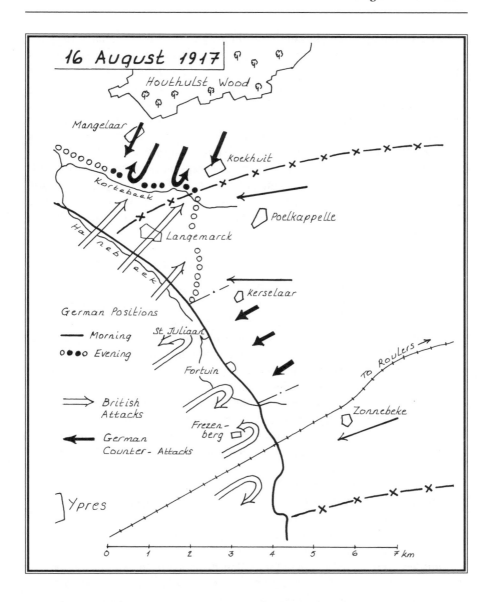

in places. However the *Eingreif* force succeeded in almost restoring the original line by means of a counter-stroke."

Launched by the British Fifth Army by no fewer than eight divisions and supported by a successful French attack by their I Corps in the area forward of Bikschote – the so-called Battle of Langemark – which opened on 16 August, in fact involved a frontage stretching south all the way to the Ypres – Menen road and beyond. Holding a key part of the line, just to the north of the 5th Bavarian Infantry Division, in and around Langemark itself, were the regiments of 79th Reserve Division, a Prussian formation which had distinguished itself on Vimy Ridge during the bitter fighting of 9 and 10 April 1917. It had been in position since 1 August, had already seen a great deal of action and was in the process of being relieved by 183rd Infantry Division as the battle opened. One of its regiments, Reserve Infantry Regiment 263, for example, was actually handing over to Infantry Regiment 184 during the early hours of 16 August, when the operation was interrupted by drum fire. As a result, 1st and 3rd Companies and elements of 11th Company, were still in the line and took part in a further defensive battle. One of the platoon commanders of 11th Company submitted a report, on 20 August, concerning the events of the day.

Reserve Leutnant Engler 11th Company Reserve Infantry Regiment 263 [42] **5**

"During the battle of Langemark I was a platoon commander in 10th Company [*sic*]. During the night 15/16 August the company was relieved by 10th Company Infantry Regiment 184. Because of the heavy artillery fire, we despatched our men back to the rear by sections and widely spaced out. The British artillery fire gained more and more in strength, until it reached the intensity of drum fire at 6.00 am and lasted until 7.00 am. As a result, the company commander, [Leutnant] Guillaume, Vizefeldwebel Böhm, two batmen, some runners and I remained on the position with 10th Company Infantry Regiment 184. At about 7.00 am the fire began to fall more towards the rear position and the British infantry launched its attack. The artillery fire had caused the companies of Infantry Regiment 184 serious casualties.

"The British succeeded in breaking in to the position of 9th Company and, as we were informed by a Gefreiter from 9th Company, most of the company was overwhelmed and captured. The few men left in 11th and 12th Companies managed to hold their positions. Small British detachments [from the British 11th Division] did manage to cross the Steenbeek, but they were forced to dig in there, thus bringing the attack in this area to a halt. Further to the north (to the right of 9th Company) the German companies could not hold out against the dense British waves, which followed each other in quick succession. As far as I could see, the British simply continued to advance without check. This meant that we were now in great danger of being attacked form the north or northeast. In order to avoid having our lines rolled up, we swung round to the north and brought the waves of British infantry under enfilade fire, which was even more effective because we were able to deploy two machine guns.

"The British response was to fire smoke, which created a dense screen. Right at the beginning of the action, two platoon commanders of 10th Company Infantry Regiment 184 were wounded. At that I assumed command. I advanced with a platoon of 10th Company towards the north, in order to conduct a reconnaissance in that direction. Despite the British shrapnel and machine gun fire, which was being fired at us from west, north and northeast, we maintained our position completely. The British were halted and forced to dig in. The attack of the British infantry was very effectively supported by a large number of British aircraft. These aircraft circled very low overhead, firing their machine guns. From 7.00 am to 9.00 am I did not see a single German aircraft. On many occasion we opened fire at the enemy airmen, but without success. On the other hand the 8th Company shot down an aircraft along the road between Poelkapelle and St Juliaan.

"The 8th Company, with which we were in contact, advanced at about 11.00 am from the *Wilhelm Stellung* in the direction of Langemark and went firm along the Poelkapelle-St Juliaan road. For us, this removed the danger of being attacked from the rear. On two occasions I observed the British displaying red lights and assembling by them. They shook out in formation once more then advanced on Langemark. This happened, for example, by the cemetery at Keerslaar-West. Unfortunately we could not engage them because groups of German prisoners were also being held there. To our south, where the Bavarians were located, the British attack also stalled. By midday there were still only a few isolated pockets of resistance. The casualties of 10th Company Infantry Regiment 184 were considerable. A large proportion of the total wounded had been wounded in the head. Towards 1.00 pm the artillery and machine gun fire slackened gradually, so we could pull back. Following a wide arc around Poelkapelle, we reached Westrozebeek after 4.00 pm."

Unfortunately, Infantry Regiment 184 did not leave any detailed account of the part they played during the Battle of Langemark. They subsequently rated 16 August as the hardest, but most successful, day of battle for the regiment. Their war diary recorded:

" Under intense fire of all calibres and through places contaminated with gas, stumbling through the crater field in the pitch dark night, the regiment, which advanced in small groups, arrived on the position to which it had been ordered [between Langemark and St Juliaan, along the Steenbeek]. 1st and 3rd Battalions held the front line, with 2nd Battalion in reserve. Before the relief in the line was complete, everywhere a major British attack occurred. It was a hard-fought battle in unknown terrain, but the regiment performed heroically, either maintaining its position or throwing the enemy back by means of counter-attacks. The casualties were extremely heavy and included some of the finest men in the regiment. The 1st Battalion was almost totally wiped out; whilst the 3rd Battalion lost all its company commanders and the regimental commander was evacuated as a result of injuries incurred during the move forward."[43]

The German defenders in and around Langemark enjoyed the least success on 16 August. The progress in that sector, limited though it was, was probably the reason for selecting it as the name of the battle. Elsewhere along the front assaults were brutally and summarily rebuffed, either by the ground-holding divisions or through the use of vigorously conducted counter-strokes, as exemplified by the experience of Infantry Regiment 84.

Leutnant C Beuck, Commander 5th Company Infantry Regiment 84 [44] **3**

"16th August dawned. For us it was to be one of the most unforgettable days of the war. During the early morning drum fire came down with a sudden crash. I woke up with a jerk and automatically pulled my belt and coat tight and ordered the company to stand to. I knew that we should be involved in a counter-stroke. Soon an order arrived form the regiment: '5th, 6th and 9th Companies are to advance on *Westhaus*, via Grotemolen and recapture the lost position …' I ordered an immediate departure. We advanced over the hill into the low ground, which was in an appalling state – bog, shell holes and broad trenches. Altogether it was extremely difficult to advance. Zonnebeke was off to our right. We came under artillery fire and began to double march forward. I looked around me, seeing the same scene I had seen so often before, especially in Poland. Widely spaced in assault formation the company was advancing with the section and platoon commanders out in front. The whole thing looked as though it had been poured out of a mould.

"A feeling of pride swelled in my breast; pride in my dear brave 5th Company. Every man knew that it was going to be a hard day, but each was filled with an iron determination to do his duty. The old *Mansteiner* spirit[45] was alive and well. Heavy fire was coming down on the hill to our front and I was gripped by concern about how the company would be able to get through it. Sharing my concerns with Vizefeldwebel Wellmann, he replied, 'We simply must get through it, Herr Leutnant!' – and we did. We got right through to *Westhaus*. Hauptmann Hofmeister was standing at the entrance to a dugout and waved at me. I told the company to take a short breather and ran up to Hauptmann Hofmeister. He beamed with joy. 'I knew you would not leave us in the lurch,' he said and shook my hand.

"His was an unenviable position. The front line and the *Wilhelm Stellung* to his front were occupied by the enemy; the British were within one hundred metres of him. The battalion command post had only one machine gun to defend it. To the left the 90th had launched an assault, but there was a gap to his front. That was what we had to fill. We pressed on, to be greeted by a torrent of small arms fire. We took cover and opened up rapid fire. I spotted that the enemy was beginning to waver and passed on the message: 'We attack at any minute,' followed by, 'Stand up! Advance! Advance!' It was a brilliant charge: a long, continuous line sprang forward – into the *Wilhelm Stellung.* The British pulled out, leaving their dead and wounded behind them. Naturally we had casualties as well.

"Vizefeldwebel Wellmann came crawling along the line to report sad losses to me. Storm, an outstanding Unteroffizier, who had been with the company from the start and who had received the Iron Cross First Class only a few weeks previously, had been killed. That was a hard blow for me – but we had to carry on. Ceaselessly we drove the British in front of us, but we had to halt in front of the Hanebeek. The enemy artillery had ranged in on this line and was deluging it with fire. The attack came to a standstill, but we had achieved a lot. We had moved the line back level with that to the right of the railway embankment. The enemy had also attacked there on the front of 8th Company but, thanks to the energetic intervention of Vizefeldwebel Hegermann, had been halted. Hegermann, a man of few words, but absolutely reliable and possessed of great presence of mind, had managed to bring a machine gun into action on top of his concrete pillbox in the nick of time and so bring the attack to a standstill.

"The hours passed slowly; all too slowly the sun completed its course, but finally it was evening. The noise of firing died away gradually. I heard about further casualties within the company; all of them caused me pain, but most of all the news of the death of my dear, courageous Wellmann. Nobody could say where or how he was killed. Towards midnight only occasional shells were exploding, but one of them crashed down right in front of me. For the first time in the war, I was wounded by enemy steel. Splinters from the same shell also hit Unteroffiziers Kaad and Hoffmann, who were near me. Hoffmann later died of his wounds. I hobbled back out of the line once Reserve Leutnant Sebold had taken over command of the company and, after searching in vain for hours, reached a dressing station."

Leutnant Hans Bromm, Commander 12th Company Infantry Regiment 84 [46] **3**

"After the British had gassed the forward positions during the night 15/16 August, they attacked on the morning of 16 August. Because the troops holding the forward positions had suffered heavily, all available regimental reserves were ordered forward. The 12th Company was directed to advance in the direction of *Rumpelkammer* and to report to Hauptmann Soltau there. Two approach routes were available. One of them, once it had cleared the first few houses in Zonnebeke, ran along the railway embankment, but this area was under particularly heavy British shell fire, so it was advisable instead to take a route straight through Zonnebeke and then to remain in the cover of the railway embankment. We set off, therefore, in single file through Zonnebeke. This village, too, was under very heavy fire, but it did at least offer protection from view. The company arrived in the shelter of the ruined church without casualties and stopped for a breather.

"Exploding shells were sending wooden beams and the remains of walls spinning up to the rooftops in the air and landing unpleasantly close to us. This sort of shelling was not going to cause us any particular damage and the shells which cleared the embankment tended to fall in the morass next to it where they were smothered. As a result, we were soon at the *Rumpelkammer* at the cost of only one man wounded. From here we were directed to move forward, to link up with the companies there so as to re-establish a continuous line, then to advance on the British attackers. Together with elements of 10th and 11th Companies and some of 6th Company, who had arrived from the *Flandern Stellung*, we established a very thin line with its right flank on the railway embankment. The front line ran along immediately behind the Hanebeek. Due to the endless shelling over time, this stream had become a swamp and an obstacle to frontal attacks. We also had a relatively undamaged block house in our area which was used as an aid post for the wounded.

"During the hours which followed we were involved in a permanent fire fight. When, as a result of a counter-stroke mounted by Reserve Infantry Regiment 90, the British were flooding to the rear in large numbers, we engaged them from our position off on the flank with rifle and machine gun fire, causing them considerable numbers of casualties. By 4.00 pm the weather was clearing and our positions began to be engaged by an increasing amount of enemy artillery fire. There were several men killed in the platoons of Reserve Leutnant Schlüter and Vizefeldwebel Schnibben, but we waited in vain for an enemy attack. At this point our reserves, who had been left out of battle in the morning, came forward. As far as the eye

could see, away to the left and right and emerging over the railway embankment, was one line of infantrymen after another – all of them endeavouring
to get forward to our lines. The enemy had also spotted these approaching
reinforcements and went to work at them with artillery and aircraft. Our
men tried to produce cover by throwing smoke bombs. Whenever an
aircraft swooped low to engage our men with machine gun fire, they took
cover in nearby shell holes, emerging once the aircraft had passed, to
continue on their way. Within a very short time the first of the infantry
was with us. They were elements of Fusilier Regiment 34, who helped us
to man a combined defensive line.

"The British began to engage our line again, concentrating especially on
the blockhouse. It does not say much for the materials used in the construction that a dud, which landed two metres in front of the blockhouse,
ricocheted straight through the wall nearest to the enemy. Unteroffizier
Birzunski, who was by the entrance, was severely wounded and a man of
12th Company had his arm torn off. Miraculously, Leutnant Schlüter was
uninjured. It was by now going dark and the artillery fire on our line died
away almost completely. Both we and the 34th despatched patrols forward
of the position. Our wounded, whom we had not managed to evacuate
earlier, were now moved away from the front line to the rear. During the
course of the evening we were ordered to hand over our positions to
Fusilier Regiment 34 and to pull back to the *Flandern Stellung* in the
morning. As dawn broke the remnants of the 12th Company arrived there
and the following night we left this position, too, and marched to St Elooi."

One of the medical officers of the regiment, who was deployed forward in support
of operations throughout this tour of duty, left a detailed account of the problems
faced by the medical evacuation chain during the August fighting, as did one of his
patients.

Dr Otto Gleue, Medical Officer 3rd Bn Infantry Regiment 84 [47] **7**

"[On 5 August] we marched forward to the front, passing Passchendaele
and Moorslede en route. As dawn broke we arrived in the Third Position ...
The following night, because 3rd Battalion was to occupy the third line, I
was ordered to take over the Regimental Aid Post in Zonnebeke. I found it
to the left of the entrance to the village. It was a small concrete pillbox,
which was completely unsuitable for use as an aid post, because the
entrance was so low and narrow that stretcher cases could not be carried
in. It was completely impossible to take care of the wounded inside it. As
a result I had to carry out my treatment outside the pill box in a shelter
made of groundsheets and there the wounded had to wait to be evacuated.

Because we had to work by candlelight at night and because the aid post was so busy, it was impossible to prevent enemy airman from spotting us and directing fire down. As a result we had several men killed and wounded.

"Right forward in the First Position was another aid post, the *Kaffeegut* [Coffee Shop], which initially was manned by the medical officer of the neighbouring regiment. However, when this regiment was relieved by Bavarian Infantry Regiment 19, it was not taken over by another doctor. As a result I was ordered to do so. Shortly after midday in bright sunshine and clear visibility over long distances, I moved forward with Sanitätsunteroffizier Hagener. We passed through Zonnebeke. What a sight it was! Hardly a single house wall was complete. Our route forward was a succession of shell craters, tree stumps, corpses and incoming shells. We had to cross the railway embankment at a point which was under very heavy fire. The *Kaffeegut*, an elongated concrete blockhouse, was located about 1,000 metres behind the front line and 400 metres in front of the embankment. We had been informed by the runners that the embankment was permanently under machine gun fire. To check this we threw ourselves into a shell hole by the embankment. We decided that we either had to find another way or to check if the British would respect the Cross of Geneva, because the entire area was under British observation. We waved the Red Cross flag and the firing ceased. We then crossed the embankment and arrived at the *Kaffeegut* completely unharmed.

"Matters were so arranged that I dealt with the wounded of those members of Infantry Regiment 84 who were forward of the railway embankment and also men from the left flank of Bavarian Infantry Regiment 19. Stretcher cases were carried back to the aid post in Zonnebeke then evacuated under arrangements made by a medical Feldwebel. During the first few days I had twenty four stretcher bearers available but later, as the number of cases increased, this went up to forty eight ... Because the enemy had constant observation over aid post *Kaffeegut*, the wounded were only carried to the rear after dark. On average the stretcherbearers had to make four to five round trips between the *Kaffeegut* and Zonnebeke per night. Their casualties were extremely high. Whilst we were there it was reported to me that sixteen had been killed or wounded.

"To help me I had the hard-working Sanitätsunteroffizier Hagener and two stretcherbearers from the company. Our workload was very great, especially on 10 and 16 August. At night the *Kaffeegut* resembled a beehive. The wounded came and went, runners on the way from the companies to the headquarters called in for a pause to catch their breath, stretcher bearers took a short rest before setting off on their risky journeys and we must not forget the ration parties, who night after night carried food and drink forward, handing it over to carrying parties from the companies at the aid post. These ration parties carried out their duties brilliantly during the Battle of Flanders. We expected them shortly after midnight and they never failed us, regardless of how heavy the artillery fire was. Certainly many of those who were wounded have them to thank for the fact that we were able to boost their spirits through the provision of plenty of food and drink.

"During the night 16/17 the ration parties brought forward supplies for 200 men, which I later handed over against a receipt to Infantry Regiment 34 who had relieved us when we pulled back to the *Flandern Stellung.* The iron rations which we held in the aid post were also very useful. Large quantities of bottled mineral water and alcohol were stored here, which helped us to refresh the wounded and give renewed strength to the exhausted. The health of the troops was excellent. There were no medical epidemics; in fact very few men reported sick. I had absolutely no cases of gas poisoning to deal with. I was told at the time that the British only fired gas shells at night and that the concentrations were so weak that they had almost no effect. This good state of health was nothing short of a miracle, because the men were forced to live in dreadful conditions. Hardly any of them had anything better than a shell hole covered by a ground sheet to live in. If the living arrangements left something to be desired, they were more than compensated for by the rationing arrangements. The carrying parties brought forward more than the troops could eat or drink.

"At 5.45 am on 16 August the most intense drum fire that I had ever experienced began suddenly. It was impossible to differentiate individual explosions. Towards 9.00 am runners reported to me that the enemy had broken into the positions in several places. At that Feldwebelleutnant Krüger launched forward with his platoon to go to the support of the threatened companies. I was deeply impressed with the grip he had on his platoon. I had the impression that Krüger was a soldier through and through. He had a real sense of duty and was quite fearless. From the aid post we had been observing the advance of the enemy on the left and right. We reckoned that we should soon be threatened by the Tommies from the rear also – to our front was an impassable swamp, which the enemy could not cross. We felt as though we in the aid post were caught in a sack and assumed that we should all be captured unless help was on the way in a very short time. Shortly before midday, however, our counter-attack was launched.

"After a short preparatory bombardment we watched and saw, as far as the eye could see, lines of our brave *Mansteiners* launching forward to throw the enemy back to their old positions. For me watching the British racing back to the rear with our men hard on their heels was the most uplifting moment of my entire war service. The following night Infantry Regiment 84 was relieved in its forward positions ... I stayed with my medical personnel for a further thirty six hour at the aid post in order to take care of the large number of wounded from 16 August."

Musketier F Lindelof Infantry Regiment 84 [48]

"The battlefield and approach routes which bore witness to the great battle were behind me. At the dressing station I was given a seat next to a driver and was taken from there to a casualty collection point. From there I was transported by narrow gauge railway to Kortrijk, where we arrived towards evening. Here in the place which housed Army Headquarters there was an enormous amount of activity. Clerks in cars or despatch riders on motorcycles roared through the streets in all directions. Everywhere there was hustle and bustle.

"A large building, which must have been a theatre or something similar, had been fitted out as a dressing station. It had room for hundreds of wounded. I was accommodated with another comrade in a small side room. My overstrained nerves would grant me no rest. All the images of the previous day kept flashing again and again in front of my eyes. Towards midnight I was finally overcome by sleep, but the cruel war even pursued me here. In the middle of the night I awoke to a dreadful scream. I shot bolt upright out of bed. The room was lit up as though it was in flames. The bed next to mine was empty. I then felt pain and something sticking to my feet. I sprang back into bed and found that I had injured my feet on broken glass. Where was my comrade? I called for help and eventually a medical orderly came. In a breathless voice he explained that there had been an air raid. An ambulance parked outside the door of the hospital had been hit by a splinter in the petrol tank, which had exploded, burning out the vehicle.

"My comrade, who had been lying there next to the outer wall, had been hit in the back by a splinter which had flown into the room through an emergency door. This caused a haemorrhage which killed him later. The orderly took me down to the cellar where the other wounded men were sheltering, dressed in whatever they had grabbed as they left. We spent the rest of the night there, because the enemy aircraft paid us several other visits. The following day I left by train for the homeland."

A member of Reserve Infantry Regiment 213, writing home after a long night on listening duty, neatly summed up the experience of the past few days and the mood of the defenders at the end of the fighting of 16 August.

Gefreiter Hinrichsen 9th Company Reserve Infantry Regiment 213 [49]

"Not far off to our front there was a cemetery; graves of our fallen comrades which, due to the advance made by the enemy on 7 June, the day of the great Wijtschate explosions, now found themselves in the area dominated by German and British artillery fire. Time and again a flare soared through the night sky, casting a ghostly light on the white crosses. There was no sign of the enemy. Whenever we saw the crosses our thoughts turned to death. So many dear comrades had already gone. Who would be hit today? Every eye strained to pierce the darkness, because every man knew exactly what was at stake when on sentry duty in the blood-soaked soil of Flanders.

"Gradually night faded into day. Dawn broke. It was 5.30 am and I was just about to crawl over to Unteroffizier Neubauer in his shell hole, when drum fire suddenly crashed down along the line. Now it was a matter of keeping alert, with rifle and hand grenades ready to hand. A short time later, rockets, announcing an attack, soared upwards. The air was full of the howling and crashes of bursting shells. Shrapnel balls showered down on our little nook; we curled up small and stuck it out. Suddenly a heavy shell landed very close. There was a terrible pressure wave. I was sent flying through the air, somersaulting backwards and lost conscience momentarily. When I came round I found myself up to my neck in the stream which ran three metres behind our position.

"I was totally deafened, I ached in every limb and my arm was numb. Summoning up all my energy I crawled back to my position on my stomach and to a scene of utter destruction. A direct hit had come down right in amongst us. I called in a low voice to my friend Neubauer, but I heard nothing in reply. Then I spotted him propped upright in the bushes three metres away. I staggered over to him, but he still did not speak. I pulled him towards me and he fell to the ground next to me as stiff as a log. I looked at him carefully and realised that I was looking at the death mask of the poor lad. It was a quick, easy death. I dragged my fallen comrade to a shell hole and covered him with my groundsheet.[50] Thank heavens, the sentries left and right of me were untouched.

"There was a battle raging off to the right; it looked as though the Tommies were not willing to risk the bog in our area. It was by now broad daylight. I now had to hang on for another eighteen hours, soaked to the skin. My boots were full of water, my coat leaked and everything was dripping. I was shivering and freezing from cold and, following this terrible incident, I could not gather my thoughts together coherently. The day dragged by. Everything I had on was soaked; it had to dry on my body. After an eternity evening drew near and, with it, relief. I hoisted myself out of my shell hole and stretched my stiff limbs. We now had to carry our fallen comrade back to the rear with us. We wrapped him in a ground sheet, which we secured with a large belt. Slowly our platoon made its way back. Carefully and quietly we picked our way along until we arrived at our blockhouse. I reported in to the Leutnant, then we carried on. There could be no question of sleep that night. At long last dawn approached and we dragged our weary frozen limbs into our accommodation. I lay down on a hard bed and fell asleep. I slept and then I dreamt – not of the war, but of love at home and the love of a young woman."

There was a relatively quiet period; then, on 22 August, the offensive was renewed and tanks were used in several places, in particular by the British 11th and 48th Divisions to the north of St Juliaan.

Reserve Leutnant Kindler
Anti-Tank Section 4th Battery Field Artillery Regiment 20 [51] **8**

"It was a fine sunny summer's day. I sat in front of my dugout observing to see if our infantry was calling for defensive fire, when suddenly a runner arrived with an order. 'Command Post, Infantry Regiment 67, 10.05 am, 22.8. To the anti-tank battery. Three tanks have broken through in the area of Infantry Regiment 67. Anti-tank guns to take up fire positions. Signed: Heil [the name of the commander]. The teams were soon on the spot and I could set off with my section, which comprised two guns and two ammunition wagons ... We passed through Beselare which, totally shot up and under heavy fire, presented a dismal sight ... Beyond Beselare the road was almost impassable. Shell hole overlapped shell hole and the same was true left and right of the road. Away from the road the ground was one mass of soft clay, so we picked out way forward as best we could.

"Suddenly I heard yells and shouts behind me. My second gun had tipped into a shell hole and was hanging from the traces almost upside down. I called a halt, but a swift attempt to right the gun failed. So as not to lose any more time, I left the gun commander and crew with the gun, ordering him to follow up as soon as the gun was ready to be moved. I continued with one gun and the two ammunition waggons. Nearby I watched a group of infantrymen hurrying forward, loaded down with boxes of ammunition for their machine guns. They were avoiding the road, because the fire was heaviest there. As I was looking at them a shell landed in their midst. Luckily it was a dud, but the air pressure sent one of them spinning into the air, still holding on to his ammunition box. I assumed that he was seriously injured until I saw him leap to his feet and continue running forwards, twice as fast.

"It became harder to distinguish the line of the road. Only because of the slightly firmer ground and the presence of cobbles strewn around was it possible to follow it. It seemed from the tangle of branches and smashed tree stumps to one side that there had once been a wood there but, apart from that, all was yellow clay, covered in shell holes with all the vegetation destroyed. My gun and the ammunition wagons swayed alarmingly as we passed through the shell holes. I had to slow everything down, in order to avoid the fate which had befallen the gun I had left behind. The way was littered with British dead from the battles of the past few days, when successive attacks and counter-attacks had caused the positions to be pushed backwards and forwards a few hundred metres. At one point my gun ran over the shoulder of a dead man, sending him rolling across the road as though he were still alive.

"The horses were sweating profusely from fear and excitement and, as we tried to cross a large shell hole, the leading horses jumped it, the middle horse, complete with driver, disappeared down into the hole, but the pole horse baulked and had the strength to halt the gun. I had them all unharnessed and was able, using the pole horses alone, to move the gun forward a further one hundred metres. It was impossible to get the gun or the other waggons any further. As I was trying to orientate myself a square black object hove into view to one side at 600 – 800 metres range. 'Half right – Tank!' I ordered then, as soon as it was bracketed, 'Rapid fire!' The ammunition carriers worked flat out to carry sufficient ammunition from the wagon. The rounds were landing right in front of the tank, then I saw a direct hit on the front of the tank. Up until then it had continued to move slowly. Now it slewed to one side and stopped. I checked fire and watched as three men jumped out and raced for cover. At that I sent a few more shots into it and there was no more movement.

"The tank was knocked out. We were so keen and worked up that we had disregarded shells landing all round us. We dived into nearby water and clay-filled craters. Shell splinters whizzed about, sending showers of filthy water over us, but only a direct hit would have been fatal. It was not that we had been located by the artillery, rather more that they were putting down a rolling bombardment in front of their tanks and we were caught up in it. All the time we were still being showered by water. Over everything the sun was shining brightly, but incongruously, on this shattered landscape and exploding shells. In the meantime I had spotted a second tank a few hundred metres to one side. It was located in the remains of a garden or small copse and stood out clearly against the dark background. I immediately brought it under fire but, after about twenty shots, I was told that all the ammunition was used up. The rapid fire had also caused the gun to jam. We had to pull back.

"The middle horses were still stuck in the crater with their heads down. 'Everyone to the horses!' The job which normally would have taken a lot of time and trouble was done in two minutes. Heaving on tails and manes, each with the strength of two, the animals were soon standing up once more on stiff legs; trembling and running with sweat. They could not be harnessed for the time being, so the gunner sitting to the rear led them on reins. We trotted gently back. One gunner and one horse were slightly wounded and several spokes on the wheels of the gun were penetrated or splintered. The gun we had left behind was upright once more, but so badly damaged that it been unable to follow up. The next day the Army Communiqué spoke of several knocked out tanks, one of which was ours."

The experience of the infantry support, or anti-tank batteries, was restricted to only a small proportion of the German artillery units. By far the greater number were condemned to remain in static positions, subject to regular bombardments with gas and counter-battery fire, such as that experienced near Warneton later in the month when a nearby 210 mm howitzer was engaged.

Unteroffizier Löffelbein 3rd Battery Guards Field Artillery Regiment 3 [52] 9

"A British battery opened up on us during streaming sunshine on 24 August. After a few scattered rounds, there was suddenly a series of quickly-fired shells that were right on target. Most unfortunately for us the British brought the entire area of the farm under fire so that we received a share as well. There had already been several casualties around the 210 mm howitzer. One by one the great shells hammered into the house and garden, creeping ever closer to our gun. Some rounds flew over us; others landed on the railway embankment behind us then, with a great crash, one landed right next to our blockhouse, shattering the window and sending clods of earth and splinters of wood flying into our bunker. Suddenly there was another explosion nearby; this time it was a little further away and accompanied by a peculiar metallic clang. I rushed out and my worst fears were confirmed. The second shell had landed right next to our gun.

"I was still taking in the sight of the shattered gun shield, when a brief whizzing sound announced the arrival of the next greetings card. This shell landed in a pile of ammunition, which promptly caught fire and blazed fiercely. To our front I could see the crew of the 210 mm howitzer scattering in all directions. Our gun layer Schulze and Kanonier Bonk were shaken by the arrival of another shell, just as they left the blockhouse. The ammunition began to rattle about and become dangerous. We do what we could to extinguish the flames, but throwing earth over them did not help any more and we did not have the time or a calm situation with which to deal with them, more rounds kept landing all the time. Naturally the telephone link to the battery was destroyed. I could see no alternative, but to follow the example of the men on the 210 mm howitzer. Each of us grabbed what seemed to be important: gun sight, telephones, steel helmets and gas masks, then we doubled away from the position.

"The thick smoke given off by the blazing ammunition provided the best possible signal to enemy aerial observers. Within a few minutes the entire ammunition stock of our gun had been burnt out. If we had left our departure any longer, it is doubtful if any of us would have escaped unscathed, because now it appeared that two enemy batteries had been bringing heavy fire down. The Tommies had brought down drum fire for about four hours and not until about 7.00 pm did it appear that they were satisfied with their work. The firing ceased and, with pain in our hearts, we could return and inspect the damage. Our gun was dragged off to the rear the following day, but I doubt if the damage was repairable. Our blockhouse was completely wrecked and burned out, together with everything which we had not managed to carry off. Of the ammunition, only a few shredded cartridge cases and some unexploded shells remained. The grass was burnt in all directions; the pear tree had half fallen over and was burned. All in all it was a dismal sight. The day had cost the lives of two of the crew of the 210 mm howitzer. The three of us had emerged unscathed. The following day we received a new gun and, with renewed courage but gloomy foreboding, we set about ranging our gun in, digging in once more and clearing all traces of the previous day. However the British did not have another opportunity to send us running, because we were relieved a short time later."

As it drew to a close, August had been nothing but a morale-sapping series of setbacks for the British army as it struggled vainly to make progress across the Geluveld Plateau. On two occasions Crown Prince Rupprecht had noted in his diary the dip in British morale, as revealed by prisoner interrogation, that the failure of the attacks was causing. On 16 August he wrote, 'British prisoners are saying – and this has never been heard before – that they wished that they had shot their own officers who were leading them into the slaughterhouse. They have had enough of this butchery!'[53] then, on 22 August, he recorded the fact that, 'Of the British prisoners who have been brought in during the past few days, the NCOs and men are complaining about the defective leadership of their officers; the officers about the failings of the staff officers. Nobody believes that there is any chance of defeating Germany without American assistance.'[54] During a visit to the 5th Bavarian Infantry Division on 25 August, he was briefed that during recent German counter-attacks, 'the British were hardly defending themselves, whereas earlier they had stood firm – even in the face of enfilade fire. Even officers had been seen with their hands up, kneeling down and surrendering without a fight.'[55]

It is a simple fact that almost always the defence had prevailed during August, but it was paying a high price in casualties to stave off the Allied advance. As the month drew to a close, there was no feeling of exultation; just a type of grim satisfaction that the line was being held. The closing days of the month saw a series of attempts to make progress to the east of St Juliaan, all of which were beaten off with negligible gains. Writing home, a gunner from Reserve Field Artillery Regiment 27 described two days of battle as seen from the gun lines:

"27 August. The British, who have been constantly carrying out local attacks, some of them in strength, against the southern part of the divisional sector [27th Infantry Division] today launched an assault on a grand scale.[56] In an instant, the broad slopes to the front of the enemy were a sea of flame and exploding shells. The crash of the exploding shells fused into one appalling racket like the roar of a monstrous organ. Soon the infantry positions disappeared in smoke and dust. Our batteries joined in at the maximum firing rate possible. Each of our batteries was under fire from one, or more often, several enemy batteries, but the losses amongst the 2nd Battalion were relatively slight and the firing rate of the batteries barely affected.

"Every gunner was aware that each man and gun counted; that the Württemberg artillery in general and Reserve Field Artillery Regiment 27 in particular, had never left their brave comrades in the infantry in the lurch. What did it matter how close the enemy shells rained down, just as long as we met the infantry's calls for defensive fire forward? Our shells hammered down on the enemy and each gun team competed to outshoot the rest. As soon as an attack was beaten off, we cooled the guns then, without further orders, engaged the enemy assembly areas. This went on all day long. We had no idea what was happening forward. We had contact via runners as far as the *KTK*, but all links further forward had been cut. Nevertheless we knew that our brave infantry would hold out; none of the gunners had the slightest doubt about it.

"All the telephone lines were destroyed and attempts to repair them were soon given up as a bad job. We were completely dependent on runners, but everything went very well. The British were not tackling newcomers; they were up against tried and tested fighting soldiers, men of experience from both the Somme and Ypres. Not until the early morning of 28 August when the enemy renewed their artillery bombardment, but lacked the infantry to conduct another attack, did the success of the previous day become clear. The enemy had attacked using enormous quantities of men and materiel, including tanks, gas and aircraft, but no sooner had they penetrated our cratered positions than they were thrown out once more – at the latest during the course of the day. Their casualties were enormous; they had lost a number of tanks and achieved nothing. The attack had gone in along the frontage of the four Württemberg divisions, (from south to north the 27th, 204th, 26th Infantry and 26th Reserve). Everywhere we wiped the floor with the British. No wonder that a sign appeared the following day in one of the British trenches: *We can wait until you Schwabians have gone.* [57]

Crown Prince Rupprecht of Bavaria: Diary Entry 28 August 1917 [58]

"Yesterday's attacks by the British were utterly defeated, thanks to the courageous resistance put up by the troops from Württemberg. However it was not possible to drive the enemy out of the western tip of the Herenthage Wood. But for the time being the attacks against Fourth Army are not expected to die away … "

In fact there was about to be another operational pause. The switch of prime responsibility for the campaign from the British Fifth to the Second Army had already taken place on 25 August following the latest series of British reverses.[59] In retrospect, the attacks which had just been defeated were regarded as minor affairs by the Allies. This was not a view shared by those directly involved, nor was it at all obvious at the end of the month that a period of relative calm was about to descend on the battlefield whilst General Plumer made the preparations for the first of a series of major 'bite and hold' operations, which were to change the course of the battle.

Notes
1. Kriegsarchiv München: Gen Kdo III AK 26/27
2. Missing from this list is the British Guards Division, which attacked just to the north of the Ypres-Torhout railway in the direction of Langemark.
3. Reymann: History Infantry Regiment 62 pp 161-164
4. The British launched no major attacks on 3 August, so this incident probably refers to an attempt to improve positions locally in preparation for a subsequent assault.
5. Christian: History Infantry Regiment 418 pp 64-65
6. Schatz: History Reserve Infantry Regiment 239 p 128
7. Reymann: *op. cit.* p 158
8. Tiessen: History Reserve Infantry Regiment 213 p 530

9. In fact the British 41st Division remained in the line longer than the Germans expected. Vizefeldwebel Pfeil of 1st Company Infantry Regiment 62 captured one of its men in thick fog on 6 August (See Reymann: History Infantry Regiment 62 p 159).
10. Tiessen: *op. cit.* p 531
11. Boldt was transferred to a field hospital in Wevelgem, where he died during 5 August. He had been an outstanding member of Reserve Infantry Regiment 213 and was sadly missed. Leutnant Kurt Boldt is buried in the German cemetery at Menen Block M Grave 2921.
12. Tiessen: *op. cit.* p 532
13. *ibid.* pp 532-533
14. Schulz: History Reserve Infantry Regiment 209 p 204
15. Kronprinz Rupprecht *'Mein Kriegstagebuch' Band II* p 235
16. Mülmann: History Infantry Regiment 140 p 157
17. Theysohn: History Bavarian Field Artillery Regiment 20 pp 84-85
18. *ibid.* pp 85-86
19. Dahlmann: History Reserve Infantry Regiment 27 p 317
20. Kessler: History Reserve Field Artillery Regiment 9 pp 205-206
21. Hülsemann: History Infantry Regiment 84 Vol 4 Nr 1 p 3
22. Pries: History Reserve Infantry Regiment 90 p 222
23. Kriegsarchiv München: Gen Kdo III AK 26
24. *ibid.*
25. *ibid.*
26. The original report noted that this statement was confirmed because machine gun fire was still being heard from this sector as late as 6.45 am.
27. Kriegsarchiv München: Gen Kdo III AK 26
28. *ibid.*
29. *ibid.*
30. Dahlmann: *op. cit.* p 320
31. *ibid.* pp 318 – 319
32. *ibid.* p320
33. There are many references to duds in the German literature. Whilst it is true that manufacturing faults, or errors of drill did produce duds, the swampy morass into which so many shells were fired tended to smother their effect completely and so convey the impression that they had not detonated.
34. Dahlmann: *op. cit.* p 321
35. *ibid.* pp 321-322
36. *ibid.* p 322
37. *ibid.* p 322
38. This is a considerable exaggeration. The British 18th Division, complete, was involved, as was 74 Brigade of 25th Division. This hardly amounts to 'several divisions'.
39. Schwerin: History Reserve Infantry Regiment 261 pp 148-149
40. Kronprinz Rupprecht: *op. cit.* p 247-248
41. Heinicke: History Reserve Infantry Regiment 263 pp 154 – 155
42. *ibid.* pp 149 – 151
43. Soldan : History Infantry Regiment 184 p 57
44. Hülsemann: *op. cit.* Vol 4 Nr 2 pp 10-11

45. The full title of the regiment was Infantry Regiment 84 von Manstein (Schleswig) Nr. 84: hence '*Manstein* spirit' and '*Mansteiners*'.
46. Hülsemann: *op.cit.* Vol 5 p 35-36
47. *ibid.* p 42
48. *ibid.* p 44
49. Tiessen: *op.cit.* pp 537-538. Gefreiter Hans Hinrichsen, promoted unteroffizier as a result of his performance in Flanders, did not live long in his new rank. He was killed on 25 October 1917 near Hulluch and is buried at the German cemetery in Carvin Block 5 Grave 1050.
50. Unteroffizier Richard Neubauer is buried in the German cemetery at Menen Block M Grave 1241.
51. Benary: History Field Artillery Regiment 20 pp 307-308
52. Collenberg: History Guards Field Artillery Regiment 3 pp 294-295
53. Kronprinz Rupprecht: *op.cit.* p 246
54. *ibid.* p 248
55. *ibid.* p 249
56. This refers to the attacks launched by the British XVIII Corps, involving 144 and 145 Brigades of 48th Division and 32 Brigade of 11th Division, which yielded only trivial results at high cost.
57. Moser: *Die Württemberger im Weltkrieg* pp 629-630
58. Kronprinz Rupprecht: *op. cit.* p 251
59. Naturally Fifth Army and the French forces on its left flank continued to be involved with operations throughout the remainder of the battle.

CHAPTER FOUR

September 1917

There might not have been any major operations in the early days of September, but locally opposing units manoeuvred for positions and took advantage of the period of dry weather to improve their positions in the muddy shell holes which made up the forward battle area, to dominate No Man's Land as far as possible and to continue to snatch prisoners. 24th Infantry Division, for example, which had been operating to the south east of Hollebeke since mid August, was called upon to carry out a raid on 1 September. It was the subject of a letter home a few days later.

Gefreiter Linke 6th Company Infantry Regiment 133 [1] **1**

" ... Once more I found myself in the rear area practising for a raid. What a patrol action that was – eighty eight men strong! But, as a result, I am now wearing a black and white ribbon. This is how it went: We were driven forward in trucks. About 10.00 pm we arrived forward and we set off immediately, just as we had practised and, in accordance with the old song, 'Quietly, really quietly ...' we advanced, one behind the other, one column to the right and the other about one hundred metres to the left. Everything was quiet, just like every other night. We lay down about sixty metres from the enemy trenches. At exactly 11.00 pm our artillery and mortars opened up suddenly and our machine guns joined in too. (It was a crazy racket!), even though the gun fire was clearly coming down behind the enemy front line trench!

"At the same moment the assault groups launched forward at the enemy trenches. In the shock, about forty of them were killed, a great many wounded were lying around and we captured eleven prisoners. These poor lads had been just about to be relieved; they had all their kit and equipment hanging on them. I myself manned a liaison post forward of the enemy trenches, so that everyone would find their way back. Once they were all on their way back, an Unteroffizier and I recovered a severely wounded man who had been hanging on the British wire and brought him back.

"We had two men missing, two seriously wounded and fifteen lightly wounded. Of course, this was because as soon as the Tommies realised what was happening, they called on their artillery (it seems to work better for them than it does for us!!) and we were hit hard by defensive fire as we pulled back. Luckily we arrived at our *KTK*. We then conducted our

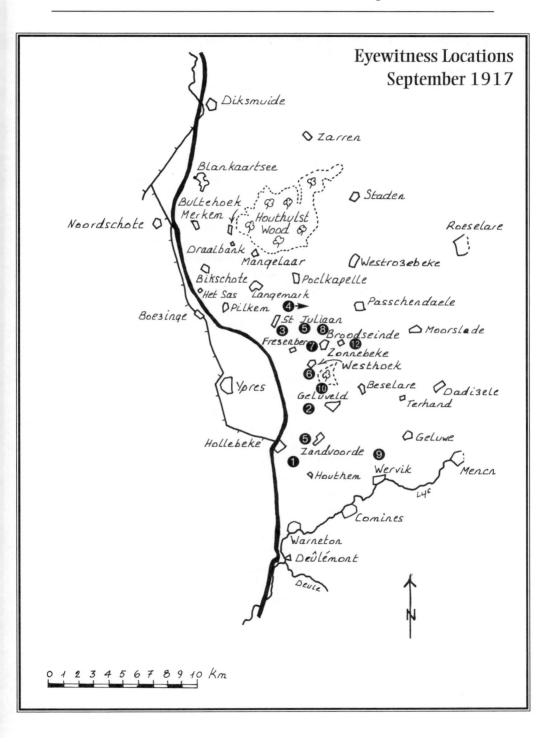

Eyewitness Locations
September 1917

prisoners to the regimental headquarters, where we were addressed by the regimental commander. There was tea and rum for everyone (including the prisoners!) and then it was back in the trucks to Wervik. This afternoon there was a big parade in front of our divisional commander, Hammer, who handed out various medals. I got the Iron Cross Second Class."

Typical of many other ground-holding formations, 9th Reserve Division spent a protracted period in the line near Ypres during the summer of 1917, latterly in and around the woods west of Veldhoek and south of the Ypres – Menen road. By early September the regiments had been in the line for some weeks and the strain was beginning to tell. This report could have come from any one of a large number of the regiments of Groups Ypres or Wijtschate. Even if there had been an inexhaustible supply of fresh divisions to replace those who had spent many days in the line, there was simply no way around the limited railway capacity leading north into Flanders. Ammunition, which was being consumed in prodigious quantities, had to take priority and the divisions *in situ* simply had to go on enduring the conditions until severe battle casualties made their replacement imperative.

Report on the Fighting Ability of Reserve Infantry Regiment 19 dated 4 September 1917 [2]

"There has been a reduction of the fighting ability of the troops as a result of the numerous gastro-intestinal illnesses which have, without exception, affected every man stationed in the trenches. During the past eleven days five officers and 165 men have been evacuated to hospital through this cause. In addition a further forty have been given medicine and duties. These gastro-intestinal illnesses are accompanied by fever, headaches and nausea. The cause is the wet conditions in the craters and dugouts and the stink of rotting corpses which is poisoning the air. Despite clearance of the area many corpses must be concealed in the mud and water-filled craters."

Despite having a similar sick list, their left hand neighbour, Infantry Regiment 395, was kept constantly occupied through the first two weeks of September. Their war diary is full of descriptions of working parties, heavy bombardments, patrol activity and beating off British probing raids. At 9.30 pm on 9 September, for example, there was a British raid in about half company strength against a forward sap. A swift counter-attack by their 11th and 12th Companies not only retook the lost sap, but recovered the body of a dead officer of '14th Battalion Royal Sussex Regiment' [sic][3]. Field Artillery Regiment 20, which was in the direct support role of the division, repeatedly sent batteries and observer groups forward during these days to come to the aid of the hard-pressed infantry.

Offizierstellvertreter Preuß Field Artillery Regiment 20 [4] **2**

"Acting as an observation officer, accompanied by an Unteroffizier and a gunner, equipped with field binoculars on a stand and sufficient rations for three days, I set off from the horse lines at 3.00 am, in order to be in the area of the support trenches manned by 11th Company Infantry Regiment 395 before day break ... Apart from the usual harassing fire we had no trouble reaching the place, where the relief took place very swiftly. Telephones and carrier pigeons were available for passing messages and the link to the [artillery group] was working. As soon as a fault developed someone ran along the line of the cable to repair it. That evening there was obvious activity in the enemy trenches, cables was being run to the rear and a group of staff officers popped up on the parapet of the enemy trench from time to time. It was clear from this activity that something was being planned for the next few days.

"During the night the infantry brought food for the company forward in [insulated] hay boxes on their backs. After midnight an intense drum fire began and continued until dawn. Thinking that all signs of life and resistance in the German trenches had thereby been destroyed, the enemy launched an extremely violent attack. Simultaneously enemy airmen launched attacks from the air. However, rifle and machine gun fire hammered into the attacking troops, tearing great holes in the ranks of the enemy. All available forces were used for the defence. Because the telephone line to Group was cut, I formed a platoon from my people and a few infantrymen. Distributed amongst the shell holes, we kept up a lively rate of fire against excellent targets and thus helped to prevent the enemy from taking any more ground. We took the rifles and ammunition from wounded infantrymen. That evening we were relieved and headed back to the battery position."

Preuß was lucky to survive his tour of duty unscathed. On 14 September Landwehr Leutnant Döbert of 6th Battery was killed by enemy shelling[5] and the following day Oberleutnant Stier, its commander, together with several junior ranks, was wounded. It was not just the infantry that was suffering as the weight of the bombardment increased inexorably.

In the middle of the month there were various changes in deployments and command and control arrangements. On 10/11 September 2nd Guards Reserve Division took over from 27th Infantry Division from Württemberg, which had fought so well at the end of August. The division deployed with all three regiments in a line. Its right [northern] junction with 36th Infantry Division was located at the Sebastopol crossroads, about one kilometre east of St Juliaan. It manned its sector in the sequence north to south of Reserve Infantry Regiment 91, Reserve Infantry Regiment 15 and Reserve Infantry Regiment 77. Despite the relatively dryer weather in September, the positions were in a terrible state as the battalions moved forward; it had been beyond the capacity of the exhausted Württembergers to make any significant improvements.

Reserve Leutnant Adolf Kümmel Reserve Infantry Regiment 91 [63]

"We reached the battle zone after a march of about one hour. The guides that the Württembergers had arranged were at the appointed place. Just as so often before, the companies advanced in single file, avoiding enemy fire wherever possible and plodding on through the crater field, which was at least one kilometre deep. The monotony of the battle zone made it extremely difficult in the dark to maintain direction. The occasional flare fired right forward in the front line was only of marginal assistance in this task. The only aids to orientation for the guides were such things as characteristic groups of closely-packed craters, a smashed concrete blockhouse, the ruins of an abandoned battery position or the wreck of a shot-down aircraft.

"There were frequent halts, either because the guides were unsure where they were, or because the columns had become separated due to the need to double march through locations which were under particularly heavy fire. Finally, after moving for hours through this wasteland and having overcome unspeakable difficulties, the troops ended up somewhere in the front line. We were still not at our objective; rather it was a case of moving laterally, sometimes for several hundred metres, until we reached the sector of the companies we had come to relieve, or had linked up with the flanking units. Whilst doing this we had to be extremely careful not to make any noticeable noise and avoid giving loud words of command. We did not want to attract the attention of the enemy, or we should have been on the receiving end of rapid machine gun fire, which would have made the relief even more difficult …

"Our Württemberg comrades were shadowy figures. We exchanged a few words and they melted into the darkness. What now? One by one, or in pairs, we climbed into craters, where the feeling was that for the time being we had been abandoned. We newcomers had many unanswered questions. Where are our neighbours? Where exactly is the enemy? We longed for dawn, so that we could survey our surroundings with our small trench periscopes. There was no question of sleep. We tried, as far as possible, to organise our craters for defence. With our rifles immediately to hand, we began to dig crawl trenches to nearby craters. Again and again, startled by an odd noise, we dropped our spades, grabbed our rifles and stared to our front. Gradually we became accustomed to the fact that we had no barbed wire obstacle to our front and that within the company there was as good as no depth to the position."

Further to the rear, on 14 September, the 236th Division replaced 3rd Reserve Division as the *Eingreif* division covering the Passchendaele sector, carrying out rehearsals and completing the necessary reconnaissance of its most probable counter-stroke tasks. Meanwhile the bombardment continued to rain down and the enemy probed the forward positions.

Reserve Leutnant Adolf Kümmel Reserve Infantry Regiment 91 [7] **4**

"At 4.00 am [14 September], following a short, sharp bombardment on the positions of our right hand neighbours (Infantry Regiment 175), the British launched a raid, which succeeded in penetrating the forward positions and establishing a nest of resistance in the front line. Our 1st Company drove them off. Of twelve members of the British 58th [*sic*] division[8] three men, including a sergeant, were captured. The remainder were killed in hand to hand fighting. During the afternoon from 4.00 pm to 8.00 pm and assisted by aerial observers, the British artillery brought down between one hundred and two hundred 240 mm shells against the concrete pillbox which housed the *KTK*. With each explosion the pillbox swayed like a ship on a choppy sea.

"There were far too many occupants for such a small structure but, because of its prominent location on high ground, they could not move away by day. It was, of course, impossible for the commander and his staff to remain there once the pillbox had been recognised as a command post, so the regiment ordered it to be moved to the hill at point 706.[9] The 2nd Company was withdrawn from the front line and went into reserve near the new command post. Their sub-sector was filled in by 1st and 3rd Companies and the 9th Company was moved from the *Flandern II Stellung* [Flanders II Position] and moved into splinter-proof blockhouses in Goudberg, 400 metres west of the regimental command post in Mosselmarkt. These moves produced greater depth within the regimental sector and ensured a swifter response if a counter-attack had to be launched."

Hauptmann Schwilden 3rd Battalion Reserve Infantry Regiment 15 [10] **4**

"Although the artillery fire was already coming down very heavily and causing casualties during the night 17/18 September when we arrived in Sector C [Gravenstafel area], during the coming days and nights it increased constantly in intensity. All the blockhouses and pillboxes were engaged systematically. Prior to 20 September five were destroyed by direct hits and, in addition, the British artillery kept bringing down huge concentrations of fire along the entire front line and the rear areas. In the early morning they would start slowly, then build up to drum fire during the space of an hour. We could easily deduce that an infantry assault would not be long in coming. The companies were put on the highest state of alert and reminded that it was their bounden duty to hold their forward positions in the event of an attack, regardless of what might transpire. They were also directed to put out a line of listening posts during the night of 19/20 September, to prevent them from being surprised."

Reserve Leutnant Metzing
3rd Machine Gun Company Reserve Infantry Regiment 19 [11] **5**

"Once the relief of the machine gun companies was complete during the night 13/14 September, I occupied machine gun posts 86 and 87 in the *Drossel* [Thrush] Position.[12] From 15 September onwards there was a great deal of fire from heavy calibre guns (up to 280 mm) on all the positions within the battle area. The *Drossel* received on average 500 – 600 shells per day, but there were no direct hits. During the evening of 19 September this was widened to include bombardment with gas and flame and the firing continued throughout the night.

With unmistakeable signs multiplying that the relative quiet of the past two weeks was about to come to an abrupt end, on 19 September command of Group Ypres passed from III Bavarian Army Corps to the Guard Corps. The change of command came in the nick of time because, during the early hours of 20 September, drum fire of ludicrous violence crashed down all along the lines, concentrating particularly on the heights from Passchendaele, south through Zonnebeke and Geluveld. The British artillery had been preparing for this moment ever since command had shifted from Fifth to Second Army. Thanks to an extraordinary expenditure of labour, the guns were correctly positioned and supplied with immense quantities of ammunition, spare barrels and other equipment.

With the first of a series of offensive operations imminent, at the appointed time fire was brought down with great accuracy all along the frontage of the attack.

Reserve Leutnant Hesse
Commander 10th Company Reserve Infantry Regiment 77 [13] **4**

"All hell broke loose. Only by bawling at the tops of our voices at one another could we make ourselves understood. The enemy also fired gas and incendiary mortar bombs of the largest calibre. My batman had prepared a sandwich for me, despite the overwhelming bombardment and, in order to keep it as clean as possible from the constantly falling showers of filth, I had to keep it covered with my other hand. Punctually at 6.00 am the artillery fire began to fall once more. It was an absolute torrent of fire, which was completely outside my accustomed experience."

Writing later, an eyewitness with Infantry Regiment 459 recorded,

"Heavy shell fire rained down on Passchendaele. Fire was coming down all round a large crucifix – *Christ covered in filth* – which stood in the middle of the main street. An ammunition column was speeding past it at a gallop. An enemy aircraft dived down on our little group, like a bird of prey; lead from its machine guns spattered against the walls and splintered trees. *Take cover!* But then, with a great howl, a huge shell crashed down into the remains of the house behind us. Pillars of earth and clouds of smoke shot up in the air – then down came a cascade of splinters and stones – *Further! Further!* – ducking low, our faces bathed in sweat, we raced on.

"There was feverish activity in the regimental command post. Runners arrived to collect orders; flare signals were fired; message dogs were despatched; a German infantry cooperation aircraft made contact. A captured Tommy was being questioned. Observation posts reported in, reports were being written, orders prepared and maps compared. Brumm – brumm – brumm droned the loudspeaker, constantly – to begin with anyway, until all the telephone lines were cut. Then the runners had to take over. *Runners!* What responsibility, what devotion to duty, what silent, sacrificial, gallantry that word covers!" [14]

Reserve Leutnant Metzing
3rd Machine Gun Company Reserve Infantry Regiment 19 [15] **5**

Drum fire came down about 5.00 am on 20 September. About 5.45am some men arrived from the 3rd and 4th Companies with the news that the front line had been overrun and the enemy was in *Westfalenwald* [Westphalia Wood – about 400 metres west of the *Drossel*]. The rate of firing increased once more: flame rounds. There was so much smoke that it was impossible to see more than two metres. Burning oil fell on the clothing of the machine gunners and the entire blockhouse was full of smoke. I sent the riflemen into cover, retaining only one machine gun, which was in position at the north entrance. Towards 6.30 am visibility improved and lines of British infantry could be seen advancing towards the northern part of *Amselwald* [Blackbird Wood – about 250 metres north of the *Drossel*]. The machine gun opened fire; the line of infantrymen came to a halt, ran back and made as if to dig in along a sunken road facing the *Drossel*. Sustained machine gun fire forced them to retreat. The majority were shot down; only about one third made it back.

"The enemy were then reinforced and began once more to conduct an advance from strongpoint to strongpoint towards the northern corner of *Amselwald* in the area of Reserve Infantry Regiment 6. We engaged them from every one of our positions. From the two platoons involved, only about ten survived. That would have been about 10.00 am. All firing died away. The visibility was very good. Individual enemy infantrymen were picked off with our pattern 98 rifles. The machine gun engaged enemy reinforcements and carrying parties in the Infantry Regiment 395 area [to the north] at ranges out to 2,000 metres with considerable success. This continued throughout the day. At about 3.00 pm an enemy machine gun crew took up a position at the northeast corner of *Westfalenwald*. We poured sustained machine gun fire onto this point, forcing the gunners to run and we shot almost all of them down.

Reserve Leutnant Kotthoff
1st Machine Gun Company Reserve Infantry Regiment 77 [16] **5**

"It was 1.00 am [20 September]. Silently we set off [to relieve the 2nd Machine Gun Company]. The thunder of the barrage and the flashes of the guns showed us the way. We soon reached the battle area. Howling and whistling the heavy shells roared overhead, searching out their targets with great crashes. On and on we marched until we reached Zonnebeke, where the ruined houses showed us that this was once a flourishing place. Now there was nothing but death. Rotting, stinking horses were sprawled all over the roads and wagons simply drove over them. On we continued, turning right onto a country lane.

"We were still five kilometres from the front and already the country-side was one massive crater field. We picked our way carefully around the shell holes. Many men fell in to them but luckily, after going wrong once or twice, we arrived at the Red House. This was, in fact, a house, reinforced heavily with concrete. It has three rooms and is located on a crest. We entered the darkened space and 2nd Company exited. We were delighted to have the terrible journey behind us and began to settle in. During the night it was relatively quiet, but with daybreak things began to get much more lively; our blockhouse coming under heavy, direct aimed fire. Round after round landed and the entire building trembled and heaved. We sat it out in silence, wondering when our mousetrap would be hit. Even a medium calibre shell, if it hit us in a vulnerable spot, would be sufficient to finish us off.

"The entire day passed in this way. During the night there were heavy concentrations of fire then, during the early hours, extraordinarily heavy artillery fire which lasted in undiminished strength all day came down. When would the shell which was intended for us arrive? I looked up at the ceiling with concern. It hung above like a nightmare. With great care, I forced a sandwich down, but I had no appetite. Their senses dulled, my men stared glassily into the middle distance, their cigarettes smouldering. I, too, was smoking in an attempt to keep control of my nerves. We were surrounded by crashes, explosions and an unbelievable racket as though we were in the midst of Hell.

"Hold on! 'I just wish that it were evening,' said one man. The minutes dragged by. Almost every minute we were looking at our watches; but the day just would not end, nor the fire slacken. Suddenly there was a dull thud! A powerful quake ran through the structure and concrete fell from the roof. Rigid with fear I looked up. 'Lord, have mercy on my people!' All turned out well. The shell had impacted on the front wall of the blockhouse and the concrete had withstood the shock. We all breathed a sigh of relief … We sat and made feeble jokes. 'The Tommies cannot wreck this place,' said one man. 'No,' cracked another, 'but I do think that they are making an attempt on our lives!'

As far as the defence was concerned, any form of communications which might have survived the preliminary bombardment was now destroyed or unusable. *KTKs* had no means of contacting *BTKs* and reserves could only be committed through guesswork. Eventually, at 8.25 am, regimental headquarters of Infantry Regiment 395, part of the 9th Reserve Division, which was operating to the south of the Ypres-Menen road, received information, carried by a message dog from the *BTK* and timed at 7.40 am: *Continuous fire on the readiness troops, coupled with heavy machine gun fire. Fire can be heard all along the front.* A little later it became clear that a major effort was being made to advance along the line of the road and that the enemy had already made significant progress.[17]

Quite apart from the power of the British artillery fire and the strength of the assaulting infantry, which would probably have been decisive in any case, the three week period of relative calm had lured the defence into a false sense of security. Holding the vital sector along the Hanebeek forward of Polygon Wood and Zonnebeke was the 121st Infantry Division – and it had been in the line for a month at that point. It had suffered heavily in local attacks on 22 August and from serious bombardments on 23 and 27 August. For the first few days of its tour of duty, it had deployed Reserve Infantry Regiment 56 left forward and Infantry Regiment 60 right forward. Now, due to losses, it had to send forward elements of Reserve Infantry Regiment 7, which had been in the divisional *Eingreif* role near the Keiberg up until then, to occupy a central sector. As the days went by, this constant exposure to aerial attack and shelling, coupled with the squalor of occupying muddy craters for days on end with only poor rations to eat, took a considerable toll on the fighting efficiency of the formation.

Gefreiter Johann Müller 2nd Battalion Infantry Regiment 60 [18] **6**

"I have been right in the thick of it for the past two days. I am with the battalion staff in the *Rumpelkammer* [a large concrete pillbox]. This is virtually the only blockhouse which is still in one piece. The constant explosion of heavy shells make it shake like a fourth class carriage! As long as one does not land directly on it, it seems all right. But what a state the area is in! – especially Zonnebeke. It is only the basalt building blocks, trees, beams and tiles which bear witness to the fact that there was once a road and a village here. Then the whole area is always shrouded in dust and smoke. And the craters here are five to six metres in diameter; one after the other; some deeper than others. Torn up railway tracks and sleepers, parts of the wrecked embankment, wagons from the narrow gauge railway piled up higgledy-piggledy: it is scene of utter confusion and it is hardly possible to pick a way through it, even by day.

"When you see the position, you would think it almost impossible to be able to get through such a desolate crater field. The shelling never ceases. Yesterday an enemy aircraft circled over us, directing fire on our blockhouse. The British fired over 300 shells at us and we thought the whole thing would collapse on us at any moment. The companies, including the officers, spend the whole time in the open, in shell holes. Normal command is impossible. Everyone has to huddle down in a crater, stay hidden and do what his neighbour does. The word 'Position' exists only on paper. Throughout the night the shells continue to rain down. But the ground is boggy, so the risk from splinters is not very great.

"Only in the morning does the shelling ease up. Then the stretcher-bearers go out with Red Cross flags and collect the wounded. When the Red Cross is shown, there is no firing from either side. The way the positions are entangled can be seen from the fact that our stretcherbearers bring in masses of British wounded and the other way round. Apart from that, nobody dares show his face by day. If he does, he brings all the artillery down around his neck. But when I see the calm way the men move around under fire, I just marvel at it; that is particularly true for the ration carriers."

By the end of August, Infantry Regiment 60 had already suffered 687 casualties, twice the number suffered by the other two regiments put together.[19] It ought to have been relieved without further delay, but the decision was to keep it in the line and efforts were made to reinforce it in various ways. The sick list lengthened and the casualties continued to mount, especially when the *Rumpelkammer* was destroyed. It was wrecked by several direct hits in quick succession, then a direct hit by a 380 mm shell on a house occupied by members of 4th Company killed eighteen and wounded forty one men. Rescuers pulled out twenty five men, suffering from light wounds or shell shock, but eighteen could not be recovered.

It is small wonder, therefore, that having beaten off a trench raid on 12 September and having been subjected to an extraordinary weight of fire for a six day period, the forward companies of Infantry Regiment 60 were down to a mere thirty to forty dazed men when they were assaulted by units of the British 9th Division on the morning of 20 September. The full weight of the assault fell on the battered remnants of 6th, 7th and 8th Companies occupying craters right forward. The remainder of the regiment was manning the *Wilhelm Stellung*, Zonnebeke and the *Flandern-I Stellung*, with the 1st Battalion ready to intervene in the local *Eingreif* role in the event of an attack.

Naturally, although it is known that the handful of men in forward positions defended their craters gallantly, they were brushed aside in the first rush and the *Wilhelm Stellung* swiftly went the same way. In accordance with their orders, 1st and 2nd Companies Infantry Regiment 60 joined up with 11th Company in Zonnebeke. The sub-units of 1st Battalion, received final instructions and immediately began to move forward to counter-attack due west to the north of the Ypres-Roeselare railway. What happened next was one of the first indications that the British had discovered a counter to the tried and trusted tactics of flexible defence.

Leutnant Vonalt Infantry Regiment 60 [20] 7

"We doubled forward; the companies receiving their orders at the regimental command post. My platoon advanced on the railway embankment to the right of Zonnebeke and soon we had no contact to our right or left. The whole area had been drenched with gas and visibility was down to less than thirty metres. The gas masks were a real handicap, so we just stuck the breathing tubes in our mouths, held our noses and pressed on. The British realised that we were counter-attacking and brought down appalling drum fire on us.[21] Only able to move in short bounds, we made slow progress forward, then it became quite impossible. We remained lying in cover, crawling about in an attempt to avoid the worst of the fire.

"We took heavy casualties. Two men of my platoon were killed and five wounded. We went and took cover in a cellar. Two men remained outside, observing. We knew that it would only take one light calibre shell landing on the rubble which covered the cellar to collapse the roof; we just hoped that it would not happen. Only after I had hung on for a full two hours outside did I seek cover in the cellar and settled down next to the stove. It was about 11.00 am when events caught up with us. There was a dreadful crash and the whirr of splinters and nose cap, then piles of stones and debris rained down. The shell had crashed down into the cellar the far side of the stove and everyone on that side was either killed or seriously wounded. I emerged with two other men and we looked around immediately for the two observers, who were outside manning a crater, so that we could begin the rescue of the others.

"It was all in vain. The screaming and moaning quickly grew quieter and we were only able to recover two men who had bled to death. Five men, two rifles and a pistol was all we could muster – what a fighting force! Moving from cover to cover, we made our way through the artillery fire from this place to a pillbox we could see further to the left. On the way we equipped ourselves with rifles and hand grenades taken from dead men. The pillbox was jammed with soldiers; several companies of different regiments were all represented. Great was our joy when we came across our company commander, Leutnant Schreyer, and one of our runners. We were allowed into the pillbox, but we had to stand by the front wall, which was already badly damaged.

"It was a case of out of the frying pan into the fire! Our pillbox was engaged systematically with super-heavy shells. Every time that one of these shells landed nearby the whole pillbox shook alarmingly. We were safe from splinters here, but it was questionable if the front wall would survive a second direct hit. Everybody kept calm – officers and men – but all were thinking about what could happen; then it did. About 2.00 pm there was an almighty crash as a shell impacted on the forward wall, piercing it and scabbing off large chunks of concrete. Thank heavens we all escaped with bruising. This hit left a gaping hole in the pillbox and nobody wanted to stay there any longer. We exited hurriedly and moved away forwards to escape the fire. We soon came under small arms fire at a range of 300 metres. Because we were not a formed group, it was pointless to try to advance any further, so we all took cover in the shell holes."

Just to the south, the situation was very similar in the sector of the Bavarian Ersatz Division, which straddled the Ypres-Menen road holding the woods to the west of Veldhoek and forward of the *Albrecht Stellung* and the *Wilhelm Stellung*. Once more, this division had been in the line from 25 August. They were huddled and packed tight into clusters of blockhouses and pill boxes, which lacked the most basic of amenities and whose protective capacity was dubious.[22] Once more, increasing losses forced the division to deploy all its regiments forward: Bavarian Reserve Infantry Regiment 15 right, Bavarian Reserve Infantry Regiment 4 in the centre and Bavarian Ersatz Infantry Regiment 28 in the south, maintaining a junction point with the 9th Reserve Division. Worn down by the bombardment and through clashes with raiding parties launched forward repeatedly to test the defences, the shattered remnants of the forward companies were largely holding a series of shell-hole positions, when two hours of drum fire of extraordinary violence was followed by wave after wave of assaulting troops from the 1st Australian Division north of the Ypres-Menen road and the 23rd British Division to the south of it.

There are very few surviving accounts from eyewitnesses in the forward companies; all were overwhelmed in the first rush, but sounds of machine gun fire were still being heard coming from the *Albrecht Stellung* at 8.30 am. The line was then overrun swiftly and it is fairly certain that by 9.00 am it was in Allied hands and that other waves were moving through to advance on the *Wilhelm Stellung*.

Unteroffizier Ludwig Schmidt
10th Company Bavarian Ersatz Infantry Regiment 28 [23] **2**

"On 20 September 10th Coy was located in the *Wilhelm Stellung*. Already the previous day we had had the feeling that something was in the air and, by 8.00 am, we received a report from battalion that the British had attacked and had seized our front line. Our company commander, Reserve Leutnant Lücking, despatched 1 Platoon under Reserve Leutnant Remy forward to reinforce the forward positions. He only got four hundred metres, before he was forced to seek cover from the British fire in a small pillbox. That was his undoing. 2 and 3 Platoons deployed left and right of the [Ypres-Menen] road. Together with other members of 2 Platoon I took cover in a ruined house, whose timbers and ruined walls offered some protection from view and splinters.

"Towards 9.00 am, British soldiers, advancing from Herenthage Park onto a small rise, were so clearly silhouetted that every one of the defenders was able to draw a bead on them. We shot as rapidly as we could and held them off for a time. They made attempts to move round to our left and right, but we kept them under fire. Unfortunately we were not supported by the machine gun which had been deployed in the company sector to our right. That was a regrettable fact. Our company, under Leutnant Lücking, held out until 1.00 pm. When the British could not get forward, an aircraft flew very low, directing the artillery fire, which then intensified. We still continued to hold. At that the British fired smoke bombs and smoked off the entire area. At first we thought that it was gas. There was a wall of smoke twenty metres to our front.

"We could no longer see to shoot then, suddenly, emerging out of the smoke, were swarms of British soldiers with fixed bayonets. For us it was all over. The few of us had no chance of resisting an assault at that range against such numbers. It was a matter of hands up, drop equipment and throw away ammunition. My pockets were still full of bullets. In consequence, when a British soldier searched me, he hit me in the groin with his rifle butt. I was relieved that nothing worse happened to me. Our main concern was to escape from the clutches of these drunken British soldiers as soon as possible.[24] I cannot express in words my own thoughts at that time. I stood and watched as a British soldier spun round and shot one of our comrades in the back as he made his way to the rear.

"As we passed our own front line, we saw that the British positions were crammed with reserves. They lay there shoulder to shoulder, waiting to advance. We were collected together by an aid post, then led further back to a holding cage. The following day we were moved to a transit camp."

The 16th Bavarian Infantry Division was located in rear of the Bavarian Ersatz Infantry Division forward of Oosthoek and Terhand in the *Eingreif* role. In accordance with contingency plan *Näher heran* [Get Closer], its regiments were brought to readiness at 5.15 am.[25] At 9.00 am on 20 September, Bavarian Infantry Regiment 11 was ordered forward to conduct battalion counter-strokes against the Polygon Wood – Herenthage Chateau sector to eject the enemy from the *Wilhelm Stellung* and to restore the old front line and so provide some relief for the hard-pressed Bavarian Ersatz Infantry Division. H Hour for the first of these operations was to be 11.30 am and the battalions set off immediately. None of them achieved a thing. Arriving level with Polygon Wood, the companies of the 3rd Battalion were torn apart by the British defensive barrage. Having suffered appalling casualties, the survivors took cover wherever it could be found. The advance of the 1st and 2nd Battalions to a start line came to a shuddering, bloody halt during the afternoon near Polderhoek, where the remnants of the companies attempted to shelter from the torrent of shell fire in scattered craters.

"Despite the immense difficulties, orders arrived for an assault to be launched by these two battalions at 7.00 pm. It was completely out of the question. An attempt was made to move forward; it petered out in 150 metres and the shattered remains of the battalions spent the next night huddled in a few battered pill boxes, or out in the open. They had suffered casualties of seventy five percent and achieved nothing whatsoever.[26] A little to the north, the battalions of Bavarian Reserve Infantry Regiment 21 also moved forward, being hammered constantly by artillery fire.

Despite all efforts, lack of any friendly artillery support, raging British barrage fire and casualties which were mounting alarmingly, meant that the attacks simply ground to a halt. Its 2nd Battalion made the most progress, penetrating into Polygon Wood, but being completely unable to traverse it and reach its western edge.[27] 16th Bavarian Infantry Division was a high quality formation, but all the skill and dash in the world stood no chance in the face of the torrent of fire the British artillery could bring to bear at the critical points.

Further to the north, a counter-attack was launched by Infantry Regiment 459, in position behind 2nd Guards Reserve Division, which despite the fact that there had been deep penetrations of its sector in places, continued to fight on throughout the day. Advancing forward from the Gravenstafel area, it was subjected to a storm of artillery and machine gun fire and was brought to a standstill, before it had had a chance to make any worthwhile progress at all. The 1st and 2nd Battalions carried the weight of the attack, but the men of its 3rd Battalion, who were not directly involved, nevertheless passed a chaotic day, before being committed forward as reinforcements that evening.

Leutnant Spahn 3rd Battalion Infantry Regiment 459 [28] **4**

"At 4.00 am we received the order, *Immediate readiness! Advance in assault order!* Half an hour later the battalion arrived in the assembly area to the north of Moorslede. On the way we were greeted by the first shrapnel rounds. For this we had an airman to thank. In Flanders they formed an absolute aerial plague ... The division [236th Infantry Division] then moved forward to launch a counter-attack. The wildest rumours were flying in all directions: *Regiments wiped out! The British have broken through! Very heavy losses!* Our infantry assault battery rattled past, complete with ammunition column. That was a beautiful sight. The infantry advanced in long single files stretching away forward. The numerous hedgerows offered good concealment from view, which was just as well; the skies were full of observation balloons.

"A direct hit in a farmyard killed or wounded our complete signals section. Instead of taking up a position in the open, they had fallen for the old mistake and sought cover in a building by the road. The 1st and 2nd Battalions deployed into position, occupying craters in the front line west of Passchendaele and the 3rd Battalion was in reserve to the right rear. Because of the smoke it was impossible to make out the crests to our front. The battalion pressed on to the *Flandern-II-Stellung*. At 4 o'clock it was to receive its orders for the attack in Mosselmarkt.

"Taking a runner with me I raced off and had the great pleasure of repeating the route up the wobbly mud-covered steps. Behind a huge blockhouse sat the battalion orderly officers at a table writing. A shell splinter landing on the table tore my muddy map and the battalion commander burnt a finger on it. The counter-attack was fixed for 5.30 pm. Too late! The enemy had already broken in during the morning. I cannot provide any accurate information about the very slight success of the attack launched by Reserve Infantry Regiments 91, 77 and 15.

"Our 1st and 2nd Battalions had ejected the enemy out of the *Flandern-I-Stellung* and thrown them back across the Hanebeek. The 3rd Battalion was to remain initially in the *Flandern-II-Stellung* as reserve to Reserve Infantry Regiment 91 and was to move in thirty minutes. My return was a journey through hell. I hardly know how I managed to leap from crater to crater and eventually regain my shell crater. The artillery battle intensified, but I had the distinct feeling that our artillery was holding back.[29] [On my return] I fell asleep. When I awoke it was pitch black. The battalion was to move left and go into support behind Reserve Infantry Regiment 77. *Leutnant Spahn is to link up with the BTK*

"The question was: who was going to provide me with directions to the *BTK*? I certainly had a map, but the area was utterly confusing and it was completely dark. Orientation was going to be a major issue! By chance I came across a man from Reserve Infantry Regiment 15 and I went along with him. We reached his regimental *BTK*, but the commander, Hauptmann von Widekind, could provide me neither with information nor an escort, but he did ply me with two glasses of schnaps. He had no idea about the situation to the front, but everything seemed to be in total confusion.

"I headed off on a compass bearing. It was unforgivable to have set off without anyone to accompany me. I had to locate a road, along which the *BTK* was located. Ah! That appeared to have been it. Now it was reduced to a chain of craters, into several of which I fell … In the *BTK* I was received in the usual manner with schnaps, mineral water and a short briefing. Moving rapidly with an escort I returned, pleased with the way this man had agreed to come with me … At the *BTK* of Reserve Infantry Regiment 15, I met the commander, who was already picking his way forward gingerly with the remains of his battalion. He had thought that I was never going to return …

"His companies were down to thirty to fifty men as a result of earlier losses and because it was extremely difficult to gather men together from a crater field position. Leutnant M___ had collected up about fifty men en route, all of whom were stragglers from other regiments, but provided us with useful reinforcements. Unfortunately, on the way to the front, most of them disappeared once more and only very few got forward. Not much troubled by artillery fire, the companies occupied positions in the craters.

"We went into a large blockhouse where a telephone was still working … A whole series of headquarters seemed to have no idea of our whereabouts and numerous confusing complaints flew backwards and forwards. *This is the Lippspringe Regiment!-That means nothing to me; I want to speak to BTK Bern! – Understood! – This is Regiment L … – Get off the line, I want BTK Bern!…Watch your language! The enemy may be listening in! Rubbish!* Frankly the enemy may as well have been listening in. They would not have understood one single thing.

"Finally I managed to get through to my own regiment: *3rd Battalion Infantry Regiment 459 is to move under command of Reserve Infantry Regiment 77 …* Oh brilliant! They were going to rest their own men and deploy [we] strangers forward."

The infantry had no monopoly on confusion on that day, as the experience of Field Artillery Regiment 7 shows. It had been tasked to provide fire support for a counterattack in the Broodseinde area, but in a classic case of order, counter-order and disorder, the battalion was scattered and its commander spent the next twenty four hours trying to regain control.

Hauptmann Blank 3rd Battalion Field Artillery Regiment 7 [30] **8**

"Initially two of my light howitzer batteries were moved forward from the assembly area and subordinated to another group (Westhoek). A little while later the last of my batteries was called forward under command of Infantry Regiment 458, so I was left alone with my staff. I immediately rode to the relevant artillery commander (11) and requested orders for me and my staff. At that we were despatched forward through extremely heavy fire to check round all the batteries, because so far no reports concerning their arrival had been received. At the same time I was ordered to take command once more of all the batteries and to form my own group. We rode forward as far as we could through the heavy fire. Then we dismounted and I continued on foot, along with my adjutant, Leutnant Wolff, my orderly officer, Leutnant Pungs, some telephonists and clerks. As far as possible we avoided heavy and super-heavy calibre fire, deviating away from it or flinging ourselves down or into shell holes as necessary.

"Enemy aircraft were operating quite blatantly over our lines and far to the rear. Descending to fifty or even twenty metres, they machine gunned everything. Eventually, by between 3.00 pm and 4.00 pm, we found ourselves in the forward area. The sun was shining and the visibility very good. I expected to come across two of my batteries, the 6th and the 8th, in forward positions, but after a long careful search, I only found one (8th), which had taken up positions next to a 210 mm howitzer battery. In answer to my question concerning the whereabouts of the battery commander, I was taken to one side and shown where Leutnant Reintjes was lying dead.[31] He had been conducting a reconnaissance with the commander of 6th Battery, Leutnant Elsner, when both were hit by the same shell. Whereas Leutnant Reintjes was killed instantly, Leutnant Elsner was severely wounded. One leg was blown off, the other was hit and he had two shell splinters in his head. He was evacuated alive, but died that evening in a field hospital, before he could be decorated with the Iron Cross First Class for gallantry[32].

"Together with Leutnant Caufin, the one remaining officer of 8th Battery, I went to find a new position. The emplacements next to the howitzer battery were untenable. I ordered the limbers to be brought forward ready to change firing positions as it went dark. Simultaneously I issued orders to 6th Battery, which had pulled back to the assembly area on the death of its battery commander, telling them to move forward once more and directing them to a position, which they occupied as it went dark. After a long search, I found barely adequate accommodation for a command post, which was only a few hundred metres from the batteries. It is in a captured dugout and there I have been operating for the past twenty four hours.

The severity and intensity of British artillery fire during the battle meant that telephone lines had little chance of surviving for very long. Throughout, commanders were plagued by an inability to communicate rapidly and accurately. There were, however, times when light signalling stations could be useful, as this account makes clear.

Unteroffizier Klußmann 5th Company Reserve Infantry Regiment 77 [33] **4**

"On 20 September, the battle flared up on our sector with the utmost intensity. My signal station was under very heavy enemy fire. The front line trenches, about 500 metres away, were under such heavy fire that they were constantly enveloped by one dust cloud after another. It was a difficult task whilst the fighting raged to remain completely out of cover in order to maintain constant observation over the front line and so be able to receive light signals sent from the front and re-transmit them to the rear. Artillery shells kept crashing down to our front and rear, whilst overhead enemy aircraft descended to harass us with machine gun fire.

"Nevertheless I maintained my position there from 5.00 am with Musketiers Hugo Kratz from Peine and Georg Helbes from Kleefeld. We were at all times ready to send and receive. Because of the dust, smoke and other filth that was being thrown up as high as houses, it was impossible to make out anything to the front. We had already lost two MS 16 signal projectors to shell fire and were left with only one small one, just as the battle reached its greatest pitch of intensity. Suddenly a message was flashed from the forward edge of the battle area. Now we strained all our senses to make out the Morse code letters – despite the numbing crashes of the shells, the dust and the clouds of smoke.

"Despite all the problems, we were able to make out the fragmented message. I dictated the letters and Kratz and Helbes wrote them down. *The British have broken in. Help urgently required!* We transmitted this message to the rear and, a little later, reinforcements arrived. In addition, at the request of the battalion commander, Hauptmann von Lüttwitz, the Richthofen wing was scrambled, because we were suffering very badly at the hands of the enemy airmen. When I flashed the message forward: *The Richthofen squadron is on its way*, we were able to note down the reply, a joyful cheer of *Hurra*, which flickered to us from the front line through the swirling clouds."

On a day of almost unrelieved frustration and disaster for the defence, there was one slight crumb of comfort: the performance of the regiments of 2nd Guards Reserve Division, backed by 236th Infantry Division. A wide gap was torn between the Reserve Infantry Regiment 15 and Reserve Infantry Regiment 91, but the survivors fought on, and the defence, which covered the vital approaches to Passchendaele, did not buckle completely. Thanks to the commitment of the very last of the regimental reserves and an extraordinarily gallant attack by the 236th Infantry Division, the defence did at least push the enemy back to the rough line of the *Wilhelm Stellung* to the west of Passchendaele. Nevertheless, the day had taken a severe toll as Kleine, an eyewitness from Infantry Regiment 459, and Tambour Wibbe, of Reserve Infantry Regiment 15, describing the situation that evening, explain: **4**

"The entire sector was under extremely heavy artillery fire. In attempting to get forward and close with the enemy on the slopes to the front, our assault companies and their supporting battery suffered severe casualties. Nevertheless the counter-attack which had been ordered was pressed home and the enemy driven back. How mundane that sounds; what a bloody tragedy these words disguise ... We, in the command post, had heavy losses as well. About 7.00 pm fourteen of our comrades were killed by a direct hit ... Killed at a single stroke and with hardly a murmur. In an instant they were covered by a thick layer of dust. I was hit in the groin by a flying fragment, but luckily it was just a piece of a tile. Next to me an

Unteroffizier of our signal detachment went off his head. We had to restrain him, binding him tightly, because he had been rushing around, lashing out and foaming at the mouth. I raced off to the casualty clearing point about one kilometre to the rear to fetch stretchers and stretcher-bearers."[34]

Tambour Wibbe 3rd Battalion Reserve Infantry Regiment 15 [35] **4**

"The pillbox housing the staff was completely destroyed by incendiary shells about 6.00 pm. It had contained a number of wounded men. All of them and the two gefreiters acting as runners were killed by direct hits. I was the only man unwounded. The pillbox had been spotted by the enemy because flare signals had been fired from the entrance. I now watched and noticed that the enemy battery was firing in a pattern of three salvoes, followed by a short pause. I grabbed up the maps and other important items, waited for the third salvo to fall, then ran for my life cross country. Luckily I came across the commander and the adjutant in a crater. They had given me up for lost!

"Because the last of the runners was dead or wounded, the commander gave me the task of using my last reserves of strength to carry a report to regimental headquarters. He promised me a reward and a long spell of leave. I carried out the job, hurried to the rear and was released to move to Rumbeke. All the time heavy artillery fire was coming down. I finally reached Rumbeke in a truck, which gave me a lift from the *Chausseegraben*, where I had been lying totally exhausted."

With the fading light, the worst of the fighting died away too, but the noise of battle continued into the night, which saw continuous activity as reserves were rushed forward, ammunition and food were replenished. Meanwhile, both sides took stock of the events of the day.

Reserve Leutnant Zimmer Adjutant 2nd Battalion Infantry Regiment 459 [36] **4**

"The day drew to a close. As the sun sank as a blood-red fireball in the west, it created a scene of weird beauty and the entire horizon appeared to glow. To our front a wrecked concrete bunker blazed as the flares which had been stored inside shot into the air in a series of red and green streaks. This was punctuated by the sound of the boxes of hand grenades exploding. Muzzle flashes which lit up the horizon betrayed the location of the British heavy batteries which were bringing down interdicting fire on the rear areas in order to interrupt the forward movement of supplies and rations. The twilight faded rapidly and soon it was difficult to make out the faint outlines of the shot-up tree stumps against the evening sky. Whenever the British concentrations of artillery fire got too unpleasant, we adopted tactics of mobile defence; that is to say we thinned out the positions to left and right."

Reserve Leutnant Kotthoff
1st Machine Gun Company Reserve Infantry Regiment 77 [37] **4**

"We were located about 800 metres behind the front and the enemy had advanced about 400 metres. Unfortunately I could not bring my weapons into action, because our own troops were still forward of us. A battalion arrived from the rear to launch a counter-attack, but was unable to get forward through the barrage. The battle continued all day, leaving the area dotted with wounded men. The poor lads had to remain where they were as the fire poured down and continued in heavy concentrations throughout the night. Towards morning there was further drum fire. I felt very sorry for the wounded, many of whom were lying in our concrete blockhouse. Silently we sat there in the candlelight. Suddenly all was deadly quiet. The fire had stopped completely, not a shell was landing.

"I raced outside to be greeted by the first rays of the morning sun. Could it possibly be true? Here where there had been nothing but death and destruction all was utterly peaceful. We could have wept for joy. Swiftly everyone rushed out and marvelled at this miracle. Softly the sun shone down on this place of death. It was too much for some of the glazed eyes to take in. Peace! Peace! What a wonderful word. I really cannot do justice to the impression it made on me; I lack the words. I breathed deeply of the wonderful air then, suddenly, I saw flags coming across our rear area. Red Cross flags! Slowly they came, stretcher after stretcher. Forward of us Red Cross flags were waving. What an amazing, overwhelming sight!"

Reserve Leutnant Metzing
3rd Machine Gun Company Reserve Infantry Regiment 19 [38] **5**

"That evening there was drum fire for another hour. The forward edge of this fire came down on the *Drossel*. During the hours of darkness the remnants of 10th Company also came and occupied the *Drossel*. [As a precautionary measure] double sentry posts were established 100 metres to the west and northwest, but they were withdrawn at first light. The night passed peacefully. During the morning of 21 September there was drumming from 4.30 am to 5.30 am, but thereafter it was very quiet. Our mortars and howitzers engaged *Westfalenwald*. One of the rounds drove away the crew of one of the newly-arrived enemy machine gun posts at the northeast corner of the wood and we shot them all down. We then spent the entire day engaging all visible targets within *Westfalenwald*. From 3.30 pm there was better-directed fire than the previous day on the *Drossel* and one man was slightly wounded. Drum fire again that evening. Towards 11.30 pm we were relieved by the 3rd Machine Gun Coy of Infantry Regiment 117. On the first day we fired 11,500 rounds and 1,000 [*sic*][39] on the second, using only one weapon at a time. The second was kept under cover in the blockhouse, cleaned and swapped over."

Making the best of the outcome of the day's fighting, Group Ypres published an Order of the Day on 23 September. It is plain that either the subtlety of the use by the British army of 'bite and hold' tactics on a massive scale was lost on the defending commander, or he chose to ignore its significance:

"The first phase of fighting of the third Battle of Flanders is behind us. Following the use of unprecedented quantities of ammunition over a period of days, on 20 September the long-expected attack by the British was launched in overwhelming strength all along the front of Group Ypres. Thanks to the heroic courage of the ground holding divisions (208th, 36th, 2nd Guards Reserve and 121st), some of whom had been in position already for a protracted period, [thanks to the] powerful thrusts of all available reserves and ground-holding divisions as well as the important counter-attack of the 234th Infantry Division and elements of 236th Infantry Division, it has been possible to throw back the enemy that had broken in and quickly to halt the major enemy offensive. All that was left to the enemy were small territorial gains in the form of a shell-shattered crater field. His intention of breaking through our line has failed utterly with heavy casualties. All the troops who participated in the fighting can look back with pride on their achievements.

"Even though heavy casualties mean that gaps were torn in our ranks in places, we can content ourselves proudly in the knowledge that we brought about the defeat of a tough, determined enemy who vastly outnumbered us and stormed forward with the intention of achieving a decisive breakthrough. This will give us the strength victoriously to hold on further. We can face the coming battles, confident that victory will still be ours. I wish to express my warmest thanks and recognition of all commanders and troops in the Group."[40]

The army group followed this up with a somewhat anodyne version of events, which contrived to gloss over the failures of the day completely and to imply that the day had proceeded for the defence in much the same way as the major battles of August.

Army Group Crown Prince Rupprecht Daily Report 20 September 1917 [41]

"Under the command of General Sixt von Armin, the fighting troops of Fourth Army have successfully negotiated the first day of the third battle in Flanders. True to the massive artillery effort made by the British during the past few days, the concentration of enemy fighting power peaked today along a twelve kilometre front. Advancing behind a wall of drumfire of extraordinary intensity from guns and mortars, came at least nine British divisions (several Australian ones amongst them) [*sic* – in fact only 1st and 2nd Australian Divisions were involved that day]. They were supported in many instances in the attack by tanks and flamethrowers. After a battle of changing fortunes, the enemy succeeded in penetrating up to one kilometre of our defensive zone and temporarily up to the outskirts of Passchendaele. Our counter-attacks drove them back to the west of Passchendaele. Just as during the earlier battles in Flanders, our commanders and troops performed to the highest standard."

During the operational pause which followed the 20 September, there were still minor attacks, but the days and nights were filled mainly with reliefs in the line, creation of and readjustment of the placing of the reserves and redeployment of scarce resources, so as to be able to counter the next major Allied push.

Unteroffizier Sauer 2nd Battery Reserve Field Artillery Regiment 9 [42] **9**

"After we had spent fourteen days, grouped together with the foot artillery in a blocking (reserve) position, we were moved forward [on 22 September] into battle positions. Offizier Stellvertreter Nagel, Wachtmeister Kippermann, Unteroffizier Sauer and a few other comrades formed an advance party which took over the position. That night the battery moved up into positions to the south of the Menen-Ypres road at *Deimlingseck* [Deimling's Corner]. It was impossible to dig ourselves in as we had at Verdun and other places, so we had to make do with rough corrugated iron shelters about seventy five centimetres high. We could lie down or crouch beneath them, but could not use them in any other way as living accommodation. When we came under fire, we had to crawl out and disperse, or shelter in a nearby bunker, assuming that there was enough room. We sometimes had to spend hours at a time in here. The physical condition of the ground also helped to reduce casualties. It was so swampy that it absorbed much of the effect [of exploding shells].

"Nevertheless, on the position, whilst laying line, collecting empty cartridge cases, or bringing up engineer stores, we suffered many casualties. Whilst in the corrugated iron shelter one night, Kanonier Woya was decapitated by a shell, which seriously wounded another comrade. Commanded by Reserve Leutnant Sauter, 1st Section (Guns Heinzel and Sauer) was ordered to relieve the infantry support section of 1st Battery Reserve Field Artillery Regiment 9 at a farm near to *Bahnhof Nachtigall* [Nightingale Station]. Responsibility for the task had barely been assumed when the highest state of alert was ordered. We harnessed up and could tell from the noises to our front that something major was happening. In the morning we were ordered to move and, in broad daylight, we made our way cross country into position via *Neu-Amerika* [New America, located on the Wervik-Beselare road].

"The drivers of my gun, Pachali, Röhr and Franke, had a very hard time of it. The first concentration of fire arrived during the afternoon. A short while later, as the entire gun crew was sheltering in shell holes, a direct hit next to a pile of ammunition set the whole lot on fire. This was the signal for destructive fire to be brought down, sealing the fate of my gun. The right hand wheel was splintered, the breech mechanism, training gear, panoramic sight and trail were all wrecked. The crew was moved onto another gun located 100 metres to the left and there we spent several days. We then heard that all the batteries were to be withdrawn. This caused immense difficulties for the 2nd Battery because all the guns had sunk in so deep that they could hardly be pulled out of the mud. We had to wait for nightfall before we could succeed, but we also managed to improvise a sledge and drag the remains of our wrecked gun back to Menen, where we were issued with a new one."

Having had some days to reflect on the latest developments, the army group commander recorded some of his current concerns in his diary. These are in sharp contrast to his thoughts when the battle began seven weeks earlier and represent some of the first indications that the course of the battle was becoming a worry to him.

Crown Prince Rupprecht of Bavaria: Diary Entries 23 and 24 September 1917 [43]

"We cannot tolerate the idea of the enemy firmly in control of the Zonnebeke heights or the Geluveld [Plateau]. They are now so close to achieving this that the fear must be that they will achieve it with their next attack. We must ensure that our counter-strokes during the next enemy assaults are driven right up to their planned objectives."

"It appears as though fresh attacks against Groups Ypres and Wijtschate are about to take place. It is to be hoped that they do not take place too soon because we currently lack reserves behind the main battle front."

Meanwhile, 51st Reserve Division, which had been deployed as the *Eingreif* division behind Group Diksmuide from 10 August to 19 September, was moved south following the battles on 20 September to the Kezelberg heights, three kilometres north of Menen; the aim being to shore up the defences around the area of Polygon Wood and to provide some forces in reserve for future operations. This was not long in coming. During the night 24/25 September, troops from 3rd Battalion Reserve Infantry Regiment 229 and 3rd Battalion Reserve Infantry Regiment 230, under the overall command of Oberst Litzmann, commander Reserve Infantry Regiment 230, moved forward to the south of Polygon Wood and, by 5.00 am 25 September, were in position along a start line, running north-south, spanning the Reutelbeek and secured by men of 1st Battalion Reserve Infantry Regiment 230.

A sharp thirty minute bombardment was followed by a vigorous attack, intended to recapture the *Wilhelm Stellung* at this critical point. The attack was reasonably successful, although losses were high due to Allied counter-attacks, artillery and machine gun fire. Reserve Infantry Regiment 229 found that enemy machine gun fire was especially heavy against its southern flank and it failed to make much progress there. Nevertheless, by 6.30 am it had captured a group of concrete pill boxes at the southwestern tip of Polygon Wood.[44] Having reorganised there, the attack was resumed and made more progress. This was followed by violent reaction and the regiment was involved in heavy local fighting for the remainder of the day.[45] The following night was spent in trying to reorganise the new defensive lines south of Polygon Wood; a task which was barely complete before the next storm broke over the defenders.[46]

First Company Reserve Infantry Regiment 231 also played a limited role in the attack. For the men involved, it was a highly dangerous undertaking.

Leutnant Heider 1st Company Reserve Infantry Regiment 231 [47] **10**

"On 25 September 1st Company Reserve Infantry Regiment 231 ... was on stand-by, located near Geluveld to the right of the Ypres – Menen road. We had already suffered several casualties due to the artillery fire. At midday I was ordered by Hauptmann Bürger to advance and occupy the line of the *Wilhelm Stellung* to the right [north] of the road. It was one of the most difficult missions that I was ever given during the war. It meant that we had to get forward several hundred metres through the heaviest imaginable artillery defensive fire – and in broad daylight. I gave my own orders to my men, adding: *The hour has come when I have to trust each and every one of you implicitly. I shall go first and you must follow me, well spread out. We shall meet up again in the front line. Go forward with God!*

"Moving with me were my two young runners, Joachim Algermissen from Hildesheim and Gefreiter Wilhelm Koch from Königsdahlum, near

Hanover. With total disregard for their lives and completely calm, they rushed with me from shell hole to shell hole. On one occasion I was almost buried by a shell. Just as we reached the front line and were pleased to have reached it unscathed, Algermissen was shot through the chest. Shouting, *Praised be the Lord Jesus Christ!* he collapsed, mortally wounded … It was uplifting to see my men arriving one by one in the front line, but one third of the company had fallen victim to the ferocious fire on the way. I was later able to establish that none had faltered. Those missing were all reported killed or wounded.

"That evening we were ordered, along with the entire division, to switch our front slightly to the left [south], so as to ensure that all units were occupying the *Wilhelm Stellung.* Reserve Infantry Regiment 230 to our right did not seem to have received this order or to have conformed to it and a gap developed on our flank. Fortunately this was not spotted by the enemy and I covered it by turning the right flank of the company [to face north]. To our front the scene was one of utter chaos. Dead and wounded lay everywhere – many of them British. We established our strongpoint around two pillboxes. The enemy were about twenty to fifty metres away and enemy machine guns pointed at us from nearby blockhouses.

"During the night a Scotsman blundered into our position. We kept him there to tend to his severely wounded countrymen, who were moaning terribly. One of them had lost both his eyes to a flamethrower. I longed to shoot him and put him out of his misery, but such action was not permitted. I estimate that my company was reduced to thirty to thirty five men. We had to maintain a high standard of alert throughout the night. As I went around the position I saw that many, who had earned the right to sleep, were sleeping their last sleep of all in the miserable muddy shell holes; these, the finest of our faithful people, had been kissed on the forehead by the Angels of Peace."

Crown Prince Rupprecht of Bavaria: Diary Entry 25 September 1917 [48]

"An operation which I directed was to be carried out to improve our positions between Polygon Wood and the [Ypres – Menen] road by Geluveld was completed satisfactorily. The next major attack will probably not take place for a few days." [49]

Only hours after the army group commander had written up his diary, his prophecy was rendered null and void when, with a deafening roar, several belts of drum fire stretching out more than 1,000 metres in depth, was brought down on the eight kilometre frontage to be attacked from north of Zonnebeke to south of the Ypres-Menen road. With the defenders weakened by the fighting of the previous day and the exertions of the night, the 5th Australian Division made rapid progress against the sub-units of Reserve Infantry Regiment 229 in Polygon Wood. At 6.20 am, Hauptmann Fischer the northern *KTK*, sent a report by carrier pigeon to the regiment which read, *The enemy is outflanking us to the right* [north] and followed this at 8.00 am with a further message, *We are holding on! Am conducting counter-strokes to the north and west.* [50]

Major Hethey, the southern *KTK*, also conducted a sharp defensive action, firing his rifle alongside his men until he was shot through the head and killed at 6.30 am.[51] Thereafter the defence of Polygon Wood splintered into tiny remnants, some of which managed to stay into action until about midday. By then Reserve Infantry Regiment 229 had taken severe casualties, including Leutnants Glaubitz and Weigel shot through the head and Leutnant Stölting, commander of the 3rd Machine Gun Company, who died, shot through the heart.[52] Leutnant Körber was the last man of Reserve Infantry Regiment 229 to break out of Polygon Wood to the rear. Everything now depended on the *Eingreif* troops.

To the left of Reserve Infantry Regiment 229 and on the southern flank of the main thrust, Reserve Infantry Regiments 230 and 231 of 50th Reserve Division held firm. Despite intense pressure and the losses it had sustained during the counter-stroke the previous day, Reserve Infantry Regiment 230 spent the day fighting hard at close quarters, with numerous local actions. A sure sign of how hard the fighting was in this area, is the fact that the regiment only captured twenty one Allied prisoners, compared with the 250 taken during its counter-attack near St Juliaan on 31 July.[53] To the rear Reserve Infantry Regiment 78 of 19th Reserve Division moved forward from a holding area west of Geluwe to forward assembly areas near Geluveld, where it was placed at the disposal of Reserve Infantry Regiment 231. It was not initially deployed, but did move to reinforce the weakened Reserve Infantry Regiment 231 later in the day.[54]

A little to the north, the regiments of 17th Infantry Division had just taken over the *Eingreif* role from the fought out Bavarian 16th Infantry Division. In anticipation of the forthcoming attack, they were in an assembly area west of Panemolen, at thirty minutes notice to move. Initially it was though that they would deploy southwest towards Zandvoorde, but once the target of the Allied attack became clear, everything changed.

Hauptmann Caspari 2nd Battalion Infantry Regiment 75 [55] **10**

"Towards 10.30 am information arrived that the enemy, attacking the inner flanks of Groups Ypres and Wijtschate, had forced their way into Polygon Wood. Orders were changed immediately; the regiment was to advance more to the north, in order to be in position behind the endangered sector. 1st Battalion was to move to Zuidhoek, 2nd and 3rd Battalions, artillery, engineers and the storm platoon to Terhand. Meanwhile the British were bringing down ever heavier fire throughout the area and numerous aircraft worked even harder to spot the move of German reserves. Our machine guns opened fire on them repeatedly. A huge shell crashed down on the house where, only moments earlier, the commander of 2nd Battalion had been giving oral orders to his company commanders. It appeared that, following their success further forward, the British had lifted their barrage fire to the east.[56]

"In the face of this brutal reality and bowed under the weight of our battle loads, we could only pick our way forward tortuously and painfully. Again and again we had to take cover to avoid the attentions of [enemy] aircraft, or wait for the machine gun and mortar teams and the carrying parties to close up ... It was 1.00 pm before we were in the new assembly areas. In the meantime, at 12.40 pm, Major Hagedorn had received orders from the headquarters of 34 Infantry Brigade, located 600 metres south of Terhand. These had been issued by 17th Infantry Division at 11.40 am and directed us to link up to the left (south) of Detachment *Quednow* [the reinforced Grenadier Regt 89] and participate in the planned counter-stroke.

"It took more than another hour for this order to be relayed down to the lowest level, especially to Detachment 'Hagedorn', whose sub-units were spread over three kilometres. As ever such matters do not run as smoothly under the fire of the battlefield as on exercise or war games! From 2.00 pm the advance towards objectives in the *Wilhelm Stellung* began (this so-called position was, however, nothing but a mass of craters) ... The cratered area stretched from Terhand forward. In the low-lying places the craters were full to the brim with water and the ground was just like a water-filled sponge, which had degenerated into a swamp in various places.

"In addition, the entire area was under heavy artillery fire, which was coming down in great depth. The first belt of fire to be negotiated was coming down level with our battery positions to the west of Terhand. Everywhere the explosions of high explosive shells and the effect of smoke shells was reducing visibility, making breathing difficult and stinging our eyes. It was impossible to follow a set route, or to maintain separation between individuals or groups of men. Commanders just led their men stumbling in a westerly direction through the roaring grey-black wall of the barrage, which was periodically lit up with flashes. Watching out for the places where the fire was falling most densely, attempts were made to pass weaker points, skirting wired-off battery positions, swamps and hedgerows, looking for crossing points across swollen streams.

"Platoons made their way forward in single file or in groups, trying to keep up with their commanders. Machine gunners and carriers boiled with sweat and cursed their way forward. To begin with casualties were only slight, thanks to the speed with which the belt of fire was tackled on the way forward. Hauptmann Krull, commander of the 1st Battalion ... was able to report at 3.20 pm, 'The battalions seem to be making good progress forward. They are approaching the eastern edge of Polderhoek.' A little later, at 4.10 pm, he reported, 'The companies are passing through Polderhoek and the 2nd Battalion has made similar forward progress.'

"The two battalions linked up approximately along the line Polderhoek Chateau – Geluveld, but as they crossed the crest line south west of Polderhoek Chateau they came under heavy artillery fire and intense machine gun fire from the front, but also from the flanks, with the fire from the right [north] being particular severe. It proved to be impossible to link up with Grenadier Regiment 89 on this flank. Ignoring the fire, the battalions advanced through the positions of Reserve Infantry Regiment 230 and set off, moving from crater to crater for the old *Wilhelm Stellung*. Groups of British soldiers, who had penetrated this far to the east, were thrown back, suffering high casualties from our small arms fire. But our own casualties were also mounting noticeably.

"As they were attempting to organise a flank guard facing north, Leutnant Brokate, commander of 4th Company, and one of his officers, Leutnant Wilhelm Thyssen, were both killed.[57] The 6th Company managed to advance as far as the *Wilhelm Stellung*, but the others could not get that far. The British simply dominated the approaches with their machine guns and mortars. Attempts were made to move individually or in small groups by rushing from cover to cover, but gradually the attack withered away. Machine gun fire hammered down from both sides, mortar bombs and artillery shells crashed down everywhere. Signal flares shot up through the smoke and dust and spouts of earth were thrown up in all directions. In this hell of steel splinters, there was no longer any question of moving during daylight. It was beyond human ability."

The experience of Grenadier Regiment 89 was almost identical. With great courage and having taken severe casualties, its forward companies reached the eastern edge of Polygon Wood and the open ground to the west of Reutel. Enemy machine fire from unseen positions then began to take a serious toll. Reserve Leutnants Kruse and Schilling were killed,[58] twelve other officers and a correspondingly high number of junior ranks were wounded. There was absolutely no possibility of achieving the given objective, but the regiment managed to cling on to the line it had reached until it was relieved by Reserve Infantry Regiment 73 during the night of 27/28 September. The trauma of these two days of battle and the courage shown by individuals made a deep impression on the survivors, as this diary entry, company report extract and letter written home show:

Fähnrich Heinrich von Alt-Stutterheim 2nd Battalion Grenadier Regiment 89 [59] **11**

"From 4.00 am [26 September] drum fire was heard. At readiness, I made an entry in my diary, which I had not done since 17 September, but no sooner had I begun than we were told, *Prepare to move ...* The Tommies had broken into Polygon Wood to the south of Zonnebeke and we were to be deployed as an *Eingreif* division. At 10.00 am we headed north out of our assembly area. About 1.00 pm we found ourselves under fire in a totally shot-up wood. We waited here for orders and tried to orientate ourselves. After about forty five minutes we moved a little further to the right ... but we were still under such heavy shrapnel fire that we moved even further right. From here we moved forward, halting behind a hedge on a hill top, where Hauptmann von Grone briefed us about the situation ...

"As we advanced, we came under very heavy machine gun fire. My platoon was in the centre of the company, with Stenglin left and Vizefeldwebel Wiese right. Leaping from crater to crater we moved forward. Immediately my company commander, Leutnant Stein, was shot in the right hand side of his stomach by a machine gun bullet. Moving on I landed in a wrecked trench, which was full of men from different regiments. I followed the trench to the right. The men in this packed trench seemed to have no wish to advance, but they had been there for three days already. At this point my platoon got split up. A few minutes later, alone in the trench, I saw some of them rush forward on my right. I raced after them and linked up in a shell hole.

"Most of them were from other companies of 2nd Battalion, one was from my platoon and one from 12th Company, who told me that Leutnant von Aspern had been wounded. One man was wounded with a shrapnel ball in the arm whilst we were in the shell hole. Once we had bandaged him up we carried on. Gradually some of the more courageous men joined up with us. There was an enormous amount of shrapnel and machine gun fire, wounding many of the grenadiers. Tending to a wounded grenadier in a water-filled shell hole, I was myself wounded by a shrapnel ball which went straight through my upper arm. It was 6.00 pm by now. I took my jacket off and a Vizefeldwebel from 7th Company bandaged me. As I was dressing again, I was hit by another shrapnel ball on the steel helmet. I took it off and felt for a wound, but the ball had not penetrated it. It just left a small dent.

"Taking off my belt and assault order, I took only my telescope, revolver, stick, ration bag and gas mask ... We crept to a dry hole to our right and stayed there until about 6.45 pm, then all three of us set off back ... Because one of the grenadiers could hardly walk, he leaned on my shoulder. We had hardly gone ten steps when he was shot in the right ear, losing his right eye ... At that I rushed back with the other two. Perhaps 100 metres back. There was just too much shrapnel fire. We waited until about 8.00 pm, then we began to make our way, along with many other wounded, back to the aid post. On the way I once more met the man who had been wounded by the machine gun. He carried my ration bag, but we got split up again and I did not see him after that. There was not much food left in it anyway.

"The aid post was already full ... I made a sling for my arm with the strap of my gas mask carrier ... I felt very weak through loss of blood ... [then I was moved back] via Moorslede and Iseghem."

Reserve Leutnant Schütt 11th Company Grenadier Regiment 89 [60] 11

"At about 4.00 pm on 26 September the company advanced as part of the second wave against Polygon Wood. It was not long before it came under tremendous artillery fire. Nevertheless progress continued to be made. A short time later a great concentration of high explosive shells, mixed with gas shells, came down, forcing the company to mask up. Soon it was enveloped in a very dense cloud of gas, which meant that contact within the company was lost and orientation became impossible.

"The company commander despatched Gefreiter Hermann Jahnke and Grenadier Ludwig von Walsleben to link up with [troops in] the front line. Both of them set off wearing their gas masks and ignoring the artillery barrage to complete their task. A few minutes later both of them were quite seriously wounded by an exploding shell, but they gathered their wits and bandaged one another up. After that, instead of pulling back to the aid post, they continued with their task. Not until they had returned to their company commander and given him a situation report did the two of them proceed to the aid post."

Grenadier Gülzow Grenadier Regiment 89 [61] 11

"On 26 September, we were launched in a counter-stroke against Polygon Wood. We advanced in column half right to the copse by the *Jägerwäldchen*. ... We reached it after force marching for about one hour and remained there for about another hour, while the Tommies poured heavy shells on us (at least 280 mm), which exploded with ear-splitting

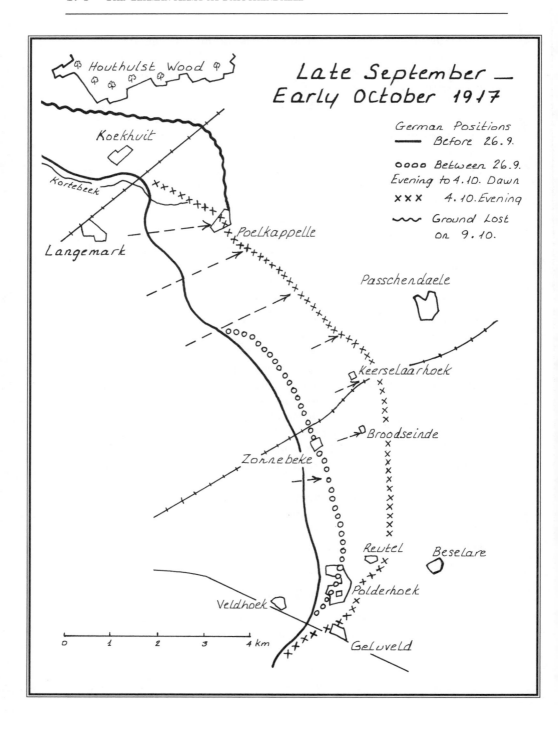

Late September —
Early October 1917

German Positions
——— Before 26.9.

oooo Between 26.9.
Evening to 4.10. Dawn
xxx   4.10. Evening

〜〜 Ground Lost
      on 9.10.

Houthulst Wood

Koekhuit

Kortebeek

Langemark

Poelkappelle

Passchendaele

Keerselaarhoek

Broodseinde

Zonnebeke

Reutel   Beselare

Polderhoek

Veldhoek

Geluveld

0   1   2   3   4 km

crashes. Unfortunately this split up 1 Platoon. Ammunition wagons raced to the rear – some of them with only one driver left for six horses, sometimes drawn only by two horses. Loose horses raced around, panicked by the fire. In the meantime 4th and 12th Companies passed through us. Because I had got separated form my mates – my glasses were covered with sweat and dust – I went forward with the 13th.

"After we had crossed a hollow my battalion, with Hauptmann von Grone and his staff, suddenly approached us from the right. After that I went forward with men of 2 Platoon. One of them was the signaller, Flashar, who was supposed to have been wounded in the leg later. Then I moved with the light machine gunners. We went through a crater field, passed through 6th Company, which was meant to be in front of us, and then we ended up in the enemy's barrage fire, which went on until 9.00 pm. After I had stopped by a wounded man of 6th Company, I went on a few more craters and ended up finally with Unteroffizier Ehrich of our 3 Platoon, together with another of our platoon and two 6th Company men in a crater.

"We dug in there with our spades. After 9.00 pm we linked up with about fifteen men of our company about fifty metres to the right. Two were from my section and there was a light machine gun … some of us moved some wounded to the rear. There were about twelve of us in a section of trench and we dug ourselves in deeper. In the morning between 5.00 am and 6.00 am heavy artillery fire came down. The same happened between midday and 4.00 pm (observed fire) then, between 6.00 pm and 7.30 pm, there was the most dreadful destructive fire. We thought that there would be an attack, but none came … We were relieved about 4.00 am [28 September] and moved back rapidly for two hours, then we met up with a 210 mm long barrelled gun that was going our way and we got a lift, because most of us could go no further …

"There were nineteen of us … The company did not have many killed, but enormous numbers were wounded. The artillery fire was extraordinary. You cannot imagine such a hail of shrapnel with high explosive mixed in. The Tommies used the heaviest calibres against the forward trenches. It was just a miracle that none of our nineteen men forward were wounded on 27 September, because the shells rained down between 6.00 pm and 7.30 pm, throwing filth up into the air. The Tommies' machine gun fire was also awful. They were a bit higher up in Polygon Wood and, therefore, could bring down fire, whilst our machine guns did not have much chance to shoot. Also our artillery seemed to be inferior, as far as I could judge in that hellish concert – at least as far as heavies were concerned, though we did fire a lot.

Our light guns, which had to change positions when we moved, were hit so hard by the enemy that they could not have had many guns left. It was no laughing matter for the field artillery ... So that is a bit of a picture of the fighting for you. Fifteen hours drum fire! By the time we were relieved I had had it."

With the defence facing a genuine crisis as a result of what the Allies subsequently referred to as the Battle of Polygon Wood, 17th Infantry Division had to be relieved as a matter of extreme urgency. 19th Reserve Division arrived to take over the line between Geluveld, northwest to a point level with the centre of Polygon Wood. Reserve Infantry Regiment 73 held the right, Reserve Infantry Regiment 92 the open ground in the centre near (Polderhoek) and Reserve Infantry Regiment 78 left (Geluveld). It was a traumatic time for all involved, as this letter indicates.

Leutnant Walsemann 6th Company Reserve Infantry Regiment 92 [62] **11**

"I am really happy to have left all the insane murder behind! May God be praised, who permitted me to survive this hellish fire! I can still barely credit how lucky I was! How was it possible to avoid the thousands of shells? I still go ice-cold when I think back to that small, water-filled shell hole in which we lay totally unprotected and acted as targets for the countless British guns. I lack the words even to describe approximately what we suffered and achieved during those days. The length of the battle made Verdun dreadful; but so concentrated was the British fire in Flanders that it was incomparably worse. Our role as defenders was simply to hold on and let it pour down on us. Nothing is a greater strain on the nerves than to have to remain defenceless in unprotected positions, for days at a time, facing an enemy bent on your destruction.

"During the night 27/28 September the regiment was called forward to conduct a relief in the line forward. We were to be deployed in the Beselare-Polygon Wood sector – a notorious spot. Even the approach march was extremely difficult. Prevented by artillery fire from using the roads, we had to pick our way across country, through the swampy, shot-up terrain. My commanders knew what to do and in single file we were making slow, but steady, progress. Suddenly dense fog descended. The commanders became uncertain. It was impossible to see two paces in front of us. Wire fences surrounding animal pastures hindered our progress, so we cut the wire. The column got split up. 'Step short in front!' came the cry from the rear. In the end the whole column came to a halt; nobody knew where we were. According to my compass I was sure that the road to Terhand was not far off to our right. I was just about to set off with a small patrol when there was an enormous crash very near to us, followed by a second. We closed up

1. Crown Prince Rupprecht of Bavaria, the Army Group Commander.

2. General der Infanterie Hermann von Kuhl, Chief of Staff Army Group Crown Prince Rupprecht.

3. General der Infanterie Sixt von Armin, Fourth Army Commander.

4. Oberst Friedrich von Loßberg, Chief of Staff Fourth Army.

5. Fliegerleutnant Karl von Allmenröder, an air ace with Jasta 11. Allmenröder was credited with 30 victories by the time of his death in a dog fight at the end of June 1917, only three weeks after he was awarded the Pour le Mérite.

6. Major Lincke, Commanding Officer, 2nd Bn Reserve Infantry Regiment 212. Severely wounded and captured on 4 October 1917, he claimed to have spoken to the commander of 1st Australian Division on his way to captivity

7. Messines Village June 1917.

8. The ruined monastery Wijschate June 1917.

9. A shelled German battlefield cemetery, similar to the one from which the body of
Fliegerleutnant Allmenröder was recovered.

10. The effect of the bombardment. A wrecked blockhouse in the Albrecht Stellung
August 1917.

11. Men of the support battalion Infantry Regiment 418 waiting for orders at the *BTK*. 16 August 1917.

12. Men of Infantry Regiment 418 about to launch a counter-stroke near Langemark 16 August 1917.

13. Zonnebeke 22 August 1917.

14. An *Eingreif* battalion advancing August 1917.

15. Sentry Position
Blankaartsee

16. Houthulst Wood August 1917.

17. The effect of counter-battery fire Geluveld Plateau September 1917.

18. The effect of counter-battery fire near Moorslede September 1917.

19. *Eingreif* troops about to launch a counter-stroke 20 September 1917.

20. Struggling to move an observation balloon through the craters on the Geluveld Plateau September 1917.

21. Men emerge from a pill box near Veldhoek in September 1917, to take a breath of stinking, poisoned air and collect a bucket of filthy water.

22. The wreckage-strewn battlefield of Polderhoek Chateau 26 September 1917.

23. A smashed blockhouse in the Wilhelm Stellung near Poelkapelle October 1917.

24. Geluveld October 1917.

25. Houthulst Wood October 1917.

26. The *KTK* of Marine Infantry Regiment 3 Poelkapelle October 1917.

27. A sentry keeps guard, whilst his exhausted comrades sleep. Passchendaele October 1917.

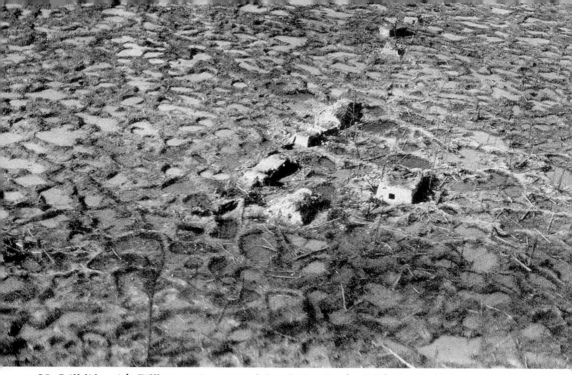

28. Still life with Pillboxes: A scene of desolation in the Wilhelm Stellung west of Passchendaele. October 1917.

29. Road Langemark-St Juliaan October 1917.

30. Road Moorslede - Passchendaele October 1917.

31. Plank road through the swamp near Beselare October 1917.

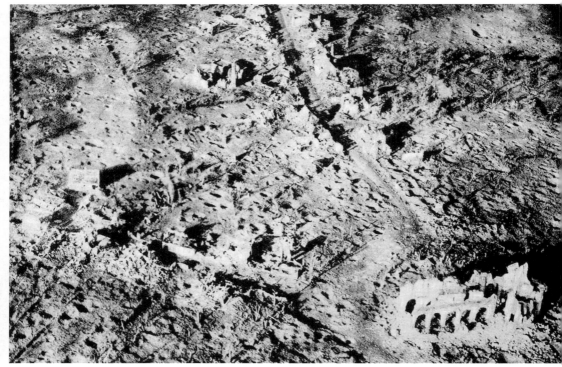

32. Passchendaele village late October 1917.

33. Passchendaele village from the air November 1917 - nothing more than a coloured smear in the swamp.

34. Passchendaele village at ground level November 1917.

35. German dead, killed by shelling.

36. German and British dead, killed in a hand to hand fight for a machine gun post.

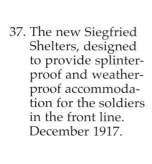

37. The new Siegfried Shelters, designed to provide splinter-proof and weather-proof accommodation for the soldiers in the front line. December 1917.

into a bunch and realised that we were right by the position of a German heavy battery. This was a hot spot and it was unwise to linger long in the vicinity, because the British would not long delay their reply. We had covered barely one hundred metres when the first great shells roared overhead. They crashed into the ground and their splinters whizzed past us. A heavy blow to my upper arm convinced me that I had been hit by one. My arm was very painful and hung down motionless. However I could see no blood, just a small hole in my sleeve. Everything must have been all right and we pressed on forwards. We moved clear of the fire zone, without suffering any casualties. In the meantime the fog had cleared and the commanders could get their bearings once more.

"With my hundred riflemen I was to occupy a 600 metre section of the front ... What met my eyes was a sight that exceeded the wildest fantasy: crater overlapped crater, often three or four of them inside each other and all full to the brim with water. Was it going to be possible at night and in the fog to balance on the small slippery edges which separated the craters? In the regiment we always used to say, 'It's going to be all right' – and usually it was. We could only make our way forward slowly; the terrain became ever more swampy and we frequently slipped from the narrow edges into the depths. The heavy loads we were carrying: machine guns and boxes of ammunition, meant that we sank in even deeper. Some of my men slid in up to their hips in the mud. Ohde, a big stocky man from Berlin, the pride of the company, became almost hopelessly stuck; only with the greatest effort could we pull him clear. It was worst at the Reutelbeek. The crossing was made on two hidden railway lines, but some, whose boots were thick with mud, fell off. The cries for help were constant as we set to to pull our comrades out of the clinging morass. It was necessary to keep this as quiet as possible. The British were not far off and would respond to the slightest sound with artillery fire. Thank God it all went well. That which was apparently impossible was completed without casualties and we arrived at our destination.

"All I found was an officer with some tens of men, who looked up at me with blank, white faces from the shell-hole where they were huddled. The company commander, utterly exhausted and apathetic, talked in a confused manner about defensive fire and men being buried alive; responding to my questions concerning how? and why? with ironic, stupid giggles. The poor wretch was at the end of his tether. He could give no information about his position, the situation to his left or right, or concerning the enemy. I quickly let him go. There was nothing else for it but to clarify the situation myself. The moonlight helped me to get orientated. After enormous trouble, I located my left hand boundary, where I linked up with

5th Company Reserve Infantry Regiment 92. As a result I could distribute my men, beginning on the left, to cover the huge gap to the western edge of the wood. To the right, despite intensive patrolling, it was impossible to link up that night, so my right flank remained in the air.

"The position consisted exclusively of shell holes; there were neither trenches, nor dugouts. The company was spread out over fifteen shell holes: 2 Platoon under Vizefeldwebel Wolf on the right, Vizefeldwebel Pierrot's 3 Platoon on the left, with 1 Platoon, commanded by Offizierstellvertreter Greiwe, in the centre and wallowing in the mud together with the company commander, the only officer forward. The enemy position followed a vague line of pillboxes up to Point 727. British sentries and patrols had pushed forward very close to our right flank. I sent a report to battalion concerning my dispositions and urgently requested a further company to fill the gap on the right flank. The runner returned quickly with the direction that closing the gap was up to me. In the meantime it was after daybreak and all movement stalled due to the need to avoid being seen by the observers in balloons and aircraft who maintained a constant watch over this totally open terrain.

"During the morning of 28th there was another two hour bombardment, which fell heaviest on my right flank. I crawled from shell hole to shell hole and discovered that Leutnant Jürgens, Vizefeldwebel Brockmeier, who saved my life on the Somme, another vizefeldwebel, an unteroffizier and two men had been wounded. During the evening the two-hour period of drum fire was repeated; amazingly without causing any damage at all. Then all fell still and the ghosts all rose out of their holes. The right flank was still my biggest concern. From way off to the right came the cries for help of a wounded man, who was certainly not one of ours. A little while later some men from 4th Company Reserve Infantry Regiment 73 appeared in No Man's Land, but they knew neither where they had come from, nor where their company was located. Together with my battle-tested, prudent Offizierstellvertreter Greiwe and my brave and eager runners, Konrad Stroh and Hermann Eggers, I donned my field cap and gas mask and went looking for the link up once more. The southern edge of Polygon Wood, which ran westwards, led us astray and we ended up too far to the west.

"We found ourselves directly in front of a British machine gun nest which sent greetings in our direction. Branching off east and echeloned way to the rear of our right flank, we came across some men of Reserve Infantry Regiment 73, which with its 4th Company was holding the left flank about 250 metres west of the sunken road in the *F[landern]- I* position. Understandably, because they were as comfortably placed as was possible in the circumstances in their deep dry trenches which were located on somewhat higher ground, it proved to be pointless to try to show their company commander that they were in the wrong place. Between the left flank of Reserve Infantry Regiment 92 and my right flank there was a 600 metre wide area of unoccupied territory. Following this useful reconnaissance we returned to the company. Great was our fury when we were informed that, during our absence, an eight man British patrol had suddenly appeared on the right flank and had taken some of the above-mentioned men of Reserve Infantry Regiment 73 and my right hand man with them. The immediate follow-up led to the shooting dead of one British soldier and the capture of a second, but we were unable to secure the release of our men.

"It really was an annoying occurrence. I provided the forward area commander with another report and made an urgent request that a company be thrown into the gap. This time my representations were rewarded with success. 2nd Company Reserve Infantry Regiment 92 under Leutnant Vigelahn was sent to extend the 6th Company [frontage] during the night 28/29 September. To the left, contact with 5th Company was maintained by means of patrols, but there was a 100 metre gap on the left in the swampy valley of the Reutelbeek. This area was, in fact, more or less impassable. Sleep was out of the question that night. Wedged together, our trousers soaking wet, our feet in water, perched on the rim of the crater, were my batman, my two runners Eggers and Stroh and my courageous stretcherbearer, Unteroffizier Jan Drücker. Hardly a word was exchanged. Each was preoccupied with his own thoughts. The physical tension was eased from time to time with a cigar or a good swig from a bottle. Hardly anyone was hungry, so much of the well-cooked food which had arrived punctually went to waste ...

"There was a considerable increase in enemy artillery fire during the morning of 29 September. Fire concentrations became more frequent, coming down particularly heavily just toward evening. It appeared as though a British attack was imminent. Then came news from the left flank that British assault forces were advancing. Some British steel helmets could be seen bobbing around in No Man's Land. The company was stood to in no time flat. The six machine guns went into action ... Forgotten was the weariness and lassitude; every man a hero, we stood ready to receive the enemy. Red flares fired in the air warned our artillery, who promptly brought down dense masses of defensive fire, which the Tommies found impenetrable. Whether we were facing an attack or a raid I cannot say. Either way our morale was boosted as we eventually dropped back into our shell holes. Unfortunately we had suffered heavy losses that day. In addition to three men killed we suffered sixteen wounded and one man missing.

"If we had expected a quiet night we were mistaken. Our artillery fired large quantities of gas between 11.00 pm and 3.00 am, which of course did not go without reply. Again and again on the enemy side the red-green-yellow signal for artillery defensive fire went up, to be followed promptly by two hours of drum fire which, following the work of our machine gunners the night before, was rather more accurate this time. During the evenings of 29 and 30 September, officers and NCOs from 2nd Battalion Reserve Infantry Regiment 93, who were due to launch an attack on the line of pillboxes to our front, as part of a more general attack between Polygon Wood and Geluveld, came forward to our position. The force itself moved to readiness during the second night, without being spotted and without suffering any casualties. The new troops made an outstanding impression: they were all young, tough lads. After a short, but heavy, barrage the infantry attack was launched at 6.00 am. 6th Company Reserve Infantry Regiment 92 was ordered to remain in the position to secure it. The attack to our front was successful: the first line of pillboxes was captured.

"For us, however, the situation got noticeably worse. Absolutely murderous defensive artillery fire came down and, whenever it appeared to stop, renewed flare signals demanded a continuation. The sectors of 6th, 8th and 2nd Companies were particularly hard hit. Immobile, frozen like stone statues, condemned to death, [the men] crouched down in their shell holes. But nobody even thought of running away. Even the wounded insisted on being brought to me in order to take their leave formally in accordance with the regulations. Speaking from the groundsheet [in which he was being carried], Vizefeldwebel Pierrot from Alsace, who had had a leg shot off, continued to give brief orders, then formally requested leave to withdraw from the company, wounded. It simply moved me to tears. Direct hits landed in several shell holes.

"My senior unteroffizier – Schaupmann from Osnabrück – was killed and four of our comrades along with him.[63] Gefreiter Faßbender dug himself out of the clay severely shell-shocked. Suddenly there was a terrible crash: our shell hole? We tumbled on top of one another, enveloped in smoke and with lumps of clay pouring down on us. A man was thrown high in the air in an arc and dumped down in our shell hole. His spine shattered, he gave off a fearful death rattle. He had been in the next hole, where a direct hit had just landed. We closed his eye lids and removed his identity discs and valuables. He was a nineteen year old batman from Reserve Infantry Regiment 93. Until it went dark we were forced to stare at his corpse. Any attempt to move it would have had bloody results. That evening we laid him to rest in a nearby shell hole. When would it be our turn? I lit a cigarette and a strange calmness and a feeling of security enfolded me. God was nigh!"

Reserve Oberleutnant Theodor Fischer,
Commander 3rd Battery Bavarian Foot Artillery Battalion 18 [64] **12**

"The 3rd Battery, equipped with its four Belgian 120mm guns took up position astride the road to Zonnebeke about two kilometres west of Waterdam [i.e. just to the north of Keiberg]. A mere stone's throw forward left was the 6th Battery. It was impossible to construct dugouts – water was hit one metre down – and there were no materials to build anything out of concrete. The gunners had to split into twos and threes and dig shallow pits, which they covered with corrugated iron, camouflaged with earth and vegetation, in order to be protected against aerial observation at least. The ammunition lay in several heaps in the open and, like the guns, was camou-flaged with branches and other vegetation. In this primitive position, the battery endured the murderous British artillery fire for weeks ...

"In the early hours of 30 September the battery was engaged with about 400 heavy shells. Most of them landed on the battery position, especially in the area of Number 3 and Number 4 gun. Wheels, trails and ancillary equipment were all destroyed. A direct hit on a pile of ammunition blew up seventy rounds. A wooden hut near Number 4 gun caught fire and threatened to jump the gap to further nearby piles of shells and cartridge cases. Unteroffizier Weishaupt, completely ignoring the heavy fire which was still falling, raced over and repeatedly fetched water from a shell hole to throw over the flames and prevent a further disaster.

"After a pause of a few hours heavy fire came down once more at 11.30 am; this time with medium calibre shells. Cries for help were heard coming from Number 2 gun. At that the battery officer,[65] Leutnant Trautner, rushed across and discovered a man from 2nd Battery Field Artillery Regiment 61, which was located 200 metres to our left. He had been wounded in the foot. Whilst the battery officer and the Sanitätsgefreiter were bandaging the man up, a further shell landed with a great crash by this group and covered them with earth and filth. The battery officer was wounded in the upper arm by a shell splinter, but carried on with his duties on the gun position. Hearing about the wounding of the battery officer, the battery commander hurried to the gun position, but the battery officer refused his offer to relieve him. At that the battery commander turned to go and was wounded in the back just as he left the position.

"The battery remained under heavy fire until 7.00 pm. At 1.30 pm a shell landed just in front of the window of the command post. Shell fragments, earth and smoke came flying in, seriously wounding in the forehead the vizefeldwebel, who was sitting next to the battery officer. Another shell exploded just by the door at 4.00 pm. A huge splinter left a gaping wound in the head of the signaller, flew red-hot past Leutnant Trautner, went straight through the chimney of the stove and embedded itself half a metre deep in the earth which formed the side wall. The call went out for a medical orderly and, at that precise moment, another shell burst, seriously wounding a gunner in the left shoulder. At 6.00 pm the fire intensified. It landed all around the pits in which the men were sheltering and smashed the aid post, burying three gunners. Once again it was Unteroffizier Weishaupt who laid his life on the line and ran over to rescue the buried men.

"During the night the battery was re-supplied with 300 rounds and put down harassing fire in accordance with its orders. It also fired in support of an infantry attack the following morning. At 11.45 am the battery came under fire once more. A splinter set on fire a crate full of cartridges in front of Number 1 gun. The fire spread at once to the withered hedge which ran along the road, leapt from there to a pile of empty packing cases and threatened to destroy the piles of shells and cartridges stored by Number 1 gun. The battery officer, assisted nobly by Unteroffizier Weishaupt, struggled to control the blaze. After twenty minutes the flames were extinguished. Throughout this time shells had been exploding constantly with great crashes in a radius of thirty to fifty metres and sending splinters flying in all directions.

"During the morning the battery was ordered to put down barrage fire, but no sooner had it opened up than it came under British counter-battery fire once more; the beautiful autumn weather meant that many aircraft and observation balloons were in action. The crews, whose nerves had already been badly stretched by the extreme demands of the past few days, fled – some of them into the command post, others to shell holes behind the position. The battery commander urged and encouraged all of them [to return to their duties] and succeeded in raising morale, ably assisted by Obergefreiter Kolmich, who played his harmonica with gusto. As a result when orders arrived to open fire at 4.00 pm and to increase it to rapid fire at 4.30 pm at all costs, because the infantry would be attacking at that time, every man was at his post.

"Within a few moments shells were landing once more only a few metres from the gun crews, who pulled back again out of the hellish rain of fire. Nevertheless, just before 4.30 pm, the battery officer, Leutnant Trautner, supported by Unteroffizier Weishaupt and Obergefreiter Kolmich and faithful to the orders received, served Number 2 gun themselves and opened fire despite the fact that the battery position remained under constant shell fire throughout. Inspired by this heroic example, the gun crew of Number 1 gun came forward once more and fired shell after shell at the rapid rate. The other two guns were unserviceable. Towards 6.00 pm the sound of battle died away, but suddenly, at 7.00 pm, drum fire came down once more. One gunner was seriously wounded in the neck and died later at the dressing station. By 9.00 pm the fire eased. There were still 241 shells on the position and the battery officer ordered them to be fired. The position was reduced to a crater field. The trees to its front were reduced to bare stumps ...

"Three guns, their wheels and ancillary equipment damaged, stood prominently like small islands rising above the surrounding shell holes, which were two to three metres deep. Apart from the command post and a couple of small pits near Number 1 gun, everything was totally smashed. The position had become untenable; the next day the orders arrived to change position ... [During the move], near Waterdam, Leutnant Trautner was seriously wounded in the thigh. A few days later he died in a field hospital in Gent, a true hero."

Losses had been so severe during the past week of fighting that, as September drew to a close, fresh troops arrived to replace both ground-holding and *Eingreif* formations all along the front. 20th Infantry Division was expecting to replace 234th Infantry Division in the *Eingreif* role (south) but, such was the importance of the defence of the Passchendaele Ridge that this was changed at very short notice. *20th Infantry Division is to relieve 23rd Infantry Division on 28 September in its positions to the west of Passchendaele*, came an order the previous day and there was a great scramble to meet the new requirement. This turned out to be much more complex than expected, because some of its sub-units involved had to relieve troops of the 4th Bavarian Infantry Division as well. There was still a need to produce a fresh *Eingreif* division for use in the southern area so, in the absence of 20th Infantry Division, it fell to the regiments of 45th Reserve Division to assume the role.

By the morning of 29 September 20th Infantry Division was almost fully deployed. Major Niemann, the new *KTK* of Infantry Regiment 79, was established in command of the new sector with Infantry Regiment 77 to the north and Grenadier Guard Regt 3 the south. It was not long before the regiment was confronted with the stark reality of daily existence in the front line at this critical point in the battle.

Leutnant Kollibay Infantry Regiment 79 [66] **4**

"The enemy artillery fire increased throughout the day. From time to time brought down in violent concentrations, it was mostly directed against the positions of the troops at readiness and in reserve. However the casualties it caused were disproportionately few, bearing in mind the quantities of ammunition fired. Forward, everybody was crouched down in shell craters, unable to move and listening hard to the crashes coming from the rear. Evening drew on. Suddenly fire crashed down violently on the front line and everyone crouched down lower in his shell hole. Suddenly one of them noticed something as he breathed in. It was the vile smell of chlorine! Quickly he looked over the edge of the crater. Great white clouds were billowing towards the shell holes. All around were dull thuds, as though duds were landing. Gas! Gas! went the shout from crater to crater. Quickly masking up, everyone dropped down low into the muddy craters and waited ... waited until the British stopped firing."

For the troops holding the forward positions, it was business as usual, despite the setbacks of 20 and 26 September. Elsewhere, however, work had been going on day and night in all the higher headquarters as the staff grappled with the analysis of the changed British tactics and sought to find a counter. The operational method seemed to them to be the launching of a series of assaulting waves, with the objective of securing a line agreed in advance with the artillery; there to go over to a deeply echeloned defence with plenty of machine guns deployed and featuring at least two distinct protective defensive fire belts further forward. It was felt that whilst their previous defensive tactics had almost had the character of an advance to contact during mobile operations and had led to considerable, if costly, German successes, the new British methods had transformed the counter-actions into a form of the far more difficult assault on reinforced field positions: hence the bloody failure of the *Eingreif* troops in late September. The results of this study were then published by Fourth Army. An extract reads as follows:

Fourth Army Operation Order, dated 30 September 1917 [67]

"According to captured orders and intelligence gained from the major days of battle (20 and 26 September) it appears that the essential characteristics of the new British offensive tactics are as follows: Three of the four battalions of each brigade form attacking waves of the same weight and attack in succession. The fourth battalion is in reserve. Each of the three battalions is allocated a definite line which it has to capture. Each line in turn is prepared for defence, reinforced by numerous machine guns and each succeeding battalion launches its attack through the line so secured.

This immediately produces a zone of defence in depth, protected to its front by defensive artillery fire, with additional barrages, through which our reserves have to pass, brought down even further forward and effective even before the attack itself is completed.

"This operational procedure can only yield minor territorial gains to the enemy each time they attack, but if these attacks continue in quick succession as they did on 20 and 26 September and if a similar amount of ground is gained each time, it must be assumed that gradually the decisive heights on the main battle front will be lost and that finally we shall be forced back from the *Wasserfront* [Water Front] and the Lys. We must bend all our efforts to avoid this. In contrast to other parts of the Western Front, therefore, we are forced to fight decisively for even the smallest piece of ground.

"In order to wear down and destroy the enemy infantry in the same way as the enemy attempts to do to our infantry, there is to be an increased concentration on the engagement of enemy infantry. Most of the field artillery is to be used in this way whilst, within the ranks of the heavy artillery, at least half of the available ammunition is to be used to attack the enemy infantry. Defensive and destructive fire missions count as engaging the infantry. It is important that bringing down random harassing fire is avoided. Instead, targets should all be identifiable places where the infantry is to be found. These include: pillboxes, command posts, machine gun nests, duckboard tracks, smoked off areas, and narrow gauge railways.

"Whenever observation is possible, destructive fire is to be brought down. If this cannot be achieved, harassing of the same targets is permissible and, because the enemy like us completes reliefs at night following heavy battles, these are the times when heavy interdicting fire is to be directed against infantry positions and the areas to the rear. Large amounts of gas are to be used against battery positions and the enemy forward battle zone. Army headquarters will issue orders separately for these 'Major Gas Engagements'. Each of the Groups will also direct smaller scale gas shoots against the infantry whenever the wind is favourable. Extensive use is also to be made of gas-filled mortar bombs.

"All the indications suggest that the enemy holds the mass of their infantry well to the rear in between major days of battle, leaving only thin outpost lines forward. We have to force the enemy, therefore, constantly to maintain larger forces in their forward battle zone and to place their reserves further forward, so that our artillery has worthwhile infantry targets to engage. This can only be done if we launch attacks ourselves, preferably during the intervals between their attacks, so that we can disrupt their plans. This will force the enemy, if they are to be able to hold on to the ground they have won, to launch costly counter-attacks, against which we can deploy maximum firepower. In addition, we must use large concentrations of fire on other parts of the front to deceive the enemy about where the attacks are to be made and also despatch plenty of patrols forward to keep the enemy on their toes. Our attacks are to be launched, either where our positions can be tactically improved by so doing, or at places where the enemy is making use of concrete pillboxes to our front and we can recapture and re-use them ourselves."

So much for the theory, but it remained to be seen if these measures would be sufficient to counter the new Allied tactics.

Notes
1.   Niemann: History Infantry Regiment 133 p 71
2.   Schwenke: History Reserve Infantry Regiment 19 pp 259-260
3.   Gerth: History Infantry Regiment 395 p 96. There appears to be a mistake here. It is possible that this officer was serving with one of the units of the British 116 Brigade from 39th Division, whose units were 11th, 12th and 13th Royal Sussex, together with 14th Battalion Hampshire. Either the number of the battalion is wrong, or possibly an officer formerly of 14th Battalion (which never served in France and was disbanded in 1916) was attached to one of the other three. The situation is further complicated by the fact that, although this division participated in the attacks on 26 September, it was not in the line on the date of the raid. There is no reason to doubt that the Germans recovered the body of an officer, as they claimed, but his identity and unit affiliation will have to remain an unsolved mystery.
4.   Benary: History Field Artillery Regiment 20 pp 311-312
5.   Leutnant Ernst Döbert is buried in the German cemetery at Menen Block D Grave 808.
6.   Kümmel: History Reserve Infantry Regiment 91 pp 313-314
7.   *ibid.* p 314
8.   From the location involved near St Juliaan, it is probable that this is a misprint for the 48th Division.
9.   This is a reference to a fixed point on a map and has nothing to do with its height.
10. Forstner: History Reserve Infantry Regiment 15 p 158
11. Schwenke: *op. cit.* p 271
12. The *Drossel* position was located about one kilometre west of Zandvoorde where the Zandvoorde-Zillebeke road crosses the Bassevillebeek.
13. Wohlenberg: History Reserve Infantry Regiment 77 p 332
14. Pirscher: History Infantry Regiment 459 pp 71-72
15. Schwenke: *op.cit.* pp 271-272
16. Wohlenberg: *op.cit.* pp 332-334
17. Gerth: *op. cit.* p 107
18. Cron: History Infantry Regiment 60 pp200-201
19. *ibid.* p202
20. *ibid.* pp 209-211
21. This is highly improbable. Vonalt himself comments on the lack of visibility. The fact of

the matter is that the protective barrage was so comprehensive that any body of men moving forward was certain to encounter it.

22. On 18 September alone 3rd Battalion Bavarian Ersatz Infantry Regiment 28 lost eleven killed and twenty eight wounded as a result of pillboxes being collapsed or wrecked by shell fire. See Brauch: History Ersatz Infantry Regiment 28 p 166

23. Brauch: *op. cit.* p 179

24. There are constant references to drunken attackers in the German literature. It is doubtful if there is much substance to them. Apart from the fact that men needed all their wits about them in the attack, many abstained from all food and drink before an operation in case they were wounded and needed rapid surgical treatment.

25. Braun: History Bavarian Infantry Regiment 21 p 75

26. Dunzinger: History Bavarian Infantry Regiment 11 pp 55-56

27. Braun: *op.cit.* p 76

28. Forstner: *op. cit.* pp 166-167

29. In view of the immense quantity of counter-battery fire which was coming down throughout the day, it is much more likely that the German artillery was simply unable to make a more powerful response. In the circumstances, it would have made no sense for them to have operated as Spahn alleges.

30. Henke: History Field Artillery Regiment 7 pp 209-210

31. Leutnant Albert Reintjes is buried in the German cemetery at Langemark in the *Kameradengrab.*

32. Leutnant Josef Elsner is buried in the German cemetery at Mangiennes Block 3 Grave 6.

33. Wohlenberg: *op. cit.* p 330

34. Pirscher: *op. cit.* p 73

35. Forstner: *op. cit.* pp 159-160

36. Pirscher: *op. cit.* pp 78-79

37. Wohlenberg: *op. cit.* pp 332-334

38. Schwenke: *op. cit.* pp 271-272

39. This is believed to be an error. 10,000 rounds fired on the second day would appear to have been more probable.

40. Wohlenberg: *op. cit.* pp 340-341

41. Kessler: History Reserve Field Artillery Regiment 9 p 212

42. Kessler: *op. cit.* pp 213-214

43. KronprinzRupprecht: *Mein Kriegstagebuch II. Band* p 265

44. This group of pillboxes was one of the few points where the advance of the I ANZAC corps was held up the following day. See McCarthy: *Passchendaele. The Day by Day Account* p 85

45. Wiedersich: History Reserve Infantry Regiment 229 pp 101-102

46. Niebelschütz: History Reserve Infantry Regiment 230 pp 173-176

47. *Festschrift: 2. Regimentstag des Reserve Infantry Regiment 231* pp 12-13

48. Kronprinz Rupprecht: *op. cit.* p 265

49. This statement appears to be a strange assessment of the situation by the army group commander. As a result of prisoner interrogation, it seems to have been common knowledge on the German side that a major operation was planned for 26 September. See, for example, Schuster, History Infantry Regiment 369 p 64 'According to a statement made by a prisoner who was captured during the night 24/25 September [and interrogated] by

Group Wijtschate, the enemy intend to renew their attack on 26 September'. Less specifically, Trebing, writing in the history of Infantry Regiment 370 notes, 'At 11.00 pm [25 September], intelligence was passed forward that, according to statements of prisoners, an attack was to be expected the next day.' Martin, in the History of Grenadier Reserve Regiment 100, states quite baldly: 'Prisoner statements were unanimous that there would be a major British offensive on 26 September.'

50. Wiedersich: *op. cit.* p 104
51. Major Ernst Hethey is buried in the *Kameradengrab* of the German cemetery at Langemark.
52. Reserve Leutnant Paul Stölting is buried in the *Kameradengrab* of the German cemetery at Langemark
53. Niebelschütz: *op. cit.* pp 172-173
54. Möller: History Reserve Infantry Regiment 78 p 248
55. Zipfel: History Infantry Regiment 75 pp 304-307
56. This was, of course, an example of the barrage fire, designed to enable the attackers to hold on to their newly-acquired gains.
57. Reserve Leutnant Emil Brokate is buried in the *Kameradengrab* of the German cemetery at Langemark.
58. Leutnants Richard Kruse and Wilhelm Schilling are buried near to one another in Block D of the German cemetery in Menen in Graves 700 and 686 respectively.
59. Zipfel: History Grenadier Regiment 89 pp 334-336
60. *ibid.* p 337
61. *ibid.* pp 338-339
62. Kellinghusen: Kriegserinnerungen pp 649 – 653
63. Unteroffizier Wilhelm Schaupmann is buried in the German cemetery at Langemark Block B Grave 18225.
64. History K.B. Schwere Artillerie pp 294-297
65. In the German artillery the title 'battery officer' was given to the officer who commanded the gun position, from which the weapons were actually fired. The battery commander was normally in his command post or manning an observation post.
66. Brandes: History Infantry Regiment 79 pp 423-424
67. Makoben: History Reserve Infantry Regiment 212 pp 398-399

CHAPTER FIVE

1 – 15 October 1917

As October opened the German High Command was forced to confront some uncomfortable truths. They now realised beyond any doubt that the Allies had changed their tactics. The ending of attempts at breakthrough, or the setting of distant objectives beyond the effective range of their field artillery and their replacement with 'bite and hold' operations, negated the German tactics of flexible defence at a stroke. As has been noted, rapid analysis of the course of the fighting on 20 and 26 September proved the scale of the changes. It now appeared to the German commanders that the new intention was to move to a series of local advances in quick succession, designed to force the defence back, slowly but surely, in the direction of the coast.

First Quartermaster General Erich Ludendorff [1]

"The fighting of the Third Battle of Flanders [i.e. the September battles] exhibited the same characteristics as the second battle and the fighting before Verdun; that is to say limitation of the depth of the penetrations in order to avoid the effect of our counter-attacks and to smash these by massed artillery fire. After each attack I had discussions with General von Kuhl and Oberst von Loßberg, either at the front or by telephone. I also travelled forward to Flanders to arrange for officers with experience of the battles to study the same questions. Our defensive tactics had to be modified in some way. We all felt the same, but it was incredibly difficult to find the correct solution. We could only feel our way forward carefully towards one.

"The proposals which were made to me by the men on the spot inclined me towards a return to our earlier tactics. This meant an, admittedly only very slight, strengthening of our forward positions and dispensing with counter-attacks by our *Eingreif* divisions. These were to be replaced with local thrusts, which were to be conducted on a wide front prior to an enemy attack by divisions deployed in a second wave close up behind our positions. This would reinforce the front line and add further to the depth of the battle area.

"For the Army High Command, it meant making a second division available behind each of the forward ground holding ones; in other words a more intensive use of forces than ever before. It was a simple matter of

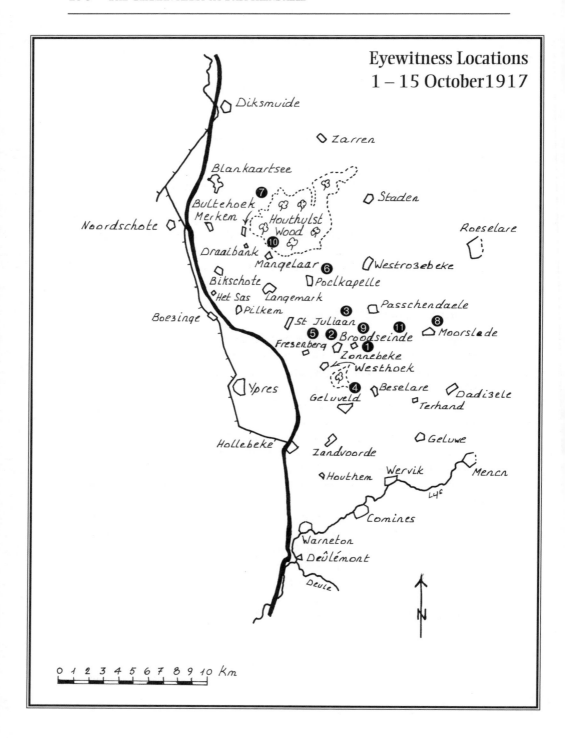

Eyewitness Locations
1 – 15 October1917

calculation to demonstrate that the use of a second division behind almost all of the front line ones, would lead to an increase in the security of the defence, but it was equally straightforward to work out that such a policy would have to lead to a much greater thinning out of the front in other places than had been the case previously ... I approved the tactical changes, even though within my own staff voices were raised against the move away from the 'defensive battle'. I believed, however, that I had to give priority to experience from the front." [2]

As a result of all the work, it was concluded that the battle conditions now demanded a shift away from the previously accepted principles of flexible defence and 'that the possession of even the smallest piece of ground must be fought for decisively.'[3] To that end the role of the *Eingreif* divisions was to change. Instead of waiting to react to Allied attacks, pre-emptive operations were to be launched with the aim of forcing the Allies to hold their forward lines more strongly and to place their reserves in forward positions where they would be vulnerable to German artillery fire in between days when major attacks were launched. Like many such ideas conceived in haste, this one was to be short-lived. Within a few days, on 4 October, it became plain that this scheme too was a failure. That realisation was still some days in the future, however, when units and formations of 4th Guards Infantry Division went forward to relieve the exhausted men of 3rd Reserve Division who had been deployed forward in the critical Zonnebeke area.

Füsilier Karl Böhme 11th Company Foot Guards Regiment 5 [4]

"The trains filled with the regiments rolled north through bleak countryside, through busy towns, up hill and down dale. Then we came to Flanders and its murderous battle ... Suddenly we came to a halt. Had something gone wrong? 'Everyone out!' We were in Torhout. It was the middle of the night and there was no light to be seen on the streets. Above us aircraft were prowling round, trying to spot the slightest glimmer. From the front came nothing but rumbling and crashes. The place was over-flowing with troops. 'Good night mate! We are not here for a rest cure. Tomorrow we shall form part of a counter-attack division and shall be sent into battle!' Every man to the front! There can be no rest now. Off to the mud of Flanders. We have to help our comrades maintain the wall and protect the Homeland.

"Leaving Moorslede we head for Zonnebeke, carrying only light assault order. Everywhere ghostly ruins loom out of the darkness and there are corpses, the stink of burning, flares and shells. Now and again someone curses softly when he is tripped up by the sticky mud. It is all part of a night march on a corduroy road to the front in Flanders. Heavy shells begin to land very close – Keep up! Things are now pretty hot! They explode with an appalling crash. Down! – Up!- Down! – Up! 'Just get through it! Don't get caught up in a bit of defensive fire! Be careful, wire! – Just keep going! We rush on through craters and the clinging morass, boiling hot and with our lungs heaving. At long last we are through it. Our breath comes a little easier. Now there is not much fire coming from the front. We are not the least bit scared by field guns, but the heavy ones! It sounds as though the world is breaking apart!

"Now down into the holes, spade in hand. The 4th Guards Infantry Division is digging in in Flanders for the third time to protect the wall, despite high explosive shells and the clatter of machine guns. By morning everything is still and the work is covered with planks of wood and branches. There is plenty of heavy stuff lying in wait to take on anything that moves, guided by airmen from the west. But death is still riding abroad in Flanders. Every so often it plucks another one from our midst. – no stopping to ask questions about tears, the homeland or luck. At night we carry the fallen to the rear in silence. Several times a day a great hurricane of fire rolls over us from the west: crashing, bursting, flames and thunderous noise! Can we survive amidst it? Is that just a crazy thought? But we have to; we are all part of the grey wall and we must protect the Homeland, our women and children against the bringers of death, because we are all German soldiers!

In an attempt to overcome the setbacks of 20 September and the additional progress made during the battle for Polygon Wood and Tower Hamlets on 26 September, the German army continued to make every effort to prevent further British progress across the remainder of the Geluveld plateau. They had had but little success on 30 September and 1 October, but in view of the continuing serious situation and in accordance with the latest thinking, a further determined counter-attack by Reserve Infantry Regiment 212 of 45th Reserve Division, in association with reserves from the ground holding 4th Guards Infantry Division was scheduled for the early morning of 4 October, with H Hour at 6.00 am. This operation, codenamed *Höhensturm* [Storm the Heights][5] was designed to move forward the front line from its current swampy position to the crest line from the western edge of Zonnebeke to *Haus Käthe* [situated in De Veldhoek, 500 metres east northeast of the north east tip of Polygon Wood].

Unfortunately for the German army this clashed directly with the third major 'bite and hold' operation, designed to secure the Broodseinde Ridge together with the Gravenstafel spur. As a result, when the opening British barrage crashed down at 6.00 am, it caught the German assault force in the open. They were more or less destroyed and the losses amongst the formations of 4th Guards Infantry Division, which were holding the line and also participating in the counter-attack, were also very high. Overall, although every effort was made later to put the best gloss on events, 4 October was a day that turned out to be yet another disaster for the defence. Occupying positions to the north of the Zonnebeke-Moorslede road just to the east of Broodseinde, was Grenadier Guard Regiment 5, with the Foot Guard Regiment 5 immediately to their south. Already severely weakened by losses they had sustained in earlier fighting, they fought hard, but were largely powerless to prevent penetrations all along their front.

Major Freiherr von Sobbe Infantry Regiment 92 [6] **1**

"In the early hours of 4 October, 4th Guards Infantry Division had completed all the necessary preparations for an attack to recapture the parts of the position near Zonnebeke which had previously been lost. They were already gathered in great masses and backed by reserves. Their batteries, supported by artillery from neighbouring sectors, opened up heavy fire at 5.30 am, only to be hit by a deluge of counter-fire, whilst they were in the middle of their preparatory bombardment. Simultaneously the enemy brought down drum fire on a fifteen kilometre front from Poelkapelle to the Wijtschate sector. The 4th Guards attack was smashed before it ever got started. Behind this wall of fire twelve British divisions were drawn up, shoulder to shoulder, ready to launch a major assault. Great steel 'birds' flew in all directions, hitting home with savage violence. An endless stream of splinters whistled and whirred through the air. Craters disappeared only to be reformed. The earth seemed to want to swallow up everything.

"The battalions clung on amidst a crazy maelstrom of flying objects. The shells crashed down faster and faster. Bodies trembled; pulses raced. Time seemed to stand still as seconds became hours. The appalling uncertainty was quite dreadful. Nameless fears caused the gorge to rise in our throats. Who can deny it? Were you going to be hit? Would you die without even having clapped eyes on the enemy? Some of the men hunched there in silence, stripped of all their emotions, taking in nothing, unable to comprehend the surrounding chaos which at any moment could blow them to smithereens. Many prayed, perhaps for the first time in a very long time: 'My God, do not forsake me' and, mixed in with their prayer was the glimmer of hope of men still trying desperately to hang on to life.

"Others held on strongly in faith; their wish for life being tempered by a readiness to die. 'Lord, thy will be done.' The image of Christ crucified appeared to their souls, conquering death for them. What strength of faith this acceptance of God's will amongst this appalling destruction demonstrated! Those who possessed it understood that they were working their earthly purpose out in the face of these overwhelming events. But could it really be that they should have fulfilled their life's work quite so soon? Possibly some of them did hope to be spared to see their families again and to work out their earthly purpose, but perhaps the Almighty had decided otherwise. The riddle of man lies in eternity. To surrender to the will of God meant that the time and space of earthly being had already been despatched in the distance towards the place where the portal to eternal life would open unto them.

"From time to time the will to live rose in each of them, causing them to seek to avoid an anonymous death [during the bombardment]. It should not end like that; far better to be allowed at least to confront the enemy face to face, to be able to pay him back for all this hate. Life had to be sold as dearly as possible. The feeling of powerlessness was awful. Faces screwed themselves into a grim fury. Hands grasped weapons tightly. Frequently the weapons were buried or made unserviceable. Each time someone rushed feverishly to repair and maintain them. Eyes and ears strained through the fog of war and the continuing racket in order to pick up the slightest sign of the appearance of the enemy in good time. The enemy batteries continued to bring down drumfire. All the mortars were buried and the same fate befell most of the machine guns. One soldier after another was hit and rolled away into a shell crater, his lifeblood seeping away from his wounds. It was not necessarily terribly painful. Those who died there were conscious of having fulfilled their life's objective, which was to die in battle. Crouched down between the dead and wounded were the living, sticking it out with parched lips and burning eyes. 'Father I call unto thee!'

Füsilier Karl Böhme 11th Company Foot Guards Regiment 5[7]**1**

"The sixth night of our tour [3/4 October], the order came round: 'Keep a sharp lookout! We are taking on the Tommies head on today. Fresh regiments have been brought forward to launch an assault. We are to hold out positions to the last man.' … The dance begins! The barrage comes crashing down, raining shells down in a wild frenzy on the ground. Forward comrades and give the Tommies what for! Celebrate the attack over there as revenge! Then a great heaving and trembling enveloped the entire place as the heavens opened in a veritable storm of steel! From a thousand guns came endless howling, crashing and banging. Great flashes lit up the sky as the earth trembled under crushing blows. Then came the screams of the dying! Dear God in heaven, let this morning be past! Pulses racing, each man held on in the jaws of Hell. Suddenly, what's that? Someone came running back, then there were others, then large numbers and, in between them, lines of Tommies. Open fire, our mates need help! OK, enemy half right! Aim! Fire! They seem to have been checked. Now, look left! Pass me a new belt – the cooling water is already boiling in its jacket – Damn it! – now the gun falls silent, it cannot fire a round – gunner over here! – clear it – it is completely fouled up, a round is jammed in the breech – there's no time to fix it – there's a spare rifle. Start firing, fire as fast as you can, fire as though your life depends on it!

"And we stood firm, shoulder to shoulder, but the enemy kept bringing up fresh troops. Our little band kept shrinking. The deadly hail of lead tore first one and then another of us away. We melted away like snow in summer. All around was death and flames! – hand grenades exploded – small arms fire was flying in all directions! Is there nobody left to plug the gap? The machine gun is choked with fouling and out of action, all the ammunition has been fired off – there are only two of us left; two from two sections – enough blood has been spilt – it is useless to fight on. There is a stark choice – pull back or be captured – Hands up! It's no contest – out of the hole and run for your life. It is always better to do that than to surrender tamely. The remnants can always rally in the rear.

"We succeed in blocking the way to the Tommies. Once more we stand firm and defend! The steam has gone out of the enemy attack. They do not attempt to get further forward. A gain of a few hundred metres is all that they have managed. Once more victory has eluded them. At long last some welcome news arrives. 'The reliefs are here!' is passed on from mouth to mouth. We head off to billets in the rear across shot up roads. Only a few have survived the battle. Dog tired we report in to the company assembly point. Three men of the hundred who were forward answer their names at roll call."

Major Lincke, Commander 2nd Battalion Reserve Infantry Regiment 212 [8] **1**

"Shortly before 6.00 am and far behind the British lines, a previously unknown light signal, comprising three blue, red and green flares was fired and hung, plainly visible in the sky for several minutes. This signal was the trigger for the sudden start of a concentration of enemy light and medium calibre shells on our trenches. The fire was of an intensity which even the battle hardened officers and men had never previously experienced. Despite this fire the companies of the centre of the attack [i.e 5th, 6th. 7th and 8th Companies] got to their feet at 6.00 am, exactly as ordered and went their final way. What actually happened in that swampy area in the dark and in the fog, no pen of a living author can ever write. No report ever reached the battalion commander, a sure sign of the intensity of the battle. Always previously, even during the hardest fights, the platoon and company commanders had always done their duty and sent situation reports to the headquarters in rear.

"On the other hand, it was not long before a runner arrived at the head-quarters of the left hand battalion and provided the information that the front of Reserve Infantry Regiment 93 had broken completely and the enemy was penetrating deep into our positions, threatening our flank and rear. This was not believed at first and the commander probed the runner about the circumstances. He explained that two members of Reserve Infantry Regiment 93, showing all the signs of shock, had rushed past them, giving only a brief explanation."

The regiment had experienced a similar situation during the Battle of the Somme, which made them disinclined to believe the story, until it was confirmed by the adjutant, who went forward to find out what was happening. All was confusion and before the situation was fully clarified, before any coherent counter-action could be arranged, Major Lincke, who had been wounded in the arm by a shell splinter, which tore into his brachial artery, together with his men were all captured by Australian troops. Their casualties were appalling. The regimental commander, Oberstleutnant Rave was killed along with thirteen of his officers and 328 of his soldiers. The numbers of wounded, missing and sick brought the total for this disastrous day, when some companies lost ninety five per cent of their strength, to forty one officers and 1,009 junior ranks.[9]

Major Lincke, Commander 2nd Battalion Reserve Infantry Regiment 212 [10] **2**

"We finally reached the old German front line, which had been torn from the possession of the Guards during the battle. Dotted around in the swampy landscape were concrete pillboxes, with space for about one section ... At one of them I saw what, for me, was the most gruesome sight of the war. Hanging from one of the four metre long vertical steel reinforcing rods by his legs was the corpse of a German soldier, headless and with his chest torn open. He must have been thrown there by a shell ... I kneeled next to a runner from 8th Company who was close to death and begged for water. I shall never forget his beaming face when he recognised me, his commander ... he thought that we must have won the battle. I gave him the last drops in my water bottle then held his hand for the few remaining seconds it took him to die ...

"As we tried to enter the inside of the pillbox, which was already crammed full, space was willingly made for us. We were offered all kinds of refreshments and I could tell from the conversations of the Australian soldiers how surprised and reassured they were by what to me was entirely normal behaviour with this dying comrade. Their own propaganda had obviously provided them with a completely different image of enemy officers.

East of Broodseinde, it was 7.00 am on 4 October before detailed news reached the commander of Grenadier Guard Regiment 5. He gradually despatched his reserves, which were drawn largely from Reserve Infantry Regiment 211 forward, with instructions to advance to contact and thereafter to conduct a delaying battle, but it was a chaotic period of fighting, marked by deep penetrations, encirclements and fights to the death by pockets of defenders. Just as the commander was rapidly running out of options, a member of Bavarian Infantry Regiment 5 from the 4th Bavarian Infantry Division arrived at his command post to orientate himself about the situation. Although the Bavarians were located only 2 kilometres east of the command post, they were in the area of another division. Nevertheless the urgency of the situation demanded decisive action and, despite the fact that he was only a major and the commander of the Bavarians was an oberstleutnant from another division, he directed his adjutant to write out a counter-attack order which he despatched together with a situation report.[11]

There then followed a nerve-wracking period of two hours where the waiting in the command post was only punctuated by the arrival of bad news: 'All the members of the ground-holding battalion are dead or captured.' 'Support battalion has been hit by overwhelming artillery fire and smoke and has been overrun.' The commander takes up the story:

Major Freiherr von Schleinitz, Commander Grenadier Guard Regiment 5 [12] **1**

"What else could possibly be done? The enemy only had to march forward and he would simply be able to break through, rarely throughout the war had the time been ticked off so slowly. Initially there was no sign of help arriving, but it had in fact come. The Bavarian Regiment had, in fact, obeyed my attack order and very skilfully had hit the flank of the advancing British [sic] soldiers, just as I had directed. At approximately 1.30 pm a report arrived from the right flank company, commanded by Leutnant von Hennig: *Hurra! Reinforcements!* There was no more, but I already knew enough. My grenadiers could take new heart, the front was closed once more and the situation saved"

In fact the request for assistance had arrived with Bavarian Infantry Regiment 5 at 11.25 am and within minutes the commander had issued a written order:

"1. The enemy is pushing forward onto the Broodseinde Heights and beyond, along the line of the railway running to the south of Passchendaele.

2. Grenadier Guard Regiment 2 is holding the line of the gravel pits 200 metres east of Broodseinde crossroads

3. In order to counteract the threat developing on the right flank of Grenadier Guard Regiment 5, 1st and 3rd Battalions are to advance, with the utmost urgency, along the axis *Kapellenhof-Keiberg*. The obstacles along the *Flandern II* line can only be crossed via the track leading to *Kapellenhof*.

4. 1st Battalion Bavarian Infantry Regiment 5 is to depart at once, followed by 3rd Battalion which, having crossed the obstacle is to advance on the left of 1st Battalion. Once contact is made, the inner flanks of each battalion are to advance northwest in the direction of the station at Keeselaarhoek ... "[13]

The attack was pushed with great vigour, contact was made with the remnants of Grenadier Guard Regiment 5, but it was not possible to make any significant progress and the assaulting troops dug in eventually on a minor crest to the north east of the Broodseinde cross roads. The immediate crisis may have been over, but intense fighting continued throughout the day, causing the regiments of 4th Guards Infantry Division very high casualty rates. It was a very similar picture on the Gravenstafel spur, when formations of 20th Infantry Division were holding positions amongst the craters. For the *Heide* [Heath] Regiment [Infantry Regiment 77] which fought with the utmost determination, it was to be one of the blackest days of the war. The companies held on grimly in the early morning whilst a hurricane of fire broke over them. Dense clouds of gas, smoke, fumes from exploding shells and dust floated above the crashing shells and pillars of filth that constantly rose from the seething crater field. As a result the sentries could barely see one hundred metres.

Reserve Leutnant Groth 12th Company Infantry Regiment 77 [14] **3**

"Far out to the right the red flares were going up; the fire became ever more frenzied. A loud uniquely endless droning racket filled the air and enveloped the positions so it was impossible to distinguish one sound from another. Many men lay silent, apathetic, pressed hard against the walls of the craters. Others crouched down, murmuring prayers; there staring eyes struggling to take in the gruesome scenes of death all around them. Suddenly above the row could be heard the voice of a blond 'Heath Man'. 'Herr Leutnant, here they come!' Reserve Leutnant Almstedt sprang to his right. It was true, the British were on their way approaching from half left in long lines; wave after wave. They were in no hurry; their artillery would have been effective! From the right at the boundary between 2nd Company and the companies of the 3rd Battalion, came the sound of intense small arms fire and the crash of exploding grenades. There the enemy, having forced a swift breakthrough in the area of the 10th Ersatz Division, had taken the forward companies of Infantry Regiment 92 in the right flank. Despite the tough resistance the men from Braunschweig had put up, they had been rolled up and now it was the turn of Infantry Regiment 77 to be taken in the right flank.

"This was resisted with all possible force. Reserve Leutnant Gain who still had two Maxim 08 machine guns in working order, poured fire into the lines of the attackers and forced them to take cover in shell holes. Reserve Leutnant Meyer took up a fire position with a machine gun of Infantry Regiment 92 which had arrived in our area. The fog began to disperse and aching eyes stared hard into it to make out the enemy. Gradually things began to move in the clouds of smoke and dust and solid forms began to be discerned in the swirling fog. At long last the enemy closed in; finally the fight was on. It was simply a matter of firing round after round from the weapons; each one found a victim. Our fire forced the Tommies to take cover. Through my telescope I could see dense masses of British soldiers attempting to by-pass the swamp and hill to our front. I ordered the machine gun to bring down fire at 500 metres. The masses scattered, stalled, formed small groups then disappeared in to cover. Further off we could see small groups of prisoners being led away. We were very few. How long could we hold them off?

12th Company resisted the pressure in this area longer than any other company, but finally the end came. Reserve Leutnant Groth continues:

"My telescope was smashed by a bullet as I looked through it. Fortunately I only suffered a few scratches. Meanwhile we were under a hail of enemy hand grenades and the machine gun was knocked out. A little later, the enemy suddenly appeared in strength ten metres behind us. We were completely surrounded! We were under heavy fire from all sides and grenades continued to be thrown. The machine crew was shot down the few remaining men were overwhelmed, bayoneted, bludgeoned with rifle butts and robbed. The four or five who were left were led away bleeding profusely."[15]

In all over 1,100 German soldiers were taken prisoner by the New Zealand Division in this area and many more were killed, largely as a result of the bombardment, despite the fact that difficulties with moving guns and ammunition forward meant that this had been rather less intense than that of the September attack. Although the main focus of the day was in the Broodseinde-Gravenstafel sector, there was also sharp fighting to the south near Polygon Wood, where Reserve Infantry Regiment 92 was defending a length of the *Flandern I Stellung* between Polygon Wood and Beselare. As was often the case during this battle, Allied operations on the flanks of an assault, even a major one, were rarely marked with the progress achieved in the centre of the attacking front

Hauptmann Wolf Reserve Infantry Regiment 92. [16] **4**

"On 3rd October I was informed that the battalion was going to be relieved that evening. Naturally that suited me well, but things were to turnout differently. Battalion headquarters had a strange experience. Our concrete pillbox had originally been built into Polderhoek chateau. When we first arrived some of the walls were still standing; gradually, however they disappeared, so this great white lump of light coloured concrete stood out on the hill top, presenting a brilliant target that the British gunners just could not leave alone. Initially we and the surrounding area were engaged so heavily by medium calibre guns that not even a mouse could have escaped it. Then, just before 4.00 pm came the first round. Blam! Good grief, what was that? We had no idea and our artillery liaison officer, whose name now escapes me, could not throw any light on the matter either. Then came the next great crash – a bit closer this time. I had a careful look outside. Blast it! There was an aircraft right overhead.

"The situation was serious and sure enough, every three minutes came a shell from an enormous gun, which we were a year later to discover had a calibre of 405 mm. On one occasion the artillery liaison officer remarked that the opposition was shooting poorly; otherwise they would have hit us by now. This observation did not earn him any great applause. Gradually all was silent within our blockhouse. I can still remember sitting at a table, constantly refilling a small pipe and drinking a schnaps every now and again. My eye was drawn constantly to my wristwatch where, following the movement of the hands I could see that that lot over there were maintaining their three minutes intervals with amazing precision. But what has happened? It is 6.30 pm. We ought to be able to hear the shell shortly. Nothing. 6.31 pm, 6.30 pm and thirty seconds. Still nothing. A voice broke the silence. I think it was that of the machine gun officer, 'Hauptmann, now they have not fired for ninety seconds.' Good Lord! The brain had got so used to three minute intervals that these ninety seconds seemed like a lucky eternity. It was 6.33 pm. The round never arrived. Ten minutes passed. I stood up and, with me, so did everyone else and accompanied me outside. The bunker was tilted a bit, but it was still upright. We much enjoyed the sunset. Every year, on its anniversary I think back to this moment, although it is always dark here at that time in East Prussia. It meant that we had been left in peace but, on the other hand, the rear areas were hit hard. As a result of all the fire the relieving battalion arrived seriously scattered and depleted and, which for me was decisive, the battalion commander had not arrived. My battalion was relieved and I assumed command of the relieving unit: not alone; my entire staff stayed too. We all knew perfectly well that something was going to happen in the morning.

"The next morning duly dawned and, with it, came the usual drum fire. Blast it! The Tommies obviously had something special lined up for us. The fire lifted. We listened hard, but detected nothing. It looked as though they were not actually going to attack. Leutnant Bode stayed outside. I wanted to have a drink of coffee and just I was raising the hot cup, Leutnant Bode yelled, 'Hauptmann: the Tommies!' Out I rushed and there – yes for God's sake – there they were and not only the Tommies. There, too, was the entire staff of 2nd Battalion Reserve Infantry Regiment 92 and the staff of the new battalion as well. It was not long before the Tommies were forced onto the back foot as the first attack was beaten off. The British then set about their minor tactics carefully. Whenever one of our heads popped up, there was the sharp crack of a British bullet. If only we had a machine gun. Do we really not have one? No, in fact we have two reserve weapons. Due to the continuing drum fire they had been withdrawn and were hoping to stay uninvolved. That soon changed and they were once again chattering away merrily and we had a period of calm.

"My faithful batman Protz disappeared into the blockhouse and soon reappeared with a large number of sandwiches which we passed round. Luckily thanks to our regimental commander the previous evening, we had a large stock of schnaps and cigars. The situation did not seem to be half as bad as it had earlier. I stood on the enemy side with Leutnants Schwier and Bode and observed the progress of the British through the telescope. They were gaining ground left and right of us. The racket was deafening; it was impossible to hear anything above it. Suddenly I received a hard blow to the neck. Blast it! Had I been wounded? Protz just laughed and removed a small stone which had lodged in my collar. But what caused it? We looked around trying to get to the bottom of it then there was a further puff of smoke between us. What about that? Leutnant Schwier maintained that it was an assault gun and that we ought to try to locate it. Aha! Over there – another puff of smoke. Suddenly our faithful battalion runner Sprik appeared in front of me and said, as calmly as ever, 'Herr Hauptmann: over there – three tanks.' He was absolutely right; it could not be denied. Three tanks – what was going to happen?

"Protz said, 'I do not think that they will be able to get through the swamp.' We shall just have to see. Oh yes – one has already bogged down. Good! The crew climbs out. Our machine gun fire deals with them. What about the second? Clang! One of those British shells which gives off a reddish smoke hits it squarely. Very many thanks for the support! As for the third, what is it going to do? It turns away, so that was that dealt with. In between times we attempted by means of light signalling to maintain contact to the rear, but the rain of British high explosive and smoke shells made that impossible most of the time. Nevertheless we were all of good courage. About midday we were once more subjected to a severe test, because our own heavy artillery began to honour us with their attentions and, I am sorry to have to report, their shooting was good. What was to be done? We fire off flares and flashed light signals: all in vain. Nothing would put the artillery off.

"The atmosphere became somewhat tense. Were we to retain this dominating point only in order to be massacred by our own artillery? Artillery Liaison Officer! What are we to do? What did the magnificent chap say? 'Because we cannot get a message through I shall try to break through to the rear and get this nonsense stopped.' A shake of the hand and I saw him race off towards the rear in great bounds, until he disappeared from our sight, enveloped in a great many small clouds of dirt from exploding shells. We waited, but things did not improve. It was clear that we had to stay, clear too that we had to get a message to the rear. Suddenly my dear and faithful runner Gefreiter Sprick appeared in front of me and said, 'Herr Hauptmann, I shall try to get through to the regiment.' Next to him stood young Utschakowski, who had only joined us in Kurland[17] and asked quietly if he could accompany Sprick. Did it have to be? Did these two also have to be sent? Could the artillery liaison officer have got through? Finally it was obvious that it was taking too long. A few more well-aimed shells brought about a decision: Go on! Break a leg! The two of them got through, got through to the regiment. Our artillery sent us no more presents.

"It may have been about 4.00 pm when I saw, far to the rear, small dots moving across the battlefield. Simultaneously a murderous weight of enemy artillery fire came down. It was impossible to see anything through the clouds of smoke and flying earth but, eventually, when it was possible to see through the murk, we could clearly recognise that these tiny dots were unstoppable and were getting closer. There could be no doubt. This was the counter-attack. It made progress forward, but slower and slower.

The British were well aware how to block it. All my officers and men were fully occupied trying to make sure that we were not thrown out of our position and fortunately, thank heavens, they were in no position to see that the counter-attack was beginning to falter and then suddenly be brought to a standstill five hundred metres behind us.

"But then things began to move once more. We flashed messages, fired flares into the air, then success! Our lines began to move once more. They advanced, they pushed on beyond us. Our job was done. In front of me stood a regimental commander in his peacetime uniform, with its stand-up red collar. I think it was a regiment from Mecklenburg. He looked at his map, then asked me, 'Is that Polderhoek Chateau? Yes? Well that's a fine thing!' It certainly was a fine thing. They had reached Polderhoek Chateau and it was still being held by German troops, admittedly and unfortunately not very many of them. I shall never forget this day or the dear comrades with whom I experienced it."

Unteroffizier Paul Stolz 4th Company Reserve Infantry Regiment 92 [18] **4**

"The 4th October dawned. It was a day which for me and many others will remain unforgettable. Already by 5.30 am the British brought down drumfire of an intensity you would hardly believe possible.[19] 320 mm howitzer rounds were sent crashing down on our positions in an un-interrupted series. The aim was to snuff out all life. Only a few unteroffiziers and their men were still holding out. On the left [south] of the Beselare-Ypres road many had pulled back to where, as I later discov-ered, the artillery fire was less intense. But we were bound to stay where we were in order to protect the battalion staff.

"Shell after shell smashed into our ranks. Several of our mates were buried by a direct hit. Others followed. Many were buried alive. Some we dug out; amongst others this included our dear friend Heinrich Gartmann. I lost half my section. Some we could only recover as corpses. Trinkler was seriously wounded and died at my side in the arms of the doctor. This terrible drumfire lasted until evening. In amongst the dark clouds of the explosions, fountains of dirty yellow soup-like clay spouted out of the craters, along with huge clods of earth, tree trunks and chunks of concrete. It was like a volcano erupting. No power of the devil could create anything more violent. Against this work of man, hell itself would seem feeble. The entire swampy earth shook when super-heavy duds, of which there were plenty, bored down into the ground.

"Meanwhile the British thrust forward with the utmost violence, advanced closer and closer and finally threatened our right flank. I never saw a performance to equal that of our artillery that day. No sooner were the coloured flares fired than the shells began to roar forward over us. A battery of close support artillery was co-located with us. Stripped to their shirtsleeves, the gunners laboured, firing until the barrels glowed red hot. Every single tank that appeared in front of us was fired at. Behind us the field artillery came forward at the gallop, unharnessed and brought the British under direct fire. The guns soon ran out of ammunition but so did the force of the British attack. At this point I must make special mention of the deeds of Vizefeldwebel Paehr, a war time volunteer, who carried all of us along by his example and bearing. We went through hours of intensive fighting, but our efforts were crowned with success. We could look back on this day with pride. The British did not succeed in capturing our position, even though they did take possession of the front line. Dead men and knocked out tanks were strewn everywhere on the ploughed up ground. Our nerves had been stretched to breaking point throughout this day of intense artillery fire. We longed for rest, having had barely an hour's sleep throughout. The following night our battalion was relieved."

On his way back to the rear and months of treatment in hospital and captivity Major Lincke, who had been captured earlier in the day and who had arrived in the rear via a regimental aid post where he and his comrades had been robbed and an advanced dressing station, had a most unusual experience as he made his way to the rear during the late afternoon. His treatment varied greatly, but initially, at least, he was well treated by the Australians. He also claimed that he was received along the way by the commander of the 1st Australian Division, who spoke excellent German with a Berlin accent, before finally beginning his journey to the rear areas.

Major Lincke, Commander 2nd Battalion Reserve Infantry Regiment 212[20] **5**

"Finally we ended up in front of a large old German command post which, it later transpired was the headquarters of the commander of the 1st Australian Division. There an orderly officer stopped us and, despite all protestations, roughly separated my batman from me and said that he had to go forward once more to help carry back British [sic] wounded. I did not see Simon Wege again until I met him at his home in the Lippe area after I had returned from captivity.

"I myself was taken to the divisional commander, who had previously been informed about me. In front of me stood a young general only a little over the age of 30, who spoke lively and faultless German with a Berlin accent. [21]He began at once to question me. I immediately explained that he could not demand of me, as an old soldier, the answer to inappropriate questions and he replied, 'OK I shall not ask you anything which you are not permitted to answer, but I am sure you will not object to a conversation about general questions.' I fainted at that point and, as I came round, British [*sic*] officers were around me, attempting to pour whisky through my tightly gripped teeth. I sat up and they offered me a cup of tea and biscuits which I accepted gratefully.

"The discussion, which I had with this senior officer, lasted for more than an hour and was, for me, one of the most interesting memories I have of the war. Its content, coupled with everything I had so far witnessed in and behind the British front and was later to experience, sowed the first serious doubts in my mind about whether we should be able to bring the war to a successful conclusion in the face of this immense commitment of men, materiel and organisation. I had the opportunity during our conversation to observe the interchange between the divisional commander and his staff, who entered and left bringing reports and orders and receiving others. I have to admit from what I saw and was able to follow, that the [work of the headquarters] was conducted in an exemplary manner.

"In response to a question from me the divisional commander declared that he had studied in Berlin and Heidelberg and had learned his good German there. He was an Australian lawyer who, before the war had already been a captain in the Australian militia. When war broke out he had gone to England and had initially enlisted in the Kitchener army, where he had made such swift progress that he finally ended up at the head of the 1st [Division] which, he added with pride, made him the commander of the best Australian division. He asked me how I had been treated by his men. I told him truthfully that apart from being robbed there were many good things to report. At that he stated that though his men were a rough lot when they were fighting, on the other hand they showed good will towards courageous opponents whom they could respect.

"It was a complete mystery to him how we expected to be able to win the war when we were opposed by the men and materiel of the whole world. He put it very bluntly: 'The cannon fodder of the entire world is at our disposal.' What he meant by this was that the manpower reserves of the enemy alliance were inexhaustible, whilst on the other side, as he stated and the events of today's battle had proved, the best soldiers of the Kaiser were being killed, wounded or captured and in any case were no longer available to fight. To his question, 'When will your revolution begin?' I parried with pride, 'Do not forget, general, that we are Germans not Russians.'

"Finally we came to the subject of the day's fighting, amongst other matters. He explained that having drawn the appropriate lessons from the battles during the spring and summer, during which our counter-attacks had certainly brought us great success, they had decided to move instead towards attacks with limited objectives. In principle the attacks would be designed to remain within the covering fire of the artillery. In this way today they had taken the crest line which ran south from Broodseinde crossroads. Their artillery was deployed, as I observed during my journey to the rear, into many groups, standing wheel to wheel. Each gun had three barrels at its disposal, so even if one suffered only superficial damage or wear, the battery commander had the possibility of changing one twice.

"This came to me a painful revelation, knowing what immense difficulties our guns were having in their efforts to achieve precision fire with worn out barrels. Finally the divisional commander took me to the map table and showed me the opposing positions in his sector and that of the neighbouring division, which were marked with coloured flags. He stated that the British objectives were thirty English miles distant. I could tell from the way the lines ran that in that area where the attack of Reserve Infantry Regiment 212 had occurred – and that was directly opposite the 1st Australian Division – the enemy penetrations of our lines were the shallowest."

Initial German assessments of the day are interesting. The Fourth Army report is factual, but the official Army Communiqué is simply full of wishful thinking and sophistry, not to say outright lies, designed to obfuscate the setbacks of the day from faulty tactics to enormous casualties.

Fourth Army Daily Report 4 October 1917 [22]

"Once again the British attacked along the line from Langemark to south of the Ypres-Menin Road. The main foci of this major day of battle were Poelkapelle, the Passchendaele area, Zonnebeke, Beselare and the village of Geluveld. The British only gained a narrow strip of territory from Poelkapelle to Zonnebeke and Beselare. This was totally disproportionate to the very heavy casualties."

Army High Command Official Communiqué 5 October 1917 [23]

"The commander and men of the Fourth Army have endured a day of battle of rare intensity, coming through it well. From early morning until late into the night the fighting went on from the area northwest of Langemark to south of the Menen-Ypres road. On a front of fifteen kilometres there were repeated British attacks. Massed artillery fire at the limit of what men and guns could achieve was directed ceaselessly on the ground where the bitter ebb and flow of the infantry battle was played out. The battle was centred on Poelkapelle, the individual farms three kilometres west of Passchendaele, the crossroads east and south east of Zonnebeke, the woods west of Beselare and the village of Geluveld.

"The enemy were only able to push forward of this line temporarily, but because of the violence of our counter-attacks could not maintain their gains, despite sending forward fresh forces into battle right up until late evening. The total gains of the British were limited therefore to a strip one to one and a half kilometres wide from Poelkapelle via the spurs to the west of Zonnebeke and along the line of the road from there to Beselare. This village, like Geluveld is firmly held by us. The bloody losses of the British divisions – at least eleven of which were involved in the early morning assault along the battle front – are universally stated to have been very high. The excellent cooperation of all arms of our army combined to break up even this massively heavy blow by the British, whose aims, despite protestations to the contrary, were not limited, but doubtless aimed at distant objectives.

"Nothing can ever surpass the heroism of the German troops in Flanders."

The private thoughts of the army group commander, although expressed in his diary in a measured way make it clear that he, at least, was only too well aware of the implications of the latest Allied advance.

Crown Prince Rupprecht: Diary Entry 4 October 1917 [24]

"A major enemy offensive was launched between the Ypres-Staden railway and the Ypres-Menen road. The enemy succeeded in advancing about one kilometre. We still hold Poelkapelle, Broodseinde was unfortunately lost, but we held on to Geluveld. The salient which has been pushed into our lines has increased the length of our front and so made the overall situation more difficult. Fortunately the break in point by Broodseinde is directly opposite the reinforced *Flandern II* position, which stretches from Passchendaele as far as Keiberg [i.e. about 3,500 metres]. Because this is the final ridge before the plain, we must push the enemy back off the heights he gained yesterday. This can best be achieved by means of a counter-attack into his right flank, launched from the direction Beselare-Geluveld."

The intensity of the fighting during the first half of October caused extremely heavy casualties amongst the troops deployed. Again and again formations had to be rushed forward to buttress the line where it was most threatened, regardless of the risks that this involved. The experiences of one machine gunner during a deployment by 240th Infantry Division near Poelkapelle, has provided us with a vivid illustration of how easily a routine operation could turn into a personal nightmare in the prevailing conditions.

Schütze W. Neißer 1st Machine Gun Company Infantry Regiment 470 [25] **6**

"Forward, near Poelkapelle, the enemy had virtually wiped out a Saxon division. Help was required urgently. We grabbed up our equipment, collected some coffee and set about launching a counter-attack. There was a flurry of activity as everyone rushed to get ready; orders and words of encouragement were hurriedly given in these early hours of an October morning and soon we were ready to set off. A broad well-made road led to the front. Returning wounded painted a lurid picture of the appalling battles they had been through. All the strain of battle could be seen on the faces of some of the chalk-faced men and yet these comrades had managed to come through. Officers hurried up and down, ambulances and ammunition columns rattled past us and we began to take our first casualties from massed British ground attack aircraft who, flying at rooftop height, greeted us with bombs and machine gun fire. Observers in aircraft and balloons began to direct the first heavy shells towards us.

"On the command, 'Prepare weapons!' we dismounted our machine guns from the wagons. The companies deployed, the machine guns split up and, making use of the small amount of cover available, we advanced. Later we moved from shell hole to shell hole. On the way, due to the frenzied weight of fire of all calibres and the attention of attacking aircraft, we lost all contact with our platoon and company, so from then on we acted independently under the courageous leadership of our gun commander Wacholz. Our company commander, Leutnant Vogelbacher, and our platoon commander, were both bravely carrying out their duties in the front line, but in such drum fire it was impossible to exercise unified command.

"Up to this point our machine gun crew had miraculously not suffered any casualties, but the further we got forward, the more dangerous the situation became. There was no sign of the enemy as we leaped from crater to crater, occasionally firing off a belt of ammunition or lay there taking cover in shell holes, half full of water from shells or aircraft machine guns. These were terrible hours and impossible to describe. Dead from various regiments lay strewn around the battlefield in heaps, whilst the wounded begged for help. Utterly heart-rending scenes were being played out, yet these were interspersed with marvellous examples of comradely behaviour and devotion to duty.

"Gradually the British pulled back, defending every single fold in the ground. For the time being the risk of a breakthrough was past. We found ourselves to the left [south] of the station at Poelkapelle and wanted to advance beyond the railway embankment. With one rush we were on the embankment then, at that precise moment, we were hit by a shell. I heard screams, was hit and blacked out as I was thrown through the air. When I came to some time later I seemed to be covered from head to foot in blood and filth. I felt a burning pain in my arms and especially in the area of my pelvis. Blood was seeping slowly from my wounds, but I was too weak to try to bandage them and the risk from flying shell splinters was too great. Three of my comrades and four or five ammunition carriers from the infantry, who had been detailed to help us, lay around, terribly mutilated a few metres from me. One was still alive, screaming pitifully, until he too fell silent. Everyone else had disappeared. The British were now bringing down an enormous weight of fire on the embankment. A heavy shell landed every minute and, in between large numbers of *Ratschbumms* [German equivalent of whizz-bangs] exploded.

"Badly wounded, helpless, almost crazy from thirst, I was in a desperate position. It was very hell, in the most dreadful meaning of the word. The minutes dragged on into eternity then, suddenly, the British defensive fire lifted towards our rear areas. I immediately thought that it signalled a British counter-attack and capture, but things were to turn out differently! About 3.00 pm I remember lying on my stomach and looking at my wrist-watch, then I lost consciousness for lack of blood. Drifting on the edge of consciousness, I assumed I was dying and was quite content with the notion because, apart from a burning sensation, I was not in any particular pain. The mountains of home appeared before me and, like lightning, my young life flashed by me. I had served the Fatherland willingly and faith-fully and was ready to die. But it was not to be.

"A British laced boot, complete with puttee, turned my head to one side as the owner tripped over my steel helmet. I regained consciousness immediately. It was night and clouds were drifting across the moon. A British sergeant (his name was Mollet and I still have a visiting card of his) bent down over me and promised me help soon. A little while later I was carried by stretcherbearers to a great blockhouse near Poelkapelle station, which the British were occupying. The sergeant brought me schnaps and biscuits and my wounds were dressed with the greatest care. I had absolutely nothing to complain about. The British soldiers made a great fuss of this young lad and, thanks to the schnaps, I was in good spirits, apart from the fact that I was now a prisoner.

"Then there was another twist. The Germans attacked once more after a short, sharp bombardment and forced the British back over their start line. The Tommies had all disappeared upwards to defend the area, leaving me and one other wounded man in the blockhouse. Suddenly loud voices bawled, 'Hands up!' through the entrance. They were German attackers, looking for British prisoners. My joy was naturally great. Two men were told off to carry me back. After a few hundred metres of extremely painful movement a British concentration of fire came down, my two carriers paused for a moment, dumped me unceremoniously on the ground, then disappeared to escape this space filled with flying steel. What now? I was utterly desperate. Huge explosions were going off all round me. At any second I might be buried alive and killed. With an immense effort I rolled over to a crater and fell in. Finding myself up to my knees in water and knowing that the risk of being buried alive was greatest low down, I summoned the last of my energy and hauled myself up so that I lay with my head just below the rim of the crater.

"What a piece of luck! A very short time later a heavy British shell crashed down four or five metres from my crater. A fountain as high as a house shot up, there was a crash and a blast of air. Something hit my head and body hard and I felt no more. When I came to it was night. I managed to free my head inside my helmet and my right arm. The reminder of my body was buried in the heavy wet ground. The outlook was grim! The few comrades who came anywhere near me, could not help. There were thousands lying around. Where could they begin? I had a roaring pain at the back of my head (my skull was fractured) and my limbs were being crushed by the weight of earth. There I lay under constant artillery fire. The bitter fighting ebbed flowed around me and there was nobody to help me!

"During the second night that I lay there buried, I saw two comrades nearby. They were working their way forward with a large container of coffee. They could not dig me out; they had no tools and no time, but at my request they gave me some hot coffee. The fact that several litres of the hot liquid ran down my face did not matter. They had no mug with them, they had to lower the great vessel down near me and shells were going off in the vicinity. Frankly it was not possible to damage me anymore. What were a few blisters on the face? The whole time I was buried I had nothing to eat, but I did not need anything. I just had his constant thirst and more thirst! Periods of unconsciousness alternated with feverish wakefulness. The cold of the nights helped me to come round, but shells landing close by made things pretty hot for me at times. I cannot explain how I kept my morale up, but I never lost hope. Then on the morning of 13 October I was freed. A Leutnant and two signallers approached me, I called out to them and they dug me out. It was very foggy and so it was possible to move about without being seen. My bones were still in one piece, but the bruising hurt terribly and my head ached with a dreadful buzzing. These comrades carried me to a wide road, gave me something to eat and drink as well as some cigarettes, which pleased me best of all. Ambulances and ammunition columns used this road constantly and the Leutnant said that someone would soon take me with them. At that these brave comrades from Saxony left me.

"I lay to one side in a ditch filled with the dead – British and German. They lay there with staring eyes and clenched fists – a gruesome sight. *In Flanders there are many soldiers, In Flanders there are many dead ...* The words of this song kept running through my head. After asking and begging for ages and after many had driven past regardless of my cries for help, at long last the driver of a motor ambulance took me aboard. His vehicle was already overflowing, but I begged him to put me on the rear step. He lifted me like a doll and placed me there. I lay, clinging on to a cross member with the desperate energy of a man reaching the end of his physical strength. The ambulance drove slowly, under constant shell fire then, after a journey of about two kilometres a heavy shell landed about 200 metres to our right. There was little overpressure but that, in combination with my weakness, meant that I lost my grip and fell off the vehicle.

"As I fell, I saw the vehicle drive on then all was black until I regained consciousness in the early hours of 17 October. I came to in the gymnasium of a school in Gent. Who picked me up I do not know. All I do know is that I was taken unconscious with many other severely wounded men to Gent. I was wounded on 9 October at about 2.00 pm and reached a field hospital about midday on 14 October."

Even for those regiments not directly involved in the contact battle, the conditions still took their toll. Holding positions centered on Jonkershoven during these early desperate days of October to the west of Houthulst Forest, Infantry Regiment 46 of 119th Infantry Division had not come under direct major attack, but had suffered from heavy bombardment on several occasions and was being worn down by the terrible wet and cold weather conditions. Its commander wrote a letter home about it, which he posted on 8 October,

Oberstleutnant Zunehmer Infantry Regiment 46 [26] **7**

"There was a great deal of rain yesterday evening and throughout the night. This was followed by the usual fog, so I had the horses brought forward through the wood and rode with Leutnant Feulgen via Jonkershove and the badly damaged, but still usable, road to Merkem and so was able to achieve more, despite our recent bad experience when enemy airman were able to direct fire on my mounted group and almost finished us all off. Luckily we initially turned to the north up the road, because I wanted to speak to the new *BTK* Hauptmann von Schaewen, 1st Battalion Landwehr Regiment 387.

"Once I arrived there I had some doubt about continuing because, despite the fog, the British, contrary to their usual practice, were bombarding the road and the Brabant Line heavily. In the end we did continue and I left the horses with the groom in a small barn behind the ruins of a house. There were already wounded men in the trenches of 1st Battalion Landwehr Regiment 387 and as we entered Sector B a shell came down right in front of us and completely blocked a section of trench, which fortunately was unoccupied. We were forced to move cross country for a while as a result.

"In the trenches of the 3rd Battalion there was hardly a soul not in the shelters and those few were pressed hard against the front wall of the trenches. Worst of all the fog began to thin out and disappear. The nearby enemy positions were clearly visible and the fire increased all the time. It appeared that we had no chance of getting through to [Major] Guischard's command post[27] and how we were going to get the horses out was a mystery.

"We turned round. Just as we emerged from the trench to skirt the previously mentioned blockage, another shell came down right in front of us. We threw ourselves down in the dirt as the splinters and clods of earth flew past. Simultaneously we saw shells landing around the ruined house, where we had left the horses and which was still one hundred metres away. Gefreiter Schön emerged riding the bay. The black horse was apparently wounded and lame, but the groom raced across the ploughed up ground to meet us.

"We made it into the cover of the wall with me riding Felgen's horse and he the groom's, which was bleeding from two wounds, but was not lame. The groom dashed into the nearest shelter, with instructions to return to us that evening. We rode off like madmen, initially across the crater field, where less fire was falling than on the road. Above us were those damned aircraft. In Jonkershoven we met up with my groom Schön. The black horse had suffered three serious wounds, which were likely to keep it out of future action, but the bay had only suffered a flesh wound."

Around 7 October the regiments of 238th Infantry Division – Infantry Regiments 463, 464 and 465 – were relieved in the line near Arras and moved north to a holding area near Oudenaarde, hoping for a period of rest and recuperation. It was not to be. Within three days it was ordered north to take over from 17th Infantry Division as an *Eingreif* division. In the light of experience gained so far,

Infantry Regiment 465, reinforced by despatch riders, 2nd Battalion Field Artillery Regiment 62, one third of the light ammunition column, one third of the divisional storm detachment, one platoon of Engineer Battalion 368 and a divisional signals troop, formed three battle groups: Laue, Baader and Wilcke and set off in motor vehicles for the front. No sooner had they arrived at the eastern edge of Moorslede, in rear of the sector of 220th Infantry Division and had begun to debus in the midst of heavy harassing fire, than they came under air attack as well. One of their number, von der Ohe, takes up the story: **8**

"The convoy halted. In no time we had debussed and were pulling our weapons and ammunition boxes behind us, when we heard, *Whoosh, whoosh, blam, blam!* as two aircraft bombs crashed down by the road. We raced for the edge of the village as fast as our legs would carry us and dived into the first barn we came to. The Tommies continued to harry the convoy as it made its escape, whilst the company dispersed by platoons and took cover behind the numerous hedges. There we settled down to await whatever might come our way. A continuous stream of vehicle convoys continued to deliver the other companies of the regiment and the others of the brigade until all were assembled. These hours of waiting were torture. We were soaked to the skin by drizzling rain. We were located in the middle of our heavy artillery batteries. As a result the Tommies kept putting down high explosive shells on us in a random pattern – quite unlike their normal routine – and thousands of fragments from the shell bursts flew in all directions.

"Of course the hedgerows were in no way bomb proof. Suddenly one hundred metres to our left there was a huge explosion, a giant sheet of flame shot up skywards and billowed out into a cloud of thick black smoke. As it dispersed there was not one single trace remaining of the house that used to stand on the site. It seemed as though an oil or petrol dump had been hit and exploded. The heavy shells of the Tommies crept ever closer. It was all extremely unpleasant. Then all of a sudden our hearts skipped a beat. A heavy shell had landed in the middle of Offizierstellvertreter Rauch's 3 Platoon.

"A large puff of blue smoke went up and we all held our breath. Something dreadful must have happened on the far side of the hedge. Then we heard a peal of laughter. Had the men all gone mad? What had happened? It turned out the shell had landed in a deep trench latrine, located in 3 Platoon's area. There it exploded harmlessly, but it distributed the entire evil-smelling contents of the latrine over everyone in the platoon, with the most generous allocation going to the platoon commander!" [28]

This incident may have lightened the day for everyone less those directly affected, but it was to be hours before orders arrived for a change of location. Finally at 8.30 pm the regiment was ordered to move to an area near Ruyter, three kilometres south west of Roeselare. This move at night, without guides, via almost invisible tracks, was an appalling strain on the already tired men. During a nightmare march, a hand grenade went off accidentally amongst the men of the 3rd Machine Gun Company, killing Schütze Dallmann, who was carrying it and wounding a large number of other men[29]. Nevertheless the regiment succeeded in arriving at the correct place and the 2nd Battalion was immediately ordered forward to reinforce 195th Infantry Division, arriving exhausted at 3.00 am.

Leutnant Wedekind 2nd Machine Gun Company Infantry Regiment 465 [30] **9**

"We left our holding area and returned to the road where we had left our vehicles. They had been shelled and had changed location – but where were they? Because it was pitch black, to search would have been pointless. We just had to set off, carrying our machine guns and their ammunition as well as our own equipment. A machine gun drained of water weighs seventy pounds and a box of ammunition forty five pounds.[31] These were heavy loads. Carefully we picked our way along the road. Totally unnecessarily it began to *Flander*, as Rittmeister Herrmann so delicately put it. That is to say it started to rain in sheets. By about 1.00 am we were about half way there. Columns of vehicles drove past us, but ours were not amongst them. After a rest of one hour, we continued on our way, but the men were so worn out that they had to rest every five minutes.

"Long before the officers had relieved the men of as much weight as possible. It was the only way to drive the company forward. Dawn had already broken by the time we reached Ruyter, our destination. At that precise time the companies were ordered forward. Rittmeister Herrmann was not impressed with [the late arrival of] his company and spoke to me very roughly. I kept my counsel. He simply did not know that we had achieved a superhuman feat, simply because were determined to do our duty to the limit of our ability."

240th Infantry Division, which had been formed around heavily reinforced elements of some of the regiments from Baden, deployed to Flanders as an *Eingreif* division during early October. On stand by from 7 October, it was alerted for action on 9 October. At 6.30 am 9 October, British drumfire was opened on the area of Poelkapelle. An attack began about one hour later, hitting amongst others the 6th Bavarian Infantry Division, which at that time was in the middle of a major relief in the line operation. The 240th was launched in a counter-stroke at about midday. It made some progress, despite the enormous weight of fire being directed against the approach routes and had managed to force its way forward of the German front line positions in places, when at about 7.00 pm, there was a further British bombardment, followed by a resumption of the attack. There was confused fighting for some hours, ground was lost and gained and then the survivors of the 240th settled down to assist in the defence of the area until they were relieved in the middle of the month by the Marine Infantry.

On receipt of the news about the partial breakthrough, reinforcements were rushed forward to seal off the gains. The situation was far from clear and this was reflected in some of the orders to the reinforcing units and formations. Reserve Infantry Regiment 233, part of the 195th Division, was ordered forward to a holding area in between the Passchendaele-Moorslede road and the Ypres – Roeselare railway. The orders were to take up a counter-penetration position behind the railway and to eject any enemy in the area. No sooner had the regiment prepared to do this than all was changed and it found itself under command on 5 October of the 20th Infantry Division and directed to relieve the remnants of Infantry Regiment 79, Bavarian Infantry Regiment 9 and Bavarian Infantry Regiment 5 in much the same area. According to its commander, Oberst von Riesenthal, the actual orders from 40 Infantry Brigade for this relief, which was to be carried out without any reconnaissance, during a pitch black night in the rain and under intense artillery fire, were, 'Get as far forward as the enemy troops will allow you, then lie down in the numerous trenches and craters there!'[32] Somehow the battalions managed to get into position where they found themselves lying fully exposed to the elements and enemy fire and subject to constant heavy attack.

Vizefeldwebel Alfred Kleysteuber 12th Company Reserve Infantry Regiment 233 [33] **9**

"Our orders came to embark for Flanders! – Flanders! The word flashed round the regiment like news of a death. Everywhere there were serious faces, because everybody knew that the fateful hour was upon them. On 3 October we passed Caudry, where the band of the Recruit Depot of the 195th Infantry Division played for us again, then we entrained for Thielt. Already during the journey we were kept awake by the sound of the dreadful bombardment along the front. The was a constant rumbling in the distance, the windows of the train rattled all the time, whilst the sky was lit up by the muzzle flashes and exploding shells of the artillerymen of both sides. Accompanied by all these impression, we arrived tired and with nerves strained at Thielt about midday. We were quickly in our billets, but it was not long before staff officers arrived to bring the regiment to readiness.

"This was serious business! We paraded in assault order and lorries arrived to move us forward. The word had got round: 'The British have broken through near Broodseinde!' Our procession made its way through pouring rain via Iseghem to Moorslede. The roaring and rumbling from the front was ceaseless. That sounded ominous for the morning! We were now travelling through the area under British bombardment. Shells and shrapnel rained down, but there was still no sign of a halt! Finally, not far from Passchendaele station, we debussed. All the weapons were gathered behind a hedgerow and everyone tried to get some rest. A flurry of shells landed in amongst the piled weapons, but because none of us was wounded, nobody paid them any attention. However, because the firing continued, people began to edge off to one side or the other, but it was impossible to avoid the 'raindrops'; the enemy was scattering shells everywhere. In the end we just stood and waited where we were.

"It was a little calmer as dawn approached. That evening we took up positions along the railway embankment. To be more precise we occupied the available craters, which we quickly developed with spades into a rough defensive position. All the time the rain continued to beat down. In order to counter that and to have a bit of protection from shell splinters, the men dug small scrapes in the forward edges of the craters, pulled their groundsheets down over their ears and stuck it out, in case they came. What a terribly long night it was! On the stroke of 6.00 am the enemy began to bring down destructive fire. All hell broke loose as we were showered with shells from the tiniest to the super-heavy calibres. Initially shivers ran through our bodies. Uncomfortable feelings of unease filled us as we shrank from the dreadful thought that our last moment might be nigh. Bit by bit the spell was broken as individuals became calmer, conquered their evil thoughts and slipped into a sort of daydreaming, which was only broken when a shell 'tore itself clear of its wrapping' in the immediate vicinity. After a couple of hours, the shelling slackened, only to open up on the neighbouring sector. Towards noon the whole thing was repeated. That evening as it began to go dark we had the same thing and it continued late into the night. All the pauses were filled with a calmer rate of harassing fire.

"During the evening of 8 October the concentrations increased to drum fire. Everything pointed to an attack in the very near future. Some elements of the reserve launched a counter-attack. But it was pointless – the enemy had still not attacked! We had been taking severe casualties, so during the night the battalions conducted a mutual relief in the line. In the early hours of 9 October drum fire began with a sudden concentration of fire. It increased gradually towards 7.30 am when it reached a truly extraordinary level of violence. Then at long last we saw them: the British infantry arm in arm, rifles slung, advancing slowly and picking their way forward across the ploughed – up, furrowed ground. In complete disregard of the mortal risk involved, the reserve battalion of our regiment moved to counter-attack straight through this hellish bombardment. Our front line positions were overrun without any difficulty by the enemy. The majority of the defenders were out of action through death or wounds, or were captured after a short period of defence. Unfortunately our machine guns failed. The rain and mud had rendered them unserviceable.

"The enemy reached the final heights before Passchendaele. Our reserve battalion then pressed forwards and brought down well-aimed fire on the advancing enemy. Ha! That brought them up short. To them it was un-imaginable that anyone could actually advance through fire like that. Our men drew ever closer. That caused concern within the British ranks. First a few, then more, turned about and abandoned the ground that they had recently won from the 233rd. Our earlier hill, though not the original front line was recaptured. It was quiet on the 10th and 11th. For the time being the opposition had had enough. On the 12th the well-known, familiar drum fire began again. Once it had made its views known sufficiently, the brown forms of the British advanced once more in their tightly packed lines. To the right of the railway embankment they made good progress. Once they passed the forward headquarters of the sector commander, the remaining men in field grey had to pull back. This time the expected counter-attack failed to materialise. Gathered at Passchendaele station, the 233rd received the order to pull back to the area of the field kitchens. Finally the regiment was relieved on 13 October and formed up on 14 October in Den Aap. It comprised three composite companies."

Jäger Battalion 4, which was part of the newly deployed 195th Division, also endured a day of serious, but ultimately successful, fighting on the Passchendaele Ridge on 9 October.

Major Ludwig von Menges Reserve Jäger Battalion 4 [34] **3**

"The 195th Division had taken over the sector of 3rd Reserve Division around the village of Passchendaele. Reserve Jäger Battalion 16 was occu-pying a forward battle position on 9 October, whilst Reserve Jäger Battalion 4 was in support trenches 800 metres southwest of the place and Reserve Jäger Battalion 24 was placed behind it in reserve. 1st Company was located in nests of resistance north of *Eckardtsgrund* [This area of low ground, through which the Ravebeek runs, is located approximately one kilometre south west of Passchendaele church]. 2nd Company was slightly to the rear in the *Grund* itself and finally the 3rd Company was located with its left flank on the road to Broodseinde. 4th Company was held in reserve, just in rear of 3rd Company, so that it was in a position to reinforce the threatened left flank. The 1st Machine Gun Company was in reserve in the centre of the position, whilst each company had two heavy weapons from 2nd Machine Gun Company allocated to it, in addition to its own six light machine guns. On the left flank, either side of the road there were two groups of three heavy machine guns. The remaining eight were unfortunately retained elsewhere in reserve.

"The place for machine guns was really to be sited in depth in the forward positions. The higher formations always preferred to maintain reserves under their control, but in fact it was impossible to have too many guns deployed in defensive positions forward. At 6.15 am [9th October] there was a further increase in the intensity of the drum fire and this was quickly followed by a British infantry attack which we soon spotted. We received the order *Reserve Jäger Battalion 4 is to reinforce Reserve Jäger Battalion 16 in its forward location.* The pulverising weight of fire meant that this was received with some trepidation. With outstanding daring, Leutnant Kretschmer set off immediately for Reserve Jäger Battalion 16. The other three companies were ordered off to the left flank, despite the fact that destructive artillery fire was tearing great gaps in the ranks of the infantry and the machine gunners. It was here along the road, just as Hauptmann Plümecke had correctly predicted, that the decisive action would be and not forward.

"Old England [*sic*] had broken through in the area of our left hand neighbours and was attempting to roll up the battalion from the south. Röhler's platoon of 3rd Company had already been overwhelmed, but 4th Company, assisted by elements of 2nd and 3rd Jäger Companies, dealt the enemy a significant blow. The breakthrough stalled. The battalion, now reduced to a third of its original fighting strength, thwarted all further attempts to win ground until 24th Reserve Jäger Battalion, reinforced by part of Reserve Jäger 4, succeeded by means of a counter-stroke to force their way forward to the original British jumping off line. The war diary noted laconically: killed four; missing fifty five; seriously wounded seventeen; slightly wounded sixty one. Altogether that added up to 137 men, or rather more than the complete bayonet strength of a company. You, dear schoolboys who read about deeds of heroism; Germans sitting around tables enjoying a beer, just think of all the blood that flowed; all that had to be performed whenever the Army Communiqué read, 'Today, too, our troops beat off all British attacks in the Passchendaele area; their meagre gains of ground were recaptured from them.'

The regiments of 119th Infantry Division were also moved forward early in October and were fully involved in the heavy fighting on 9 October. The day before the attack was renewed, Infantry Regiment 58 relieved Fusilier Regiment 86 in the Houthulst Forest area, with its 3rd Battalion forward in the Draaibank position, 2nd Battalion in support and 1st Battalion back in reserve in Terrest. There was not even time for the two regimental staffs to complete their handover/takeover, so Fusilier Regiment 86 remained in command during the day of heavy fighting.

Leutnant Hermann Schmidt Commander 6th Company Infantry Regiment 58 [35] **10**

"Just on midnight 8/9 October 1917, four small groups of men crossed this road in [Houthoulst Forest]. They were the four companies of 2nd Battalion Infantry Regiment 58 advancing at 300 metre intervals ... Almost unscathed, though constantly expecting a visit by the Spirit of Death, we arrived at the Melane café on the western edge of the Forest. Here we were met by guides from the troops we were to relieve and were led forward by individual companies to the various sectors. We had barely covered a few metres when a cry of *Gas!* livened up the trail of weary nervous men making their stumbling way forward.

"Exploiting the west wind, the French had sent over a few salvoes of gas shells, which had no effect whatever – our masks were always carried at the ready. The restriction on our breathing did, however, make our forward progress over the soaked clay soil a good bit more problematic. Our brave lads pressed on forwards; none of them shirking just because the visibility was dramatically reduced in the dark and the fog. The appalling danger in which we found ourselves bound us together. If anyone could not reach forward and touch the man in front, he shouted out loud to make him wait.

"Eventually at 4.30 am we reached our appointed sector. It was the so-called *Papegut* which had often featured in the army communiqué and comprised a massive concrete blockhouse, divided into four sections which rose out prominently like an arch in the midst of the ruins of the flattened walls of the farm and could be seen from a long way off ... Within the blockhouse, the section closest to the enemy was occupied by a machine gun sharp shooter group. Next to them was an infantry section of 3 Platoon 6th Company Infantry Regiment 58. Further to the right in the third room was a platoon commander, telephonists and stretcher bearers and on the far right the company clerks, my batman and me.

"The other two platoons of the company, which were only in section strength, took up positions in the crater field left and right of the block-house. [Once settled] we lay down, thinking to catch up on lost sleep. We had hardly settled down when it started to become light and suddenly the entire bunker heaved under the impact of a heavy shell. This shell alone would probably not have been sufficient to disturb our rest had it not been accompanied by the drone of an aircraft. About three minutes later came the sound of a second detonation. This was followed by another then shells began to fall with ever-increasing frequency. We began to be able to distinguish between the arrival of shells of different calibres and saw that three artillery cooperation aircraft, circling very low, were in the sky above our pillbox. I attempted without success to engage them and in return we were machine gunned from the air. It was clear to us what was happening. Ranging shots would be followed by drum fire and a major day of battle.

"Once ranging in was complete, the fire increase constantly until it became drum fire, which by 9.00 was so intense that the only variation in the endless thunder was the intensity of particular explosions. All we could do was to sit still next to one another and mull over how long our concrete shelter could withstand this crazy bombardment and what was happening outside. We exchanged brief speculations, but decided that there could be no question of a change in the overall situation. We then settled back silently, staring to our front or puffing nervously on a cigarette. The shells continued to plough everything up and gradually it became darker as the piles of earth thrown up by the explosions began to cover the small window which looked out to the rear of the pill box ...

"About four hours must have passed like this when an almighty crash above our heads caused us all to jump to our feet. We could only guess at what had happened. On the enemy side the ferro-concrete had taken an enormous blow from ceiling to floor and at the same time ground water began to flow in. The overall situation led me to suggest that we evacuated the bunker despite the drum fire. I felt it better to die than to be buried alive. There was resistance to my suggestion; the men felt more secure in this swaying pill box than outside and we had to stick together. I opened the door and left it slightly ajar, so that at least we had an escape route. In the meantime the water had risen twenty centimetres.

"It must have been about 4.00 pm when two tremendous, almost simultaneous explosions rocked the blockhouse to its foundations. We were certain that the bunker next to us had been blown in. We continued to sit as though we were rooted to the spot, when the door flew open and a man tumbled in. We hauled this prostrate man to his feet. Slowly he came round and explained to us, gasping for breath between each word, that two great incendiary rounds had landed, which had immediately set everything on fire and raised the temperature so high that he thought that he was going to suffocate. He had only saved himself by diving at the doorway and at least getting his head inside. He declared that the remainder were dead or lying wounded in the shell holes.

"The barrage hammered on in undiminished strength. To have set off to try to rescue the wounded would have been tantamount to suicide. All we could do was pin our hopes on the evening and a slackening in the artillery fire. Suddenly the adjacent room, which was connected to ours by a window, was full of fire and suffocating smoke. Two telephonists immediately leapt over to join us, but one did not have the courage to attempt to pass the blazing doorway. He ran backwards and forwards and tried to use his gas mask – which of course allowed the smoke to pass in. Despite our shouts, he did not seem to want to save himself. Not until I bawled at him that he would be burned to death did he jump towards us through the fire.

"Now we had to close the armoured window, because the fire, which was being fed by timber in the blockhouse, grew constantly in intensity and started to set off ammunition and hand grenades. Towards 7.00 pm we could hear once more the distinctive sound of aero engines of several enemy aircraft which were circling low. They seemed to be satisfied that the blockhouse was hopelessly on fire. We clearly heard the Tak! Tak! of a few sharp bursts from their machine guns then they disappeared. About 7.30 pm the fire slackened and died away to desultory shelling by 7.45 pm. Our moment had arrived. We dashed outside and brought in those in the worst condition. There were eight in all, some of whom were almost totally buried and had only managed to prevent themselves from suffocating under the weight of earth pressing down on them, by keeping a hand in front of their hands and mouths.

"We then tended to them, bandaged them up and placed them in twos on the bunks. I sent four men to the rear immediately, to be collected by the medical company. The barrage was resumed, sometimes at high intensity for up to ten minutes at a time, which rather demonstrated that the French and the British had no intention of attacking before the following morning. I sent one man off in both directions to link up with our neighbours. One of them returned after two hours, stating that he had seen no trace of another living thing within a large radius. The other man simply did not return. I decided to stay until all our wounded had been collected then to go and conduct a personal reconnaissance of the area.

"Hour after hour went by. We sat in this hole, dead beat and with wet feet. Every so often the overpressure of exploding shells would snuff out our candle stub, until we had no matches left. Previously, in order to ensure that no light escaped, we had kept the upper window blocked up with sandbags. At 1.30 am I sent an unwounded clerk and a telephonist to the rear to summon medical assistance urgently. That left my drummer, my batman and me alone forward. I set 5.00 am as our time for departure. At about 5.30 am we set off, promising the wounded that we would send help to them. We picked our way over the pock marked ground, accompanied by gas shells. At the Melane café we bumped into our counter-attacking force, told them where our wounded were and fell asleep."

Leutnant Hasse 12th Company Reserve Infantry Regiment 46 [36] **7**

"The breathing spaces that the Tommies allowed us became ever shorter. On 4th October there was another utterly murderous major day of battle, but the British did not enjoy much success. However, they did not permit us much of a rest, because they still hoped for success before the onset of winter and only four days later an enormous weight of fire came hammering down on the regimental sector. The same applied to the 12th Company near Bultehoek, which was under fire for hours from the *Eselsbatterie* [Donkey Battery], situated so close that the shell was heard to burst before the firing report of the gun arrived ... the air shook, the stink of powder was everywhere and for hours we were blinded by bright red flashes ... What idiot had betrayed the company whereabouts by ill-judged movement? It was immensely annoying.

"The battalion commander, who had been watching the endless fire from his bunker off to the right, was heard to observe that he hoped that he might some time link up again with the remnants of 12th Company. All around Bultehoek the terrain was completely open and devoid of cover. One by one the men raced from their shelter to join the company commander in his. This shelter, with its roof made out of tree trunks covered in fifty centimetres of beaten earth, certainly offered better protection than the other shelters ... but the commander was less than happy to have fifty six men all crowded together in one small space ... and so he ordered each man to race individually through the heavy fire and to reassemble in the communications trench 100 metres further forward.

"Leutnant Hoffmann and I were the first to go. We had not covered twenty metres before the pressure wave of the first exploding shell had hit us. There were red flashes everywhere. Blinded and somewhat shaken, we rushed on and gained the security of the trench. Not every member of the company risked the dash. Some stayed where they were. Once in the trench the company spread out to the right and thus escaped the arc of fire of the *Eselbatterie.*

"It was evening before the remainder of the men arrived and then the company commander could report to battalion that the 12th Company, which had not suffered any casualties, was established north of Bultehoek and that it intended to spend the night in bunkers in front of the swamp area near Jonkershoven. The night was pitch black. It was impossible to organise ration carrying parties, because there was a fear that they would stumble into shell holes and drown. In the bunker the two rough beds were placed upright and fifty five men wedged in for the night. The final section to arrive maintained the sentry duty with hourly reliefs. At first light they were directed to rouse the carrying party. Jamry, the company cook, would certainly be ready and waiting with rations and it was essential that coffee and bread as a minimum were collected.

"It was still not daylight when the enemy guns opened up. They roared on endlessly, which meant that an attack was imminent. At first light 12th Company moved out to do its duty. Passing the headquarters shelter, where the commanding officer was standing in the doorway looking at the weather and yawning, the company commander reported that the company would be on stand-by in the ruins of some houses north of the Melaene road. With empty stomachs, everyone was shivering with cold. To the south of the road the enemy artillery fire was coming down much more strongly, which rather telegraphed the enemy intentions. To the front our heavy machine guns had already opened up, which meant that the attack had already begun. The officers of 12th Company strained their eyes looking to the south and, to a lesser extent, to the west. This was because at the front here the priority was to defend against an enemy advancing on the left flank of the regiment.

"Suddenly a well-known Vizefeldwebel from Engineer Company 237 appeared, wounded in the leg. He was hopping along with the aid of a stick. I went over to him to enquire about the situation at the front. He reported that the British and French were attacking and that the boundary between the two was directed at the regiment. He added that the attack had been halted; mainly because the heavy machine guns of the *KTK* of 2nd Battalion Reserve Infantry Regiment 46 had completely mown down the enemy in their sector. Having thanked him and wished him luck I set off to return to the company. Near the road my luck ran out. The report of the *Eselbatterie* always came too late. I tried to leap up, but my arm hung uselessly below me. I thought that I had just been hit by a flying lump of clay, then somebody told me that I was bleeding. Yes, sure enough blood was dripping down from the little finger of my left hand.

"A medical orderly came rushing up, scissors in hand. I was not about to let him cut off my sleeve, so I pulled off my jacket and shirt. A small entry wound was visible on the inside of my upper arm. I felt totally drowsy in the midst of all these explosions [because of shock]. The medical orderly bandaged me up. By now it was 8.00 am and the Leutnants continued to maintain a look out. A little while later the medical NCO persuaded me to head off to the dressing station, if only to receive an anti-tetanus injection. This he repeated at ever decreasing intervals until I handed over to

Leutnant Hoffmann and went with my drummer to battalion headquarters formally to take leave. On the way to the bunker housing the aid post we sought out a crossing through the swamp. Once more shells came flying through the air at us. Fortunately they did not all explode and three of them were swallowed up in the bog.

"In the aid post bunker, I met up with Leutnant Ratte of 10th Company, who had been wounded by a shot through the thigh. Whilst we were being treated, Offizierstellvertreter Figger, mortar commander of the 1st Battalion, was carried in. His mortar line had been established in the reinforced concrete artillery position by the *Kloster Schule* [Monastery School] and he had been hit by a splinter as he observed through a vision slit. He had been hit in the thigh. The bone was broken, he had lost a lot of blood and he looked terribly pale. Together with Leutnant Ratte I headed off to the field hospital via the transport lines. In our room, Leutnant Sasse, 2nd Company, was in bed and Leutnant Montua, 11th Company, sat next to him, his face burnt and his head bandaged. In a single room and too ill to be moved was our Hauptmann Benecke. The nurse permitted us to see him for a very short while and, noticing that he had a dozen tubes hanging from the right hand side of his chest, we brought him quickly up to date. He quickly slipped into a delirious fever, during which he exhorted us to be careful. The nurse signalled to us and we crept out.

"Offizierstellvertreter Figger arrived in a vehicle. His leg was amputated immediately, but he had lost too much blood. Towards evening the nurse called us to close his eyes for him.[37] Overstrained, the doctors worked feverishly. Wherever we looked or heard there were men from Reserve Infantry Regiment 46. That night enemy aircraft appeared overhead. All the lights of the hospital were extinguished. The wounded men who had just cheated death breathed heavily. It was like a nightmare to lie there helplessly. There was no way of escaping; it was just a matter of trusting to luck.

"In the collection point for the lightly wounded, everyone was woken up so they could seek shelter in the cellar. The shaking did not wake Gefreiter Boesel of 8th Company Reserve Infantry Regiment 46. He lay on the floor and continued to grunt and snore. The others went below. A bomb landed right by the entrance to the building, exploded and blew out the windows and all of the ground floor. About twenty of the lightly wounded men were killed or wounded again, but the Gefreiter carried on sleeping soundly on the first floor. He was a runner, who was constantly on the go and he needed to catch up on his sleep."

There was to be no let up in the tempo of operations, despite the extreme difficulty the Allies experienced in trying to manhandle guns and ammunition into position for a resumption of the attacks. On the German side, rushed forward to make good losses sustained by 10th Ersatz Division during the fighting of 4 October, the regiments of 18th Infantry Division found themselves defending positions in the *Flandern I* line one kilometre east of Poelkapelle during the battles of 9 and 12 October. The Allied artillery might have been finding it difficult to provide the same weight of fire as it had to cover the operations on 4 October, but it still made life extremely difficult for the defence. On 9 October, during a day of intense close-quarter battle, Infantry Regiment 68 succeeded in beating back numerous minor incursions, but it suffered the majority of its 287 casualties up to 10 October that day. As a result, 3rd Company as regimental reserve was ordered forward as it went dark to reinforce the front line. This was easier said that done.

Fähnrich Britten 3rd Company Infantry Regiment 68 [38] **6**

"At 7.00 pm, when the firing had died away slightly, 1 and 2 Platoons (of which I was a member) went forward, commanded by Offizier-stellvertreter Braune (who was later killed at Passchendaele), to strengthen the front. We marched for about an hour. Suddenly a group of pillboxes loomed up in front of us through the gloom. We must have strayed too far to the right. That was the edge of Poelkapelle and – over there voices speaking in English. Left and right of us flares went up in all directions. Suddenly British machine guns opened up to our left and right rear. In a flash we had disappeared into a huge shell hole, where we took cover. Did Braune know where we were? I at least had no idea where the British lines and our own were.

"All of a sudden we heard British voices directly to our front. Two men were approaching a very young British soldier who was stuck up to his waist in the mud. They could not free him and had to leave him to his fate. Damned flares! We could hear the sound of German voices to our front and behind us a British machine gun. Everything here seemed to be hopelessly entangled. Braune approached a pillbox cautiously then a German machine gun opened up. Slowly, one at a time, we climbed out of our hole and headed for the pillbox. The ground was unbelievably boggy, we just hardly got forward. The man to my front threatened to disappear into the darkness, so I moved quicker, only to get stuck up to my knees in the morass.

"Blast it! 'Step short', came the call from behind. This was followed by the noise of a British machine gun firing from the rear once more. I used my rifle as a walking stick to get me through the swamp, but then the man behind me got stuck as well in the filthy mess. The British gun went on spraying bullets, which sent up splashes from the muddy mess next to us. At long last the two of us were extracted from the bog with the help of our comrades. A few more steps and we were in the concrete pillbox. Four of my men were missing, amongst them Fahnenjunker Hövel. They must have been hit by the British machine gun; not there was much we can do about it for, as a lanky Unteroffizier in the pillbox told us, the whole place was crawling with British soldiers. Braune decided that we were to retrace our steps and in the early morning we were back on the edge of Westrozebeke."

It was not only on the battlefield that the strain was beginning to tell. Concern about the failure of the tactics of flexible defence during the battles in late September and the amended tactics on 4 October was also a source of considerable anxiety within the German command structure which, collectively, was responsible for the integrity of the defence.

First Quartermaster General Erich Ludendorff [39]

"An infantry battle began on 4 October. We survived it, but only at enormous cost. It showed that the strengthening of the front line which had been introduced after my last visit in September was not a cure-all. I then followed my own judgement, without asking any further questions and recommended to Fourth Army that it introduced the use of a narrow strip of territory between the enemy front line and the line where our own troops were to conduct a mobile defence. If the enemy wished to launch an attack, they would have to cross it. This would gain our artillery time to engage them, before they closed with our main defensive line. The great difficulty lay in withdrawing the forward garrison in the event of an attack … The principle was simple and clear. Fourth Army was reluctant to follow my proposals about the use of an area of advanced posts; only gradually were they convinced about it."

Having made this decision, Ludendorff was quick to issue a memorandum, which was distributed down to divisional level all along the Western Front.

Chief of the General Staff of the Field Army 1a. Number 67059 op. dated 9 October 1917 [40]

"The failures at Verdun as well as in the Battle of Flanders have, amongst other reasons, been caused by inappropriate deployment of the *Eingreif* divisions held in reserve. Penny-packeting, premature or delayed deployment, unclear missions and failure to guarantee the cooperation of the attacking formations with the artillery have been the main failures of operational procedures …

"Correct and timely concentration of the *Eingreif* divisions, unity of

deployment of the individual regiments or the entire division, clear distribution of orders, limitation of the objectives to be achieved and correctly
arranged cooperation with the artillery are the principles which must be
applied in order to make really effective use of the *Eingreif* divisions."

These initial remarks were followed by a series of examples where incorrect
methods had led to failure. Addressees were warned to avoid falling into the same
trap then the document continued:

"Consequences: **In principle it is the task of the organic reserves of
the ground-holding divisions** [41] to eject the enemy out of their own areas
of responsibility. If this is not possible, counter-strokes by *Eingreif* troops
are only possible if the operations are launched by **powerful** forces (both
infantry and artillery), are **concentrated and swift** (within a few hours)
and **well supported by artillery**. To facilitate this it is important that the
troops are placed in good accommodation outside the range of the mass of
the enemy artillery. They should be concentrated by regiments and have
good communications with the artillery.

"Wherever these pre-conditions cannot be met (which is often the case),
counter-strokes by the *Eingreif* troops to bring about the immediate recapture of lost ground in the forward battle area must be renounced. The
operational methods to be used and the size of deployments must be
matched to the tactical situation. In particular this question must always
be posed, *Are the likely casualties proportional to anticipated regaining
of ground?* It is an error to use *Eingreif* divisions unnecessarily to reinforce
ground holding ones.[42] It is pointless and damaging in terms of the
outcome of the battle, because it simply increases the number of troops
deployed and brings in its wake higher casualties, which cannot be justified. **The art of command** comprises **sparing** deployment of the *Eingreif*
divisions and the **maintenance of their fighting strength**."

Crown Prince Rupprecht, the Army Group commander, irritated by the unspoken
implication that his handling of the battle was in some way deficient, confided his
reservations about the material emanating from the Army High Command to his
diary on 9 October.

Crown Prince Rupprecht of Bavaria: Diary Entry 9 October 1917 [43]

"I have some concerns about the new defensive procedures recommended by the Army High Command and the same applies to their
directive to engage the enemy artillery strongly in future during a battle.
Up to now we have always taken the view that the entire artillery is best

used to break up the infantry attack. Because it is always difficult to determine after a period of drum fire if the enemy is only going to probe forward with strong patrols, or intends to launch an assault on a broad front, the new defensive procedures mean that there is risk that in some circumstances the forward outpost line will be withdrawn in the face of an advance by a few companies and that there will be break-ins in certain places.

"The difficulty of shortening the range of the artillery after the withdrawal of outposts is linked to the fact that, depending on the ground, it is impossible to withdraw them all equally. If to these difficulties is added the fact that reporting of the withdrawal of the outposts and adjustment to the rear of artillery fire is bound to be uneven then it is probable that there will be gaps or weak points in the defensive fire, causing a chequerboard effect, which will be to the advantage of the attacker. General Ludendorff does not accept that this will cause difficulties and refuses to discuss any of the questions which have been telephoned through."

Whether it was a result of his dissatisfaction with Ludendorff, or the feeling that the battles of 9 October had not gone as well as they might have done for the men under his command, Crown Prince Rupprecht struck what for him was a very pessimistic note in his diary entries during the middle of the month.

Crown Prince Rupprecht of Bavaria: Diary Entries [44]

10 October 1917

"There was very high wastage within the divisions of Fourth Army yesterday and we fired off the equivalent of twenty seven trainloads of ammunition. This time it is still possible to bring forward sufficient troops to conduct the necessary reliefs in the line, but if, as is to be expected, the French attack the Seventh and Third Armies simultaneously with the British continuation of attacks against the Fourth Army, the Army High Command will not be in a position to despatch sufficient fresh troops forward to help us. If this happens we shall have to get by with what we have and that would mean giving up our less important positions to the enemy and pulling back slowly and gradually from one position to another.

11 October 1917

"Our forces along the main battle front in Flanders are still thoroughly mixed up and confusion reigns in the various formations. It is really worrying that the fighting ability of our troops is reducing all the time and that all the means we have employed to attempt to counter the oppressive superiority of the enemy artillery have failed to have any effect. Because we are involved in a battle for time, there remains nothing for it, but repeatedly to give ground in order to force our opponents to waste time as they move their artillery forward."

That same evening, the units of Infantry Regiment 68 were engaged in a delicate relief in the line operation to the east of Poelkapelle.

Reserve Hauptmann Biernatzki 3rd Battalion Infantry Regiment 68 [45] **6**

> "So I set off at 11.00pm in pouring rain through the pitch black night across unfamiliar territory towards the front. The ground was like nothing that I had ever seen or experienced before. Crater overlapped crater, most of them filled to the brim with water. The edges of these shell holes, along which we picked our way, were one great oozing morass. Repeatedly that night I asked my guide where he was leading me. It was literally impossible to see your hand in front of your face, but after a march of one and a half hours, he brought me to a concrete pillbox where the commander whom I was to relieve was located. However he was not there. For the past two days he had been located in a different pillbox from which he could better exercise control over his troops. After much wandering to and fro, during which I once more made the acquaintance of the water in a shell hole; this time not just me, my adjutant also did the same thing. At long last we reached the concrete pillbox. Here, if we sat at a bench, we were up to the calves of our legs in water. We knew that the enemy, due to the small territorial gains he had made left and right, would be putting our position under enormous pressure."

By the end of the night some of the regimental machine gunners had been relieved and considerable reinforcement had taken place, which meant that when the drum fire began at 6.30 am on 12 October, this sector, which was just over 1,000 metres wide, was being defended by no fewer than seventeen heavy machine guns, not to mention large numbers of the lighter Maxim 08/15 weapons held by the infantry companies. This was a formidable force with which to confront the assaulting troops. Patrols sent forward established the enemy lines were crammed with troops and Infantry Regiment 29, the neighbouring regiment managed to capture two Scottish soldiers from a newly-deployed division who stated that H Hour was scheduled for 6.00 am.[46] This made it certain that an attack was about to take place, a fact which was confirmed when Infantry Regiment 28 also captured a man from the British 48th Division.

From 4.00 am, therefore, the positions were fully manned and the regiments stood ready to repel the assault which was pushed forward with the utmost determination as this description shows.

Fähnrich Britten 3rd Company Infantry Regiment 68 [47] **6**

"With a crash, shrapnel rained down on our lines at 6.30 am. It stopped equally abruptly five minutes later and British barrage fire started coming down behind us. 'Here they come!' Laboriously, slowly, working their way forward step by step through the swampy ground the British attacked. One of our light machine guns was knocked out right at the beginning. A shrapnel round had filled it with filth. Just as the crew was opening the top cover, a second round crashed down smashing the gun and wounding several of the crew. The second gun to the left from me hit the enemy with great force. The comrade who was sharing my shell hole (the second man was killed by a shell splinter through the heart right at the beginning of the bombardment) and I fired as fast as we could and it was much the same story from the other shell holes.

"The Tommies pressed forward to within grenade throwing range. They had taken enormous casualties. On the other hand on the left they had closed right up and, on the far side of the stream, they seemed to have broken in to the 4th Company position. Our artillery defensive fire was crashing down fifty metres to our front and doing great damage to the Tommies. But we too had significant casualties, mostly from small arms fire and especially on the left flank amongst Lukomski's platoon. Having been briefed on the situation by an Unteroffizier, I crawled over to the left flank, where the Tommies were within ten metres. In the meantime, it must have been about 10.00 am, the power had ebbed away from the attack. On the other hand British airmen, flying at very low level, were pouring fire into our holes.

"We also came under fire from a machine gun located to our left rear. There was firing in all directions. A man next to me, who had just shot a British soldier through the head, collapsed, also with a head wound. Two Tommies who were shooting whenever a helmet appeared were making life very unpleasant. Von Lukomski's batman lobbed two hand grenades across and everything went quiet. I waved, 'Come on over! And as I did so, a shot cracked past a hairsbreadth from my head."

There was some slight progress in this area, but that dense network of machine guns did the trick. The British troops lost the barrage, the attack faltered and later in the day the survivors were withdrawn. There had been some slight progress in the areas of Infantry Regiments 28 and 29, but by dint of deploying all the reserves and at the cost of not inconsiderable casualties, the so-called First Battle of Passchendaele had first faltered, then failed, in this area and it was the same story all along the front that day. Objectives set to the east of Passchendaele were simply unattainable in the prevailing circumstances. The Allied artillery had failed to deliver the necessary destruction and neutralisation, the German defenders had fought effectively and bravely and the weather, that great leveller, worked more in the favour of the defence than the offence.

Crown Prince Rupprecht of Bavaria: Diary Entry [48]

12 October 1917
"The weather has taken a sudden turn. Happily it has turned to rain, which is our most effective ally. This morning the enemy renewed his attacks against the Fourth Army all along the entire front from the Langemark-Houthulst road to the Zonnebeke-Moorslede road. It is less a cause for concern that they gained ground to the north of Poelkapelle than the fact that they pushed up close to the *Flandern II* position which runs along the ridge from Passchendaele to Drogenbroodhoek. In order to keep a tight grip on the heights between Passchendaele and Moorslede, the last before the flat hinterland, a division was despatched there from Menen and a second was moved to Roeselare in order to occupy the heights from Westrozebeke to Stadenberg."

Elements of Grenadier Regiment 9, which was part of 3rd Guards Division, had been forward in the Keiberg area to reinforce the front line of Reserve Infantry Regiment 94 from the evening of 12 October. The conditions were simply appalling. They occupied a random series of water-filled craters. There were no trees to be seen, not a patch of green, no sign of a trench just rain, rain and more rain. The grenadiers stretched their groundsheets over the craters in an effort to keep dry, but it was hopeless. They were up to their waists in filthy water and mud. Some men tried vainly to bale out the holes using mess tins or steel helmets, but soon gave up the unequal task. Shells continued to rain down and the casualties went on mounting. One of the platoon commanders of the 1st Battalion wrote up his impressions of the conditions and the state of the fighting as the First Battle of Passchendaele died away. He could have been acting as the spokesman for all the forward troops.

Vizefeldwebel Zaske 1st Battalion Grenadier Regiment 9 [49] **11**

"If you wished to find one single sentence to encapsulate what it meant to endure the worst drumfire imaginable, to hang on in ploughed-up terrain which made a mockery of every attempt at orientation, where there was a lack of food, where life was lived out in shell holes and mine craters, where it was impossible to distinguish the clay from the water, where all appeared to have been reduced once more to the primeval swamp from which our planet developed millions of years ago, this was the best attempt that could be made: *Yes, we were in the Carpathians and took part in the breakthrough in Galicia; we were there on the Somme, we have got to know the worst of the Eastern and Western Fronts, but here ...* and words failed everyone.

"When we emerged from our holes, we looked like animals whose natural camouflage made them indistinguishable from the surrounding earth, even for the sharpest eye. Our grey uniforms were coated with mud and earth and it appeared as though every man was encased in terracotta from his steel helmet to the nails on his boots. Here we endured to the uttermost limit of that which was humanly possible; our daily entertainment an endless stream of shells, most of them heavy calibre, which crashed down everywhere that the enemy suspected we earthworms were lurking.

"Over there is the crew of a light machine gun, in their 'dugout', which comprises a medium-sized shell hole, featuring a sheet of corrugated iron spread across the portion nearest to the enemy as protection against the endless Flanders drizzle for the weapon that the five man crew treat as sacred. The wet conditions gradually turn outer and underclothes into an unpleasant leathery substance sticking to the limbs. A shell impacts two metres in front of this austere shelter. The corrugated iron sheets flies up in a great arc, to land more than ten metres away. One member of the crew is killed and two others seriously wounded. The remaining pair clean the fallen mud and clay off their gun, mount it on the lip of the crater once more and soon it is chattering away at lines of enemy infantrymen who have been careless enough to expose themselves to it. That is a typical example of defence when the enemy acts as though all life has been extinguished and our men demonstrate that they are still there.

"Yes, they stick it our in their thin, wavy defensive lines; on their own or in twos and threes. Self-absorbed, their voices barely able to make themselves understood to their neighbour above the hellish racket. They are fully aware that in Flanders they are right at the focus of the fighting throughout the full length of the Western Front, of the war itself and that the outcome is entirely up to them. Suddenly all falls silent ... Does it mean an attack all along the line? Hands grip rifle butts tighter, the security screws on grenades are checked. Yes, it is an attack! It is a moment of liberating relief! Rifle and machine gun fire is poured into the enemy and our artillery brings down violent concentrations. Over-keen Tommies, who have already pushed forward in front of the crater, are dealt with using grenades. It lasts half an hour then the attack is beaten off, with casualties amongst both the courageous Pomeranian soldiers and the enemy, whose losses are even higher.

"The attack is renewed after two to three hours. The images and the result are the same. The next day the official Army Communiqué reports that the Pomeranian Grenadier Regiment has smashed every enemy assault."

Crown Prince Rupprecht of Bavaria: Diary Entry [50]

13 October 1917

"The course of the fighting yesterday was far more favourable to us than early reports indicated. In particular the hills around Passchendaele and Drogenbroodhoek remained in our hands. Fourth Army has been allocated another division by the Army High Command, but due to overloading of the railways there can be no troop transport to Flanders before 18 October.

"Whilst only recently General Ludendorff directed us to preserve our forces by yielding territory in the event of major assaults, he is now of the opinion that we should give up only the minimum amount of ground to the enemy, because the battle is going to be decided in our favour within fourteen days. What has led him to this optimistic assessment is beyond my comprehension. I am convinced that the British will continue to press home their attacks as long as they possibly can; that is to say for another four to six weeks. They certainly do not lack the troops. On the Somme they did not give up until the weather towards the end of November prevented a continuation of their attacks."

Fortunately for the defence, which was now severely stretched, it was clear that the state of the ground, the appalling wet weather and general exhaustion meant that there was no choice for the Allies but to impose an operational pause until the situation improved. The defenders were not to know that of course and as the first two weeks of the October fighting drew to a close, there was little optimism, despite the relatively favourable outcome of the battles on 9 and 12 October, that they would be able to hold until they would be saved by the onset of winter.

Notes
1. Ludendorff: *Meine Kriegserinnerungen* pp 389-390
2. This is an interesting line of argument by Ludendorff. The change in tactics was swiftly proved to be ineffective and this reads as though Ludendorff was trying subsequently to distance himself from a decision for which he himself bore the final responsibility.
3. Gieraths: History Reserve Infantry Regiment 210 p 330
4. Stosch: History Foot Guards Regiment 5 p 355-356
5. Makoben: History Reserve Infantry Regiment 212 p 401
6. Sobbe: History Infantry Regiment 92 pp 411-413
7. Stosch: *op.cit.* p 355-356
8. Makoben: *op.cit.* pp 407-410

9. *ibid.* pp 431-432
10. *ibid.* pp 407-410
11. The root of Schleinitz's concern was that the Bavarians belonged to another division. Had they been part of the same division then an order from the *KTK*, never mind the regimental commander himself, would have been quite sufficient to ensure compliance, regardless of any rank differential.
12. Stosch: *op. cit.* pp 437-438
13. Weniger: History Bavarian Infantry Regiment 5 p 92
14. Viereck: History Infantry Regiment 77 pp 455-456 and 458
15. This was clearly a bloody fight with no quarter given. Reserve Leutnant Redel of 11th Company Infantry Regiment 77 reported, 'After a hard fight, the last six or eight men had to surrender. The British were not knightly opponents, however. Blind with rage they shot the few remaining Germans out of hand as they plundered the contents of their pockets. The British medical orderlies were not interested in evacuating the German wounded. They just shot them. British civilisation celebrated these orgies.' *ibid.* p 458
16. Kellinghusen: *Kriegserinnerungen* p 653-654
17. Kurland is the German name for the northern part of Latvia.
18. Blankenstein: History Reserve Infantry Regiment 92 pp 314 – 315
19. According to the divisional report after the battle, 232 British batteries were firing on the divisional front, countered by only 64 German batteries: odds of almost 4:1 against. See Kellinghusen *op. cit.* p 655-656
20. Makoben: *op. cit.* pp 407-410
21. Assuming that this incident did occur as Lincke claims, he cannot have been speaking to the divisional commander, the then Major General HB Walker, who had been born in 1862 and was a British regular officer. Possibly the conversation was with a red-tabbed staff officer and Lincke was confused deliberately or accidentally as to his identity.
22. Jordan: History Field Artillery Regiment 95 p 113
23. Makoben: *op. cit.* p 428
24. Kronprinz Rupprecht: *Mein Kriegstagebuch II. Band* p 267
25. Müller-Loebnitz: *Die Badener im Weltkrieg* pp 296-298
26. Zunehmer: History Infantry Regiment 46 pp 315-316
27. At the time Guischard was in command of Reserve Infantry Regiment 46, a post he had held since 30 August 1917.
28. Gottberg: History Infantry Regiment 465 pp 114-115
29. *ibid.* p 116
30. *ibid.* pp 115-116
31. A metric pound weighs 500 grams, so the weights involved were thirty five and twenty five kilograms respectively.
32. Brendler: History Reserve Infantry Regiment 233 p 211
33. *ibid.* pp 231-233
34. Menges: History Reserve Jäger Battalion 4 pp 228-229
35. Schmidt *et al:* History Infantry Regiment 58 pp 193 – 196
36. Puttkamer: History Reserve Infantry Regiment 46 pp 159-160
37. Offizierstellvertreter Otto Figger, who died of his wounds on 9 October 1917, is buried in the German cemetery at Hooglede in Grave 6714.
38. Pafferath: History Infantry Regiment 68 p 474

39. Ludendorff: *op. cit.* p 391
40. Kriegsarchiv München: HGr. Rupprecht 93
41. Bold = original emphasis.
42. This had been a common procedure earlier in the battle and indeed was still occurring right until the fighting died away in November 1917.
43. Kronprinz Rupprecht: *op. cit.* pp 269-270
44. *ibid.* pp 270-271
45. Pafferath: *op.cit.* p 477
46. Presumably they were from the 9th (Scottish) Division which had just returned to the line after a two week break.
47. Pafferath: *op. cit.* pp 480-481
48. Kronprinz Rupprecht: *op. cit.* pp 271-272
49. Hansch: History Grenadier Regiment 9 pp 414-416
50. Kronprinz Rupprecht: *op.cit.* pp 271-272

CHAPTER SIX

16 – 31 October 1917

During the heavy battles of 12 October, the regiments of 195th Infantry Division succeeded in holding onto their positions around Passchendaele more or less intact, but their casualties had been so high that they had to be relieved. The regiments of 238th Infantry Division were used for this purpose; Infantry Regiment 465 moving up to occupy a sector 800 metres wide on the right of the divisional front, running south from a point just east of Wallemolen, about two kilometres west of Passchendaele. The relief began during the early hours of 13 October and was carried out only with extreme difficulty, due to the terrible going underfoot.

Schütze Behrens 3rd Machine Gun Company Infantry Regiment 465 [1] **1**

"The battalion was due to relieve the forward position. It was a long approach march, so initially we loaded the machine guns on the wagons. At first all went reasonably well, but suddenly wagon one pitched into a shell hole in the dark. We pushed it back onto level ground and continued on our way. Then the same thing happened to wagon 5. We had great difficulty in extracting it. Suddenly wagon 1 stopped. There were two overlapping craters in the road and water filled trenches on either side. We were stuck. There was nothing else for it; we had to unload the machine guns and carry them forward, together with their ammunition. Moving partly on the road and partly to one side, we made slow progress – yet speed was essential if we were to reach the infantry to our front. We constantly had to get out of the way of motorised trucks which were driving towards us.

"One occasion I fell into a ditch over which I was attempting to jump and sank in up to my hips. I climbed out carefully and we continued. Once again we encountered vehicles and stood there on the edge of the road cursing them [especially because] they flattened two of Gerecke's water containers. Gradually we reached a point where vehicles no longer bothered us – over the hills near Passchendaele. We headed on westwards, turning off at a bend in the track which led to the position of the *KTK*. Here there was desultory harassing fire, but we traversed it safely, [unlike the] numerous corpses which littered the locality.

"The jäger unit which we relieved seemed to have suffered very badly, a

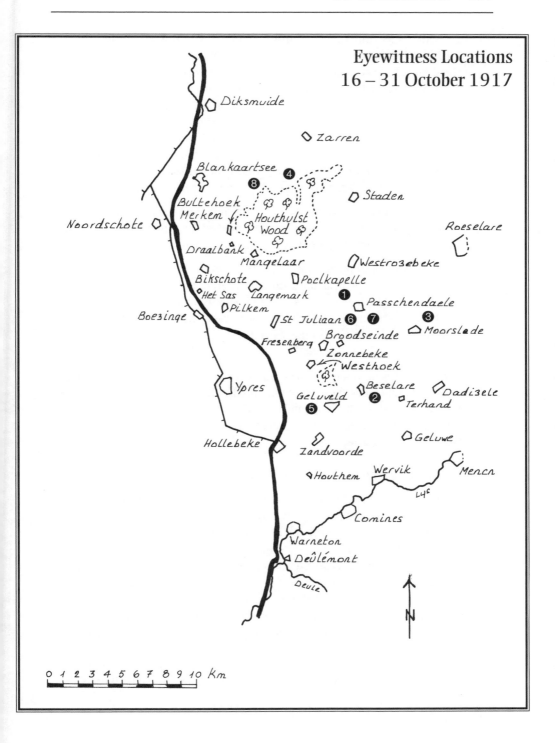

Eyewitness Locations
16 – 31 October 1917

fact which was confirmed the following day as I crawled around the position to locate one platoon of the company which was occupying some ruined houses. Everywhere lay bundles of green or grey rags of clothing which covered the bodies of German soldiers whose hearts had ceased to beat. The bunker of our company commander was not too far from that of the *KTK*, but despite the short distance I still managed to fall into a mud-filled crater ... Naturally I was received in the blockhouse by a gale of laughter – but they would of course have preferred me to have stayed outside. As it was there was barely room for Leutnant Schmidt, our commander, Leutnant Kunkel and his entourage, Eggers, Weser and me."

Naturally there was no position as such to occupy, just a series of concrete pill boxes, both large and small, which acted like a magnet for Allied artillery fire. One eyewitness from 1st Company Infantry Regiment 465 wrote,

"The company commander and the entire platoon were jammed into one small blockhouse. The heat and stink as a result of the press of bodies and the soaking and filthy clothing and equipment was terrible. To that must be added the constant firing. Each time there was a direct hit, we all jumped involuntarily and our heads rang. Nevertheless we were all poised to race out when an attack threatened." [2]

Not everyone was accommodated in pillboxes in this area. A few made use of isolated deep dugouts, but these were not popular. It was far from clear that they were proof against heavy shells or bombs and their use carried the additional risk of death through suffocation if the entrances were collapsed. Leutnant Wedekind describes one narrow escape:

Leutnant Wedekind Infantry Regiment 465 [3] **1**

"In the forward area I made use of a half-finished dugout, located not far from the concrete bunker being used by the *KTK*. A slight local rise in the terrain had made the construction of a reasonably deep dugout possible – a rarity in Flanders. The two entrances were, however not connected, which was a very unpleasant situation for us. One particular day we came under very heavy fire and one super-heavy shell blew in our entrance. We sat there in the darkness filled with a sense of foreboding. A match was struck which showed us that the entrance had fallen in as far as the seventh step. Wild thoughts raced through my head. We had been buried – buried alive!

"More thoughts rushed through my brain. There were ten of us, company headquarters and a gun team, all trapped in a very small space.

The air could not possibly last long. It would not even have been possible to try to dig out the entrance; the earth would have collapsed in and buried us completely. Like lightning I weighed up the situation and decided on a course of action. Everyone was to stay calm, so we used up as little oxygen as possible and no lights were to be lit. I then took up a pick which had been used during the construction of the dugout and started to tap with regular rhythm on the wall of the chamber. Would the men in the next dugout hear us?

"An ear pressed to the wall detected only the noise of drumfire and the trembling and heaving of the suffering earth. From time to time I could hear the dull individual explosions of super-heavy rounds falling nearby and sounding doubly menacing to us. Then I began to hear knocking at regular intervals; our message had obviously been understood. Once more I signalled and once more received a reply. We kept absolutely still and soon we noticed that someone was working on the entrance of the dugout then, finally, a shaft of light shone down on our cell. A hole began to appear and we could see the sky. Saved! But there was still a long wait until the hole could be enlarged sufficiently for me to be pulled clear past the two unfortunate lads who had been on sentry duty at the dugout entrance and had been crushed flat by the explosion of the shell.

"I realised how bad the air had already become once I could breathe freely again. I was utterly nauseated and my head spun. However, I could think of nothing else at that moment than my gratitude to our heroic rescuers, Gefreiter Koltes and his men, who, with complete disregard for the torrent of artillery fire, had dug us out. I dragged myself over to the bunker. Rittmeister Herrmann did not want to allow me into this small space, which had long since been overflowing, but eventually I won his sympathy and, as the ninth member, I joined the existing eight in a space of four square metres, one metre high. I could hardly speak, but after a large swig of schnaps and a few biscuits I recovered a little. Wedged in with my knees drawn up and my steel helmet propped against the wall, I lolled there completely apathetically and dozed off for a short nap"

Despite the fact that the regiment had not been involved in a major action, when it was relieved by Bavarian troops on 21 October after a week long deployment, the regiment had lost thirty five men killed and ninety nine wounded, not to mention five officers and 127 other ranks evacuated sick. Unfortunately it was impossible to withdraw it for rest and recuperation, so it remained in forward bivouac areas, remained on immediate standby for further deployment and was subject to endless air attacks, until it was called forward again, after several false alarms, on 27 October, once more to take over from the Bavarians.

Routine administration was rendered extremely difficult. The rainy, overcast skies made the nights pitch black and, with all the landmarks shot away, orientation for carrying parties was at times next to impossible. Troops moving forward into position carried as much in the way of drinks and rations as they could in addition to all their ammunition, which certainly helped, but the regular provision of hot food was important for the maintenance of morale Almost superhuman efforts were made to meet the need; sometimes these were crowned with success, sometimes not, but always they were attended by the risk of casualties from harassing fire.

Sergeant Kreibohm 10th Company Lehr Infantry Regiment [4]

"The 4th Platoon was made the ration party. Each evening it had to go forward. As far as Moorslede it's fairly quiet, then it really starts. I send the kitchen wagon back to the rear. The carrying containers and bread are distributed then, putting ourselves in God's care, off we go: not through Moorslede itself; nobody would get through, but off to the left of the village through the crater field and the gun positions. A bit of luck, there is some moonlight, but it's an awful route – beyond description. Something like this can only be understood by someone who has carried heavy loads, squelching forward through exploding shells and the craters they leave behind. Fortunately we succeed in getting through to the company. After the rations have been issued, we return at a trot. Almost cooking ourselves, we get back to our kitchen wagon. I feel full of joy because I still have all my men with me; there are no casualties."

The Lehr Infantry Regiment was fortunate to receive rations in this way. In many other instances along the line the carrying system broke down in the dreadful conditions, even in well organised and disciplined units. A few days earlier, Reserve Hauptmann Biernatzki, commander 3rd Battalion Infantry Regiment 68, wrote to his regimental commander complaining, 'In view of the immense exertions of the troops, the rations are currently completely inadequate. [The situation] is worse than it was in Moerkerke. In the last three days, we have received two days' rations of fat substitute and jam on one day only. In addition instead of receiving 1/10 litre of schnaps per head per day, we have received only 3/20 litre [*sic*].[5] There are a great many cases of gastro-intestinal illness.'[6]

Feldwebel Kubeile 1st Company Grenadier Regiment 9 [7]

"For days no rations had been got forward to the company, so it was essential that somehow food was got to them, if the grenadiers were to be able to hold their positions. Men were assembled from the transport lines and quartermaster's department, but there were very few of them; most were only 'fit for garrison duty'. Grenadier Kelm volunteered for this duty even though he fell into this category. He had been severely wounded in the foot and had to wear an orthopaedic boot. Despite our reservations, because he could barely walk, he insisted on being allowed to proceed; he was determined to take food forward to our comrades. However, on his way back, he met a hero's death." [8]

It was not only at the tactical level that problems continued to mount as the month went by. Despite the reservations that Crown Prince Rupprecht and General der Infanterie Sixt von Armin had about the Ludendorff directive of 9 October, they had no choice but to implement both its broad thrust and detail within the formations engaged in the defence of Passchendaele. On 11 October the commander of Fourth Army, General Sixt von Armin, signed off an order which did not arrive until after the fighting was over on 12 October, but it certainly laid down the tactics that the defence was to deploy for the remainder of the battle.

Fourth Army Order Ia/g. No. 420/October, Secret, dated 11 October 1917 [9]

"The major battle on 9 October has demonstrated that, providing the enemy assault is not totally overwhelming, powerful ground holding divisions can maintain their positions from within their own resources, (e.g. 16th Infantry Division, 22nd Reserve Division, 10th Bavarian Infantry Division and 25th Infantry Division), or at least manage to regain their original positions with some assistance from the *Eingreif* division (for example, 195th Infantry Division). Where, on the other hand, the enemy has succeeded in making a deep penetration (e.g. 18th Infantry Division, 227th Infantry Division), not even a fully battleworthy division supported by its *Eingreif* division is able to fully recapture its position. It is as important, therefore, to deny the enemy further progress as it is to recapture lost ground completely.

"From these considerations two principles emerge regarding command in battle:

> a.   Ground holding divisions must be fully up to strength and battleworthy.
> b.   Restraint by higher headquarters in the calling forward or deployment of the *Eingreif* divisions.

"Formations committed to the contact battle usually emerge from it badly mauled. At the end of a major battle the forward troops comprise a mere scattering[10] of riflemen, who lack either unified command or deployment in depth. Almost always order can only be restored by means of a complete relief by fresh troops.

"Of even greater importance is the maintenance of the strength of our infantry between the major days of battle. Wastage is almost as high as when fighting is taking place, due to a combination of constant enemy fire and the consequences of the [bad] weather conditions. If we wish to maintain our ability to fight, we must relieve troops more quickly. Within the ground holding divisions this is not currently possible because of the width of the sectors. Because of the rapid tempo of operations, with major days of battle following one another in quick succession, it is generally not possible to achieve this; it must be limited to special cases.

"I can see a possible method of maintaining the performance of the forward troops and that is by means of a ceaseless system of reliefs operated mutually by the ground holding and *Eingreif* divisions. This has two advantages; it prevents the forward troops from becoming exhausted and it ensures that all the troops who may become involved in major battle in a particular sector gain a good knowledge of the ground. These planned reliefs can only apply to infantry and engineers, because the artillery is divided into two thirds permanently in fire positions and one third ready to support assaults.

"To this end I order the following:

1. In accordance with arrangements to be determined by the corps commanders, planned reliefs are to be introduced between the ground holding and *Eingreif* divisions in the entire areas of Groups Staden and Ypres and the right flank division of Group Wijtschate.[11] The divisional commanders are also to change over simultaneously with their divisions. Intended exchanges are to be discussed with Army Headquarters, by means of telephone conversations between Group Commanders and the Army Commander, in order to ensure that in particular cases what is planned can be discussed in the context of the overall situation. The details of the arrangements for relief are to be reported by telephone.

2. As far as possible the relief of all the infantry of a division is to be completed in one night.

3. In the case of *Eingreif* divisions, whose deployment is decided by the corps commanders, I recommend that, in order to conserve the strength of the troops, the rule should be to maintain one third near the front, with the remaining two thirds only to be moved forward from their accommodation onto the battlefield once a major battle has begun. In the event that the *Eingreif* divisions are deployed, every effort is to be made to ensure once the major battle is over that at least the battalions who have been

directly involved in the fighting are replaced by troops who have not been engaged.

4. At the latest by the time the reliefs of the current ground holding divisions by the *Eingreif* divisions are complete, [the forward battle area] is to be divided into an outpost zone and main defensive position. The relieving troops of the *Eingreif* divisons are to be briefed in detail before their deployment about the reason for this operational procedure.

5. Relief arrangements for Group North, the new Group Diksmuide,[12] the three southern divisions of Group Wijtschate and Group Lille will only be made by Army Headquarters.

6. On the basis of reports received from divisional and corps commanders I note that both between and during major days of battle there has been notable increase in the tendency for [those deployed forward] to trickle back towards the rear.[13] I require this evil to be countered by resort to the sternest measures, regardless [of any excuses] and for punishments inflicted to be made known to all troops. The sealing off of the rear areas [and the designation of a line] which leaderless soldiers are only permitted to cross if they are in possession of written authority proved to be successful during the Battle of the Somme.

> Signed: Sixt von Armin
> General der Infanterie

It is interesting to note from paragraph 6 of the order that the constant fighting coupled with the bad weather was taking a noticeable toll on the morale and willing-ness to fight of at least some of the German troops as the October fighting dragged on. There may, therefore, have been some substance to the intelligence briefings which Haig was receiving at the time, concerning the ability of the German army to absorb the constant pressure to which it was being subjected, but care should be taken not to read too much into this type of statement. The great majority of the defenders fought with the utmost self-sacrificial determination right through until the campaign was finally called off.

The autumn fighting placed great demands on the artillery as well. On 4 October Bavarian Field Artillery Regiment 20 returned, along with the other formations of 10th Bavarian Infantry Division, for a second tour of duty to the east of Beselare. It was in action constantly in support of its infantry, but also took part in counter-battery fire and in the major gas bombardment of 15 October.

Reserve Hauptmann Brügelmann
2nd Battery Bavarian Field Artillery Regiment 20 [14] **2**

> "The battery position could not be described as beautiful. It was near the Potterijebrug forward of Dadizele. We were surrounded by a lovely swamp. There was no accommodation to provide protection, just a small cellar (the so-called Mousetrap) to provide shelter from the rain. There was barely enough cover to provide screening even from the eyes of ground based observers. We already had fourteen strenuous days of battle behind us when on 15 October from 1.00 am to 3.30 am we fired 2,000 gas shells and followed up with a further 200 until 5.00 am, by which time all the guns were out of action. It was the greatest firing performance by the battery throughout the entire war.
>
> "After these extraordinary exertions we rested a little. We had rearranged the position, carried out necessary work and had finished ranging in. It was a pitch black night and the rain was pouring down. During the day enemy fire had been quite heavy, but it had eased off somewhat. The telephone rang. The battery commander was to report at once to the group commander. That meant something unusual and probably not pleasant. I picked my way carefully through the swamp, the shell holes and the barbed wire and arrived at the concrete blockhouse where the staff was accommodated. I received the following order: '2nd Battery is to change the position of two of it guns tonight two kilometres forward. The position – as shown on the map – has been reconnoitred by Leutnant X. Unteroffizier Y will lead the way.'

To organise the move and carry it out at short notice was immensely difficult. After all sorts of problems, the guns were some distance to the west of their original position. Hauptmann Brügelmann continues:

> "Forward along what used to be a road! Now it was ankle deep in water and right in front was an upturned wagon of the foot artillery … We could not move past it. We needed some advice, but it was hard to come by. What was the route that the guide was supposed to know? He explained that it was hopeless to the left and right and he had no suggestions to make. That was a marvellous situation! Something had to be done quickly, so I raced off to the nearest battery and telephoned Group. Report: 'The guns of 2nd Battery are stuck. The guide does not know the way.' Reply: 'Leutnant X is to do the guiding. The guns must be got into position at all costs.'
>
> "Leutnant X was found and made his way to us, only to announce that we had taken completely the wrong route. There was nothing for it but to

retrace our steps and an hour later we were back at our start point ... full of anger and full of concern because it was getting lighter."

Eventually the guns of 2nd Battery were established in the correct position and, because it was so far forward, it was spared a great deal of artillery fire and was never subject to counter-battery fire. Hauptmann Brügelmann once more:

"That evening a small wagon was despatched forward. It was carrying stoves, rations, wine, cigars and cigarettes to ease the existence of those hanging on forward in their holes in the ground. Once per day their warm food was brought forward, but they had to brew their coffee themselves. Reliefs were arranged every third or fourth day. Leutnant Hochrein and Leutnant Gaymann took it in turns. The section fired with great industry out to their maximum range at batteries, advancing lines of British soldiers and also in support of the forward infantry on 26 October when the large-scale attack was launched. The British made no progress [that day] in this area. Everything went well for the section. The British assumed that no guns could be that far forward and, whilst there was an endless stream of shells roaring overhead in the direction of the rear areas, they themselves were barely troubled. The only [problem] occurred when a direct hit struck the courageous ammunition column when it was in the process of unloading. Four men and five horses were killed."

Reserve Leutnant Peistrup 8th Battery Field Artillery Regiment 62 [15] **3**

"On 18 October 1917 8th Battery was moved forward through extremely heavy fire and, despite unspeakable difficulties, close behind the forward infantry positions, in order to carry out a gas shoot. The limbers moved into position nearby. Everything was done as silently and calmly as possible. As the ammunition column came forward one man and two horses were killed. A further two horses and another man were killed where the limbers were located. The battery had to remain silent until the appointed hour for the gas shoot arrived. Punctual to the minute, along a front of four kilometres, hundreds of guns opened fire and in about one hour, the mission, to fire one thousand rounds, was complete.

"As we prepared to move our guns, one of the limbers slid down into a huge shell crater. Officers and men attempted, in some cases up to their necks in icy water, to free the horses. Despite the greatest efforts this proved to be impossible, because the horses were trapped by the mud. There was nothing else for it but to put them out of their terrified misery with a revolver shot. Hardly one hundred metres further on, another team fell into a crater where, before it could be rescued, all the horses were drowned. The driver himself escaped only by the narrowest of margins. Because of these losses the battery had to leave an ammunition wagon behind.

"The following morning Vizefeldwebel Könnecke and six drivers arrived to recover the wagon, but because of heavy fire this proved to be impossible and Fahrer Tiburski was killed during this attempt.[16] Könnecke volunteered to try again. He was lucky the following night to be able free to the wagon, but hardly had it begun to move than Könnecke was hit by a shell. His outstanding men could only transport his corpse to the rear. All too soon this courageous man had to lay down his life for the Fatherland. Honour his memory!"

Unteroffizier Keil 9th Battery Field Artillery Regiment 115 [17] **4**

"I was returned to duty with Field Artillery Regiment 115 on 18 October 1917 in Flanders and was posted to 9th Battery. I reported to the battery office that evening then made my acquaintance with the crew of Number 2 Gun which had been allocated to me. The battery was at rest that evening but, as luck would have it, the rest period ended that night ... About 9.00 pm the battery moved off to its new fire position in the open near the white chateau by the cemetery. Vizewachtmeister Wagner allocated the gun positions in the dark. I did not carry out this order exactly. Instead, on my own initiative, I moved the gun about fifty metres further forward ... .We then began the usual digging duties; the scene being illuminated from time to time by flares ... We dug fast, spurred on by the urgency of the situation. Firing could begin at any time. Suddenly, oh dear! Vizewachtmeister Wagner appeared at our gun position and delivered me, a newcomer to the battery, a serious dressing down for having placed the gun there without his knowledge and agreement. All this complaining was pointless. Our gun pit was ready and could hardly be changed now. We registered ourselves swiftly by firing three rounds.

"After that I received an order to report to the battery commander. I was half way there when I heard the order, 'Defensive fire!' and rushed back in a flash to my gun, where we worked feverishly. The whole crew laboured hard to get the very greatest performance out of the gun. The enemy attack seemed to have been beaten off and there was a short pause in the battle. Night was past and we worked to maintain the gun, bring up more ammunition and then took a break. We looked around for water, found some in a shell hole and settle down to have a wash. Unfortunately our peace was disrupted by the arrival of an enemy shell which landed next to our limber, parked behind the gun. Fortunately nothing really happened, though our rucksacks, which had been placed on it, were rather the worse for wear. I noticed some stirrings within my crew. 'Korporal,[18] we can't stay here,' called out someone, but I replied, 'We are in exactly the right place!' They were astounded, but the enemy had attempted to knock us out and his fire for effect had failed completely. The battery had suffered almost no casualties.

"That shoot might have been over, but with sharp eyes in the enemy's captive balloons observing us, we had to be careful what we did. Otherwise we should have suffered badly from their fire. The place where I had been ordered to place my gun already looked terrible, so great was the joy amongst my crew. Nevertheless we were not allowed to settle down for long during this battle and we quickly received the order, 'Battery prepare to pull back to new position further to the rear!' Personally I could not quite understand the order, but that did not help much; every order was holy. Because the ground was now virtually impassable and because we could not get our teams of horse forward, it was a matter of the whole battery pulling one single gun. The performance we achieved on empty stomachs was unforgettable! Just as we positioned the first gun near the crossroads, the morning mist dispersed. My gun was the last to be moved. We had hardly got into position than the enemy opened fire on us once more. Despite everything we got on with the job. But the fortitude of the crew was first tested then failed them as they raced for cover with the arrival on the position of gas shells. I stood my ground, virtually alone, and looked around.

"At that moment I saw Vizewachtmeister Wagner standing there courageously at the cross roads. 'Where is your gun and what's happened to the crew?' he shouted. They were nearly his last words; an enemy shell landed directly in front of him. Some infantrymen, who were passing at the time were also hit … I could only react to his call of 'Help me somebody!' I bawled, 'Medical orderlies!' and Unteroffizier Otto rushed up, closely followed by Reserve Oberleutnant Schulze, the battery commander. Another man arrived and the courageous Vizewachtmeister Wagner was carried away. This was how I first met the battery commander and that was how my first day and night with it were spent … The following morning we once more heard, 'Stand by to change position!' Under the command of Wachtmeister Eichler, the teams galloped up and, after a short march, we took up new positions where Major Burde, the regimental commander himself, was waiting for us. As soon as I heard his word of command I was transported back thirteen years to my time as an active soldier when he was a captain and my battery commander. It was the first time I had seen him for thirteen years when he was my Hauptmann and battery commander with Field Artillery Regiment 12 …

"Nothing good came out of the evening of 25 October. The battery had plenty of ammunition at its disposal and we had all fed well from the field kitchen. We were all ready to thwart the British plans with plenty of 'blue beans' [artillery slang for shells]. We soon became certain that something was afoot as heavy shelling began. We loaded and fired tirelessly, as fast as we were able, spending the entire night in intense action. The hour of fate was drawing ever closer for me. At 4.00 am on 26 October there was an enormous racket. My gun seemed about to fail [mechanically], but by dint of cooling it and freshly lubricating it, we soon had it ready to fire once more. Before the first shell left the barrel, I checked the sighting arrange-ments, at which my gunner shouted, 'Open your eyes! There is no aiming mark! In his excitement the [gunner who had placed it] had overlooked the fact that the light was extinguished. Now it was essential for me, making sparing use of my torch, to indicate the correct direction. I shouted, 'Can you see that?' but the only reply was Crash! Bang! The worst had happened; a shell had landed right in front of our gun, but I was barely aware about what had happened. Bleeding profusely from a head wound I was thrown several metres. I was picked up and taken back to a casualty collection point. The young, brave Kanonier Graich, who later gave his life for the Fatherland, had not shrunk from moving me back to the rear, despite the heavy fire which was landing all around us."

For the three weeks from 7/8 October to 28 October the 24th Infantry Division held the line just to the south of the Ypres-Menen road. Infantry Regiment 133 was located left forward and Infantry Regiment 179 right forward, with its right flank just forward of Geluveld. The division was affected directly by the major battles but, as in so many other instances, it was the incessant and ubiquitously lethal artillery fire that ground the regiments down. Nevertheless, it is worthy of note that this tour of duty still lasted a full three weeks, despite the casualties the regiments suffered and it was finally only relieved after being seriously weakened by the fighting on 26 October. Timed to coincide with a major effort against Passchendaele, the attack that day by the British X Corps with 7th Division astride the Ypres-Menen road and 5th Division to its north, was intended to wrest Geluveld village and the final piece of high ground in this sector from the German army. In a day of hard fighting with serious casualties on both sides, the attack was totally repulsed.

The defence was thoroughly alerted in advance. Not only was a great deal of preparatory movement detected but, just before 5.00 am, all final doubt was removed when 1st Company Infantry Regiment 179 captured, 'a wounded British soldier of the 7th Division (Regiment Queen) [sic: i.e. a member of 2nd Queen's of 91 Brigade], who was shot by one of our sentries manning a light machine gun. He was a member of a British assault group.'[19] After intense drum fire, the attack was launched north and south of the main road. The German machine guns were swiftly brought out from the protection of the pillboxes and opened up with devastating effect against the British infantry struggling forward through the mud, despite the fact that there had been extensive use of smoke to shield the movement.

Nevertheless the attack was pressed with the utmost determination. Small penetrations were made, British assault groups reorganised then began to consolidate in small pockets of resistance in the western extremity of Geluveld. The nearest German sub-units launched immediate counter-attacks, suffering badly at the hands of Lewis gunners, but by mid-morning heavier counter-strokes began to be mounted by the battalions back in support and reserve. The *KTK* ordered a major effort by 10th, 11th and 12th Companies Infantry Regiment 179 to restore the line. The usual British barrage fire forward of Geluveld cost them very heavy casualties during the march forward then, as they closed up on the forward British positions, their movement was severely hampered by the mud and ploughed up terrain, made worse by the pouring rain.

Ignoring the hail of small arms fire, Leutnant Winkler on the left flank and Feldwebel-Leutnant Schubach on the right rallied the troops who had managed to get forward, then launched them forward in a wild charge at 11.30 am, which succeeded not only in restoring the line, but sending the few British survivors racing back to their start line. The scene was one of utter chaos, with dead and wounded lying everywhere in heaps. Nevertheless, that was far from the end of the fighting that day. There were several further attempts by the British to introduce reinforcements and to continue the attack, supported by the enormous weight of artillery fire which continued to rain down on the area. It was all in vain. All the attackers had to show for their efforts was the fact that they had so reduced the strength of 24th Infantry Division that it had to be relieved the very next day; there being a very real fear that it would be unable to withstand a renewal of the assault in this critical area.

1st and 3rd Battalions Infantry Regiment 179, which had borne the brunt of the assault against the village itself, were down to cadre size: the 1st Battalion only mustered two officers, four NCOs and twenty eight OR and 3rd Battalion was hardly better off, having been reduced to two officers, twelve NCOs and fifty eight OR.[20] Infantry Regiment 133 to the south of the road had also suffered badly, but not quite to the extent of Infantry Regiment 179.

Reserve Leutnant Oschatz Infantry Regiment 133[21] **5**

"Our regiment was deployed south of the main road from Ypres to Menen … in bog-like terrain which was littered with the bodies of British soldiers. On 9 October, a British attack launched after heavy drum fire was beaten off with heavy casualties. Because the heavy machine guns were soon rendered inoperable due to the mud, the crews were located in the few concrete pillboxes which were scattered across the position. These buildings were constantly targeted by the British heavy artillery. As a result they were frequently upended and sank into the mud.

"The regiment maintained one battalion in the front line with the so-called *KTK*. There was a further battalion behind with the *BTK* and finally, located in the C Position, was a third battalion. Here every effort was made to produce some sort of weatherproof accommodation, using curved corrugated iron sheets as protection from the rain. The endless artillery fire to which we were subjected meant that casualties were high everywhere. The rain and the cold, wet conditions meant that the extended period in the open led to a considerable worsening of the state of health of the men.

"On 22 October the British launched a strong attack which was shot to pieces by our artillery and machine ground fire and increased yet again the number of corpses in front of the positions. During the night 25/26 October there was a great deal of movement in and behind the British lines, which indicated that an attack was in the offing. At 6.30 am drum fire of utterly unprecedented weight crashed down on us, causing extremely heavy casualties. Nevertheless our defensive fire beat off the assault and counter-strokes by the 'B' and 'C' battalions threw back those attackers who had managed to break in. The main thrust of the attack was along the line of the Ypres-Menen road, where tanks were employed to assist the movement forward as far as the ruins of Geluveld. In the course of this attack our sister regiment Infantry Regiment 179 suffered appalling casualties, but our 1st Battalion, which was manning the front line, was almost completely wiped out as well. Nearly all the officers were killed, including Reserve Leutnant Fritzsche, who had proved himself repeatedly during many battles."

Apart from the wounded man from the Queen's regiment, of whom no more is heard, the German 24th and 15th Divisions captured no fewer than sixty one men of 20 Brigade and six of 91 Brigade that day. The interrogators of Group Wijtschate went to work on them rapidly and by the following day a very detailed five page report was circulated by Oberleutnant Müller-Albert, one of the interrogation officers.[22] The interrogations yielded a full and accurate breakdown of the organisation of the formations and units of X Corps, together with complete details about preparations for the attack, the equipment, its objectives and the tactics used. The interrogators were interested in details of previous attacks (e.g. Polygon Wood in early October) the casualty rates and how they had been replaced.

'The prisoners,' commented the interrogators, 'especially the NCOs, made a good impression. Almost half of them arrived in France before or during autumn 1916 … most spoke willingly; the information appears to be reliable … Morale among the men was said to be good. Naturally they all wish that the war will soon be over; some, in common with the people of England, hope that it will be finished by Christmas. Only the newspapers in England and those who are profiting from the war wish it to continue.' The report concludes with a direct quote from an unnamed prisoner: 'Lloyd George is a very competent, hard-working man. If, however, he was to spend twenty four hours participating in an attack like that, he would be even better!'

Despite the casualties and the terrible conditions during October, the morale of some individuals remained remarkably good. On 20 October a member of 6th Company Infantry Regiment 133 wrote a very reassuring message home to his family. It was a letter in sharp contrast to most of those being sent back to Germany at this time, which were altogether more pessimistic in tone. He was clearly a tough man of few needs and happy with his lot.

Gefreiter Linke 6th Company Infantry Regiment 133 [23] **5**

"Despite a great deal of mud and other strenuous efforts, I am still fit and well! You simply cannot imagine what it is like here!! I have been made a runner again and that is not exactly fun! At night we go out with a flare pistol and if we do not know what is going on, we light things up, by firing a white flare. We always go out in twos because it quite often happens that one of us sinks up to his armpits in the mud of a shell hole! The *KTK* fires a white flare every five minutes. If there is a lot going on then it is every three minutes. This is to help runners orientate themselves or we should never find the way. We are living in the company commander's concrete pillbox. Despite a lot of work it has ten centimetres of water in it and it is 300 metres in a straight line to the *KTK*. All the ground is ploughed up by shells.

"The food is really good and there is plenty of it (battle supplement!). It is just that in the A Position, because of difficulties moving it, the food is cold. Each day we get one iron ration (400 grams), one litre of coffee, 750 g of bread and something to spread on it for a snack in the evening. We get solid fuel stoves delivered so we can warm the food up. In this position the food is brought up by another company. We runners have to guide these carriers from the *KTK* to the company. You ought to hear them complaining and muttering if we are not there at the right time!! Also there is enough tobacco in the positions."

The following letter, which was written on 25 October, is far more serious in tone:

Offizierstellvertreter von Gelshorn 6th Battery Field Artillery Regiment 62 [24]

"We were pulled out of Biache, immediately loaded and transported to Renai, which is a beautiful, friendly region. – Unfortunately we only spent a day there and had to set off for the front. We were deployed near Tenbrielen to the west of Menen. Just as we were taking over the position Leutnant Pütz was wounded in the head. The same shell killed Böttcher and seriously wounded Dillich. Dillich was badly hit in the shoulder; apparently he is no longer at death's door and is said to be in Oldenburg. I handed Böttcher over to the field hospital in Wevelgem where the limbers were housed. He was later buried at the cemetery in Menen.[25] His wound must have been mortal; it was a serious neck wound.

"It upset all of us. Böttcher was an excellent chap; I shall never forget what he did during those hard days at Biache. A few days later Sprenger was slightly wounded in the neck at the same spot. He is in Germany as well. The position was really bad, in full view of ground observation with filth and mud everywhere. The last few days we were there the British kept us under heavy fire and we were fired at continuously for seven days. The crews were withdrawn so that there were no more casualties. A house immediately by the position burnt down and, with it went everyone's kit; it was a sad sight. Some of the guns were unserviceable and could not be pulled out of the position. We took the guns from the battery that relieved us and are now deployed a bit to the north near Vierkavenhoek. The position is good. We get hardly any fire; we are a long way back. Sadly we have lost two men next to one of our advanced guns. Kanonier Lampe is dead (head wound)[26] and Kanonier Hinz slightly wounded (neck wound).

"Yesterday the whole battery went forward to fire a gas shoot, but because of the stormy weather nothing came of it. It would probably have gone badly for us. It is really busy here. Almost everyday there is drum fire and attacks, both great and small. I do not know what the overall situation is like. We never hear anything here ... The Hauptmann has [recently] said, 'May the Homeland prove itself worthy of our army.' It made a deep impression on me. We have all been talking about it a lot. A lot of what has been going on in Germany is shameful for our Fatherland. All the blood would have flowed in vain. We must now win or go under. That is what I feel anyway. The guns have just opened up once more ... "

Further north, the men of Infantry Regiment 164, the left forward formation of 111th Infantry Division, who had been occupying a position in the craters west of the Goudberg, found themselves confronting the attack by 8 Brigade of the 3rd

Canadian Division on 26 October. The 3rd Battalion had already endured a terrible night move forward in miserable conditions.

Gefreiter Pühse 1st Machine Gun Company Infantry Regiment 164 [27] **1**

"One behind the other in a seemingly endless line, we made our way forward. Every step was heavy and laboured and our bodies were bent right forward. All our faces were serious, but determined. Nobody spoke a word; all were pre-occupied with their own thoughts of parents, wife and child. Everyone knew that we were to be confronted by an utterly appalling and chaotic situation. Initially we made reasonable progress, because the craters were not too tightly packed together and it was possible to go round them. Now and again a salvo of shells disturbed our movement. Now and then there was the sound of cursing and above the monotonous tramp of the feet could be heard low shouts of, 'Wire!' From the rear came the call of, 'Step short in front!' to be matched by calls from the front of, 'Keep up!'

"Detachments which had already been relieved loomed up towards us. In passing there were many exchanged whispers, but nobody stopped because they were in a hurry to reach their well-earned billets. The concentrations of fire became heavier. A stifled cry and muffled moaning told of the first wounded. The way forward became worse and worse. The soft earth which was raised up above the water had become trampled by the passage of the feet of hundreds of soldiers into a uniquely saturated and almost bottomless morass. It was rare to cover more than a few paces without sinking in over the ankles. Right and left were craters full of black filthy mud and water. They represented a terrible danger. We negotiated them with the utmost care in the darkness in order to avoid slipping and falling into the water-filled holes, a fate which soon befell one of our number.

"It was important not to make too much noise during the rescue, but unfortunately the involuntary cry of the man who fell seemed to have alerted the enemy, because suddenly there was a burst of firing. Once having begun, the firing never let up. In the end we arrived and occupied the muddy shell holes. In order to make ours as homely as possible, we shovelled the water out, then erected a platform for the gun and tried to orientate ourselves with our surroundings as well as we could in the darkness. The sky was full of lights, flashes and flares and heavy bangs and crashes were heard from near and far. Spread out among the craters the men maintained a sharp look out forwards, for the enemy was not far away. The cold night air was viciously cold, so we huddled close together in our crater for warmth. From time to time we were forced to shift our position because the water kept running in over the tops of our boots."

Uncomfortable their position may have been, but they did not have long to wait before they were fighting for their lives.

Melder Pagenkämper 3rd Company Infantry Regiment 164 [28] 1

"When the drum fire began I was on my way between the *KTK* and the front line. The only man I could find there was Leutnant Hartmann who was ducked down in a shell hole. All the other company commanders had been forced to change positions because of the weight of fire. I took cover in the hole of Vizefeldwebel Einig. The fire was coming down so heavily on the rear that it was completely unthinkable to try to get through. In any case every man was needed forward. Towards morning shells started landing one after the other right on our position. Gas and smoke clouds blocked any view of the ground to our front. Then came the moment of relief, as shells started landing beyond us. It was the sign for an attack.

"'Look, here they come through the fog!' bawled Einig, 'Fire! Fire!' One assaulting wave after another flooded up over the crest of the hill. Pack animals were moving ammunition and trench stores forward, amongst them wooden hurdles, which the assaulting troops threw down over the shell holes and patches of mud in order to get the assaulting troops forward faster and more concentrated. Everybody leapt up, aimed their weapons and started firing. The machine guns then opened up as well. Red flares curled upwards. I took a quick glance to the rear. The signal for defensive fire was being repeated and passed on everywhere.

"With a crash the German guns opened fire. When it arrived it was exactly on target, all along the hills in front of Passchendaele and right in amongst the enemy lines of assaulting troops. The combination of artillery fire, machine gun fire and the courage of the brave fighters in the front line kept the British [*sic*] at bay, but more and more columns swarmed over the hill."

The Canadians succeeded in penetrating the forward positions of 11th and 12th Companies, but 9th Company was already on standby to launch an immediate counter-stroke.

Reserve Leutnant Pätz 9th Company Infantry Regiment 164 [29] 1

"An appalling weight of barrage fire cut us off from the front line. As soon as we set off a direct hit landed on the company, but notwithstanding all the fire and the mud, which made progress extremely difficult, the counter-attack succeeded, despite the gaps that had been torn in its ranks.

The front line was restored. The British [*sic*] who, because of the mud, could only pull back slowly, offered amazing targets. As a result numbers of escaping British [*sic*] were brought down by German bullets."

This small-scale action was typical of many that day as the companies tried individually and collectively to force back the attack across the full width of the regimental sector. At times the fighting was hand to hand, but in the end the Canadians were beaten back with heavy losses and barely perceptible gains in this area.

Melder Pagenkämper 3rd Company Infantry Regiment 164 [30] **1**

"There was no more ammunition. We had fired off the lot and the first of the enemy attackers were within thirty metres. Vizefeldwebel Einig fired off the last of the flares. We had to leave our pillbox. Racing from shell hole to shell hole, we broke free of the enemy, but they continued to press us hard. Suddenly we were saved. Our airmen had understood our signals from the bunker and threw out ammunition and food to us. In a few paces we had both collected it and were once again resupplied. Then we saw that the enemy had turned away. They were pulling back all along the line.

"Reaching a swift decision we headed back to the concrete pillbox. There we ate the iron rations that the airmen had thrown to us. Oskar Winkelmann had brought in a sandbag which contained several water bottles full of rum. We all took a good drink but, while we were still eating, we heard the crash of hand grenades once more. For a moment we were taken aback. Had the Tommies not had enough? Our machine gun opened up immediately. The enemy attackers had thrown their grenades too early, which alerted us in good time. Nevertheless, a section of ten men fought their way right up to our pillbox, despite the machine gun fire. We killed them all in hand to hand fighting and the remaining British [*sic*] soldiers withdrew once more through our destructive defensive artillery fire."

A few days earlier, during the night of 20/21 October, 11th Bavarian Infantry Division had taken over the key sector which ran northwest – southeast from Wallemolen to the railway embankment of the Ypres-Roeselare railway south of the southeast tip of Passchendaele village. This was quite a broad area, so it was necessary to have all three regiments in the line in the order from north to south: Bavarian Infantry Regiment 22, Bavarian Infantry Regiment 3, Bavarian Reserve Infantry Regiment 13. The edge of Poelkapelle still formed part of the newly created Outpost Zone, with the villages of Passchendaele, Beselare and Geluveld just in rear of the main defensive position. This deployment meant that on 26 October, 11th Bavarian Infantry Division was directly responsible for the defence of Passchendaele.

Each regiment was echeloned deeply. One battalion was deployed forward,

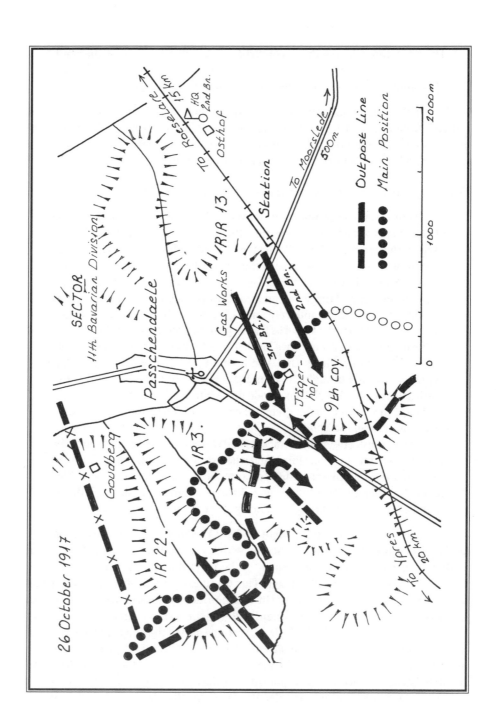

26 October 1917

SECTOR
11th Bavarian Division

Passchendaele

Goudberg

IR 22.

IR 3.

Gas Works

RIR 13.

Station

Jäger-
hof

9th coy.

3rd Bn.

2nd Bn.

HQ
2nd Bn.

Osthof

To Roeselare 15 km

To Moorslede

500m

To Ypres
20 km

Outpost Line
Main Position

2000m

1000

0

manning the outpost zone with one company and the main defensive line with three more.[31] Behind each were the immediate readiness support battalions and the reserve ones even further to the rear. The entire sector had been under heavy artillery fire throughout the four days since the fighting of 22 October. This rose in intensity to drumfire several times during the night 25/26 October, only to slacken in the early hours of the morning, before coming down once more with full force at 6.00 am. Simultaneously the men of 9 Brigade, 3rd Canadian Division and 10 Brigade of 4th Canadian Division were observed advancing towards the Bavarians in three distinct waves.

Out in front of Bavarian Infantry Regiment 3 in the outpost line was their 8th Company, one of whose platoons was commanded by Vizefeldwebel (Offizierstellvertreter) Leonhard Abt of 8th Company, who came originally from Bobingen. Such was the speed of the Canadian advance that the outpost line was overrun so swiftly that it contributed almost nothing to the defence.[32] However, Abt was quick-witted enough to pull back rapidly, together with a sizeable part of his platoon, as far as the ruins of a house forward of Passchendaele. Despite being wounded in the arm and being pressed severely from three sides by the Canadians (who were described as British in his medal citation), he held this pocket of resistance for ten hours, defeating all attempts to destroy it and acting as a considerable thorn in the side of the attackers, until he was relieved by a local counter-attack mounted during the afternoon. Even then he led a charge at the head of an assault group which succeeded in recapturing a machine gun that had had to be abandoned that morning. His leadership and gallantry, on a day marked by remarkable courage on both sides, was quite outstanding. Appropriately, he was awarded the Bravery Medal in Gold, the highest award available to other ranks in the Bavarian contingent and one of only 1,003 won throughout the war. [33]

Although Abt's work was clearly in a class of it own, there were numerous other acts of bravery during a day of close quarter fighting in filthy weather and a largely featureless swamp. Reserve Leutnant Michael Melzl was awarded the Iron Cross 1st Class, as was Offizierstellvertreter Michael Schild of 6th Company, whose citation praised his exemplary bravery and for repeatedly leading local counter-attacks throughout the day with complete disregard for his own safety. This remarkable platoon commander was later awarded the Bavarian Bravery Medal in Silver for his conduct throughout the heavy fighting in Flanders. On a day when the defence buckled, but generally held, on the Passchendaele front, the Canadian 46th Battalion, of 10, Brigade succeeded in capturing a key hill, which provided observation over the entire front of 11th Bavarian Infantry Division. The divisional commander, Generalmajor von Kneußl, ordered a counterattack to recapture this hill and an eyewitness from 2nd Battalion Bavarian Reserve Infantry Regiment 13 has left us a vivid account of the savage cost of this successful operation which was launched in the late afternoon: [34] **6**

"Our regiment was deployed to Flanders on 20 October, On a small rise alongside the railway line from Roeselare to Ypres lay the village of Passchendaele. The first time we saw it it was lit up by the glare of the morning sun. The smashed walls reached up towards the sky, as did the wrecked and torn remains of the destroyed church. Lower down and close to the railway were the remains of a destroyed gasworks; whilst amidst an expanse of swamp lay the foundations of the *Jägerhof* and the demolished station. In all directions there was yawning emptiness, ruins, rubble and destruction. Between the railway and the village was where our 2nd Battalion had its position. In fact there was no position at all; there were no trenches, just shell holes in which our men took cover. The crater field stretched forward for three kilometres. There was barely any cover, no accommodation for the artillery, the infantry, or the machine guns and almost none for the staffs.

"Our battalion headquarters was located at *Osthof*, a mean farmstead, which did have some trees and bushes which provided cover from view, but the wooden ceiling was virtually useless as protection. Every morning and evening drum fire raked across our position. On the rear areas, especially where the enemy assumed that staffs were located, fire came down almost all day long. Hauptmann Eidam, heroic, tireless, always faithful to his duty, could not rest until he had seen the entire position for himself.

"The first great day of battle came on 26 October. Enemy drum fire started coming down at 5.00 am. This was not the noise of thunder; rather it was an incessant [drum]roll. The 3rd Battalion was in the front line, with Leutnant Fleischmann of 9th Company manning the outpost line. We of 2nd Battalion were in reserve. The fire roared on. Passchendaele could no longer be seen through the dust and smoke. It was 7.00 am when suddenly a white cloud rolled over the ground as far as the artillery positions, which were under heavy fire. The enemy had smoked off the entire battlefield.

"The first information arrived at 8.00 am. The British [*sic*] had been thrown back by Bavarian Infantry Regiment 3, but had broken through in the sector of Bavarian Infantry Regiment 22. There was still no news from our forward troops. To our front it seemed to be somewhat calmer, but the artillery battle was still in full swing. At 2.00 pm a carrier pigeon arrived bearing information from our regiment. The enemy had overrun and captured the outpost company, so quickly that it had no time to react. The hill between Passchendaele and the railway had been captured. From there the enemy had an overview into the rear area and could observe all our movements. They simply had to be driven off. At 4.00 pm our battalion received the order to launch a counter-attack. Autumn mist was already settling gently on the ploughed-up terrain, the rubble and the corpses.

"Our companies lined up along the railway embankment. All our batteries concentrated a short period of drum fire on the enemy. Then we stormed forward. Of course it was nothing of the kind. Wading up to our knees in the bog, we made our way forward from crater to crater and on up the hill. Enemy machine gun fire mowed down many, but the courageous troops pressed on, with Leutnant Schmitt, who had heard only one hour previously about his promotion to officer rank, in the lead. Suddenly flares went up! The enemy had fled; the position was ours once more. Some prisoners – they were Canadians – and a few machine guns were the extent of the booty.

"But many, many, faithful comrades, including the courageous Leutnant Schmitt lay still on the captured field and much noble blood mingled with the water and mud of the captured position. Shells were still howling overhead in the direction of the *Osthof*, which the morning after our departure collapsed in ruins, burying all its occupants. Out on the railway embankment entire sections of men lay dead next to the shell holes. We were relieved at 2.00 am and were very happy about it. It had become an eerie experience, rather as though we could hear the beat of the wings of death, which had already reaped a dreadful harvest earlier that day. Dog tired and exhausted, our little band, those who were still alive, stumbled along the road in the pale moonlight. Nobody spoke a single word. Deadly serious, the dark forms with the heavy helmets on their heads, headed back to their billets, sick to the heart with mourning for the fallen"

The casualties on this day of intense fighting were extremely heavy. Writing in his diary, Generalmajor Paul Ritter von Kneußl, commander of 11th Bavarian Infantry Division, recorded them as follows:

	Killed		Wounded		Missing	
	Offr	OR	Offr	OR	Offr	OR
Infantry Regiment 3	1	58	6	204	2	135
Infantry Regiment 22		114	4	267	13	298
Reserve Infantry Regiment 13	2	64	1	239	1	96
Totals:	3	236	11	704	16	529

The total battle casualties, therefore, were thirty officers and 1,469 junior ranks. To this grim total he added 2 officers and 203 junior ranks sick in hospital, meaning that the price of holding on at Passchendaele as the month drew to an end was thirty two officers and 1,672 men, a casualty rate mirrored by the experience of other divisions during the October battles and quite unsustainable over a long period.[35]

Throughout the day enormous numbers of casualties accumulated in holding locations all over the battlefield. They lay packed into concrete pill boxes where they could be squeezed in, in folds in the ground and shell holes and, in some cases where the stretcherbearers had been hard at work moving them to the rear, they were assembled at collecting points waiting for transport to the rear. Inevitably, such were the delays, that many who might have been saved succumbed to their wounds and in any case, all the time that they remained in the forward battle area, they were still vulnerable to being wounded or killed by random shell fire. A padre from 234th Infantry Division, which only formed up on 16 January 1917, but which was heavily engaged in the autumn battles, left a dramatic account of an attempt made during the night of 26/27 October to clear some of the backlog of casualties from 11th Bavarian Infantry Division.

Feldgeistlicher K Foertsch, Padre 234 Infantry Brigade [36] 7

"I was on night duty at the main dressing station, which is where all the wounded arrived having received initial first aid right forward. Because all the wounded had already been sent back to the field hospitals I had nothing to do, so I lay down on a camp bed. It must have been about 10.00 pm, when I heard the senior doctor say on the telephone 'Seriously wounded? How many? Fifty? OK! I'll come forward with some ambulances.' At that I thought that I might as well go too. The senior doctor agreed and a few minutes later we were rattling forward with two ambulances, each towing a trailer. The senior doctor drove the leading ambulance and I followed on in the second, sandwiched between the two drivers. Initially the journey went well, but then we arrived in the area covered by enemy fire. Crashes and flashes came down to our right and left. On one occasion there was an enormous thump as a shell landed to the right of the road, sending up showers of earth. A large shell splinter whirred glistening through the air towards the vehicle, smashing our lamp and hitting the steering wheel. As one, all three of us ducked. That was our introduction. The journey became harder all the time; great shell craters in the road slowing us right down, as our lead vehicle attempted to find a way forward.

"After a long journey we arrived at an aid post, where a great many wounded were waiting to be evacuated. We could have loaded up in no time and been on our way back, but this was not the casualty collecting point that had sent for us, so we had to continue the search. We carried on forward, branching off to the right towards Passchendaele. The first of the houses loomed up then we saw a vehicle coming towards us. It was our lead ambulance. 'Turn round!' shouted the senior doctor, 'the houses have collapsed into the road and behind them the road is completely destroyed. It is nothing but craters.' There was nothing for it but to try to find another route to Passchendaele station where we were expected. It got even darker. We came across some soldiers. 'Who are you?' I called. 'Ration party from the Bavarian regiment.' It was my old Würzburg regiment. I asked them if my nephew was amongst them, but he was not. Did they know the way to Passchendaele station? Yes one Gefreiter did. He lit a cigarette and held it up as a lantern to guide us. The first vehicle followed him and we stuck close behind the dark monster that threatened to disappear at any moment from view.

"The road was extremely narrow. We suddenly skidded and slid into a ditch and got stuck and unable to drive straight out. The ambulance in front disappeared into the night. I called and shouted, but they did not hear me and continued on their way. The engine roared, one driver and I pushed with all our might, the other drove and cursed. Suddenly, with a lurch, we were free and back on the road. We set off hurriedly, hoping to catch up. Our route met another at right angles. Which way now? Right or left? I got out and shouted, but there was no reply. Something moved in the bushes nearby. 'Who's there?' It was a gunner who was guarding the horse and limbers of his battery. 'Which way did the ambulance go?' Of course, he had seen nothing. I went a little way to the right. No, that could not be the way, so we set off left. We had hardly covered any distance when we were called on to halt. It was the senior doctor. 'Stop there is a hole here.' Sure enough our vehicle was just in front of an enormous hole in the road. We could just make out the outline of the other vehicle.

"We cannot drive to the station. We shall leave the ambulances here and fetch the wounded,' the senior doctor decided. In about ten minutes we arrived at the casualty collection point. The worst cases were selected, the stretcherbearers took up their burdens and we set off to follow the railway embankment. 'Padre, take this Leutnant with you,' called a young doctor, with whom I had spent eight months at Field Hospital 190, 'he must be got to the rear without delay.' He had been shot in the back, but could still walk. I took him by the arm and led him away. He had been a young student who had been studying for the priesthood, but had become an officer during the war. We spoke animatedly, picking our way carefully past boggy areas and deep holes; not even the occasional shell splinter whizzing through the air to bury itself in the ground near us, put us off and we arrived safely at the place where the ambulances had parked.

"All too soon the ambulances were full to capacity and we had not even collected half of the wounded, so I gave up my seat for a wounded man and stayed behind. 'I shall be back in an hour or so,' said the senior doctor. You can come back with the next load. I accompanied the medical orderlies back along the railway embankment. This time it was so pitch black that Lichterloh had lit an enormous torch in Passchendaele from the flames of a burning house. The sparks flying up from it looked strangely beautiful in the dark night. I was soon standing amongst the wounded in the station yard. There they were laid in rows in the open air … Initially I checked all of them. Some were lying completely still; others were unusually animated in their pain and anxiety to be evacuated. All I could do was offer words of comfort: 'Be patient. You will be taken to the rear in an hour's time.' One was calling for water. Fortunately I was able to find some coffee. Another groaned that the ground was so hard to lie on. I was able to place my coat under his shoulders.

"Then I saw a Bavarian, deathly pale, with his arms folded across his chest. I whispered a short prayer of comfort to him … and over there was another man from near Würzburg. Wracked with pain, he called repeatedly on Our Lady, 'Mary, Help!' I sat along time with him until he became quiet and resigned to his fate. Then there was another man, cold as ice. I laid my hands on his forehead and cheeks. 'Your hands are beautifully warm,' he said. He, too, was a Bavarian. Later when I was making a further round, he greeted me cheerfully: 'Oh you're the one with the warm hands!' So naturally I spent a bit longer with him that time. Over there was a man of my regiment. He recognised me from my voice. 'I know your voice from the church service in the park at Remaucourt.' Yet another cried out for thirst. I went and fetched him some water and, as I lifted his head to give him a drink, I found that my hand was covered in thick fresh blood. I fetched the doctor who, by the light of a torch discovered a deep gash to the rear of his head, which had not been treated. The poor lad's arm had been broken in three places and, in the haste to treat that, the wound to the back of his head had been overlooked – either that or he had perhaps fallen back on a sharp stone. Later a medical orderly had to stay with him permanently. In his delirious state he kept trying to crawl away.

"Hour after hour slipped by, but the vehicles did not return. The regimental medical officer checked his watch anxiously. 'They cannot afford to leave it much longer, because the artillery fire will soon begin again.' Close behind us there was a battery of field artillery, immediately to our front the guns of a heavy battery were dug in, whilst the limit of the British defensive fire zone was located only a short distance from the station. Sure enough the firing soon started. Odd shells had already been landing nearby from time to time, but now things really started to happen. Ker-rump! Left, right, over and behind us shells were landing, then there was a noise like a thunderclap and I was blown straight between the doctor's legs. There was clatter of splintering beams and the crash of breaking glass. Stones were being sprayed everywhere and the air was full of powder smoke: the station buildings had taken a direct hit. I quickly made the rounds of the wounded. Nothing had happened, nobody had been wounded again. Not the tiniest splinter had hit the poor lads.

"However, the shells had unsettled them. 'Padre, where's the vehicle?' 'Padre, get me out of here.' 'I cannot stay here. Move me somewhere else.' There really was nowhere safer, but we moved them to by the wall of a wooden hut where the first aid equipment was stored. 'Don't leave me Padre,' said one young man. So I dropped down on the ground next to him and took his hand. There was a short roar and another thunderclap. It was the second direct hit. Quite involuntarily I ducked down towards the wounded man who lunged up and threw his arms round me. Finally he lay still, but he would not let go of my arm. As I crouched next to him he talked to me about his home, his parents, his relations with his God and we recalled church services we had both attended. We managed a really intimate discussion despite the fact that all hell had broken loose around us. The British barrage roared away ceaselessly answered by the duller, but lighter, tones of our guns. Everywhere there was the crashing and droning of shells, with bangs and flashes in all directions.

"Another three direct hits landed on or around our aid post. This continued for about another two hours, but I must admit that I did not spend the entire time with our dear comrades. After half an hour I was aching in every bone. I was already completely soaked, a light rain began to fall and the temperature dropped gradually towards zero. 'Comrade, you will have to let go of me. I am really stiff. I'll come back later.' He was happy at that. I made my way down into the deep cellar beneath the station from where my regiment was being commanded. I warmed up a little then obtained a jug of red wine and went back up. The poor lad, who had had his arm shot off, had need of a stimulant, as did that pale-faced one over there. In no time the jug was empty. In the meantime night was fading; day was dawning and the whole misery of the situation became clear. The poor young Pole, with the wounded foot, was lying across a path way and every now and then someone tripped over his foot. I moved him somewhere else.

"Fortunately the questions about the ambulances ceased. They had still not arrived. It was now daylight and the shooting had stopped. Now troops began to arrive from Zonnebeke, three kilometres from the station. There had been bitter fighting there in the village the previous night. Now gathering at the station were several companies of the regiments from Bamberg and Würzburg, together with companies from my two regiments. Lots of happy greetings were exchanged, but there was not much time for talking.

They had brought wounded with them and they were very thirsty. I brought a large can of water up and some of them were able to take a large swig from it. At long last the ambulances arrived. 'What took you so long?' Then I heard all about the terrible return journey. The dark night and damage to the road meant that it lasted five hours. Now it was matter of loading them up quickly and, in between, to carry out a sad task. Next to the station square we laid in a line on the grass the dear comrades who had succumbed during the night. Seven brave men had died of their wounds.

"Soon we were ready. The wounded were all arranged in the ambulances and the little convoy rattled off back to the main dressing station. Believe me I shall never forget the night of 26/27 October as long as I live. Nevertheless I am grateful that I experienced it."

As the end of the month drew near, there had still been no major set piece attack against the men of Infantry Regiment 465, but the loss of the line of blockhouses and pill boxes a few days previously meant that conditions were truly appalling for the forward troops. Sheltering in water filled, muddy shell holes were the men of the 1st Machine Gun Company.

Unteroffizier Behne 1st Machine Gun Company Infantry Regiment 465 [37] **1**

"From daybreak we lay in our holes, which were almost full of water. Anybody who tried to straighten up was immediately shot by a British sniper. One of our comrades who attempted to put on his coat was shot through the stomach and another who looked over the rim was shot in the arm. Lacking a Red Cross flag, the medical orderlies tied a newspaper to the handle of a spade and carried the wounded men to the rear. When at long last it went dark, we emerged to stand up out of our flooded positions, we were so wet and stiff that we had pain in every joint. Constantly lying on our backs in these conditions meant that I lost a large amount of skin. But the worst night was yet to come.

"The artillery fire was unusually heavy. Machine guns opened up and flares began to dance in the sky. The company called for defensive fire, but when the fire landed, it came down behind us. We fired yellow flares: *Increase the range*, but the next shells still came down close behind us. We shot off another yellow flare and the next salvo landed in amongst us. We had no more yellow flares, but we were determined to stick it out, so we stay where we are. To our front a sentry on listening watch shouted for help. Initially nobody wanted to go to his aid – but we had to. First one man then another [volunteered] and came forward with me. We carried him part way and the medical orderlies took him further back. Towards morning we were relieved."

After the heavy fighting of 26 October, the regiments of 238th Infantry Division were once more moved forward to attempt to continue the defence of Passchendaele. Still not recovered from their previous deployment, the tired men of Infantry Regiment 465 found themselves once more moving up to the firing line,

Leutnant Albert Schmidt 2nd Company Infantry Regiment 465 [38] **6**

"We made our way forward successfully through heavy barrage fire. This was because we avoided the roads and worked our way forward instead from shell hole to shell hole. Everywhere was in utter chaos. The British had wrested our fine pill boxes from the Bavarians who had relieved us and, of the entire battalion which we were due to relieve, we found only twenty men still on their feet and hanging on obstinately in a fold in the ground. Apart from that the entire sector was unoccupied; the British could simply have marched calmly through.

"As quickly as possible we linked up to our right and left. The line was once more continuous, but under constant raking fire from British machine guns in advanced positions."

Schütze Steinlandt 1st Machine Gun Company Infantry Regiment 465 [39] **6**

"We relieved the Bavarians, but in fact we could not find a single trace of them. Occasionally a few lads covered in filth from top to bottom hurried by us. We cursed them roundly. We did hear later that the Bavarians had fought until they were annihilated, but in the meantime all the swearing got us back on an even keel. Our former concrete bunkers were in the hands of the British, so we were forced to take cover in four man groups in the shell holes on the hill. Pleis, Gorges, who was as well known for his unshakable calmness when things got hot as for his unsoldierly demeanour when behind the lines, another comrade and I shared a crater. I recognised a few faces from our time at Lockstedt Camp and was amazed to see how they had changed in six months. They no longer looked like nineteen year olds, but like real old soldiers: fined down, with pinched faces and determined looks.

"Leutnant Schäfer came and checked our position in the dark. His visit pleased us; we felt that we should not be left to wallow alone in the filth. Gorges, who had such profound respect for Leutnant Schäfer that he would have died for him on the spot, spoke up [after he had gone] *Junge – der Schäfer, datt is doch noch een!* [Hey, what a man Schäfer is!]. That said we still looked on the monstrous Battle of Flanders, which devoured lives in an appalling manner, from a young perspective. It was war and it had to be fought. We were not soldiers to be having a good time. There was not a man in our crater who need hang his head in shame."

Leutnant Sonsalla Commander 8th Company Infantry Regiment 465 [40]

"Accompanied by my trusty men: Nottemeyer, Kaiser, Trenkner and Müller amongst others, I stumbled across ruined walls and went down into a half-destroyed cellar. The relief and hand over of the position proceeded swiftly and there were no casualties. The company we relieved was glad to get away. It was soon twelve o'clock and punctual to the minute the artillery opened up. I took a look around my cellar and what I saw was definitely not reassuring. The corner nearest to the enemy was blown in; the two metre gap having been temporarily stopped up with tiles, rubble, tree trunks and food tins. Although this provided the illusion of security and concealment, we all knew that one direct hit would be sufficient to bring down all the rubble and crush us. To find a hero's death in that way was certainly not a pleasing prospect. Nevertheless we made ourselves as comfortable as possible in our 'Heroes' Cellar' and tucked into the bread, canned food and schnaps that our cooks had issued to us and waited for whatever the future might bring.

"Suddenly a systematic barrage came down on Passchendaele village, the block of houses where we were located, the aid post bunker and the cross tracks. The bunker, located about 100 metres to one side of my cellar, was also in use as the command post of the *KTK*. The earth heaved and trembled after each explosion, then the bursts became too numerous to count. The fire continued to increase. Wooden beams and rubble were thrown into the air and came crashing back down on our cellar. Our nerves were strained to breaking point. Everyone kept a firm grip on his weapon and ammunition, ready for the moment when it would be necessary to race out of this hell hole. All of a sudden there was a tremendous impact, a dazzling column of flame shot up and twisted faces could be seen grimacing through the powder smoke and dust. This was followed by a great rumble, bangs and crashes.

"In seconds we had vacated the cellar and were stumbling and tripping over piles of rubbish and splintered beams. I lurked in a corner and waited for the next salvo. The remains of one wall which faced the enemy were still standing. I reached the doorway and was about to race towards the aid post, but decided to remain where I was until the next salvo arrived. Sure enough shells crashed down into the ruins of the right hand wall. I then made a dash for it, stumbling over dreadfully mutilated corpses. I felt the pressure wave as the next shells burst overhead and I dived into the blockhouse. It was immediately obvious that I was an unwelcome guest in the post which was already crammed with men. It was almost impossible to get into a comfortable position. Groans and moans filled the tightly packed space. The doctors certainly had a great deal of work to do."

One of the features of the fighting in Flanders was that from mid-morning each day the artillery fire died away for a couple of hours, whilst the stretcher bearers and medical orderlies from both sides were at work, together with their search dogs, recovering the wounded from the battlefield. This brief respite was used by all the combatants to emerge from their shelters, stretch and get some fresh air, before hostilities recommenced. Commanders and runners were able to move, weapons could be cleaned and personal administration attended to.

Leutnant Schäfer Infantry Regiment 465 [41]

"Looking out from a small concrete bunker, I was able to survey the battlefield and observe one of the strangest scenes of the Battle of Flanders: the undeclared truce for the collection of the wounded and the dead. All the guns fell silent and a deep peace descended on the battlefield, which was ploughed up as no earthly plough could ever achieve, turning every-thing into a ghastly chaos. From both sides medical teams and their dogs criss-crossed the area slowly and systematically. Away in the distance the red crosses of both friend and foe could be seen completely intermingled. I watched the sad work through a telescope. For once this was not a scene of butchery or the destruction of our fellow men. Here purely humanitarian impulses held sway."

Although the main focus of the fighting by this stage was on the final approaches to Passchendaele, the French army continued to conduct several sharp actions ten kilometres to the northwest where the Battle for Houthulst Wood was bitterly contested. The Saxon 40th Infantry Division suffered serious casualties during fighting in that area on 26 October and two days later they began to be relieved by the 8th Bavarian Reserve Division.

Reserve Leutnant Käsbauer
2nd Battalion Bavarian Reserve Infantry Regiment 23 [42] **8**

"During the morning of 27 October 2nd Battalion Bavarian Reserve Infantry Regiment 23, which was located in Zarren, was ordered to advance to the heights near Klerken, there to await further orders. Despite the fact that we were hours of marching time behind the front line, the shells of the British super-heavy howitzers still found their way into our rear areas. This meant that as the companies picked their way forward through the swampy terrain towards the hills near Klerken, they were constantly threatened by 280 mm shells. Not until towards evening did the fire slacken off, then guides arrived from the Saxons up front, to lead us forward for the relief. This was the beginning of a ghastly journey.

Moving along the crammed roads were ammunition columns, artillery and infantry reliefs. There was tendency for movement to stall at the heavily shelled crossroads which was nerve wracking.

"Finally we were past the artillery zone and we began making our way through the shattered landscape. We crossed swamps and streams, moved through ploughed up cemeteries and wrecked bivouac sites until after wandering for hours in the darkness, we reached the forward rendezvous. Strewn about between the smashed trees were crates about one metre high which had held shells. We crawled inside them in an effort to keep dry. It was terribly cold, but we stayed there all day without rest, because enemy aircraft kept circling overhead, ready to direct artillery fire down. Our crates were camouflaged with branches and leaves and nobody dared leave them in case the movement was spotted. The battalion which later relieved us failed to do this and paid for it with casualties of twenty one killed and forty six wounded.

"An order reached me during the evening of 28 October to go with Oberleutnant Gipser and reconnoitre the situation in the 1st Battalion Bavarian Reserve Infantry Regiment 23 area. We had barely set off when we were caught up in frenzied defensive fire, which some nervous person had called down. We pushed on without being hit over craters, barbed wire, fallen trees and bogs until we were able to gain the shelter of a pillbox in the front line. Hardly had we arrived than extremely heavy enemy fire started to come down. Everyone who was anywhere near the blockhouse piled in, until there were about fifty apprehensive men crammed into a space four metres by four metres. At regular intervals heavy shells crashed down near the blockhouse, extinguishing the lights. Men who could not find a place in the blockhouse clustered against the wall furthest away from the enemy for protection. Even the entrance was full. Then suddenly a heavy shell exploded right by it. All the candles went out and there was loud shrieking and shouting. The press grew worse as wounded men, dripping blood, forced their way in. We had to bandage them up in a standing position; there was no room to sit.

"Unterarzt Rebl and Leutnant Kupfer did their utmost to maintain calm, whilst Oberleutnant Gipser and I, our task complete, left the place which made a little more space and took our chances to return through the storm of fire to our own men. In the meantime my batman Georg Pretzl had been killed. He had been waiting for me outside the blockhouse and had fallen victim to a shell. We had to postpone his burial until the relief was complete, because we were driven back through the moonlit night by fierce high explosive shell fire mixed with gas. Wearing our gas masks hacking and coughing, we made our way with difficulty through the almost unbelievable obstacles back to our battalion commander, who had long since abandoned any hope of seeing us alive again.

"We returned to the bivouac to spend yet another night in the crates and although shells were bursting all around, none of us was touched. At 4.00 am we were wakened by our sentries, warning of more gas and a hurricane of fire. Wearing our gas masks, we miserably awaited the dawn. The following night was somewhat calmer. We picked our way forward once more through the mud and the bogs and the relief was completed. The block-house was used only by our reserves; everyone else had to spend the three days forward in shell holes and trenches filled with water. For three days the men had to stand, without any possibility of sitting, in this damp, stinking space, whilst Leutnant Fiedler and I took it in half hour turns to sit on a chair and so the endless nights without sleep passed. On 29 October, we who had been in reserve (5th and 6th Companies), moved forward into the front line itself, where, split into groups of six to eight men, we occupied water-filled shell holes. In the event we were not involved in a battle, but having to sit it out, enduring these awful conditions, had a far worse effect on morale and spirit than even the most difficult fighting."

During the night 28/29 October the final reliefs and alterations in deployment and role prior to the major battle on 30 October took place. Infantry Regiment 164, which as part of 111th Infantry Division had been holding the spur just to the north of the Goudberg, with its battalions changing over every three days, was relieved by Bavarian Reserve Infantry Regiment 7 of the 5th Bavarian Reserve Division. After the strain of the past few days, it came not a moment too soon.

Gefreiter Pühse 1st Machine Gun Company Infantry Regiment 164 [43]

"Our withdrawal was made more difficult by heavy concentrations of fire. Making good use of the crater field, but with immense difficulty, we finally reached the first concrete blockhouse to our rear. There we met our fate. A heavy shell exploded right next to us, burying us in a great mountain of clods of earth. Someone was groaning to my right. It was our gun commander Unteroffizier Grundmann. When I asked him if he had been hit, he replied that he had not, but then he felt a stabbing pain in his leg which was streaming with blood. A shell splinter had torn off his lower leg. We bandaged him up as well as we could and applied a tourniquet. We then set off with our wounded comrade. Carrying him through the craters was extraordinarily difficult and we frequently had to take cover from the fire, which never eased up. We bid our great comrade farewell at the dressing station in Westrozebeke – for ever. A little while later, he succumbed to the wound caused by the shell." [44]

Musketier Kording 1st Company Infantry Regiment 164 [45]

"We had not slept for four days and four nights. Carrying the machine gun on my back I tottered across country, swaying like a straw stalk. Every time there was a short pause, I fell asleep standing up. Having arrived at the billet I had to get several men to help me pull my boots off. My feet felt as though they had been tortured and my socks were one sticky mass of mud. I swigged down a mess tin full of coffee and slept a full twenty four hours."

In a letter home to his family a few days later, by which time it had been established that regimental losses during their tours of Flanders had cost them fifty seven officers and 1,735 men, Hauptmann Heines, who was on the regimental staff of Infantry Regiment 164, wrote.

"26 October was a day of honour for the regiment. Not one scrap of ground was lost. I take my hat off to the simple musketier, who held out in the mud and rain (sometimes sunk in up to his waist) and endured, despite the heaviest artillery fire imaginable. He is a true hero. There can be no greater heroism than this."[46]

In accordance with the new policy of divisions swapping roles, the formations of 39th Infantry Division moved up to take over from 11th Bavarian Division, which had to be withdrawn temporarily from the battle for rest and reconstitution. Infantry Regiment 132 took over from Bavarian Infantry Regiment 22, Infantry Regiment 172 and Infantry Regiment 126 from Bavarian Infantry Regiment 3 and Bavarian Reserve Infantry Regiment 13 respectively. Once complete, it assumed the *Eingreif* role behind 238th Infantry Division.

Leutnant Sonsalla 8th Company Infantry Regiment 465 [47] **6**

"Prepare! Advance! Leutnant Meyer's 6th Company took the lead, followed by my 8th Company, the 7th Company of Leutnant Esders and finally the 5th Company under Leutnant Schwirr. Man followed man in an endless procession. The silence of the evening was broken by the Tak! Tak! of an undamaged machine gun. On our left sides, bayonets and spades were strapped together. Our gas masks hung on a short strap just beneath our chins. Our packs hung down to our stomachs under the weight of ammunition bandoliers and hand grenades, whilst our bread pouches and water bottles were fixed on our right hand sides. We leaned forward slightly under the load and our steps were heavy. Our faces were serious and determined, drawn and pinched by neglect and privation. Nobody spoke; all were occupied by their thoughts, back home with parents, wives and children. Everyone knew that he was heading forward into the morass and that a grim reality faced him.

"For the first few hundred metres all went well. Our boots only sank in the mud up to our ankles and the craters were not so close that we could not skirt them. But soon it was impossible to advance in any sort of ordered ranks. Craters overlapped craters. We sank into the mud and crept forward stumbling and falling. Complaints and curses could be heard in all directions. Here a boot was lost, there a machine gunner fell head over heels. We looked like walking lumps of clay, moving in a ghostly manner. An appalling stink of corpses hung in the damp air. I was completely nauseated by it, but by midnight we had managed it.

"We occupied our holes and muddy shell craters situated on a fold in the ground.[48] Not a hundred metres to our front were the British positions. Although we were dog tired, we could not think about rest. First we had to put out listening posts then the muddy craters had to be made inhabitable. We began by baling out the water, then shovelled all the remaining filth out to our front where it served as parapet and weapons stand. The experienced hands then continued to dig in further. I lay there together with my batman Nottmeyer and my runners in a roomy hole about three to four metres square. The base of it was naturally thick with mud and filth. The usual firework display to our front went on until dawn. Sometimes there was a sharp report that broke the silence and the ensuing flare lit up the horizon. We threw ourselves down in the filth and slept until dawn."

There was a great deal of aerial activity during the afternoon of 29 October and, as night fell, a considerable increase in the bombardment. This was followed by a disturbed night with numerous concentrations of fire all along the Passchendaele front. By 6.00 am on 30 October, a lull had fallen over the battlefield. It was the calm before the storm. At 6.45 am a barrage of stunning intensity crashed down on the positions of the 238th Infantry Division, reaching right back into the depth of the rear areas. All normal sounds were drowned out by the whirring and howling of shells fired from hundreds of guns and incessant explosions as they crashed to the ground. With the ground heaving and trembling beneath them, the men of Infantry Regiments 463, 464 and 465 called for destructive fire from their own artillery. Soon the racket of the defensive fire was added to the deafening roar of the Allied fire. Vulnerable in their open craters and shell holes, the defenders attempted to take cover in the liquid mud, but such was the intensity of the fire that many fell victim to the shells and fell back dead or seriously wounded to sink beneath the mud which closed over them and formed their graves.

By 7.45 am, masses of attackers from the Canadian Corps were seen forming up to the front of Infantry Regiment 464 and then advancing in a large number of small groups and columns towards their positions. The lifting of the barrage came as a great relief and the survivors prepared to defend their line vigorously. However the barrage had ripped holes in the defence. Where nobody was alive to resist the advance the attackers exploited these gaps and headed for Passchendaele, where the attack lapped around the perimeter of the bitterly disputed wreckage of the village. To the north, in the area of Infantry Regiment 465, the barrage continued until 8.30 am, then it began to creep to the rear in a series of lifts, which were followed closely by the attacking Canadian troops. The forward sentries pulled back into the front line, where the survivors scrambled to prepare their machine guns for action. Despite the fact that many guns and their crews had been destroyed by the final drum fire, sufficient numbers of weapons remained to bring down lacerating fire against the attackers – much of it at very short range. On the right flank, 7th Company under Leutnant Esders was very proud of the fact that the attackers failed to reach his position and he made much play of it in his after-action report. 'In the end only one machine gun was still firing, but it performed extremely well and made a great contribution to our success.'[49]

Throughout the day hard fighting went on everywhere in the Infantry Regiment 465 area, with many acts of courage displayed by both sides. 'The crew of a machine gun located very close to me behaved extremely bravely', wrote Leutnant Schwirr, commander of 6th Company, later. 'To begin with Musketier Freise acted as gunner until he was shot through the head. Musketier Dempewolf quickly replaced him and he was followed by Musketier Auge until he too was wounded. Musketier Wulfes then continued to fire the gun until it was buried [by a bursting shell].' It was a similar story in 8th Company, where a series of gunners managed to maintain a high rate of destructive fire.

To the north of Infantry Regiment 465, Bavarian Reserve Infantry Regiment 13 of the Bavarian 11th Infantry Division had been hit hard and had yielded ground to the attackers. The right flank of Infantry Regiment 465 would have been ripe for rolling up, had it not been for the presence there of an extensive pond of filthy water surrounded by an impassable swamp. As it was, both 7th and 5th Companies were able to pour flanking fire into the ranks of the attackers and check them, but 3 Platoon of 7th Company was almost wiped out.

Reserve Leutnant Harms 7th Company Infantry Regiment 465 [50] **6**

"Our 3rd Platoon was located behind the others in a shelter made of tree trunks. No fewer than thirty three of us were crammed into one small damp space, but we were glad enough to have some protection. Towards 7.00 am a hellish drum fire broke out, but after the initial shock which sent our pulses racing we felt quite secure in our bunker. Soon somebody was telling a funny story and this was followed by another which was even better. I can still see our dear Feldwebel Ipkendanz as he told a humorous story and then began laughing so uproariously that he carried everyone along with him. Nevertheless everyone had the feeling that it was all gallows humour.

"Suddenly there was a dull thud by the entrance to the shelter. An incendiary round had set fire to the wood. We set to and extinguished the flames with water intended for the machine gun. Hardly had we finished when there was an enormous crash as a shell exploded on the roof sending a shower of splinters in amongst us. My great friend Gefreiter Knost, with whom I had stood shoulder to shoulder and shared everything, gave a shout. A splinter had torn open his thigh. I quickly applied an emergency dressing to him. A young recruit with a serious stomach wound lay on the ground screaming and moaning for a whole quarter of an hour, then fell silent for ever. We sat there profoundly silent; we knew what was coming to us.

"Once again a tremor ran through our bodies. There was a shaking and a crash. Splinters rained down into the shelter once more and six or eight men were hit, including the platoon commander. Whilst he calmly allowed himself to be bandaged up, a further shell showered us with steel fragments and the medical orderly who was kneeling in front of him had half his head sliced off. Miraculously I and another four men were uninjured. Outside the barrage raged on. A runner rushed in: *3 Platoon deploy immediately!* Quickly we fastened on our equipment. Oh what an imploring look my dear comrade Knost gave me when he realised I was leaving him, but my duty was clear *I cannot give you my hand ... my great comrade.*[51] A short time later another shot claimed him. [52]

"Just at the moment we were leaving this place of death another round killed our comrade Grimme. Now for the rest of us it was a matter of launching ourselves into the hell outside. What a sight it was! That which had been a green field that morning was now completely ploughed up. Due to the smoke of the exploding shells, visibility was down to less than twenty metres. An immense weight of fire was still coming down. It was quite impossible to link up with 1 Platoon, so we took cover in a shell hole. Suddenly a shell exploded on its rim, burying us with earth. It took me a few seconds to regain my senses then we dug ourselves out – the other two were wounded. I felt a dreadful pressure on my chest and stomach. Death had once more missed by a hair's breadth. Now all we could do was to make our way to the aid post. Crawling from crater to crater in amongst the exploding shells we finally reached the post, which was a bare three hundred metres away."

The battle continued to rage throughout the day. Desperate counter-strokes were mounted and these enjoyed some success. The regiments of 39th Infantry Division were brought to immediate readiness at 9.45 am, when a report reached them that the Canadians had penetrated as far forward as the church in Passchendaele. The first of their attacks was launched about two hours later. About 2.30 pm, 21 Infantry Brigade summarised the known situation:

> "There are massive artillery concentrations throughout the area. Strong British attacks have taken place against the Passchendaele heights. In the northern sector the enemy is pressing against our right flank and advancing to the south of the *Turmhof*. Towards midday the main line of resistance in the centre was pushed back 200 – 300 metres; whilst in the southern sector the line had reached the western edge of Passchendaele. Passchendaele and the surrounding area are still under moderate fire. We have no definite junction point with the neighbouring Bavarian brigade (right formation Bavarian Infantry Regiment 5). Counter-attacks by 1st and 3rd Battalions Infantry Regiment 172 are continuing." [53]

Gradually each battalion joined in and, by 5.00 pm, 5th and 7th Companies Infantry Regiment 172 had swept through Passchendaele village where, despite curtains of machine gun fire and extremely heavy shelling, they had linked up with the remnants of Infantry Regiment 465, who were desperately hanging on to their positions just to the northwest of the village.[54] The gap between Infantry Regiments 464 and 465 was finally plugged by Storm Battalion 4 and the risk of encirclement was removed thanks to decisive work by a battalion from Infantry Regiment 463 and elements of Infantry Regiment 464 who, attacking from just east of Passchendaele, forced other Canadians to give up their gains. The cost had, however, been immense – on both sides. The six Canadian battalions which had attacked had lost over fifty per cent of their strength[55] and for the time being 238th Infantry Division was finished as a fighting force; it had to be relieved that same night.[56]

"Fortunately reinforcements were readily to hand. 39th Infantry Division had already been told off for the duty, Infantry Regiment 172 was able to take over from Infantry Regiment 465 and Infantry Regiment 132 was despatched forward to relieve the shattered remnant of Infantry Regiment 464.

Leutnant Seldte Adjutant 1st Battalion Infantry Regiment 132 [57] 1

> "We were called forward during the evening and, in accordance with the order, were to relieve the front line positions of Infantry Regiment 464. We advanced to the final telephone point and from there, guided by two men from Infantry Regiment 464, the battalion made its way forward in single file. An unnatural stillness had descended on the battlefield from 7.00 pm onwards. How far forward the battle lines were, nobody really knew. It was at any rate clear that the front line had been pushed back some-

what, because the forward regiment had even called forward men of the quartermaster's department to fill up the gaps. The battalion made its way onto a spur northeast of Passchendaele and had to wait there until the relief could be arranged with the *KTK*.

"It had been arranged with the advance party of officers and guides that four companies would occupy the front line. There could be no question of there being an outpost position because, as the *KTK* explained to us, there was so little strength forward that we could count ourselves fortunate if we managed to hold on firmly to Passchendaele. The relief operation was extremely problematic. It was a clear moonlit night, but the companies had to deal with the colossal difficulty of moving through the ploughed up terrain. The guides' knowledge left much to be desired and they were completely disorientated. 3rd Company, under Reserve Leutnant Schulze, under the false impression that the line was a few hundred metres further forward than was the case in reality, blundered unluckily straight into a hail of British [*sic*] machine gun fire and the entire company was either captured or mown down at short range by the fire. Although he was seriously wounded, the commander managed to extract himself from the crater into which he had fallen. The other companies, having taken casualties, occupied a line corresponding more or less to the western edge of the village of Passchendaele.

"So began four incredibly strenuous days for the battalion. Battalion HQ was located in an extremely small cellar by a hedge which only had very thin overhead cover. This it shared, separated only by a thin wall, with the headquarters of 3rd Battalion Infantry Regiment 132, which under its commander, Major Schieß, was acting in the support role. There was an immense amount of work to do, not to mention the most important requirement, which was to guarantee the defence and the maintenance of links [left and right]. The village of Passchendaele was just a heap of ruins dotted with innumerable craters."

The success of British offensive tactics was continuing to be source of serious concern to the higher command. On 30 October 1917, General der Infanterie Hermann von Kuhl, chief of staff of Army Group Crown Prince Rupprecht, signed a paper entitled 'British Offensive Procedures'. This was intended primarily for Army and Group Headquarters which had not been involved in the fighting in Flanders to update them but was also apparently distributed down to divisional level locally. It arrived too late to be off much assistance for the remainder of the battle. Nevertheless, because it is based on observation of the battle, prisoner interrogation and captured documents, it usefully summarises the German state of knowledge as the battle for Passchendaele drew to an end.

British Offensive Procedures:
Army Group Crown Prince Rupprecht Ic No. 31500 dated 30 October 1917 [58]

"Attached is an account of offensive procedures, which the British have been employing in Flanders since 20 September 1917. It is based on reported observation by the troops, prisoner interrogation and captured orders …

"Artillery [Prior to the attack, the enemy will bring to bear] against the entire front of the intended attack and the sectors which border it, a barrage fired by guns of all calibres. This will increase day after day and the concentrations will make use of massive quantities of ammunition. Most of the shells will be high explosive, but smoke and gas will be mixed in.

"Destructive fire is brought down against concrete blockhouses, command- and observation posts; in other words against all identifiable targets. Systematic counter-battery fire seems to be restricted to certain sectors; though it remains to be seen if this is simply because these particular batteries are the most visible ones.

"Harassing fire, which often arrives suddenly in violent concentrations, is brought down throughout the zones occupied by the infantry and the artillery. Fire is also directed far into the rear areas by long-range guns directed against the zone of approach and billeting areas.

"Some days before the initial attack, then again on most days between major attacks, the fire of several batteries is concentrated into drumfire. These fire missions are directed against the full depth of the infantry zone of a sector two to three kilometres wide and last from forty five minutes to an hour. The entire width of the attack frontage is subjected to such bursts of drumfire at irregular intervals; often two to three times per day. During these times, the remainder of the area is still engaged with heavy harassing fire. As a result of these tactics there are areas, especially in front of our guns, where the fire is fairly light. Generally speaking the British only seem to spare individual areas in the depth of the positions which they consider to be impassable. Despite this they have never succeeded in stopping our ammunition re-supply; on the contrary sometimes this has even been possible during the day …

"Artillery Operations during Attacks Either before the infantry assault, or simultaneously, the entire front to be attacked is suddenly and violently deluged with the heaviest possible high explosive drumfire. Frequently smoke shells are mixed in. At the same time extremely heavy harassing fire of all calibres is brought down on our artillery positions and all approach routes. According to documents which have been recovered, the activities of the artillery break down as follows:

"Five barrages are produced. These are designated A to E and are engaged by the following weapons:

A and B:	These are each engaged by half the available field guns
C:	Machine guns
D:	150 mm howitzers; one every seventy metres
E:	200 and 230 mm howitzers; one every 110 metres. (127 mm guns are also employed).

"Initially the fire of all five types is concentrated on the German front line. Later the different barrages diverge. A continues to fall on the German line. B, D and E come down at 180 metre spacing, so that the total depth of artillery fire covers 500 – 600 metres. C is directed centrally between B and D. At a pre-determined time this fire begins to move towards the enemy, covering a particular distance in a designated time. It continues to move until the A barrage reaches a final protective line just in front of the initial objective. Here smoke is included in the A barrage to show the infantry, which is following closely behind, that the rolling barrage will pause and form a curtain behind which the infantry can complete its final preparations. The length of this pause is also pre-determined. As soon as the time is up, the barrage rolls on, to be repeated in the same way in front of each objective. The move of the barrage [in this manner] has been repeatedly observed by us; that is to say, whenever the dust, smoke, fumes and other battlefield obscuration has permitted observation.

"Once the rolling barrage has reached the protective line beyond the final objective, it continues to fall defensively along this line for four to six hours after Zero Hour. At that point B is withdrawn to A and D and E are lifted towards the enemy. Throughout the entire battle some guns are set aside to engage machine gun nests and other opportunity targets. The 127 mm guns are used against targets throughout the area to the front of the rolling barrage. Ammunition is allocated in advance to all calibres of gun, but batteries are not committed to staying within the upper limit.

"Infantry: In the overwhelming majority of instances the infantry attack is prepared with the utmost care. There are, however, cases when divisions are thrown into the attack without any preparation at all. In preparation the infantry moves as close to the German front line as possible, in order that the first wave can avoid German defensive artillery fire. It advances immediately behind its own artillery fire. Several objectives in depth have to be taken. One wave is allocated a particular objective in advance. The waves in rear leapfrog the forward waves in turn. The objectives are generally set close together; so that the amount of ground gained each time is slight. Having taken its objective, each wave organises itself immediately for hasty defence. No other general points which represent a development of previously known British tactics can be derived. That which follows concerns methods used in particular cases and, although there are sometimes similarities, these cannot be taken as generally applicable.

"Whenever necessary, the troops prepare their attacks on specially designed exercise areas. The role of each man in an attack is laid down exactly. In one place it was noticed that two men took up positions in front of a blockhouse, whilst the remainder continued calmly on their way. The two men prevented the garrison from emerging until the arrival of a flamethrower, which smoked out the position. On one captured sketch the location of a machine gun was laid down exactly in advance. It was to be deployed between the different objectives in order to strengthen the deployment in depth.

"On the main front of the attack, a division is allocated a sector slightly over one kilometre in width, but this does tend to vary according to the task and the terrain. Within these boundaries one or two brigades are in the front line and they in turn deploy one to three battalions forward. Generally speaking, however, only two battalions are used forward but, if the sector is wide, several may be employed. This means that battalion frontages may be as wide as 500 metres, but in most cases these do not exceed 250 – 300 metres. Only one example of deployment in depth of a battalion on the main attack front is known. In this case three battalions were distributed across a 700 metres brigade frontage. One battalion organised itself so that it had three companies up. Two platoons from each company were pushed forward. They were followed at eighty paces distance by two platoons in section columns, which were in turn followed at a further eighty paces interval by a platoon of the fourth company in single file.

"It appears as though, within the brigade, one or two battalions form a wave, but this depends on the width of the attack frontage and the number of objectives. In isolated instances, a single battalion has formed two waves. In the case of the deeply echeloned battalion, the various parts were not intended to be considered waves with their own objectives; rather that the two waves were partially split [during the approach]. Advances in up to eight waves have been observed, but it has so far not proved possible to distinguish such a large number of objectives. This suggests once more division into waves for convenience during movement. Recently movement in column has been observed behind the forward waves.

"The objective is built up from several lines, one behind the other, which are colour coded on the abundance of sketches which are issued in advance … If several intermediate objectives are to be taken, the distance between the start line and the final objective is usually 1,000 – 1,500 metres and

2,000 metres at the most … According to intelligence, the attacking force is moved about midnight to within two to three kilometres of the front; frequently those allocated to the attack are not moved forward until the night before. It appears that some divisions are moved up only for the day of the attack and are immediately withdrawn again afterwards. Movement is aided by generous use of white marker tape and small flags. These mark the route and direct the advancing troops around impassable marshy areas …

"The rolling barrage protects the infantryman so effectively that he only needs to follow it with his rifle slung. According to various accounts, the waves advance, often on a broad front or in column, in section groups from shell hole to shell hole. Signal panels are deployed to indicate the progress of the attack to infantry cooperation aircraft. Once the final protective line has been reached and the artillery has fired smoke to indicate the fact to the infantry, it is often marked with tape and the infantry digs in. A second group then passes through and also digs in at the agreed distance. Then by means of light signals, often in the designated colour of the relevant objective, messages concerning progress are passed to the rear …

"The British assault depends to an extreme degree on the exploitation of the power of the artillery. Through use of absolutely rigid procedures, carefully prepared to the last detail, it is able to make limited geographical gains with the greatest possible degree of security. When it follows the rolling barrage, the British infantry believes that it does not have to capture the enemy positions; simply to occupy them."

As October came to an end, the successful defeat of thrusts at Geluveld and north of Passchendaele meant that on the battlefield the situation on the flanks had been stabilised, at least temporarily. On the other hand, the Canadians were progressing slowly, steadily, but inexorably towards Passchendaele and the German High Command seemed powerless to prevent it. Fourth Army and Army Group Crown Prince Rupprecht floated plans for major counter-attacks to reclaim the lost ground north of Broodseinde, but the tempo of Allied operations prevented forces from being concentrated for such a purpose, the divisions which were available in the area were being ground down by the fighting and no more could be made available. Maintaining the same pessimistic note, typical of his mood throughout the month, on 25 October, Crown Prince Rupprecht had recorded in his diary,

"My sole consolation is the fact that only one month remains for operations. If the weather is favourable, the final blows will have the worst consequences of all. The brilliant mood of the British troops will confront the rapidly sinking morale of the German troops."[59]

It is doubtful if any soldier enduring the unutterable misery, hardship and danger of the heartbreakingly slow slog up the Passchendaele Ridge would have shared this view; indeed Sir Philip Gibbs, the well-known war correspondent, summed up the state of Allied morale during the latter stages of this campaign later by writing, 'For the first time the British Army lost its spirit of optimism and there was sense of deadly depression among many officers and men ...'[60] Nevertheless, although the performance of the soldiers defending Passchendaele, those who actually managed to survive the ferocious bombardments, surpassed anything which their commanders could reasonably have expected – witness the enormous casualties inflicted on the Canadian assault troops – the fact remains that nothing wrecks the morale of an army faster than the realisation that, collectively, it is being required to face up to overwhelming force to which it can make no effective reply. That October the German army had no workable answer to 'bite and hold'. The commanders in the field knew it, even if Ludendorff would not accept it. As for the soldiers on the ground – their horizon did not extend beyond exhaustion, maiming or death and there was still no end in sight to the fighting.

Notes
1. Gottberg: History Infantry Regiment 465 pp 118-119
2. *ibid.* p 118
3. *ibid.* p 118
4. Mülmann: History Lehr-Infantry Regiment p 428
5. The bad weather must have affected his ability at mental arithmetic. It must be assumed, however, that there had in fact been a reduction in the amount sent forward.
6. Pafferath: History Infantry Regiment 68 p 487
7. Hansch: History Grenadier Regiment 9 p 416
8. Grenadier Bruno Kelm is buried in the German cemetery at Menen Block C Grave 576
9. Kriegsarchiv München HGr Rupprecht Bd 93
10. The original German word used here was *Schützenbrei*, meaning literally and rather contemptuously, something like 'infantry stew' or 'riflemen slurry'.
11. This order was amended by means of a supplementary order issued by Generalmajor von Loßberg, chief of staff of Fourth Army, on 30 October to include also the two southern divisions of Group Diksmuide.
12. This directive to Group Diksmuide was amended on 30 October, as mentioned at footnote 8.
13. The German phrase used is *das abbröckeln nach Rückwärts*, meaning literally 'the crumbling away to the rear'
14. Theysohn: History Bavarian Field Artillery Regiment 20 pp 93-95
15. Westerkamp: *Unser Regiment* pp 186-187
16. Kanonier Richard Tiburski is buried in the German cemetery at Menen Block M Grave 1401.
17. Kees: History Field Artillery Regiment 115 pp 38-41
18. 'Korporal' is an old German rank, equivalent to 'Unteroffizier.'

19. Goldammer: History Infantry Regiment 179 pp 201-202
20. *ibid.* p 204
21. Niemann: History Infantry Regiment 133 p 73
22. Kriegsarchiv München Pi Btl 17 Bd 9
23. Niemann: *op. cit.* p 72
24. Westerkamp: *op. cit.* pp 195 – 196
25. Unteroffizier Friedrich Böttcher was killed in action 12 Oct 1917. He is buried in the German cemetery in Menen Block M Grave 1678.
26. Kanonier Lampe was killed in action on 25 Oct 1917. He is buried in the German cemetery in Menen Block C Grave 1450.
27. History Infantry Regiment 164 pp 411-412
28. *ibid.* pp 412-413
29. *ibid.* p 413
30. *ibid.* pp 415-416
31. This was quite unusual. Normally the outpost zone was much more lightly held than this by this stage of the battle.
32. This was one of the first serious tests of the new tactics laid down by Ludendorff's directive of 9 October and it, too, proved to be, if not a total failure, certainly no panacea.
33. Stengel: History Bavarian Infantry Regiment 3 p 169
34. Dellmensingen: *Das Bayernbuch vom Weltkriege* pp 445-446
35. Kriegsarchiv München: Nachlaß Paul von Kneussl (Tagebuch Nr. 15)
36. Plagenz: History Infantry Regiment 452 pp 39 – 40
37. Gottberg: *op.cit.* p 132
38. *ibid.* p 128
39. *ibid.* pp 128-129
40. *ibid.* pp 129-130
41. *ibid.* pp 130-131
42. Roth: History Bavarian Reserve Infantry Regiment 23 pp 151-152
43. History Infantry Regiment 164 pp 417-418
44. Unteroffizier Heinrich Grundmann is buried in the German cemetery at Vladslo Block 5 Grave 876.
45. *ibid.* p 418
46. *ibid.* p 420
47. Gottberg: *op. cit.* pp 132-133
48. This was almost certainly in the area of Meetschele.
49. Gottberg: *op. cit.* p 137
50. *ibid.* pp 139-140 N.B. Harms was still an NCO at the time.
51. Here Harms is quoting the final line of *Ich hatt' einen Kamaraden* by Ludwig Uhland, which is the traditional German soldier's farewell to a fallen comrade.
52. Gefreiter Hermann Knost succumbed to his wounds and is buried in the *Kameradengrab* of the German cemetery at Langemark.
53. Steuer History Infantry Regiment 132 p 325
54. Wegener: History Infantry Regiment 172 pp 206-207
55. BOH 1917 Volume II p 354

56. The rifle companies were almost wiped out by this battle. For example, after withdrawal only Leutnant Sonsalla and nine men of 8th Company Infantry Regiment 465 were still on their feet.
57. Steuer: History Infantry Regiment 132 p 328
58. Kriegsarchiv München Gen Kdo III AK Bd. 26
59. Kronprinz Rupprecht: *Mein Kriegstagebuch II. Band* p 277
60. Gibbs: Realities of War, London 1920 p 396, quoted in Terraine *The Great War 1914-18* p 187

CHAPTER SEVEN

November and December 1917

The average strength of a German infantry battalion on the Western Front in November was 640 men.[1] However, this reduction in numbers was more than compensated for by a considerable increase in firepower. In the modern jargon, the German army had ceased simply equipping the man; rather it was now manning the equipment. On 1 November, the men of Infantry Regiment 49 of 4th Infantry Division found themselves on the way north to Flanders to relieve the 5th Bavarian Reserve Division north of Passchendaele. Arriving in a concentration area behind the lines on 2 November, they were immediately issued with an additional twenty four light Maxim 08/15 machine guns, to be distributed at the rate of two per rifle company. Organised and deployed in accordance with the latest tactical thinking, each infantry regiment now disposed of an awesome weight of fire power.

In the case of Infantry Regiment 49, four companies manned the main line of resistance to the north of Passchendaele and each pushed forward one or two sections and a machine gun forward into the outpost zone, which was up to 600 metres deep. The companies of the forward 3rd Battalion (9th, 10th, 11th and 12th) distributed their remaining light machine guns, so as to complement the seven Maxim 08 weapons of their machine gun company, which had been deployed right forward. Behind them, in and around the lines holding the support battalion, some of them in overwatch positions, were deployed a further forty one heavy Maxim 08 machine guns. These comprised the balance of five from the machine gun company of the forward battalion, the twenty four weapons of the machine gun companies of the supporting and reserve battalions and an additional twelve belonging to Machine Gun Sharp Shooter Detachment 70.[2] This, in combination with the numerous Maxim 08/15 guns of the other rifle companies, gave real substance to the concept of a mutually supporting defence in depth and goes a long way to explaining why such a seemingly thin defence could still remain effective, even after being subjected to an appalling weight of artillery fire and when being attacked by overwhelming numbers.

On this late autumn battlefield, where the state of the ground made a mockery of fire and manoeuvre, where it was frequently almost impossible for attackers to make their way through the deep, clinging, clay and mud at anything above a snail's pace, they could be in real trouble if they lost the rolling barrage. One or two machine guns, which had survived the bombardment and were in the hands of skilled crews in good firing positions, could (and frequently did) bring entire battalions to a bloody standstill. Nevertheless, the fearsome reputation of the

Passchendaele battlefield was beginning by now to have an effect on the motivation of the German army. The commander of Fourth Army had already drawn attention to the problem of preventing soldiers drifting back from the front in his directive of 11 October, which suggests that matters were already causing concern then.

Now, in early November, an even more disturbing report reached the army group commander. Writing in his diary on 3 November, Crown Prince Rupprecht noted, 'Out of two train loads of Prussian replacement troops from the east, intended for Fourth Army, ten per cent went absent without leave during the journey.'[3] He returned to the same theme on 11 November writing, 'The fact that the trains coming from the east are full of soldiers from a wide range of units is extremely bad for discipline. The arrival of one of these trains in the station at Valenciennes led to disgraceful scenes, when officers attempting to take control of the situation were whistled at.'[4] In the short term, all that could be hoped for was that the pressure being exerted by the Allies on the battlefield would not lead to a more general collapse of morale, but it was hardly the type of news the commanders wished to receive as the battle entered its fifth month.

Following the events of 30 October, in and around Passchendaele, there was the usual operational pause, as guns and ammunition were manhandled forward and the Canadian Corps prepared to continue its step-by-step attack onto the high ground. Nevertheless, at local level, there was ceaseless activity and continuous minor operations.[5]

Leutnant Möhring 2nd Battery Field Artillery Regiment 62 [6]

"[During late October 1917] 1st Battalion Field Artillery Regiment 62 regularly relieved 1st Battalion Bavarian Field Artillery Regiment 21. 2nd Battery Field Artillery Regiment 62 [on one occasion] had to despatch an anti-tank platoon to Passchendaele ... The order for relief arrived on 1 November, together with an order to withdraw the platoon from Passchendaele. An attempt to carry out this order on 2 November failed. All it produced were several dead and wounded horses. On 2/3 November I undertook another attempt. I went forward with Unteroffizier Hemmieoltmanns, Kanoniers Alten, Klaus, Lünnemann, Schneppe, Friedrich and Andere as well as the necessary drivers.

"Under extremely heavy fire, we set off at night from de Ruiter. We passed Kalve and the position of 8th Battery. Shortly after 7.00 am we picked up the two teams of horses in the sunken road by the field cemetery, which was under quite extraordinarily heavy fire. To this day I still marvel at the calmness shown by both men and horses that day. Whilst I took the kanoniers and headed off along the (to me) only too well known cross country route to Passchendaele, I directed Hemmieoltmanns to await the slackening of the artillery fire – I was thinking of the usual medical pause from 8.00 am to 9.00 am – then to take the road to Passchendaele, which ran parallel to the front, with the drivers dismounted and to keep well spread out.

"To the great amazement of the infantry we arrived at the command post of the *KTK*. Like lightning, both guns were pulled out on to the road. A quick look at the watch showed that it was past 8.00 am. The Tommies had not stopped firing, so it was a matter of dismounting the breech blocks and preparing hand grenades to render the barrels useless. Suddenly someone shouted, *Here they come!* Sure enough they were coming, but not as I ordered with drivers dismounted and well spread out; rather they were one behind the other with the drivers up on the horses. One, I think it was Schröder, was calmly smoking his pipe. I held my breath as I watched the teams negotiate their way round the craters. They were in luck! The teams swung round, the guns were hooked up, the breech mechanisms loaded and we bid the infantry farewell.

"Then – the firing stopped, all of a sudden. Slowly the teams headed off, presenting a perfect target to the British. Surely this piece of cheek would upset the Tommies. How much longer would the pause in firing last? My heart was permanently in my mouth. Would we get away with it, or not? It turned out that the good Lord was with us and we regained the road leading eastwards, which took us out of view of the enemy. At a brisk trot we headed out of the shelled area. Only then did I notice that a shell splinter twice the side of a hand had slammed into the cross beam between the first pair of pole horses. I am delighted to say that my men performed excellently and that they received the decorations and promotion that was their due.

"For my part I should certainly like to know what faces the British[7] were pulling and what they were thinking as they saw us tow two guns at a gentle pace along the front … "

Leutnant Seldte Adjutant 1st Battalion Infantry Regiment 132 [8]

"Every day for one to two hours, especially during the morning between 8.00 am and 10.00 am and in the afternoon from 5.00 pm to 6.00 pm, the British brought down drumfire by guns of all calibres. This made our shelter shake and rock and we lost a considerable number of officers and men. The links between the artillery liaison officer and the heavy and field artillery were as good as useless. We were fortunate to have a wireless set with us, so whenever this equipment was lucky enough not to have its antenna shot off, we did at least have communication with regimental

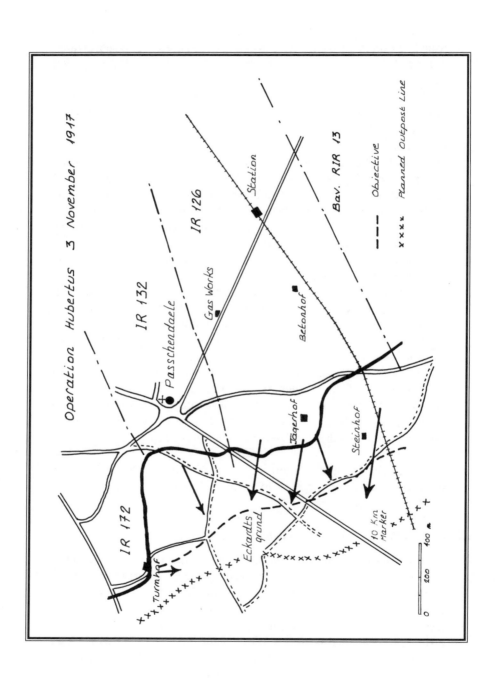

Operation Hubertus 3 November 1917

IR 132

IR 126

IR 172

Bav. RIR 13

Passchendaele

Gas Works

Station

Betonhof

Jägerhof

Steinhof

Eckardts grund

Turmhof

10 Km Marker

— — — Objective

x x x x Planned Outpost Line

0 200 400 m

headquarters. Usually, however, the heavy blessings bestowed on us by the artillery meant that both we and our antenna were generally buried!"

Even on days when there were no major attacks, the Allied artillery continued to pound the defences, paying particular attention to the heights around Passchendaele and the village itself. As a result, the regiments of 39th Infantry Division suffered badly. Infantry Regiment 132 was already pressed up hard against the western extremities of the village and Infantry Regiment 172 was forced to hold an extended line, because the Germans did not want to give up the Goudberg feature to the west of Mosselmarkt and this meant, in turn, that 2nd Battalion Infantry Regiment 172 was stretched out in a line running east-west and facing south, in order to maintain the continuity of the overall divisional frontage. They were clearly overstretched. During the early hours of 1 November there was yet another heavy bombardment of the German lines, but this died away at 8.00 am and the 'medical pause', used by both sides for the treatment and evacuation of wounded, lasted most of the morning, only to be ended by a violent concentration of fire directed on the village itself. The bombardment went on throughout the day and the following night, pausing only briefly as the Canadians pushed reconnaissance patrols forward.

Sensing that something of the sort was occurring, 3rd Company Infantry Regiment 172 sent a fighting patrol out, which succeeded in snatching a prisoner at about midnight. There was then a further period of shelling, followed up by strong Canadian probes forward onto the Goudberg at 3.45 and 5.00am.[9] The net was closing tighter and one of the problems now for the defence was that the constant Canadian pressure was making it impossible to maintain the desired outpost zone in any recognisable form near Passchendaele village. In general, the opposing forces were a mere fifty metres apart, which did not bode well when the next and inevitable push to take the village occurred.

Nevertheless, the defenders did attempt to tackle the problem. In order to create some room for manoeuvre and in a repeat of an earlier failed attempt on 31 October, 39th Infantry Division had ordered that a local counter-attack was to be carried out at 5.50 am on 3 November. Code named *Hubertus*, it was intended to push the Canadians back from the ground they had captured to the west of Passchendaele village and to straighten the line once more. The operation was to be carried out by Infantry Regiments 126 and 132, who each provided one battalion as an attacking force. Infantry Regiment 172 contributed two flank protection parties under Reserve Leutnants Reuter and Lassen. Also directly involved were the Assault Detachment of 39th Infantry Division, eight teams from Storm Battalion 4 and a full complement of support weapons. In addition, the neighbouring divisions, 5th Bavarian Reserve Division to the north and 11th Bavarian Infantry Division to the south, were directed to support the attack with artillery fire and machine gun fire wherever possible and also to launch forward diversionary assault groups to disguise the width of the attack frontage.[10]

Considerable care was taken over the preparation of the operation. Infantry Regiment 132 appointed Reserve Hauptmann Fastje, commanding officer of the 2nd Battalion, to command Assault Group *Passchendaele,* whilst Assault Group *Jägerhof* was the responsibility of 3rd Battalion Infantry Regiment 126 and the whole operation was commanded by 61 Brigade. The plan was to bring down a hurricane bombardment at 5.50 am for five minutes, the assault groups to creep forward as close to the barrage as possible, then for the entire line to rush the Canadian defenders simultaneously as the fire moved forward. A second wave would then follow up to carry out any necessary mopping up. The limit of exploitation was the road running more or less north – south, two hundred metres west of Crest Farm. Assuming that the operation was successful, the overall plan was to restore the main line of resistance along the line *Turmhof – Eckardtsgrund – Steinhof.*

In order for the operation to succeed there had to be absolute precision in each aspect of its execution, which was in itself a tall order. The ground over which it was to be conducted was in a shocking state. German reconnaissance patrols the previous night reported it to be, 'swampier than ever', with 'countless shell holes, some containing water up to the armpits'. In short, it was, 'practically impossible to traverse it'. Despite this unpromising intelligence, the preparations went ahead. Through almost superhuman efforts, the two assault group commanders got their men into the correct positions during the night, but then things started to unravel. The Canadians launched yet another raid during the early hours of 3 November. Preceded by a twenty minute fire plan, this group from what the Germans later described as the 'Royal Highland Canadians' [*sic.* i.e. 42nd Battalion, 7 Brigade, 3rd Canadian Division], clashed at 4.30 am with the Infantry Regiment 172 flank guard at the *Turmhof* = Graf House, the precise point where the front swung through ninety degrees to head east straight towards Passchendaele.

Oberleutnant Klein of Infantry Regiment 172 was at that moment discussing the final arrangements for the attack with Leutnants Reuter and Lassen. Within moments, although the two flank protection groups charged the Canadians, all three officers were wounded. Unteroffizier Wilms of 5th Company kept his head and succeeded in ejecting the raiding party from the *Turmhof,* but by then the damage had been done. The Infantry Regiment 172 groups effectively played no more part in the operation. Regardless of this setback, the assault was launched at the planned time. Initial reports were not encouraging, then information dried up completely, because dense fog had shrouded the battlefield and it was impossible for the forward observers to follow the course of events. Within minutes of the start of the attack, Leutnant Doert, commander of 6th Company Infantry Regiment 132, was seriously wounded and Leutnant Fusch, commander of the 5th Company, was killed. A little later Leutnant Weiss was also killed.[11] The officer casualties here and in Infantry

Regiment 172 had been proportionately very high, which cannot have helped maintain the momentum of the assault.

Eventually the bad news, in a report by the commander of Assault Group *Passchendaele*, despatched at 9.40 am, reached the command post of Infantry Regiment 132 at 11.15 am.

Hauptmann Fastje 2nd Battalion Infantry Regiment 132 [12]

> "The attack has failed. Our own artillery fired too short on the left flank of the attack, bracketing the two left hand companies so comprehensively that they could move neither forwards nor backwards. As soon as our own fire lifted forward, such an immense weight of defensive fire came down in depth that it was impossible for 7th and 8th Companies on the left flank to move at all. The British [*sic*] trenches on the Passchendaele heights were not engaged by our artillery, which meant that the British [*sic*] were able to bring down heavy machine gun fire on the two right hand companies, which had advanced about 200 metres. As a result it was not possible to advance here either … "

The attack by Assault Group *Jägerhof* to the south also ran into trouble quickly – and for much the same reasons. Punctually, at 5.55 am, the assault groups of the first wave began to rush forward, but came under heavy machine gun fire immediately. They did get forward to the boggy *Eckardtsgrund* area, but there the attack stalled, because they had no way of overcoming the machine gun posts. Following up, the second wave did not even advance 200 metres. The attempt by the 11th Bavarian Infantry Division to advance was completely thwarted by the state of the ground. Although elements of the assault groups carried on fighting for some time, just to the west of Passchendaele, by the evening of 3 November the Germans had been forced back to their start lines. At 12.15 pm the divisional commander, hearing that the counter-attack had stalled, ordered a repetition over the same ground at 6.00 pm. However, following a discussion with the commander of 61 Brigade, during which he learned of the full extent of the cumulative losses suffered by the regiments of the division, Generalleutnant von Böckmann postponed any thought of another attempt until after the 39th Division had been relieved on 4 November. [13]

This failure is a perfect example of how the Canadian Corps gained and maintained the initiative at Passchendaele. The raid on the *Turmhof*, for example, was not a lucky one-off event; it was entirely consistent with the pattern of pressure which had been maintained during the previous days. The precision of the artillery defensive fire and the speed with which it came down, was typical of the skill by this stage of the battle displayed by the Allied gunners in the face of enormous difficulties. Operation *Hubertus* was believed at the time by the Canadians to be an immediate reaction to the raid on the *Turmhof* blockhouse. It was nothing of the kind. On 3 November 1917 it represented the best effort the defence could mount – and it was not good enough to match the determined Canadian troops.

This latest tour of duty, including Operation *Hubertus*, had cost Infantry Regiment 132 no fewer than twenty officers and 418 junior ranks killed, wounded or missing, not to mention a large number evacuated sick. The commander of Infantry Regiment 132 summed up the condition of his men for the brigade commander on the eve of its relief. His report was later supplemented, as part of the overall after action report, by the regimental medical officer.

Major Schieß Infantry Regiment 132 [14]

> "The morale of the troops is good. It seems to me, however, that the lengthy stay in the front line has had a somewhat depressing effect on the 12th Company. The men are alert and are attending to their duties with care. However, because of the strenuous nature of the past few days, many of them are suffering from lack of sleep. This means that the NCOs are having to spend the nights constantly moving from sentry to sentry to make sure that they are awake and alert, which in turn is wearing them out. Whilst fully recognising the difficulty of carrying out a relief in the line of this company, from consideration of the security of the entire line, I regard it as urgently necessary."

Regimental Medical Officer Infantry Regiment 132 [15]

> "The following illnesses are currently the most common: colds and chills, gastro-intestinal problems, but above all skin problems caused by the plague of vermin and the total lack of means of caring for the body. As a result of the immense physical effort, lack of sleep and constant mental strain which place extraordinary demands on the nervous system and as a consequence of the appalling accommodation, all the officers and men exhibit the signs of utter exhaustion. A period of rest and recuperation would seem to be absolutely essential."

Infantry Regiments 126 and 172 were no better off so, for the time being, 39th Infantry Division was finished as an effective fighting force. It was not withdrawn completely from the Passchendaele area, but it was at least withdrawn from the battle, once 11th Infantry Division had completed its preparations and was ready to relieve it.

Leutnant Jürgens 7th Company Fusilier Regiment 38 [16]

> "4 November was a Sunday, not that it was marked in any special way by anyone. Because we were definitely due to move forward onto the

position that evening, I called a full company parade, carrying weapons, side arms and iron rations. Around midday all the company commanders were called to battalion headquarters. Hauptmann Beyer informed us that we would be relieving the frontline in the Passchendaele area. 5th, 6th and 7th Companies would be right forward, with 8th Company in reserve. To our right would be units of 4th Infantry Division and to our left Grenadier Regiment 10 ... when the other company commanders had left I spoke to the adjutant and asked him about conditions at the front. He told me that it was a scene of chaotic desolation. Just as I thought, someone had chosen the right place for us!"

As it went dark during the late afternoon of 4 November, Grenadier Regiment 10, Fusilier Regiment 38 and Infantry Regiment 51 of 11th Division left the harbour areas they had been allocated when they were carrying out the *Eingreif* role during the past couple of days and moved to relieve 39th Infantry Division. Grenadier Regiment 10 was tightly packed in the centre of the divisional sector, guarding the approaches to Passchendaele village, with its 1st Battalion forward. Infantry Regiment 51 occupied the former sector of Infantry Regiment 126 immediately to the south and Fusilier Regiment 38 took over from Infantry Regiment 172 just to the north. The men of Infantry Regiment 51 were unimpressed with their lot, describing their situation as, 'being in a soft, boggy sea of mud which was lashed by ceaseless rain and overflowing with filthy water. It was punctuated by countless shell holes, which gave the whole monotonous area the glazed look of a death mask. Our 1st Battalion occupied saturated holes in the ground, shrouded by the grey Flanders fog; hungry, wringing wet, freezing cold, and plastered with all the filth of the battle-field.'[17] Experiencing the same conditions, the companies of Fusilier Regiment 38 occupied the rough line of shell holes that skirted the Goudberg, with 7th Company responsible for the line to the east of the *Turmhof*, a recent cornerstone of the defence, but so often a magnet for artillery concentrations and hostile patrol actions.

Leutnant Jürgens 7th Company Fusilier Regiment 38 [18]

"My company held a position facing south. Immediately to its front was an impassable swamp. My right flank rested on the *Turmhof*, a concrete blockhouse which the British [*sic*] had attacked frequently. The 6th Company had occupied it and took up a front facing west. Further to the right was the 5th Company. To my left, also front facing west, but separated from me by 400 metres of swampland, was Grenadier Regiment 10. 8th Company was located astride the Westrozebeke – Passchendaele road to my left rear. The company commander I was relieving explained to me that his battalion had suffered such heavy casualties that I could relieve what was left of it with my company alone.

"He gave me a good piece of advice, which was to stay down in the shell craters throughout the day to avoid the enemy snipers, who lay in wait to detect any movement. Only between 9.00 am and 10.00 am, the so-called 'medical pause', could I get round the sector without difficulty. This was the time when both sides observed the unwritten rule that there would be no firing to permit the recovery of the wounded. At that he took his leave and disappeared into the darkness with his men. My ration party attached themselves to them and set off to find accommodation in a farm behind the lines.

"Whilst it was still dark I went along the length of the position with Reimann. Carefully, we picked our way forward around the rims of countless craters. My men were split up, two or three to a shell hole. The two light machine guns were distributed along the line. I sited one of the heavy machine guns on the right flank and placed the other in the same shell hole as myself. We made our way to the *Turmhof* on the right flank. It seemed to be in a rather poor state. I then discovered, to my surprise, that it was being occupied by Leutnant Ciolek of 8th Company together with his platoon. The 6th did not appear in the line until further to the right. I then picked my way back to my crater, rolled up in my groundsheet and tried to sleep. Unfortunately it was too cold and I kept waking up. The British maintained harassing fire throughout the night.

"As soon as dawn broke on 5 November, I pulled the groundsheet over my head and wrote the morning report by the light of my torch. Fortunately there had been no casualties so far. Whilst a runner headed off to battalion headquarters, I made my way round the position once more. This was to make sure my men were all right and to have a chance to orientate myself about the ground. To our front the crater-strewn landscape dropped away gently to a swamp-filled hollow, on the far side of which, just beyond my left flank, a few piles of broken tiles and shattered tree stumps marked the pitiful remains of Passchendaele. To the right I could see the damaged *Turmhof*. Other than that there was nothing but craters full of mud and water as far as the eye could see. Of the enemy there was not a trace, but they were there all right. As I rather foolishly made my way back to my hole, above cover, bullets immediately whistled past my ears.

"Towards 8.00 am the enemy began to increase the rate of fire and, shortly before 9.00 am, I had three men wounded by shrapnel. I assumed when the artillery fire ceased at 9.00 am that the medical pause had begun and I went over to the wounded accompanied by a medical orderly to treat their wounds. During this my gefreiter, who was clearly wearing a Red Cross brassard, was wounded in the wrist. This rather demonstrated that it was not safe, even between 9.00 am and 10.00 am, to appear above the edge of the crater. The medical pause came to an end and once more the enemy began to sweep the shelled and ploughed up area with shrapnel. I sheltered under a groundsheet in my crater, together with my runners and smoked cigarette after cigarette.

"In between times, I also attempted to warm myself up with a cup of coffee we had heated over solid fuel, but without success. The wet and cold November air chilled me to the bone. During the afternoon the sun broke through the heavy cloud cover and we were immediately plagued by enemy aircraft. Circling low, they were observing the exact line of our positions. They then fired off yellow flares and we were soon under fire from the British heavy guns. Finally it was evening and the firing died away. By then I had lost another twelve men killed and wounded. My company was now down to forty one brave men."

As the attack frontages narrowed and the defenders were pushed back more and more, the number of protected observation posts was reduced dramatically. The situation was made worse by the loss of various dominating heights which had been used previously to overlook the Allied lines. Often there were no suitable pill boxes and the artillery was forced to make use of the ruins of buildings, which were highly vulnerable to shell fire. Reserve Field Artillery Regiment 44 had moved into the Passchendaele area at the beginning of November along with the rest of the 44th Reserve Division and, very soon afterwards, had a bad experience as a result of this deficiency.

Vizewachtmeister Schwietzke 3rd Battery Reserve Field Artillery Regiment 44 [19]

"Throughout the day the Tommies were harassing the rear areas. I could not help but wonder what would happen if something landed on our house and, with that thought in mind, I went to the observation post in the house, in order to study the battle area. I had hardly got into position on the upper floor, than I heard a droning sound. Initially it was quite quiet, but then it got louder very rapidly and was followed by an ear-splitting crack and the shouts of those who had been hit.

"To begin with I could not work out what had happened, especially because there was so much smoke that I could not see my hand in front of my face. I gradually realised that a shell must have landed in the house. Before I rushed away, I said a quick prayer to Him above for protecting me from death, then I got out of the house quickly. A little while later, once everything had calmed down, we re-entered the house. What a shock! On the floor in the entrance hall the adjutant lay dead, his skull smashed. The battalion commander himself was also severely wounded and about six infantrymen were also slightly wounded. Once we had bandaged everyone up, we left this place of horror and returned to the battery position."

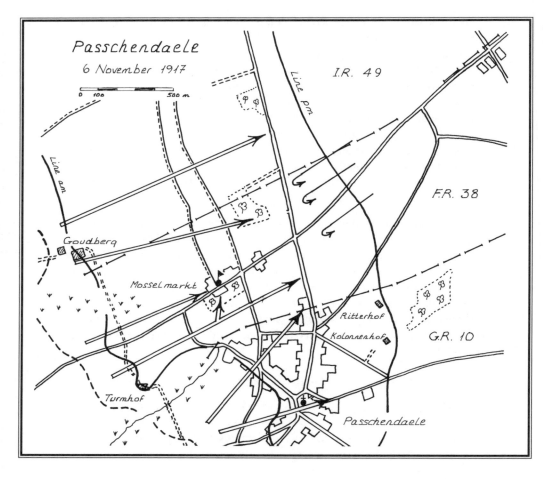

The dismal weather continued right through 5 November. The morning was foggy but, as visibility improved, the prospect for the men in the forward trenches was anything but pleasing or reassuring. From horizon to horizon there was nothing to see but brown earth, which looked as though it had been turned over by a giant plough. Artillery fire continued ceaselessly, increasing considerably during the early hours of 6 November. The Canadian Corps despatched a number of patrols forward in order to test the strength of the defences and one Canadian soldier was captured by an ambush group from 5th Company Fusilier Regiment 38. A swift battlefield interrogation confirmed the unpalatable fact that the expected assault was due to take place later that morning.

At around 5.30 am the enemy artillery fire increased to a frenzied drumfire. The defenders of Passchendaele made what final preparations they could, the fire died away slightly, then increased once more only to reduce in intensity yet again. Finally, just before 7.30 am, the attack began, supported by a complex fire plan and with the infantry of the Canadian Corps hard up behind a rolling barrage. Within five minutes the first reports of a break in a little to the north of Passchendaele were arriving at command posts in the rear and, during the next hour, more progress was made by the attackers, despite the fact that the German defenders had launched local counter-attacks in several places. It was a fight to the death for the men of 2nd Battalion Fusilier Regiment 38 and more than some men could take.

Leutnant Jürgens 7th Company Fusilier Regiment 38 [20]

"The first part of the night passed off quietly. The ration party came forward without casualties and withdrew successfully, evacuating the dead and wounded as they went. Just after midnight our artillery, which up until then had not fired much, started to bring down a heavy weight of fire – much to our satisfaction. Towards 2.00 am a runner from battalion headquarters arrived bringing me the news that a Canadian prisoner captured by our 5th Company was reported to have said that the Canadians planned to conduct an attack on Passchendaele in the morning. Our artillery was informed. I called together my platoon commanders and briefed them about the forthcoming attack. Because of the swamp, it was certain that my company would be attacked not frontally, but from the right, I gave orders, therefore, that that the company was to take up a position about 150 metres in rear of 6th Company, front facing west as a second line of defence. Casualties among the crews of the two heavy machine guns had been such that I was only able to man them in a skeleton fashion, but I placed them on the flanks. I despatched Reimann to the right and remained myself on the left flank.

"I reported to battalion what I had done and passed the information also to 6th and 8th Companies. The runner returned with battalion approval of my action. After a while things became totally calm and our own artillery also stopped firing. I had just crawled back under my groundsheet to write the morning report, when the British suddenly brought down drumfire of indescribable intensity throughout the crater field. The explosions of the shells came so thick and fast that it was no longer possible to distinguish between them. Soon the entire area was blanketed with smoke from the explosions. Splinters whined through the air and great clods of earth rained down on the men sheltering in the shell holes.

"In addition, shrapnel with a low bursting point was fired, sending a hail of lead balls down at us. All around me there were heavy casualties, but I could not establish what was happening on the right. The minute the drumfire began, I fired flares demanding destructive fire. I fired off every flare of that type that I had, but our batteries seemed not to spot them. I then called for defensive fire until I ran out of these cartridges as well. After about one hour, the enemy fire seemed to die away somewhat and to concentrate more on the rear areas. Now only shrapnel was coming down to our front and, meanwhile, dawn had broken. From the front I could clearly recognise from their open coats that some of our men were pulling back. I made them stay and reinforce our line. Hardly had they taken up position than the first dense assault wave of Canadians could be seen not more than 200 metres away.

"I immediately ordered fire to be opened and opened up myself with the machine gun, an Unteroffizier of the 2nd Machine Gun Company acting as loader. The stream of bullets was coming down effectively and causing the Canadians casualties, but I noticed at the same time that the rifle fire of my little band was extremely weak. Suddenly someone shouted, *Herr Leutnant! The right flank has cracked!* Looking over I could see that men to our right had indeed stood up and were running to the rear. I ordered the Unteroffizier to go on firing and raced over to the right flank to restore order. In the meantime the enemy had closed to within eighty metres. Desperate measures were called for, but I had not covered more than a few paces when I received a heavy blow on the right thigh and was thrown to the ground. Simultaneously two shells exploded right next to me.

"As I came round the second enemy wave had already passed me. This was followed by a further four at one hundred metre intervals. The advance stalled momentarily at the Passchendaele-Westrozebeke road. Probably this was due to resistance from our 8th Company, but then the attack continued. Some time later I saw lines of our infantry advancing on the enemy near Mosselmarkt. This caused the Canadians to pull back to positions near to me. I was already hoping that I should be liberated if one of the 'automatically launched counter-attacks', about which we had heard so much made sufficient ground. However, the enemy received reinforcements and pushed forward once more. To my acute disappointment, our infantry withdrew under this pressure. I lay there waiting and hoping for a second counter-attack in greater strength, but nothing happened and about midday I was taken prisoner."

In Passchendaele village itself, 1st Battalion Grenadier Regiment 10 had also taken a prisoner during the early hours, reporting this information by radio at 5.05 am and adding that the man had stated that the attack was due to begin at 7.00 am, a piece of intelligence which turned out to be absolutely correct. The artillery fire was already heavy, but it increased to drumfire on both the forward and support battalions from 5.30 am. The reserve and artillery positions in rear were harassed severely and drenched in gas at the same time. The already weakened reserve battalion of Grenadier Regiment 10 suffered severely at this time, forcing the regimental commander, Major von Fumetti, to inform 21 Brigade that it was out of action. Five minutes before the Canadians were due to launch their assault, Grenadier Regiment 10 called down artillery defensive fire forward of its positions. At 7.35 am the *KTK* sent a wireless message by Morse code, 'Attack is taking place. Enemy has broken into the sector of our right hand neighbour.' This was followed at 7.55 am by a request from the *KTK* for reserves, but that was the last message received before communication with the front was broken.

As the regimental commander attempted to obtain reserves, bitter, hand-to-hand fighting was taking place in Passchendaele village. Without orders, but reacting automatically in accordance with regimental standard operating procedures, 3rd Battalion Grenadier Regiment 10 launched a counter-attack, during which the commander of 10th Company, Leutnant Schaefer, was mortally wounded. One positive aspect of the close quarter battle in the village was that the quantity of artillery fire was reduced considerably. Considerably outnumbered, the defenders fought hard in the ruins and the attack made only slow progress. Unfortunately, in accordance with classic 'bite and hold' tactics, Passchendaele village was totally sealed off and no German reinforcements could pass through the intense fire. It was impassable to individuals and organised counter-attack forces had no chance whatsoever of assaulting through it.

Meanwhile, the Canadian progress to the north, through the Fusilier Regiment 38 sector, was causing great concern to the chain of command, which was totally preoccupied with assessing if, with the forces available, it would be possible to hold either the village, or even the high ground to the east of it. In an effort to assist the defenders to hold on, every artillery piece within range, including the long range guns belonging to Groups Diksmuide and Wijtschate, brought down rapid fire forward of the Passchendaele sector. An infantry cooperation aircraft reported to the regimental command post of Grenadier Regiment 10 at 12.20 pm that Fusilier Regiment 38 had been pushed back, so that its front line, manned by its 2nd Battalion, which had been in reserve, was now to the east of the Westrozebeke-Passchendaele road and that a gap had opened up between the two regiments. 3rd Battalion Fusilier Regiment 38 had already been launched and completely destroyed in a counter attack; its commander, Hauptmann Ulrich, dying at the head of his men.[21]

As the situation in and around Passchendaele continued to worsen, urgent action had to be taken. Despite the fact that the 3rd Guards Infantry Division had seen much hard fighting during October and had only recently been relieved, such was the pressure on resources that a composite force, comprising 3rd Battalion Lehr-Infantry Regiment and 2nd and 3rd Battalions Fusilier Guard Regiment, had been deployed forward, ready to conduct a counter-attack towards Passchendaele if required. Early on the morning of 6 November they began to advance from their holding area near Mager Merrie. There were no communications forward so, although it was obvious that the situation was serious, no exact information was available. Gradually they met up with odd individuals returning from the front. The trickle increased as more and more individuals, frequently unwounded, but lacking weapons or equipment, made their way to the rear. [22]

They could provide no coherent reports and not even threats issued by officers with drawn pistols, or the actions of low-flying German pilots firing their machine guns, could stem the flow to the rear.[23] At that precise, unpromising, moment an order arrived, directing 3rd Battalion Lehr Infantry Regiment to counter-attack the western section of Passchendaele village and to push forward onto the hills beyond it. Just as the commanding officer was giving out his orders in the shelter of a wall, the British artillery brought down an enormously heavy barrage. The dense curtains of fire searched backwards and forwards across the area with the utmost precision. The companies were pre-occupied, wondering how they would get through this concentrated barrage when, suddenly, a further order arrived, cancelling the attack. Instead the troops were to go into an assembly area and await further orders. An order to send two companies to plug the gap which had appeared northeast of Passchendaele also came to nothing; instead 3rd Battalion Fusilier Guard Regiment came under the orders of Fusilier Regiment 38 and linked up with its 1st Battalion in Sector North.

At around 7.00 pm two battalions of Infantry Regiment 51 arrived, relieving the fought-out 3rd Battalion Lehr Infantry Regiment. This allowed the latter to withdraw, leaving the newly-arrived battalions to carry out the necessary counter-attack to the north of Passchendaele, together with 2nd and 3rd Battalions Fusilier Guard Regiment. Hastily scrambled together, launched in the dark over a vast muddy crater field which was unknown territory to most of the attackers, it is no surprise that the attack achieved very little.[24] Describing the action later, Oberstleutnant Nollau of Infantry Regiment 51 wrote:

> "Then it was afternoon. It was impossible to get the field kitchens forward. There was nothing to eat or drink then, at 5.00 pm, came the order to launch a counter-attack. Speed was essential; it would soon be dark. Various formations were supposed to come together for the operation, but where were they? How was contact to be made with them in the short time available? In the end everything depended on 2nd and 3rd Battalions Infantry Regiment 51. Direct support was to be provided by a complete battery. The task demanded was simply the hardest of the hard, but it had to be done and it was done.
> "The battalions advanced. Those who are familiar with the crater field

of Flanders will understand what was involved at any time in trying to manoeuvre large forces here and maintain command and control – and now it was November! The landscape comprised crater after crater, full of a mixture of water and heavy clinging clay. Only with the greatest care was it possible at the best of times to avoid slipping in to one of these, or even drowning – and this was in the dark. There was no moon and no stars, just heavy rain. Even without enemy interference, it took well trained troops to move in this area. We had to cope as well with a storm of British fire, which opened up suddenly. Exploiting their good observation, the British [*sic*] must have spotted the attack very early and every available weapon was brought to bear to halt it.

"We had to focus on the need to produce a good position from which to resume the attack the following morning, so we continued to pick our way forward, stumbling and falling into the filthy mud and water, through a storm of shell fire and blood. The rain continued to pour down ceaselessly. Heavy British naval guns joined in. A direct hit landed on 12th Company, killing its outstandingly brave commander, Reserve Leutnant Grünig, and one of the platoon commanders, Leutnant Ogrosske, as well as many other members of the company. For the time being the company was scattered and out of action, but gradually the brave survivors assembled and rejoined the advance.

"To our front there was nothing but the shattered remnants of various divisions. There was a clear need for the gap to be filled by fully effective troops. Then the attack clashed with British [*sic*] infantry along the line of the main road to the north of Passchendaele. Before the matter could be resolved, an order arrived halting the advance. The line which had been achieved with such heavy losses was to be held and held it was, despite the fact that the following days were difficult and much blood was spilled."

The move forward could hardly be described as an attack, no matter how gallantly it had been carried out and, in any case, it came far too late to help the beleaguered Grenadier Regiment 10 in Passchendaele village. A reconnaissance patrol sent forward during the late morning by 2nd Battalion had reported back at 2.00 pm, 'An extraordinarily heavy artillery barrage is falling on the low ground to the east of Passchendaele, which has cut off the village completely. The line of the heights by the battalion headquarters is still occupied by our men and the sounds of an intense fire fight can be heard coming from the village.'[25] It was the last information to be received. Within the village the defenders fought on until, split into small groups, they ran out of ammunition and were overwhelmed. Many were killed, but it appears that the surrender of a fair number of them was accepted and they went into captivity.

Desperate attempts were made to pull together some sort of relieving force, but once Infantry Regiment 126 informed divisional headquarters at 4.15 pm that enemy penetrations to the south of Passchendaele had forced its right hand company to pull back to the line of the gasworks, it was obvious that nothing could be done. The fight for Passchendaele had cost Grenadier Regiment 10 a total of twenty eight officers and 566 junior ranks killed, wounded or missing. Leutnants Schaefer, Steffler and Thomas were known to be dead[26] but, of the total, no fewer than nineteen officers and 325 junior ranks were missing: the majority killed or captured in Passchendaele.

During the night the line achieved by the 2nd Canadian Division consolidated along the line Westrozebeke – eastern edge of Passchendaele village – west of the road Passchendaele – Passchendaele Station. The slight salient formed in the sector Gasworks – Passchendaele Station had had to be pulled back to conform. There, for the next few days, the defenders hung on in their water-filled shell holes, soaked to the skin and half frozen, while the artillery fire beat down on them ceaselessly by day and night.

Crown Prince Rupprecht Diary Entry 6 November 1917 [27]

> "This morning the enemy launched an attack with strong forces against Passchendaele. Simultaneously attacks took place against our positions near Geluveld. The attack against Geluveld was beaten off; in Passchendaele, however, the enemy succeeded in breaking in. Whether it will still be possible to win back Passchendaele and to hold it, along with the ten kilometre ridge which runs behind it, without too high an expenditure of troops remains questionable."

In the event, delays in transporting troops to Flanders meant that the Army High Command decided to make no effort to win back Passchendaele through counter-attack. This meant adjusting the front line of the defence to bend back further to a point along the reverse slope position which was now being held to the east of Passchendaele.

Army High Command Official Communiqué 7 November 1917 [28]

> "Yesterday there was bitter fighting in Flanders. After intense drumfire in the early morning, British [sic] divisions attacked along a line from Poelkapelle to the Ypres-Roeselare railway and against the heights of Beselare and Geluveld. To the north of Passchendaele, the attacks collapsed in the face of our defensive fire. The enemy forced a way into Passchendaele. In close-quarter fighting the eastern part of the village was retaken. Towards midday the enemy introduced fresh troops into the

battle. They were able to extend the breach, but only locally. Our position runs along the eastern edge.

"The assaults, which were launched in strength against the heights of Beselare and Geluveld, were generally brought to a halt forward of our lines. Where there were enemy penetrations, these were overwhelmed in hand to hand fighting. Destructive fire brought down by our artillery neutralised later attempts to attack."

With the focus of the fighting clearly around Passchendaele and losses amongst the defending regiments mounting rapidly, 44th Reserve Division, comprising Reserve Infantry Regiments 205, 206 and 208, which had originally taken over the role of *Eingreif* division in the south of the Group Ypres area from 220th Infantry Division on 27 October, was moved north from the Beselare area on 4 November, but was initially held back in the *Eingreif* role. Reserve Infantry Regiment 205 spent the whole of 6 November ready to move forward, but the call never came.[29] As a measure of the extreme difficulty of plugging gaps in the front line caused by the heavy fighting and continuous shelling of the past few days, once the entire division had arrived on 7 November, each of the regiments had to give up one battalion, to form a hastily-produced 'Regiment Gärtner'.[30] This composite formation was subordinated to 11th Infantry Division, which had suffered so heavily on 6 November, and rushed forward under command of Fusilier Regiment 38 to bolster the sagging defences to the north of Passchendaele that same night.

It was only a temporary measure. 11th Infantry Division was so totally worn down by its brief tenure of the sector that the following day the remainder of 44th Reserve Division marched forward to relieve it completely. Arriving in the forward area during the night 8/9 November, its regiments had little time to orientate themselves before the massive bombardment began on 9 November, preparing the way for the final push on 10 November. Reserve Infantry Regiment 205 occupied the critical central area, with its forward positions just to the east of Passchendaele village. When the companies arrived at the front there was still a complete lack of clarity about the precise location of the line to be defended. This led to one of the luckiest escapes of the entire battle.

In the early hours of 10 November, Sanitätsunteroffizier Hempel, accompanied by six men of the 3rd Company, arrived in the German lines from the direction of the enemy, having spent almost twenty four hours undetected in Passchendaele village. To the amazement of their comrades they explained that, during the march forward in the dark, they had met no friendly forces and had walked straight through both the main defensive line and the outpost zone by mistake. They had only become aware of their error when they found themselves in amongst the ruins of Passchendaele. By this time it was nearly dawn and there was no time to try to escape. They managed to find a cellar in which to hide and, although they were seen entering it, they were not recognised as German soldiers. Having spent a nerve-wracking day hidden away, they emerged cautiously the following night and were lucky enough to avoid detection and the torrent of artillery fire which was coming down. With considerable difficulty they made their way back to their own positions, where they were greeted with considerable enthusiasm. Every man would shortly be needed to bolster the defence.[31]

Not long after Hempel and his little group returned, a prisoner was captured and brought in. It transpired that he belonged to the 2nd Canadian Division and that he had only arrived in the line the previous evening. The German chain of command interpreted this to mean that another major attack was about to take place.[32] In a pre-emptive effort to disrupt final preparations, all the German heavy guns and howitzers in range brought down a concentration of fire from 5.45 am to 6.00 am just to the

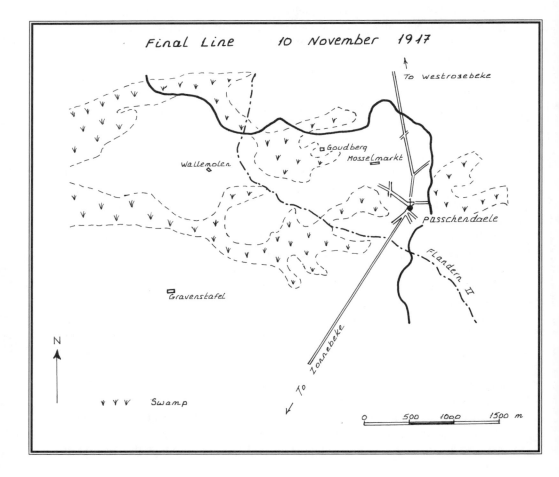

east of Passchendaele. It is not entirely clear how effective this was, because the main thrust was further to the north. At 7.00 am, the Allied artillery began to bring down extremely heavy drum fire, directed in particular (though probably by chance) at the junction between Reserve Infantry Regiments 205 and 208. Most of it fell in the outpost zone, but enough damage was done to the companies in the main defensive line for the positions to be rolled up partially later to the left and right.

After an intense bombardment in the pouring rain which lasted forty five minutes, the attacks by 1st Canadian Division and 1st British Division to its north were launched. Not that the defenders knew it, but this was the final major set-piece attack of the campaign. In an assault launched on a narrow front, the Canadians achieved their aim of gaining 500 metres of the high ground to the north of Passchendaele village. Not surprisingly, the designated objective was taken within forty five minutes, because the ground captured comprised a section of the outpost zone, occupied only by very light forces. The need to deal with machine gun fire coming from the main defensive line forced the Canadians to push forward a further three hundred metres during hard fighting later in the day. Exploiting the potential of the outpost zone, in accordance with Ludendorff's directive of mid-October, the attackers were engaged as they crossed it by every gun the defence could bring to bear and suffered serious casualties as a result.

Although it was now forty eight hours since 44th Reserve Division had relieved the battered 11th Division around Passchendaele, the artillery regiments of 11th Division were still in the line and contributing to the fire support. As a result, the artillery liaison officers of Field Artillery Regiment 42, such as Leutnant Reinbach of 6th Battery, who was located with Reserve Infantry Regiment 208 and Vizewachtmeister Kowalski, observing for 4th Battery, were able to direct fire with great precision, causing considerable losses to the attackers. Kowalski was decorated later for his skill and courage.

Thanks to the artillery fire referred to above and its own aggressive defence, 2nd Battalion Reserve Infantry Regiment 208, which was occupying the forward positions on the right of the 44th Reserve Division sector, beat off at least four separate attacks. These were timed at 6.00 am and 7.10 am and were completely smashed. 11th and 12th Companies Reserve Infantry Regiment 208 were rushed forward prior to the third attack, which came in behind a rolling barrage at 9.45 am. This time there was a minor penetration on the regimental left flank, but a determined counter-attack by the companies of the 3rd Battalion across the ploughed-up muddy terrain, was able once more to throw the attackers back to their start line. A fourth attack at 2.00 pm was broken up mainly by artillery fire, as was a fifth, which was mostly directed to the sector of the neighbouring regiment and was also beaten off. Despite the fact that the day witnessed the loss of several hundred metres of territory near Passchendaele, Reserve Infantry Regiment 208 was rightly proud of its performance.[33]

In this sector, however, the day still belonged quite clearly to the Canadians. The defending infantry lost heavily. Altogether, during the period from the end of October to 16 November when they were relieved, Reserve Infantry Regiment 205 had lost seven officers and 438 junior ranks, whilst Reserve Infantry Regiment 208 suffered casualties more than twice as high.[34] Losses in the artillery were also serious, due to the constant gassing of gun positions and almost incessant counter-battery fire. Field Artillery Regiment 42 suffered badly on 10 November, its most notable loss being Leutnant Walter Vogel, commander of 6th Battery, who was hit in the stomach with a shell splinter and killed. His place was taken by an officer of 4th Battery.

Leutnant Wennrich 4th Battery Field Artillery Regiment 42 [35]

"During the morning of 10 November I was ordered by the regiment to assume command of 6th Battery following the death of Leutnant Vogel. Whilst the gun position of the 4th Battery was relatively free from enemy fire, that of 6th Battery was an absolute witch's cauldron of exploding shells of all calibres. It was tricky enough to get to the place through all the heavy drumfire. When I arrived at 6th Battery, I discovered that two guns were hit and out of action. Because the left hand wheel of a further gun was also badly damaged, the battery was barely operational. Together with the unteroffiziers, I assembled the gunners who had gone and sought shelter in nearby ruined houses.

"During the day, despite the fact that it was suffering under heavy bombardment, the battery had fired on tirelessly with the two remaining guns and, because only two guns could be fired simultaneously, a sort of system of reliefs had been used, enabling some of the gunners to take shelter, [whilst the others operated the guns]. Towards midday a runner from one of the forward battalions reported to me. He had an important message for his regimental headquarters and, because he did not know the way, I went a short distance with him. Just as we were passing the building where Leutnant Vogel had been killed, a heavy shell exploded near to us, and a large splinter almost completely tore off one of the runner's lower legs.

"Some of the gunners from the battery carried the seriously injured man off to the rear. I myself received a splinter in the right shoulder. The medical orderlies established that my wound was not serious, but I could not use my right arm. I was the only officer available, so in fulfilment of my duty, I stayed where I was until evening, when I was relieved."

The part played by Field Artillery Regiment 42 was fully acknowledged the following day by Infantry Regiment 208, which sent the following message on 11 November:

Command Post Infantry Regiment 208 11 November 1917
To: Artillery Sub-Group North

> "At 7.20 am the enemy was massing in front of the regimental sector, prior to launching an attack, which was spotted in time by the outpost line. The defensive and destructive fire, which was called for immediately, came down without delay, smashing down into the ranks of the British. The attack fell apart, with bloody casualties, as a result of defensive fire from artillery and machine guns."[36]

Unaware of the depth of the objectives set by the Canadian Corps for 10 November, Reserve Infantry Regiment 205 believed that it had held the first of the attacks on its sector. Only in the narrow sense that its main defensive line was not initially involved was that the case and, unlike on previous occasions, this time there were no *Eingreif* troops rushing forward to launch a counter-stroke into the outpost zone. The Allied artillery fire slackened noticeably during and after the time that 3rd Battalion Reserve Infantry Regiment 208 had carried out its assault, but it came down again with full force at 10.30 am. The Canadians had obviously realised that they needed to push on beyond their original line and there was further fierce fighting beginning at 12.30 pm and 2.00 pm, when yet another counter-attack by a battalion of Reserve Infantry Regiment 208 made some progress.

Nevertheless the Canadian pressure had told once more. In all the confusion of bombardments, attacks and counter-attacks, a gap had opened between Reserve Infantry Regiments 205 and 208. The right flank of Reserve Infantry Regiment 205 was (luckily for it) resting against an impassable swamp, but beyond the boggy area there was a sizeable gap, which the Canadian troops exploited to push out a series of outposts, some 250 to 300 metres forward. Hearing of this, the regimental commander of Reserve Infantry Regiment 205 immediately ordered his *BTK* to despatch forward 5th Company to seal off this sector. Despite the heavy artillery fire, which continued to fall on the rear areas throughout the following night, as it began to go dark, the 5th Company struggled forward, heading initially towards Passchendaele, then bearing off to the north. Hit by several shells on the way, it had already suffered substantial casualties by the time it reached the appointed point. In conformity with best practice, the company commander, Leutnant Meßke, accompanied by Vizefeldwebel Kräuter, patrolled out to check how far forward he could place his men. In a final tragedy of the day for Reserve Infantry Regiment 205, they must have bumped into one of the Canadian outposts. Shots were heard and neither man returned.[37]

The story of 10 November was somewhat different just to the north where the 1st British Division assaulted the sector of 4th Infantry Division, held originally by Infantry Regiment 49 left forward (and adjoining Reserve Infantry Regiment 208), Infantry Regiment 14 in the centre and Infantry Regiment 140 right forward.

This division had been forward in the ground-holding role for almost a week at this stage and had already been heavily engaged during the battle on 6 November. 3rd Battalion Infantry Regiment 49 in the front line had suffered badly, losing its 12th Company entirely, whilst the 1st and 2nd Battalions were so weak that 2nd, 3rd, 4th, 5th 6th, 7th and 8th Companies were combined to form one composite company. On the eve of this second major battle, the regiment was down to a strength of sixteen officers and 602 junior ranks, but it still had twenty three serviceable machine guns.[38] In view of the weakness of Infantry Regiment 49, Infantry Regiment 140, which was hardly in a better condition itself, relieved it on 8 November, placing its battered 3rd Battalion in the front line.

It was clear for all to see that the 4th Infantry Division should have been pulled out of the line and replaced but, once again, lack of transport capacity was affecting the ability of the Army High Command to conduct the battle in the most effective manner. Crown Prince Rupprecht, who had listed one problem and difficulty after another in his diary during the first week of November, recorded on 7 November, 'Due to the great delays in moving new divisions, the Army High Command is not in a position to allocate fresh troops to Fourth Army. Because of this [the Army] has decided not to attempt to recapture Passchendaele. As a result, the left flank of Group Staden has had to be bent back to conform to the reverse slope position which is being defended to the east of Passchendaele.'[39]

There was no question of improving the defensive positions, which by now comprised a random selection of shell holes. Each time a spade went into the ground it hit water and, in any case, the rain of shells quickly ploughed up the ground and nullified each attempt to dig trenches to link up the small groups of men stationed right forward. Throughout 9 November and the night which followed, the regiments were subjected to endlessly repeated concentrations of artillery fire, causing severe casualties amongst the already weak companies and totally disrupting all forms of communications. Not even the runners could operate, as the rate of enemy fire increased to the absolute maximum possible. The report despatched by Infantry Regiment 140 to 8 Brigade that evening provides a graphic account of the events of the day's fighting. [40]

> "The regiment was deployed in Sector B (left) when, at exactly 7.00 am on 10 November 1917, drumfire came down along the entire front. A second barrage was brought down behind the main defensive line on the support troops. At 7.10 am the regiment alerted 1st Battalion Infantry Regiment 140 at Point 1442.[41] A similar warning order arrived later from 8 Brigade. Machine gun fire could be heard coming from the front line, indicating that an infantry attack was underway. As a result, the regiment ordered 1st Battalion Infantry Regiment 140 at 7.25 am to set off immediately in the direction of the *Nordhof* and to be prepared to launch a counter-attack.

"Meanwhile, the enemy had attacked the regimental sector in dense masses. They had been largely beaten back by the troops in the outpost zone. Troops which broke through were dealt with in front of the main defensive line by 3rd Battalion Infantry Regiment 140. This fighting went on until 10.00 am. In the meantime, 1st Battalion Infantry Regiment 140 reported that it had arrived at the Westrozebeke – Passchendaele road, had crossed it and was ascending the hill to the *Nordhof*. Here the battalion clashed with the enemy which had broken through in the Infantry Regiment 49 sector. The garrison of the *Nordhof* was trapped in its shelters. 1st Battalion Infantry Regiment 140 launched an immediate counter-attack, reporting the fact to Brigade by means of light signals. [The troops] fired from a standing position then charged. The enemy did not stand and fight; they flooded back to the rear and some British soldiers surrendered.[42] At 9.20 am 4th Company Infantry Regiment 140 reported that the *Nordhof* had been secured.[43] The battalion pressed on, followed by elements of Infantry Regiment 49 as far as the outpost line and beyond.

"It then had to withdraw to the main defensive line, because it came under friendly artillery fire and suffered casualties. Here prisoners were taken; 3rd Company Infantry Regiment 140 capturing thirty five British soldiers. A message was passed to the artillery informing them that the *Nordhof* was in our possession and that they should lift their fire forward to the former defensive fire tasks. At 10.10 am the enemy launched a fresh attack in considerable strength against the front of 3rd Battalion Infantry Regiment 140. The attack was beaten off with extremely heavy casualties amongst the attackers. Around midday, the enemy launched a strong attack from Passchendaele in a northeasterly direction. This attack hit the left flank of the regiment (10th Company Infantry Regiment 140) where, after considerable fighting, it was driven off with serious casualties.

"To the front of Reserve Infantry Regiment 208 the enemy pushed on beyond the outpost line, taking prisoners. This attack was halted by means of a counter-attack from elements of 10th Company Infantry Regiment 140, supported by overhead machine gun fire. This threw back this part of the enemy attack and they withdrew in disorder, having suffered many casualties. The commander of Reserve Infantry Regiment 208 immediately expressed his thanks for this strong support. The deployment of 1st Battalion Infantry Regiment 140 meant that the frontage of the regiment had doubled. During the afternoon 1st Battalion Infantry Regiment 140 defeated another British attack against this sector. At this point the regiment only had 7th and 8th Companies available, but the 8th Company was committed to maintaining the link between us and Reserve Infantry Regiment 208 and so could not be deployed directly for any other purpose.

"8 Brigade made available to the regiment two companies of 3rd Battalion Infantry Regiment 114 and Machine Gun Sharp Shooter Detachment 39. During the afternoon, the enemy made a further attempt to launch an attack against Reserve Infantry Regiment 208 and our left flank. The regiment, therefore, ordered the two companies of Infantry Regiment 114 to thrust forward along the line of the road towards Mosselmarkt and, if necessary, to throw back the enemy by means of a counter-attack. This movement, carried out together with elements of Reserve Infantry Regiment 208, caused the enemy to bring down defensive fire, but the actual British attack was not carried out ... From that point on there was no change in the situation of the regiment and darkness fell.

"The regiment had not only retained every part of its own sector, beating off several attacks, but had also intervened in the neighbouring sector, pushing back enemy penetrations and rendering valuable support to the neighbouring regiment. The regiment which, with the exception of 8th Company, was fully committed, suffered very considerable casualties – especially in wounded. This was because destructive artillery fire came down all day long on its positions. It is not yet possible to produce exact figures. The British casualties must have been truly enormous, because our rifle and machine gun fire was seen to have an appalling effect on the dense masses of attackers both while they were advancing and also retreating. Relatively few prisoners were taken. The whole regiment fought in an extraordinarily courageous and self-sacrificial way."

Striving to put the best gloss on recent events east and north of Passchendaele, the Army Communiqué for 11 November read,

"The cratered landscape between Poelkapelle and Passchendaele was yesterday once more the scene of bitter fighting. The British introduced fresh divisions into the battle with the aim of gaining the heights north of Passchendaele. Widely spaced, their regiments went into action. In the centre of our defensive front they penetrated our defences and stormed the heights they were seeking to take, There they came up against counter-attacks from Pomeranian and West Prussian battalions which threw them back, They renewed their attacks five times but, in the face of our defences, most of them faded away forward of our lines. Wherever the enemy gained ground they were brought down by the infantry with cold steel ... " [44]

Although infantry operations were now scaled right back, the same could not be said for the artillery. Trapped in a narrow salient, the British VIII Corps, which had assumed responsibility for the Passchendaele area from the Canadian Corps, was subject to constant heavy bombardment; partly because the German defenders did not know if further offensive operations were being considered. Major set-piece gas shoots had been a feature of the entire campaign for the German artillery. Now, on 17 November, the last of the series was carried out under the code name *Winterstürme* [Winter Storms]. This was targeted against identified Allied battery positions and was carried out because there was a fear that another major assault might be in the offing. Field Artillery Regiment 20 was one of the regiments involved. Following careful preparation and a large scale ammunition dumping programme, during a two hour timed programme, each four-gun battery fired 700 rounds. Given the conditions under which this was carried out, it was felt to be an outstanding performance and, for once, there was no instant retribution from the Allied guns.[45]

Within two weeks of the battles of 10 November, the focus of attention was moving away from the daily intensity of the battle. It was becoming increasingly clear that there would be no more major assaults in Flanders that year. On 20 November, the very day that British tanks were rolling forward to challenge the Hindenburg Line at the Battle of Cambrai, the commander of Group Wijtschate chose to address a personal communication to the commanders of all battalions and independent sub-units:

Group Wijtschate (Headquarters IX Reserve Corps) Ia No. 8990 Personal, dated 20 November 1917 [46]

> "Recently, the standard of saluting by officers in the Group sector has left a great deal to be desired. It is a rarity to come across junior officers who consider it necessary to salute senior officers first. In many cases the salute itself is extremely sloppy. Some gentlemen do not consider it necessary to take their left hands out of their pockets and others salute, riding crop in hand or with a cigarette between their fingers ... The dreadful discipline on the street of the men is caused to a large extent by the bad example set them by their officers. It is also a consequence of the fact that officers frequently either do not even acknowledge the salutes of the men, or only return them in an extremely perfunctory manner ...
>
> "This is not just a matter of external appearances. Discipline is one of the essential foundations of our successes. It must be maintained to the highest standards by even our most junior officers ... I require all regimental commanders to brief their officers and acquaint them with my instructions ... [and] require all commanders in future to correct immediately any officer who transgresses these rules."

The dying flickers of what the German army referred to as the *Flandernschlacht* and the British, ever after, as Passchendaele, dragged on into early December, despite the fact that the Battle of Cambrai was in full swing further south.

In an effort to maintain the offensive spirit and to give the troops something to think about, other than the vile weather, a full programme of patrolling was maintained. One notable effort by an eight man patrol from 7th Company Infantry Regiment 116, led by Leutnant Bode, penetrated one night as far as the church in Passchendaele. There was not much activity from the British side of No Man's Land, but the artillery on both sides remained extremely active. Command posts and headquarters continued to be sought out and engaged, whilst bombs were dropped on troops at readiness in Mager Merrie on more than one occasion. The British even took advantage of clear moonlit nights to fly over the German positions, bombing and machine gunning them.[47] Inevitably these bombardments took a toll on the defenders; one direct hit on 3rd Company Infantry Regiment 116 on 30 November, for example, killed Reserve Leutnant Wüst, Vizefeldwebel Rothermel and four men outright.[48]

The German defence let out a collective groan when the artillery fire rose to drum fire one last time on 1/2 December, hammering down on the positions of the regiments of 25th Infantry Division from Hessen. The constant artillery fire had already been causing a great many casualties during the weeks since the battles of 10 November, but this latest barrage was almost the last straw for the men of Infantry Regiment 115, whose 2nd Battalion, manning the front line to the east of Passchendaele, was already reduced in strength to a mere one hundred riflemen.[49] The positions that the division had been occupying to the north and east of Passchendaele since 26 November when it relieved 44th Reserve Division were, if anything, more dismal than they had been in mid-November.

There was even more groundwater slopping around in the shell holes and the weather was noticeably colder. A huge effort was being made to equip the front line troops with the so-called 'Siegfried Shelters.'[50] These structures comprised eight to ten sheets of bent corrugated iron bolted together on a flat base, reinforced with steel pillars and covered with earth one metre thick. These rough field constructions provided rudimentary shelters for four to six men. They were largely splinter-proof and weather-proof. Placed against the remnants of hedges, bushes or buildings, they were difficult to spot, even from the air, and proved to be very useful through the winter but, by early December, there were still relatively few of them and most of the defenders were still clinging on to their lines in the open and completely unprotected.

There was a sudden increase in the rate of fire at 3.00 am on 2 December all along the line north and south of Passchendaele then, only fifteen minutes later, two British brigades attacked in four or five waves against Groups Staden and Ypres. The outpost zone was quickly overrun and at one point the attackers penetrated swiftly into the main defensive positions at the boundary between the right flank of Infantry Regiment 116 and the left flank of Infantry Regiment 117. In the darkness, 2nd Company Infantry Regiment 116 and 9th Company Infantry Regiment 117 were soon engaged in a desperate hand-to-hand battle, which cost the lives of the two company commanders, Reserve Leutnants Schade[51] and Fuchs. Despite the efforts of these two companies, the attackers pressed on, expanding the break in.

At 3.45 am, Leutnant Fuchs' batman rushed into the command post of Hauptmann von Arnim, commanding officer and *KTK* of Infantry Regiment 117. Breathlessly, he gasped out the news: 'The left hand platoon of 9th Company has been attacked. Leutnant Fuchs has been killed, shot through the heart at point blank range. Unteroffizier Balz smashed the British soldier's skull in, but in the same instant he was shot in the stomach and mortally wounded. It was the same everywhere. The British have broken in on a broad front.'[52] Despite considerable confusion, both regiments took immediate action to secure the shoulders of the break-in, to rush forward troops to seal the breach and to conduct immediate counter-attacks. Hauptmann von Arnim despatched one platoon of 1st Machine Gun Company Infantry Regiment 117 to set up a blocking position and sent 4th Company forward to counter-attack. Trying to get forward in the pitch black night, through the trackless crater field and in heavy rain, was almost beyond the capacity of the soldiers, loaded down as they were with machine guns and other heavy equipment.

Eventually, about fifteen to twenty of them arrived at the breakthrough point. A counter-attack was out of the question, but the British gains were sealed off as more men came trickling in. In the meantime, Infantry Regiment 116 had reacted by also placing five machine guns and some riflemen in a blocking position and launching its own 4th Company forward. Reserves, comprising 7th and 8th Companies Infantry Regiment 116, were called forward from Mager Merrie to the *KTK* but, running into barrage fire on the way, ten men and the company commander of 8th Company, Leutnant Meier, were killed.[53] Forward, the counter-attack made slow progress, with heavy casualties on both sides. As it became light, it was clear (to the Germans at least) that the position of the defenders was extremely precarious. Stretcherbearers from both sides moved into the area of the breakthrough and began to recover the wounded. The Germans stretcher bearers were quick to inform their commanders that there were about 150 British troops occupying the area, with a good many more ranged behind them. Despite this considerable local superiority, there was no reaction when Gefreiter Spieß of 9th Company Infantry Regiment 117 led eight prisoners away.[54]

Taking this as an indication that no further offensive action was likely, at least for the time being, Hauptmann von Arnim raced back to organise a systematic counter-attack, leaving Vizefeldwebel Woeste of 2nd Company in charge. Noticing that the British were being driven back by 4th Company Infantry Regiment 116, Woeste seized his opportunity about midday and launched an all-out attack with the few men he had left. The British withdrew hurriedly and a number of them were taken prisoner. The breach was sealed along the original line and contact was regained with 9th Company Infantry Regiment 116. It was not quite the end of the story. There were exchanges of artillery fire during the afternoon, then the British launched another attack at last light about 5.00 pm. It was driven back after further heavy, close-quarter fighting and a further attempt to renew the attack on 3 December also failed. Completely exhausted, the survivors of the 25th Division were relieved by 16th Infantry Division that same night. Finally, the long drawn out agony was at an end. It was a time for reflection; for drawing lines beneath one of the most ghastly episodes of the entire twentieth century.

Two days later, the army group published an order for distribution throughout the formations and units that had fought in Flanders.

Special Order of the Day Army Group Crown Prince Rupprecht 5 December 1917 [55]

"The major battle in Flanders appears to be over. In consequence the moment has arrived for me to express my thanks and recognition to all commanders and troops who participated in the Battle of Flanders. Eighty six divisions, twenty two of which carried out two tours of duty, the greater majority of all our army artillery formations and other arms and services took part in this, the most violent of all battles fought to date. The sons of all branches of the German race have, through their heroic courage and tough endurance, succeeded in wrecking the attempts at breakthrough by the British and French, which aimed at the conquest of Flanders and our U Boats.

"Despite the deployment of immense quantities of men and materiel, the enemy achieved absolutely nothing. A narrow, utterly smashed strip of ground represents his entire gain. He has bought this outcome at the cost of extraordinarily heavy casualties; whereas our losses were far fewer than for any previous defensive battle. As a result the Battle of Flanders has been a serious defeat for our opponents and a great victory for us. Whoever was there can be proud to be a Flanders soldier. Each individual man may be assured that he has the thanks of the Fatherland. It was only because our Flanders front withstood every attack that was launched at it, that we were able to conduct massive blows against the Russians in the east and the Italians in the south.

"My special thanks go to the command structure of the army in Flanders, to the commander of Fourth Army [General der Infanterie Sixt von Armin] and his tried and tested chief of staff [Oberst von Loßberg], whose strength of will, and sharply focussed tactical and organisational measures made a decisive contribution to the successful outcome of the battle. But I must also express my thanks to the other armies within the Army Group. They have sacrificially kept their demands to a minimum, offered up the maximum number of forces and accepted the most serious difficulties; all in order to assist those fighting in Flanders.

"Let our enemies gird themselves up for fresh assaults! We shall be well aware how to counter them.[56]

The Commander in Chief
Rupprecht, Crown Prince of Bavaria, Field Marshal"

The British army took heavy casualties during the campaign. Particularly controversial was the fact that a very high proportion of them occurred during the six weeks from 1st October when, despite the tactical success of 'bite and hold', the appalling weather and the narrowing of the frontage under attack meant that the attackers presented ever more attractive targets for the German artillery and the law of diminishing returns began to apply. Contrary to popular belief, the attackers still lost heavily during these limited-scope operations. There were, for example, approximately 20,000 casualties from the first day of the well-prepared Battle of the Menin Road (20-25 September). The British War Cabinet was greatly exercised by these heavy losses and it took the decision to retain in the United Kingdom, during the winter and early spring of 1918, its plentiful manpower reserves, in order to prevent them from being used in further offensive operations. They were to be sorely missed when, in April 1918, the German army took back in three days what the British army had spent several painful months the previous year trying to gain.

But the German army had suffered severely as well. Writing in May 1917 in the wake of the Battle of Arras, in his report to the chief of staff of Sixth Army, Oberstleutnant Otto von Lossow, chief of staff to I Bavarian Reserve Corps, was already under no illusions about the precarious nature of the German manpower reserves. Reflecting a widely-held view, he stated, 'The wastage of manpower, such as occurred on the Somme, certainly cannot be repeated this year without seriously endangering the ability of Germany to wage war and without bringing about the exhaustion towards which the enemy is aiming through his massive deployment of men and steel.'[57] This is precisely what the costly offensive in Flanders had caused so, regardless of the absolute figures for German casualties, the fact of the matter was that they were completely unsustainable over time – especially with the Americans flooding into the European theatre in ever greater numbers.

There has always been sharp controversy about the number of casualties each side suffered during the Passchendaele campaign, much of it stoked up by attempts to inflate one or other set of figures and to extrapolate from these shaky foundations, who 'won' or 'lost'. The compilers of the British Official History were notorious for their creative accounting in this respect. Brigadier General Sir James Edmonds, writing in *Military Operations France and Belgium 1916: 2nd July to the End of the*

Battles of the Somme, which was published in 1938, exaggerated German losses during that battle in a manner which has been widely discredited since. It is just possible to understand that assessment, because Edmonds does not seem to have made use of a key text which became available in Germany in 1934; namely the *Sanitätsbericht über das Deutsche Heer im Weltkriege 1914/1918* [Medical Report concerning the German Army 1914/1918], which was published in three volumes in Berlin by Mittler & Sohn in 1934.

However, the accounting for German casualties in *Military Operations France and Belgium 1917 Volume II 7th June – 10th November Messines and Third Ypres (Passchendaele)*, published in 1948, contains equally cavalier handling of the facts and here the plot thickens. At page 362, is stated, 'The German casualty figures have never been divulged. They must be conjectured.' However, the bibliography of the above volume of the British Official History contains, at page xxxvi, a mention of the *Sanitätsbericht*, but only Volumes I and II. Edmonds writes that this is, 'The official report on the German medical service in two volumes. Volume I deals with general organization; Volume II with the field forces and armies of occupation year by year and Army by Army in the different theatres. Percentages but few absolute figures are given.' It is difficult to know what would have caused Edmonds to write this, because the report appeared in *three volumes*, fourteen years before Edmonds published the Passchendaele volume and Volume III deals mainly with exact figures, derived from analysis of the casualty returns produced throughout the war every ten days.

Whatever he states or omits, Edmonds should have known of the existence of this volume, because there is a prominent note on the title page of Volume III stating, 'The index for Volumes I-III is to be found in Volume II.' We shall probably never know for sure what possible motivation he had for thus ignoring readily available facts and figures, but it is hard to escape the conclusion that the information was not used, because it did not suit the case he was trying to make. Had he chosen to refer to Table 47 on page 55 of Volume III, entitled, 'Losses sustained by Fourth Army in the Western Theatre of Operations from 21 May to 10 December (Battle of Flanders), according to the Troop Casualty Reports' he would have been presented with a very useful summary of the facts, which would have enabled him, for example, to draw a comparison of sick rates, which might have been in his favour. According to the British Official History, at page 361, 'there was very little sickness in Flanders … Most of the patients were treated in divisional or corps rest stations, although an average of 0.3 – 1 percent of strength had to be evacuated to the base' On the other hand, according to Table 47, of an average daily ration strength of Fourth Army of 609,035, 14,943 men, or 2.45 per cent, were evacuated sick in each ten day period and there were, inevitably, occasions when the figure went higher.

Be that as it may, the figures of killed, wounded or missing, which are the normal measures of casualty rates, for Fourth Army for the entire Table 47 period (i.e. forty days longer than the dates Edmonds was using), work out as follows: killed 32,878, missing (killed and captured) 38,083, wounded and evacuated 165,280. For the period 7 June to 10 November it would be possible to get close to Edmond's assertion of 400,000 casualties (British Official History page 363), but it would be necessary to include all men with minor cuts and wounds, who were treated in the forward areas by unit medical officers and those who reported sick and were given 'medicine and duties.'[58] The worst fatal casualties were sustained during the ten day period which included the Battle of Messines (10,374 killed and missing, 12,614 wounded) and the second worst, the first ten days of October (9,034 killed and missing, 14,217 wounded). Interesting though these figures are, they are, in themselves, irrelevant. The German army knew before the battle that it could not afford to lose serious quantities of manpower, or have its freedom of action constrained by having to fight yet another battle on ground of the Allies choosing, but it happened and its significance was fully acknowledged after the war by General von Kuhl.

General der Infanterie Hermann von Kuhl *Chief of Staff Army Group Crown Prince Rupprecht* [59]

"It would be quite wrong to deny the British credit for the courage with which they fought and for the obstinate way they brushed aside the heaviest casualties and kept renewing their assaults. It would be equally wrong to suggest that there was any possibility that they might have broken through. The fact that, despite this, they continued their offensive was justified by the British on the basis of the overall situation. After the total collapse of the Russian offensive in July, the Russian army as a fighting force had fallen completely out of the picture. The Italian front was in complete tatters in October. Above all, the hitting power of the French, after the failure of the offensives on the Aisne and in Champagne, followed by the mutinies and internal disturbances was so greatly reduced that they urgently needed relief.

"The United States was still not in a position to do anything. The one and only army capable of offensive action was that of the British. If they had broken off their offensive, the German army would have seized the initiative and attacked the Allies where they were weak. To that end it would have been possible to have withdrawn strong forces from the east after the collapse of the Russians.[60] For these reasons the British had to go on attacking until the onset of winter ruled out a German counter-attack.

"Today, now that we are fully aware about the critical situation in which the French army found itself during the summer of 1917, there can be absolutely no doubt that *through its tenacity, the British army bridged the crisis in France.*[61] The French army gained time to recover its strength; the German reserves were drawn towards Flanders. The sacrifices that the British made for the Entente were fully justified."

The Passchendaele campaign may have fixed the German army in Flanders, it may indeed have seemed at times like von Kuhl's, 'The greatest martyrdom of the war'[62] but, despite all that, there was a feeling that there had been a job to do, that it was duly done and done well.

Reserve Hauptmann Chapeaurouge 1st Battalion Reserve Infantry Regiment 94 [63]

"There was no daredevil, 'up and at 'em' spirit in Flanders and smiling successes were not to be expected either. Warfare in Flanders was conducted in a tense and serious atmosphere. What was quietly done and achieved there and how much was suffered is not the stuff of ephemeral entertainment, rather it formed a fleeting page in the annals of the German army; one which need not fear any comparison with other proud, shining feats of arms of ours. It writes a new page in the history of our people, one to which all strands and levels of our society have contributed. It tells of faithful comradeship-in-arms through danger and unto death; of the noblest characteristics of our German race and carries with it the hope that out of all the petty ugliness and squabbles of the here and now, this war will, in the end, deliver to our people richer blessings appropriate to the coming years of peace."

First Quartermaster General Erich Ludendorff [64]

"Extraordinary quantities of ammunition, far beyond anything imaginable before the war, were launched at men who were eking out a miserable existence, scattered around in deep mud-filled craters … That was no longer living; that was simply unspeakable suffering. Then, out of the world of mud, the attacks would come in; slowly, it is true, but constantly and in great strength. Hammered by us in the forward area with hails of fire, these attacks often collapsed and the lonely man in the crater field could breathe a sigh of relief. But the masses kept coming. Rifles and machine guns became clogged with mud, but battle would still be joined, hand to hand – and, all too often, the mass prevailed.

"That which the German soldier performed, experienced and suffered during the Battle of Flanders will stand for all time as a brazen monument to him: one which he himself constructed on the territory of the enemy!"

Bent and battered, but by no means broken and helped by the weather, the German army had once more been equal to the defensive challenge it faced from enemies with their sights set on objectives of strategic importance, but who were no closer to a breakthrough in November than they had been in July. It was a considerable achievement against the odds and the sodden *Feldgrauen*, shivering and freezing in their water-filled shell holes that hard winter 1917-1918, had no reason to be ashamed of their efforts.

Ein ruheloser Marsch war unser Leben
Und, wie des Windes Sausen, heimatlos,
Durchstürmten wir die Kriegbewegte Erde

Our life was one long restless march
And, like the soughing of the wind, homeless,
We fought our way through the war-torn world.

Schiller[65]

Notes
1. Von Kuhl: *Der Weltkrieg 1914/18 Band II* p 131
2. Duncker: History Infantry Regiment 49 pp 235-238
3. Kronprinz Rupprecht: *Mein Kriegstagebuch II. Band* p 281
4. *ibid.* p 284 In fact subsequent investigations revealed that the transportation of these particular reinforcements had been grossly mishandled. They had not been equipped for the five day journey.. They were moved in unheated coaches, often with broken windows, and some did not even have coats. There were no proper arrangements for them to be fed or given drinks during the journey. Many were men over forty five years of age, who had been assured that they would not be sent to fighting units in the west. It was a sorry tale of incompetence in an army which normally prided itself on its administrative efficiency.
5. Naturally operations, including those conducted by the French army, continued unabated on the flanks, but the most important fighting during November took place in the Passchendaele area, so that is the focus of this chapter.
6. Westerkamp: History Field Artillery Regiment 62 pp192-195
7. The faces would more probably have been Canadian at that time and place.
8. Steuer: History Infantry Regiment 132 p 328
9. Wegener: History Infantry Regiment 172 p 208
10. Glück: History Infantry Regiment 126 p 265
11. Leutnants Otto Fusch and Günther Weiss are buried near to one another in the German cemetery at Menen Block C Graves 1280 and 1269 respectively.
12. Steuer: History Infantry Regiment 132 p 333
13. *ibid.* p 333
14. *ibid.* p 335
15. *ibid.* pp 336-337
16. Burchardi: History Fusilier Regiment 38 pp 330-331
17. Nollau: History Infantry Regiment 51 p 205
18. Burchardi: *op. cit.* pp 332-333

19. Boesser: History Reserve Field Artillery Regiment 44 p 331

20. Burchardi: *op.cit.* pp 335-337

21. Hauptmann Herbert Ulrich is buried in the German cemetery at Menen Block H Grave 1451.

22. In all probability these were the men of Fusilier Regiment 38 who had broken earlier.

23. Mülmann: History Lehr Infantry Regiment p 431

24. Schulenburg-Wolfsburg: History Garde-Fusilier-Regiment p 188

25. Schütz: History Grenadier Regiment 10 p 217

26. All three officers are buried in the German cemetery at Menen. Leutnant Kurt Schaefer lies in Block G Grave 3218, Leutnant Walter Steffler in Block G Grave 1238 and Leutnant Alfred Thomas in Block M Grave 3217. Of the missing officers, only the whereabouts of Offizierstellvertreter Friedrich Gleisberg is known. He is buried in the *Kameradengrab* of the German cemetery at Langemark.

27. Kronprinz Rupprecht: *op. cit.* pp 282-283

28. Boesser: *op.cit.* p 332

29. Appel: History Reserve Infantry Regiment 205 p 198

30. Haleck: History Reserve Infantry Regiment 208 p 75

31. Appel: *op.cit.* p 199

32. His captors drew the right conclusion, but for the wrong reason. The 2nd Canadian Division had been responsible for the capture of Passchendaele on 6 November. If the prisoner's story was true, he must have been left out of battle earlier for some unknown reason.

33. Haleck: *op. cit.* pp 75-76

34. Appel: *op. cit.* p 201

35. Schoenfelder: History Field Artillery Regiment 2 pp 212-214. Despite his wound, Wennrich was only away from his battery for fourteen days.

36. Schoenfelder: *op.cit.* p 215

37. Appel: *op. cit.* p 200

38. Duncker: *op. cit.* p 243

39. Kronprinz Rupprecht: *op. cit.* p 283

40. Mülmann: History Infantry Regiment 140 pp 163-165

41. '1442' is an example of reference point overprinted on German trench maps. These simplified the passing of locations; *viz. '200 metres west of 1442'*. It was also a simple matter to encode this information by adding to, or subtracting from, the printed number, a daily changing figure. For example, on 10 November 1917, the figure might have been +1003, so all references to 1442 would have been passed as 2445. The level of security thus provided would have been low but, in the prevailing conditions, was certainly better than nothing and the most that could have been hoped for.

42. This counter-attack occurred at a timely moment, just as 2nd Battalion Royal Munster Fusiliers, one of the leading units of 3 Brigade of 1st British Division, was in the process of pushing forward onto the hill where the *Nordhof* stood. See McCarthy *Passchendaele* p 139

43. According to Duncker *op. cit.* p 244, Hauptmann von Döhrenof Infantry Regiment 49 had also ordered a counter-attack, so the probability is that the *Nordhof* was counter-attacked by elements of both regiments.

44. Duncker: *op. cit.* p 245

45. Benary: History Field Artillery Regiment 20 p 325
46. Kriegsarchiv München: R. Pi.Kp. 17 Bd 3
47. Ludwigsdorff: History Infantry Regiment 115 p 163
48. Leutnant Heinrich Wüst is buried in the German cemetery at Menen Block C Grave 993, but the remains of Vizefeldwebel Erich Rothermel were repatriated to Germany. He is buried in Block 1 of the war cemetery in Bischofsheim.
49. Ludwigsdorff: *op. cit.* p 164
50. Hiß: History Infantry Regiment 116 p 157
51. Leutnant August Fuchs is buried in the German cemetery at Menen Block H Grave 1457
52. Offenbacher: History Infantry Regiment 117 p 195
53. Leutnant Richard Meier is buried in the German cemetery at Menen Block C Grave 965
54. Offenbacher: *op.cit.* p 196
55. Stosch: History Footguard Regiment 5 pp 354-355
56. Connoisseurs of Orders of the Day following major battles may care to compare this one with that produced by army group headquarters following the Battle of the Somme and quoted on pp 395-396 of *The German Army on the Somme 1914-1916* (Jack Sheldon, Pen & Sword Ltd 2005). The need to draft the order must have had the staff reaching for the files from the previous year. The format is identical and much of the content is repeated virtually verbatim. From 'Operations appear to have come to a halt in the Battle of the Somme' / 'The major battle in Flanders seems to be over,' via 'The only gain being a narrow strip of utterly ruined terrain' (Somme) / 'A narrow, utterly smashed strip of ground represents his entire gain' (Passchendaele) and 'Everyone who was there can be proud to have been a warrior of the Somme' / 'Whoever was there can be proud to be a Flanders soldier', followed by 'Each individual man may be assured that he has the thanks of the Fatherland' (Somme and Passchendaele), the same phrases leap up off the page repeatedly. The other armies are thanked for their sacrifices and the army group commander looks forward to new challenges. Cynics may feel that few of the men who read the order after the Somme would have been in a position to do the same after Passchendaele, but it would probably be unfair to assume that Crown Prince Rupprecht was only going through the motions. He had every reason to be proud of his men and what they had achieved and was too much of a gentleman not to thank them sincerely.
57. Kriegsarchiv München: HGr Rupprecht Bd 93
58. If casualties before 1 June and after 10 November 1917 are excluded, the corrected figures are: killed or missing 67,272; wounded 149,922. This means that, by their reckoning, the Fourth Army battle casualties attributable to the period 1 June – 10 November 1917 are 67,272 + 149,922 = 217,194. If the 182,396 slightly wounded and sick, who were not struck off unit strength, are included, the total rises to 399,590. Note that those sick and medically evacuated are not included. The debate really comes down to the question, 'When is a casualty not a casualty?' The German reply would be, 'When he does not leave his unit' – especially because the group that Edmonds included in his version of the casualty figures was officially described in the *Sanitätsbericht* as *dienstfähig* [able to carry out their duties]. It is hard to see any merit in insisting that a man remaining with his unit and capable of carrying out his duties, must be regarded as a battle casualty of the same significance as someone evacuated with serious or life-threatening injuries.
59. Von Kuhl: *op. cit.* p 126

60. This is presumably because transport would have been freed up for the purpose.
61. Original emphasis.
62. Von Kuhl: *op.cit.* p 129
63. Richter: History Reserve Infantry Regiment 94 p 274
64. Ludendorff: *Meine Kriegserinnerungen* pp 391-392
65. The quotation is from Act 3 Scene 15 of *Wallensteins Tod* [The death of Wallenstein] by Friedrich von Schiller (1759 – 1805).

German – British
Comparison of Ranks

Generalfeldmarschall	Field Marshal
General der Infanterie	General of Infantry ⎫ General
General der Kavallerie	General of Cavalry ⎬

N.B. The holder of any of these last two ranks was at least a corps commander and might have been an army commander.

Generalleutnant	Lieutenant General.

N.B. The holder of this rank could be the commander of a formation ranging in size from a brigade to a corps. From 1732 onwards Prussian officers of the rank of Generalleutnant or higher, who had sufficient seniority, were referred to as 'Exzellenz' [Excellency].

Generalmajor	Major General
Oberst	Colonel
Oberstleutnant	Lieutenant Colonel
Major	Major
Hauptmann	Captain
Rittmeister	Captain (mounted unit such as cavalry, horse artillery or transport) It was also retained by officers of this seniority serving with the German Flying Corps
Oberleutnant	Lieutenant
Leutnant	Second Lieutenant
Feldwebelleutnant	Sergeant Major Lieutenant
Offizierstellvertreter	Officer Deputy

N.B. This was an appointment, rather than a substantive rank.

Feldwebel	Sergeant Major
Wachtmeister	Sergeant Major (mounted unit)
Vizefeldwebel	Staff Sergeant
Vizewachtmeister	Staff Sergeant (mounted unit)
Sergeant	Sergeant

Unteroffizier	Corporal
Korporal	Corporal (Bavarian units)
Gefreiter	Lance Corporal
Musketier	
Grenadier	
Garde-Füsilier	
Füsilier	
Schütze	N.B. These ranks all equate to Private Soldier
Infanterist	(infantry). The differences in nomenclature are due
Jäger	to tradition, the type of unit involved, or the class of
Wehrmann	conscript to which the individual belonged.
Landsturmmann	
Soldat	
Ersatz-Reservist	

Kriegsfreiwilliger	Wartime Volunteer. This equates to Private Soldier.
Kanonier	Gunner
Pionier	Sapper N.B. These ranks all
Fahrer	Driver equate to Private Soldier.
Hornist	Trumpeter
Tambour	Drummer

Medical Personnel

Oberstabsarzt	Major (or higher)
Stabsarzt	Captain
Oberarzt	Lieutenant
Assistenzarzt	Second Lieutenant

N.B. These individuals were also referred to by their appointments; for example, Bataillonsarzt or Regimentsarzt [Battalion or Regimental Medical Officer]. Such usage, which varied in the different contingents which made up the imperial German army, is no indicator of rank.

Sanitäter	Medical Assistant N.B. These two ranks both
Krankenträger	Stretcherbearer equate to Private Soldier.

Frequently the prefix 'Sanitäts-' appears in front of a normal NCO rank, such as Gefreiter or Unteroffizier. This simply indicates that a man of that particular seniority was part of the medical services.

Bibliography

Unpublished Sources

Kriegsarchiv München

HGr. Rupprecht Bd 93:	Generalkommando I Bayer. Res. Corps Chef des Stabes No. 15290 12.4.17 'Gedanken ueber die Ursachen der englischen Erfolge vom 9.4 u. ueber etwaige Abhilfe.'
HGr. Rupprecht Bd 93:	Chef des Generalstabes des Feldheeres 1a. Nr. 67059 op. Gr. H. Qu., den 9. Oktober 1917
HGr. Rupprecht Bd 125:	Wochenmeldungen 01 – 05 1917
Gen Kdo III AK Bd 26:	Reserve Infantry Regiment 90 Gefechtsbericht über den 10 VIII 17, den 13 VIII 1917
Gen Kdo III AK Bd 26:	Heeresgruppe Kronprinz Rupprecht Ic No. 31500, 30.10.17
Gen Kdo III AK Bd 26/27:	Gruppe Ieperen Ia Nr. 29658 'Beurteilung der Lage und Kampfwert' von 2.8.917
Gen Kdo III AK Bd 83:	'Heeresbericht'. Großes Hauptquartier, den 8. Juni 1917
Gen Kdo III AK Bd 83:	Gruppe Ieperen (Gen. Kdo. III B.A.K.) 'Nachrichtenblatt für 31.7.1917', Gr.H.Qu., 1.8.1917
Gen Kdo III AK Bd 100:	Gruppe Ieperen (Gen. Kdo. III B.A.K.) 'Vorderste Linie' Ia Nr. 26341 von 20.6.17
Gen Kdo III AK Bd 135:	Heeresgruppe Kronprinz Rupprecht Lagemeldungen 01 – 05 1917.
Pi Btl 17 Bd 9:	Vernehmung von Gefangenen der 7. Division gefangen genommen am 26.10.17 durch 24.I.D und 15 I.D. westlich Geluvelt, beiderseits Strasse Menen-Ieperen
R Pi Kp 17 Bd 3:	Gruppe Wijtschate (Generalkommando IX. Res. Korps) Ia No. 8990 persönlich H.Qu. 20.11.1917
Nachlaß: Paul von Kneußl	Tagebuch Nr. 15

Printed Works (German: author known)

Appel Dr Friedrich *Das Reserve-Infanterie-Regt. Nr. 205 im Weltkrieg* Berlin 1937

Balck Generalleutnant W *Entwicklung der Taktik im Weltkriege* Berlin 1920

Benary Oberstleutnant a.D. *Königlich Preußisches 1. Posensches Feldartillerie-Regiment Nr. 20* Berlin 1932

Beumelberg Werner *Flandern 1917* Oldenburg 1928

Bezzel Oberst a.D. Dr. Oskar *Das Königlich Bayerische Reserve-Infanterie-Regiment Nr. 6* München 1938

Blankenstein Oberleutnant a.D. Archivrat Dr. *Geschichte des Reserve-Infanterie-Regiments Nr. 92 im Weltkriege 1914–1918* Osnabrück 1934

Boesser Oberstleutnant a.D. Karl *Geschichte des Reserve-Feldartillerie-Regiments Nr. 44* Berlin 1932

Bölsche Arnold *Sturmflut: Das Erleben des 7. Thür. Infanterie-Regiments Nr 96 im Weltkrieg* Zeulenroda 1935

Brandes Ltn. d. Res. Heinz *Geschichte des Kgl. Preuß. Infanterie-Regiments v. Voigts-Rhetz (3. Hannov.) Nr. 79 im Weltkrieg 1914-1918* Hildesheim

Brauch Dr. Karl *Erinnerungsbuch des Ersatz-Infanterie-Regiments Nr. 28 Weltkrieg 1914/18* Mannheim 1936

Braun Generalmajor Julius Ritter von *Das K.B. Reserve-Infanterie-Regiment Nr. 21* München 1923

Brendler Leutnant der Reserve Wilhelm *Kriegserlebnisse 1914 bis 1918 im Reserve-Infanterie-Regiment 233* Zeulenroda 1929

Bülowius Hauptmann a.D. Alfred and Hippler Hauptmann Bruno *Das Infanterie-Regiment v. Boyen (5. Ostpreßisches) Nr. 41 im Weltkriege 1914-1918* Berlin 1929

Burchardi Oberst a.D. Karl *Das Füsilier-Regiment Generalfeldmarschall Graf Moltke (Schlesisches) Nr. 38* Oldenburg 1928

Christian Leutnant d.R. Karl *Das Heldenbuch vom Infanterie-Regiment 418* Frankfurt 1935

Collenberg Oberstleutnant a.D. Karl Freiherr Rudt von *Das 3. Garde-Feldartillerie-Regiment Seine Geschichte* Berlin 1931

Cron Oberstleutnant a.D. Hermann *Infanterie-Regiment Markgraf Karl (7. Brandenburgisches) Nr. 60 in dem großen Kriege 1914-1918* Berlin 1926

Dahlmann Hauptmann a.D. Reinhold *Reserve-Infanterie-Regiment Nr. 27 im Weltkriege 1914/1918* Berlin 1934

Delmensingen General der Artillerie Kraft von and Feeser Generalmajor a.D. Friedrichfranz *Das Bayernbuch vom Weltkriege 1914-1918* Stuttgart 1930

Dieterich Generalleutnant a.D. Alfred *Geschichte des Grenadierregiments König Friedrich der Große (3. Ostpreußischen) Nr. 4* Berlin 1928

Duncker Oberleutnant d.R. a.D. Hans and Eisermann Oberleutnant d.R. a.D. Heinrich *Das Infanterie-Regiment v. Kluck (6. Pomm.) Nr. 49 im Weltkriege 1914-1918* Oldenburg 1927

Dunzinger Hauptmann a.D. Albert *Das K.B. 11. Infanterie-Regiment von der Tann* München 1921

Foerstner Wolfgang *Wir Kämpfer im Weltkrieg* Berlin 1929

Forstner Major a.D. Kurt Freiherr von *Das Königlich-Preußische Reserve-Infanterie-Regiment Nr. 15 2. Band* Zeulenroda 1931

Fromm Oberst a.D. *Das Württembergische Reserve-Infanterie-Regiment Nr. 120 im Weltkrieg 1914-1918* Stuttgart 1920

Gerth Leutnant d. Reserve Max *Geschichte des Infanterie-Regiments Nr. 395* Dessau 1933

Glück Generalmajor a.D. & Wald Generalmajor a.D. *Das 8. Württembergische Infanterie-Regiment Nr. 126 Großherzog Friedrich von Baden im Weltkrieg 1914-1918* Stuttgart 1929

Goetze Generalmajor a.D. von *Das Marine-Infanterie-Regiment 2 im Weltkriege 1914/18* Oldenburg 1926

Gottberg Kgl. Pr. Generalmajor a.D. Döring von *Das Infanterie-Regiment Nr. 465 im Weltkriege* Osnabrück

Großmann Generalleutnant a.D. August *Das K.B. Reserve-Infanterie-Regiment Nr. 17* Munich 1923

Hansch Oberleutnant Johannes and Weidling Leutnant Dr. Fritz *Das Colbergsche Grenadier-Regiment Graf Gneisenau (2. Pommersches) Nr. 9 im Weltkriege 1914-1918* Berlin 1929

Hartmann Hauptmann Alexander von *Das Infanterie-Regiment Großherzog von Sachsen (5. Thüringisches) Nr. 94 im Weltkrieg* Berlin 1921

Heinicke Lt. d. Res. a.D. Karl and Bethge Lt. d. Res. a.D. Bruno *Das Reserve-Infanterie-Regiment Nr. 263 in Ost und West* Oldenburg 1926

Henke Oberstleutnant a.D. Carl *Das 1. Westfälische Feldartillerie-Regiment Nr. 7 1816 – 1919* Berlin 1928

Hiß Prof. Albert *Infanterie-Regiment Kaiser Wilhelm (2. Großherzoglich Hessisches) Nr 116* Oldenburg 1924

Hoffmann Generalmajor a.D. Traugott and Hahn Oberstleutnant a.D. Ernst *Geschichte des Infanterie-Regiments Graf Dönhoff (7. Ostpreußischen) Nr. 44 1860 – 1918* Berlin 1930

Hülsemann Oberstleutnant a.D. *Geschichte des Infanterie-Regiments von Manstein (Schleswigsches) Nr. 84 1914 – 1918 4. Folge* Hamburg 1922-23

Jordan Generalleutnant a.D. *Die Geschichte des Feldartillerie-Regiments Nr. 95* Zeulenroda 1936

Jürgensen Leutnant d.R Dr. Wilhelm *Das Füsilier-Regiment 'Königin' Nr. 86 im Weltkriege* Oldenburg 1926

Kees Oberleutnant d. Res. Dr. Hermann *Das Kgl. Sächs. Feldartillerie-Regiment Nr. 115* Leipzig 1934

Kellinghusen Hauptmann d. Res. Wilhelm *Kriegserinnerungen* Bergedorf 1933

Kessler Major a.D. Wilhelm *Das Königl. Preuß. Res.-Feldartillerie-Regiment Nr. 9* Berlin 1938

Kinder Leutnant d.R. a.D. Theodor *Das Marine-Infanterie-Regiment 1 1914-1918* Kiel 1933

Klähn Leutnant d. Res. Friedrich *Geschichte des Reserve-Infanterie-Regiments Nr. 86 im Weltkriege* Oldenburg 1925

Kohl Leutnant d.Res. a.D. Hermann *Mit Hurra in den Tod! Kriegserlebnisse eines Frontsoldaten 17. bayer. Infanterie-Regiment 'Orff'* Stuttgart 1932

Kuhl General d.Inf. a.D. Hermann v. *Der Weltkrieg 1914-1918 Band II* Berlin 1929

Kümmel Leutnant d.Res. a.D. Adolf *Res.-Inf.-Regt. Nr. 91 im Weltkriege 1914-1918* Oldenburg 1926

Laeger Oberleutnant a.D. Alfred *Das Feldartillerie-Regiment 'Prinz August von Preußen' (1 Litth.) Nr. 1 1772-1919* Zeulenroda 1939

Lennartz Oberstleutnant d. Sch a.D. J. *Geschichte des badischen (später rheinischen) Reserve-Infanterie-Regiments 240* Zeulenroda 1938

Liedtke Major d.Res. a.D. Prof. *Das Füsilier-Regiment Graf Roon (Ostpreußisches) Nr. 33 im Weltkriege 1914/1918* Berlin 1935

Ludendorff Erich *Meine Kriegserinnerungen 1914-1918* Berlin 1919

Ludwigsdorff Oberleutnant Alex-Victor von Frankenberg und *Das Leibgarde-Infanterie-Regiment Nr. 115* Stuttgart 1921

Makoben Reserve Leutnant Ernst *Geschichte des Reserve-Infanterie-Regiments Nr. 212 im Weltkriege 1914-1918* Oldenburg 1933

Martin Leutnant d.R a.D. Dr. A. *Das Königl. Sächs. Grenadier-Reserve-Regiment Nr. 100* Dresden 1924

Menges Oberstleutnant a.D. Ludwig von *Kriegsgeschichte des Königl.Preuß. Reserve-Jäger-Bataillons Nr. 4* Oldenburg 1927

Möller Hanns *Königlich Preußisches Reserve-Infanterie-Regiment Nr. 78 im Weltkrieg 1914/1918* Berlin 1937

Moser Generalleutnant Otto von *Die Württemberger im Weltkrieg* Stuttgart 1928

Müller-Loebnitz Oberstleutnant Wilhelm *Die Badener im Weltkrieg* Karlsruhe 1935

Mülmann Oberst a.D. Paul von *Geschichte des Westpreußischen Infanterie-Regiments Nr 140.* Berlin 1930

Mülmann Oberst Paul von & Mohs Oberleutnant *Geschichte des Lehr-Infanterie-Regiments und seiner Stammformationen* Zeulenroda 1935

Niebelschütz Major Günther von *Reserve-Infanterie-Regiment Nr. 230* Oldenburg 1926

Niemann Oberstlt. a.D. Johannes *Das 9. Königlich-Sächsische Infanterie-Regiment Nr 133 im Weltkrieg 1914-18* Hamburg 1969

Nollau Oberstleutnant a.D. Herbert *Geschichte des Königlich Preußischen 4. Niederschlesischen Infanterie-Regiments Nr. 51* Berlin 1931

Offenbächer Hauptmann Kurt *Die Geschichte des Infanterie-Leibregiments*

Großherzogin (3. Großherzoglich Hessisches) Nr. 117 Oldenburg 1931

Pafferath Leutnant der Reserve a.D. Fritz *Die Geschichte des 6. Rheinischen Infanterie-Regiments N. 68 im Weltkriege 1914-1918* Berlin 1930

Partzsch Oberst a.D. *Das Kgl. Sächs. 3. Feld-Artillerie-Regiment Nr. 32* Dresden 1939

Pirscher Oberst a.D. Friedrich von *Das (rheinisch-westfälische) Infanterie-Regiment Nr. 459* Oldenburg 1926

Pflugbeil Hauptmann Hanns *Das Kgl. Sächs. 15. Infanterie-Regiment Nr. 181* Dresden 1923

Plagenz Leutnant d.L. Otto *Feldzugs-Erinnerungen des Infanterie-Regiments 452* privately published 1919

Preusser Major a.D. Wilhelm *Das 9. Westpreußische Infanterie-Regiment Nr. 176 im Weltkrieg* Berlin 1931

Pries Hauptmann d.R. Arthur *Das R.I.R. 90 1914-1918* Oldenburg 1925

Puttkamer Oberstleutnant d. Res. a.D. Oscar-Jesco von *Das Königlich Preußische Reserve-Infanterie-Regiment Nr. 46 im Weltkriege* Zeulenroda 1938

Reymann Oberleutnant a.D. H *Das 3. Oberschlesische Infanterie-Regiment Nr. 62 im Kriege 1914 – 1918* Zeulenroda 1930

Richter Oberst a.D. *Das Reserve-Infanterie-Regiment 94 im Weltkriege 1914/18* Jena 1934

Riegel Hauptmann a.D. Johann *Das K.B. 17. Infanterie-Regiment Orff* Munich 1927

Rohkohl Leutnant d.R. Walter *Reserve-Infanterie-Regiment 226 Teil II* Berlin 1926

Roth Major a.D. Karl *Das K.B. Reserve-Infanterie-Regiment Nr. 23* Munich 1927

Rupprecht Kronprinz von Bayern *In Treue Fest. Mein Kriegstagebuch, Zweiter Band* München 1929

Schatz Leutnant d.R. Josef *Geschichte des badischen (rheinischen) Reserve-Infanterie-Regiments 239* Stuttgart 1927

Scheer Leutnant d.R. a.D. Carl *Das Württembergische Infanterie-Regiment Nr. 413 im Weltkrieg 1916-1918* Stuttgart 1936

Schmidt Major a.D. Walter, Winkelmann Oberltn. a.D. Otto & Altermann Oberleutn. a.D. Martin *Das Königlich Preußische 3. Posensche Infanterie-Regiment Nr. 58 im Weltkriege* Zeulenroda 1934

Schoenfelder Generamajor a.D. *Das 2. Schlesische Feldartillerie-Regiment Nr. 42* Berlin 1938

Schulenburg-Wolfsburg Generalmajor a.D. Graf v.d. *Geschichte des Garde-Füsilier-Regiments* Oldenburg 1926

Schulz Oberleutnant d.R. a.D., Kißler Oberstleutnant a.D. & Schulze Leutnant d.R. a.D. *Geschichte des Reserve-Infanterie-Regiments Nr. 209 im Weltkriege 1914-1918* Oldenburg 1930

Schuster Oberst a.D. Hans *Geschichte des Infanterie-Regiments Nr. 369* Oldenburg 1928

Schütz Generalmajor a.D. & Hochbaum Leutnant *Das Grenadier-Regiment König Friedrich Wilhelm II (1. Schles. Nr. 10)* Oldenburg 1924

Schwenke Oberstleutnant a.D. Alexander *Geschichte des Reserve-Infanterie-Regiments Nr. 19 im Weltkriege 1914 – 1918* Oldenburg 1926

Schwerin Rittmeister a.D. C. von and Schmidt Oberleutnant d.R. a.D. Dr. Karl *Reserve-Inf.-Regiment 261 in Ost und West* Berlin 1932

Sobbe Major a.D. Fr. v. *Geschichte des Braunschweigischen Infanterie-Regiments Nr. 92 im Weltkriege 1914-1918* Berlin 1929

Soldan George *Das Infanterie-Regiment Nr. 184* Oldenburg 1920

Stengel Generalmajor a.D. Franz Freiherr von *Das K.B. 3. Infanterie-Regiment Prinz Karl von Bayern* München 1924

Steuer Major a.D. Joseph *Das 1. Unter-Elsässische Infanterie-Regiment Nr. 132 im Weltkriege* Berlin 1931

Stosch Oberstleutnant a.D. Albrecht von *Das Garde-Grenadier-Regiment Nr. 5 1897-1918* Oldenburg 1925

Stosch Oberstleutnant a.D. Albrecht von *Das Königl. Preuß. 5. Garde-Regiment zu Fuß 1897-1918* Berlin 1930

Sydow Hauptmann a.D. Herbert v. *Das Infanterie-Regiment Hamburg (2. Hanseatisches) Nr. 76* Oldenburg 1922

Tannen Oblt. d.R. a.D., Illing Lt. a.D. Rudolf, Schütz Lt. d.R. a.D. Aug. & Forstner Major a.D. Kurt Freiherr von *Das Kaiserliche Marine-Infanterie-Regment Nr. 3 in den Stürmen des Weltkrieges von 1914-1918* Zeulenroda 1936

Theysohn Generalleutnant a.D. Karl *Das K.B. 20. Feldartillerie-Regiment* Munich 1934

Tiessen Lt. d.R. Studienrat Max *Königlich Preußisches Reserve-Infanterie-Regiment 213. Geschichte eines Flandernregiments* Glückstadt 1937

Trebing Oberleutnant d.R. a.D. Emil *Geschichte des Infanterie-Regiments Nr. 370* Berlin 1929

Viereck Oberleutnant a.D. Helmut *Das Heideregiment. Königlich Preußisches 2. Hannoversches Infanterie-Regiment Nr. 77 im Weltkriege 1914 – 1918* Celle 1934

Voigt Oblt. d. Res. Hans *Geschichte des Füsilier-Regiments Generalfeldmarschall Prinz Albrecht von Preußen (Hann.) Nr. 73* Berlin 1938

Wegener Hans *Die Geschichte des 3. Ober-Elsässischen Infanterie-Regiments Nr. 172* Zeulenroda 1934

Weniger Generalmajor a.D. Heinrich, Zobel Oberst a.D. Artur and Fels Oberst a.D. Maximilian *Das K.B. 5. Infanterie-Regiment Großherzog Ludwig von Hessen* München 1929

Westerkamp Major a.D. *Unser Regiment. Eine Sammlung von Briefen, Tagebuchblättern und Aufzeichnungen aus der Zeit des Grossen Krieges (Feld Artillery Regiment 62)* Melle 1925

Wiedersich Leutnant d.R. Dr. Alfons *Das Reserve-Infanterie-Regiment Nr. 229* Berlin 1929

Wohlenberg Oberleutnant d.R. a.D. Rektor Alfred *Das Res.-Inf.-Regt. Nr. 77 im Weltkriege 1914-18* Hildesheim 1931

Wurmb Major a.D. Herbert Ritter von *Das K.B. Reserve-Infanterie-Regiment Nr 8* Munich 1929

Zipfel Hauptmann a.D. Dr. Ernst *Geschichte des Großherzoglich Mecklenburgischen Grenadier-Regiments Nr. 89* Schwerin 1932

Zipfel und Albrecht Dr. *Geschichte des Infanterie-Regiments Bremen (1. Hanseatisches) Nr. 75* Bremen 1934

Zunehmer Kgl. Preuß. Oberst a.D. *Infanterie-Regiment Graf Kirchbach (1.Niederschlesisches) Nr. 46 im Weltkrieg 1914/1918* Berlin 1935

Printed Works (German: author unknown)

Festschrift zum 2. Regimentstag des Reserve-Infanterie-Regiments Nr. 231 Braunschweig June 1925

Mitkämpfer *Geschichte des 4. Hannoverschen Infanterie-Regiments Nr. 164* privately published 1932

Oberkommando des Heeres *Der Weltkrieg 1914 bis 1918. Die militärischen Operationen zu Lande. Zwölfter Band* Berlin 1939

Offizier und Kameradenverein *Geschichte des Feldartillerie-Regiments von Peucker (1. Schles.) Nr. 6 1914 – 1918* Breslau 1932

Reichswehrministerium *Sanitätsbericht über das Deutsche Heer (Deutsches Feld- und Besatzungsheer) im Weltkriege 1914/1918* Berlin 1934

Waffenkamaraden *Die K.B. Schwere Artillerie im Großen Kriege 1914-1918* München 1928

Printed Works (English)

Edmonds Brigadier–General Sir James E *History of the Great War. Military Operations France and Belgium 1917 Volume II 7th June – 10th November Messines and Third Ypres (Passchendaele)* London 1948

McCarthy Chris *The Third Ypres. Passchendaele. The Day by Day Account* London 1995

Passingham Ian *Pillars of Fire. The Battle of Messines Ridge June 1917* Stroud 1998

Prior Robin and Wilson Trevor *Passchendaele. The Untold Story* London 1996

Steel Nigel and Hart Peter *Passchendaele. The Sacrificial Ground* London 2000

Index